TIM BUR

TIM BURTON

Jim Smith and
J Clive Matthews

This edition published in Great Britain in 2007 by
Virgin Books Ltd
Thames Wharf Studios
Rainville Road
London
W6 9HA

First published in Great Britain in 2002

A catalogue record for this book is available from the British
Library.

ISBN 978 0 7535 1278 4

Typeset by TW Typesetting, Plymouth, Devon
Printed in the UK by CPI Bookmarque, Croydon, CR0 4TD

Dedicated to

My Mom and Dad – for films and fairy tales,
and always keeping me safe.

JES

&

My parents for all the support down the years
(financial and otherwise) –
it really is appreciated, Eri for everything,
and to the memory of
Doris Millie Sant (1907–1991).

JCM

CONTENTS

ACKNOWLEDGEMENTS

Kirstie Addis (our editor), Scott Alexander, John Burnstein (at Disney/Touchstone), Mark Clapham, Lucy Cohen, Jason Douglas, Tom Duffield, Johanna Duffy, Gary Gillatt (at *Starburst*), Rick Heinrichs, Mike Jackson (at www.timburtoncollective.com), Gerard Johnson, Larry Karaszewski, Martin Landau, Stephen Lavington, Christopher Lee, Beverly Magid (at Guttman Associates), Johnny Minkley, Eri Miyazaki, Lance Parkin, Eddie Robson, Ben Russ, Mark Salisbury, Jim Sangster, Glenn Shadix, Catherine Spooner, Melvyn Stokes, Matthew Symonds, Ben Williams, and the staff at the William Morris Agency, Bumble Ward & Associates, the British Film Institute Library, the British Library, the University of London Libraries, and GOSH! Comics.

FOREWORD BY MARTIN LANDAU

As an actor, I am asked scores of questions all the time. These questions are usually proffered by journalists during interviews and press junkets relating to the latest film in which I am appearing and that is about to open imminently in theatres and cinemas across the country and around the world.

The questions are usually related to the actualities of working on the film, and my personal experiences with the on-camera and behind-the-camera personnel with whom I rubbed shoulders during the making of the movie. Usually, the memories are quite vivid and I have little trouble in articulating and recounting these experiences – they seem to roll off my tongue quite readily. During these sessions the journalists are often curious about some of the people with whom I've worked in the past. Many of them are icons such as Hitchcock, Woody Allen, Francis Coppola, Joseph L Mankiewicz and George Stevens. Most of my answers are spontaneous and spring forth with little effort.

Be that as it may, there is one question that has repeatedly stopped me dead in my tracks. I mention it because I've noticed this same question, whenever asked, reduces me to silence time and again. Why? Because it is a question that has no simple or pat answer and derails me every time!

'What is Tim Burton really like?'

I can't really tell you what he's like! I can only tell you what he *isn't* like. He isn't like anyone I've ever known or worked with before. He isn't like anyone I ever expect to meet again. He doesn't see things the same way anyone else in the world sees that same thing. His vision is his alone: unique and different enough to make anyone who is allowed the gift of witnessing it, wonder how any living human being could conjure up such a vision.

Pee-wee's Big Adventure, Beetlejuice, Edward Scissorhands, the *Batman* films, *Ed Wood, Mars Attacks!*, *The Nightmare Before Christmas, Sleepy Hollow, Planet of the Apes* – has there ever been a more divergent group of films? Each is so totally different in theme, so disparate in texture, yet each has a special, indelible stamp. Each jumps off the screen in a singular and unique way. Each film is an artistic whole, with every unfolding frame proving to be a unique and rich visual feast. No doubt about it, each of these wholly individual films had to have been conceived and directed by Tim Burton.

One would be hard-pressed to name another filmmaker in the Hollywood mainstream, working regularly within the system, creating big and expensive studio films, who chooses only to work on projects that attract his sensibilities, and arouse his own special predilections and personal tastes.

There is no other filmmaker with the latitude that Tim enjoys!

I stand corrected. There are a handful of artists working on 'labour of love' projects. But the entire budget for their films is probably a mere one-hundredth of a Tim Burton film's bottom line.

Tim Burton stands alone.

I have had the privilege of working with Tim on two occasions. Both were totally joyful, creative experiences for me, mainly because Tim, himself, was always having such a good time. There were 'takes' that were ruined during the filming of *Ed Wood* because of someone giggling aloud. Guess who?

I could go on and on about the splendours of my friend Tim Burton, but I won't, as I am eager for you to get into the heart of this book which will hopefully cast some new light on Tim and give you the answer to that fateful question that I have struggled with for years. This book has brought me much closer to being able to answer that elusive, oft-asked question, 'What is Tim Burton really like?'

After reading this book, I think you'll have a much better idea, yourself!

Read on, and enjoy!

Martin Landau
7 March 2002

Martin Landau appeared in Tim Burton's films *Ed Wood* and *Sleepy Hollow*. His portrayal of Bela Lugosi in *Ed Wood* won many acting awards, including the Best Supporting Actor Oscar at the 1995 Academy Awards.

INTRODUCTION

'I know I'm not an *auteur* because I try to listen to people. But the things I've felt strongly about, as I look back on my brief career, and had to push the hardest for, are usually the best work I've done. I don't go too far, I just do what I feel strongly about. All the moments I've fought for are the shining ones in every movie I've directed.'[1]

'I don't really consider myself a director. When I read about these old directors who went from one kind of movie to another and could do – I really can't, so everything I've ever done, I have to really love it and respond to it.'[2]

You always know when you are watching a Tim Burton film – whatever the setting or story. From the streets of Gotham City via the Hollywood of the studio era to the planet of the apes, a unique artistic sensibility, somehow both dark *and* mischievous, sinister *and* childlike, overtly, almost *distractingly* visual, affects every frame. There is simply no other American filmmaker who could, in little more than a decade, produce a love story about a man with blades for hands, a biography of a much-derided director, a not-exactly faithful adaptation of an American literary classic, and a comedy in which the lead characters die within the first reel. Across less than a dozen features, Tim Burton has demonstrated a willingness to take mainstream cinema audiences to places where they would not have gone without him. Sometimes punters and critics alike have been grateful, sometimes they haven't quite understood. Sometimes critical and commercial success have come together. Some times they have come separately or not at all. But the journey is always interesting.

This book goes through Tim Burton's remarkable directorial career, film by film and in chronological order, incorporating *The Nightmare Before Christmas* which Burton created and produced, but did not direct, and his Internet cartoon series *Stainboy* because they are works of huge significance to the public perception of Burton. Although this is the sort of book that can easily be read in any order, favourite projects first, a narrative should emerge when progressing through the films in sequence. Burton's small number of television productions are not accorded their own chapters, but covered within the section for the theatrical feature or short film of most relevance to them.

The section breakdowns within each movie's chapter feature such basic information as title, cast and year of release, and then draw on the following categories as and when appropriate.

TAGLINE AND TRAILER: A brief discussion of cinema and television marketing campaigns for Burton's films, whether he was involved with them or not.

TITLE SEQUENCE: Burton's movies frequently open with a distinctive, specially designed sequence over which the opening credits run. They are always thematically relevant to the movie, and are almost always journeys of some kind.

STORY: What happens in the movie. Obviously. The length of this will vary depending on the film under discussion.

SOURCE MATERIAL: The majority of Burton's films have been adaptations or progressions of pre-existing material. Here we discuss his approach to his sources.

REFERENCES: Particularly noticeable visual, audio and conceptual references to other works abound in Burton's productions, even though he argues that 'it's a subliminal process. Maybe the ten-year-old deep inside me is showing himself, but I'm not egging him on, consciously. Movies work on levels so deep down in your brain that it doesn't help to calculate the sources and influences. Just let it happen, creatively.'[3]

PRODUCTION: Why and how the film was made.

CASTING: The players: who they are, why they were asked and what they bring to the movie at hand.

BURTON REGULARS: Tim Burton often works with the same people several times, 'It makes it easier, when you work with somebody more than once ... because you don't have to verbalise, you don't have to talk about every single thing, so it's collaborative ... you have a feeling about something and they do it, and it's their own thing and it fits with everything, so it's very exciting; it creates a positive momentum.'[4] Here we draw attention to some of his more esoteric multiple collaborations, highlighting them from the film on which the partnership was formed.

CRITICS: The critical reception of the movie. Burton admits that 'the films I've done have always been *very* mixed critically, and I think that's very healthy.'[5] Thus comments positive and negative, valid and invalid are presented here.

MUSIC: A film's score is integral to its atmosphere. The success of the music, or lack thereof, can have a profound effect on a motion picture. It is perhaps the single most important collaboration in modern film. Long-time Burton composer Danny Elfman has described film scoring as providing 'unity where there wasn't [any] with a melody ... it's keeping that thread always going in our minds, even if it's subliminal.'[6]

CINEMATOGRAPHY: Here we discuss the visual style of the film.

PLOT PROBLEMS: Burton's interest in visual art over narrative occasionally means the finer points of storytelling get overlooked. When asked about this Burton is dismissive, 'It's like a given now, why even mention it anymore?'[7]

DEATH: A constant presence in Burton's work. This category describes each individual film's attitudes to life, death, and the hereafter, plus the multiple methods of dispatching his characters that Burton often appears to relish.

CHILDREN AND FAMILIES: Another recurring motif: the world's view of children, and their view of the world, especially in relation to their (frequently dysfunctional) families, a topic which fascinates Burton. For him the interest of childhood is that people are not yet aware of the world, 'on an intellectual level . . . you're reacting to things more emotionally which . . . is an interesting thing . . . [it's] nice to try to keep that sense of . . . everything [seeming] a little strange and weird and unusual.'[8]

CLOWNS AND THE CIRCUS: Another apparent obsession – these white-faced circus performers and their environs are a frequent source of inspiration. According to Burton's mother, this started in his childhood, when 'The only thing that ever scared him, and yet he was fascinated by it, was Bozo the Clown. He watched him every day . . . but through the crack in the door.'[9]

DOGS: Mutts, canines – pooches turn up quite a bit in Burton's films. Here we note their appearances and assess their importance.

LOVE TRIANGLES: A repeated motif across many of Burton's films is a three-way split of affection, romantic or otherwise.

CHECKS, STRIPES, DOTS: In many Burton films, simple, usually black and white geometric patterns crop up. Tom Duffield, who has worked in a design capacity on four Burton films, explains: 'that's his graphic background . . . his movies all have that graphic sense.'

AUTOBIOGRAPHY?: Many critics have underlined the similarities in appearance and outlook between Burton and characters. Indeed, one commentator has even devoted an entire book to the assumption that within Burton's films lies the man himself: 'an artist – such as I am convinced Tim Burton is – may be less than wholly forthcoming in his personal statements, he is inescapably more open in what he says in his art.'[10] In places this is hard to deny, yet in others critics have stretched this point so far as for it to become meaningless. This can hinder rather than help an understanding of the films. Here we try to assess such pop-psychological assertions, in an attempt to distinguish between Burton's 'personal' and 'impersonal' films. After all, the man himself has claimed that 'although I see similarities in retrospect between the films and the characters in them, I've never really consciously thought about it.'[11]

JUST PLAIN WEIRD: Really, *really* strange stuff: 'I remember when I had pneumonia, and I got into a kind of hallucinatory state. I stared at a doorknob for two hours and I got a lot out of that. Those are the things I want to let in, in my movies, the fever dreams.'[12]

DIALOGUE TO SKIP BACK FOR: The choicest snippets of dialogue.

DIALOGUE TO SKIP PAST: Lines that make you cringe. And then hide.

AFTERLIFE: A section dealing with such matters as how well the movie has stood the test of time, post-production considerations, financial matters, and the effects of the picture on the careers of many involved.

AWARDS: Burton's films have been nominated for many awards, and even won some of them. This category is not – nor is it intended to be – comprehensive. There are so many award ceremonies and prize-givings these days that that would be impossible. This is just a guide to some of the most significant, and some of the most wonderfully insignificant, gongs.

EXPERT WITNESS: A few select quotes from people in the know, both on the individual project under discussion, and on Burton's films as a whole.

TRIVIA: Random interesting facts which can't be fitted elsewhere.

ANALYSIS: Our own two cents' worth on what the film's *about*. Sometimes we may get carried away and spend a few bucks . . .

AVAILABILITY: Where to get it; how to get it; what you get *when* you get it. For the most part we're only dealing in DVDs, not VHSs.

THE BOTTOM LINE: Our own highly subjective opinions of the movie in *qualitative* terms, boiled down to its very essence.

EARLY LIFE AND DISNEY TIMES

Tim Burton's childhood remains a mystery, despite the fact that much of his work seems to find itself returning to the town in which he grew up – Burbank, California. Effectively a more run-down offshoot of Hollywood, the town is in essence much like any other that consists largely of suburbs – aside from the fact that most of the major Hollywood studios have lots there.

The same basic facts are always trotted out about Burton's childhood: his father used to play minor league baseball, before becoming an official for the Burbank Parks and Recreation department; his mother ran a shop that only sold cat-related items; the young Burton won a poster-designing competition whilst in the ninth grade, and his anti-litter design adorned the sides of Burbank's rubbish trucks for a year; he claims not to have been close to his parents, who bricked up his bedroom window for no readily apparent reason; he rarely mentions his younger brother; he wanted to be the actor who plays Godzilla; he played sports, but has since described himself as 'pushed' into this; he produced a number of Super-8 home movies that have since been lost.

In many ways, this is unsurprising. Burton himself has gone on record about the uneventful nature of his early life saying, 'It's weird, but the only experiences I remember from childhood are the ones which had a major impact: fearful things, like from a scary movie.'[1] Going through numerous interviews, it does indeed seem that the only things from this time to have truly stuck with him are scary movies and the odd cult TV show, be it *The Prisoner* or *Gilligan's Island*. Only when he's asked by interviewers to explain the origins of his images of a bleak, bland suffocating suburbia (*Frankenweenie, Edward Scissorhands, The Nightmare Before Christmas, Ed Wood*), alienated children (*Vincent, Beetlejuice, Batman Returns, Mars Attacks! The Melancholy Death of Oyster Boy and other stories*), or heroes who seem 'weird' to the people around them (pretty much all of his films) does Burton, seemingly bored by such a line of questioning, roll out the usual anecdotes that seem to be accepted as representative of his childhood.

When pressed, Burton's most regular description of his youth is to state something along the lines of, 'if you didn't speak well, if you didn't hang out with the other children or didn't play sport, if you liked monster movies, you were strange.'[2] To the young Burton though, this outside status had advantages. The very fact that 'they' categorised him so 'allowed me to see the world from an external point of view. That meant my perception of normality was strange. For me, reality is bizarre.'[3]

However, Burton clearly didn't see this aspect of his childhood as unique, nor did he consider that he was a special, isolated case. 'Every time I looked around . . . it looked like everyone had their own private world. You didn't see too many people . . . paying attention. They were in their own special worlds.'[4] This was an idea that he would soon be able to explore in his short film, *Vincent*. Even Hanke's conclusion to Burton's early life can only go as far as to claim that he 'turns a bleak suburban childhood into a dark myth where the imaginings of a lonely or misunderstood child become a dark reality.'[5]

It could be suggested that Burton has reshaped his own experiences of childhood to suit his later media image – that of the shy yet talented young artist – and has now come to rely on them, maybe even *believe* them, exactly as another imaginative young man comes to believe *his* fantasies in Burton's first film to receive any kind of commercial release, *Vincent*. As Burton's friend and frequent collaborator Glenn Shadix put it, 'the magazine idea of Tim is this weird, wigged-out, crazy person, and he's not like that; there's something very solid about him – yes, I think he always felt like fish out of water growing up, but that doesn't mean his creativity is fuelled by pain or anger.' Caroline Thompson, again both a friend and a collaborator, feels the same.

For her, Burton's work has a 'real affection for neighbourhood life
... although he perpetuates this perception of himself as ...
damaged, from my perspective it's just the opposite ... he's
escaped some fundamental damage that shuts most people
down.'[6]

Burton's life begins to be better documented from the time he
first moved into the film world, having won a scholarship to the
Disney-backed California Institute of the Arts (CalArts) in 1976.
One of his short film projects while at CalArts, *Stalk of the Celery
Monster* was soon deemed good enough by Disney to warrant
offering him a job as an animator, and he shifted base to Disney's
Burbank lot. It seemed like a dream come true: 'like a lot of
people who grew up liking to draw, I thought Disney would be a
great place to do it.'[7] Yet at the same time, the experience was 'so
weird ... at Disney ... I could look out the window, and see the
hospital where I was born ... and the cemetery where my
grandfather is buried. It was like the Bermuda Triangle.'[8]

Soon he began to realise that the reason for the Bermudan
feelings he was getting came from more than mere triangular
geography. 'It was a strange place because everybody was smiling
and really nice and there was a charming atmosphere ... it was
like being in ... *The Prisoner*.'[9]

His problems with working at the studio were, in essence,
existential. Burton felt that 'they were saying, "This is Disney –
the most incredible gathering of artists in the world" [and yet at]
the same time they were saying "Just do it this way; shut up and
become like a zombie factory worker".'[10] Faced with such an
attitude he soon came to feel that 'Animators were pretty much
treated like freaks ... As long as we were wearing clothes, it was
okay. You know, anything goes.'[11]

Burton's first assignment at Disney was *The Fox and the Hound*
(Art Stevens, 1981), hardly the sort of film that anyone would
associate him with in hindsight. He felt that 'it was pretty quickly
obvious that I was not cut out for it. It was, like, oh man, I
couldn't do it,'[12] and he even began to wonder if his restaurant
job was still available. Fairly soon, his dislike for his work got to
the stage where he realised he'd 'rather be dead than work for five
years on this movie,'[13] the general length of time Disney animated
features then spent in production. The only benefit of the project
was that he made a number of friends, many of whom helped out
as both cast and crew on his after-work films (see **Luau**).

Luckily for Burton, he got a transfer to another project, one that initially appeared to better suit his sensibilities, and gave him an opportunity to indulge his love of drawing his own things. He was engaged in a design capacity on *The Black Cauldron* (Ted Berman and Richard Rich, 1985). Burton spent a year sitting at his desk drawing 'any idea I wanted to . . . weird characters, weird props, weird furniture . . . doing whatever I wanted. But at some point I realised they had no intention of using any of it.'[14]

However, although Disney didn't seem prepared to use any of Burton's ideas, his co-workers had already begun to notice his talents. Henry Selick (later the director of *The Nightmare Before Christmas*), who had already managed to develop some of his own, equally bizarre ideas into a film, *Phases* (1978), by the time he met Burton, thought that people, 'especially kids, would love his work in the way that they loved Charles Addams. But nobody recognised that at Disney. They thought, Oh, this is just too weird.'[15] Selick, as well as a few others at the studio, saw in Burton someone 'really exciting, whose ideas and drawings were like a breath of fresh air coming to the studio'. But, unfortunately, for Burton's professional career 'management at that time was just terrified of taking any risks whatsoever'.[16]

Both Burton and Selick would eventually leave the studio, frustrated at the lack of opportunities to break out of the timeworn Disney mould. As Burton explained, 'I just wanted to get out. The talent was there, but they didn't have the foresight to see that people have a sense of quality and would respond to it.'[17]

Regardless, he still managed to get the studio to fund two of his short films, and also found himself commissioned to direct a short film for television. Even Burton himself doesn't quite seem to understand his time at Disney, calling it 'weird, but at the same time . . . great, because I got the chance to do . . . *Vincent*, which would have been unheard of at any other studio. It's . . . a funny place in that respect.'[18]

During his time at CalArts and Disney, Burton produced six short films of note: *Stalk of the Celery Monster*, *Doctor of Doom*, *Luau*, *Vincent*, *Hansel and Gretel* and *Frankenweenie*. Of these, the studio funded just three, and only two are currently available to the public.

STALK OF THE CELERY MONSTER (1979)

SUMMARY: A vicious scientist, conducting experiments on a tied down woman with the assistance of a hulking, hunched giant beast, is revealed to be a contemporary dentist when he pulls back the window into his waiting room and cackles 'Next, please . . .'

EXPERT WITNESS: Rick Heinrichs: 'Every year at CalArts they have a screening of all the films students have made throughout the year: *Stalk of the Celery Monster* was Tim's, it was kind of his final thesis there – and the film that got him into Disney. Most people at CalArts just used their short films to perfect various animation techniques, but Tim went for producing something entertaining. Everybody else was just exploring their animation technique, but Tim was actually trying to make a film. It was beautifully drawn, but it wasn't about the technique, it was about the people in it.'

CINEMATOGRAPHY: Deliberately washed out and pastel-coloured to the point of being nearly sepia, *Stalk* is brief but beautiful. Its characters stand out in stark contrast to their backgrounds which, as with many of Burton's films, feature black and white checked patterns, and their movements are always fluid and varied. The dentist's eyes are particularly emotive, aided by the rough, half-finished drawing style that is strangely reminiscent of many of Gerald Scarfe's satirical cartoons.

AVAILABILITY: Inaccessible in any form, a clip is included on the biographical video *Tim Burton: Trick or Treat?*

DOCTOR OF DOOM (1980)

SUMMARY: A besuited Victorian-style scientist (Burton) reveals his creation, an elephant-faced beast.

REFERENCES: Unsurprisingly there's a resemblance to the laboratory of *Frankenstein* (James Whale, 1931). The long-trunked, big-eared creature may be a jokey reference to John Merrick, the subject of *The Elephant Man* (David Lynch, 1980) who, of course, didn't *actually* look like an elephant.

EXPERT WITNESS: Rick Heinrichs: 'Tim and Jerry Rees did *Doctor of Doom* – it's another early classic, amateurish maybe, shot in black and white and on videotape, with deliberately bad over-dubbing.'

AVAILABILITY: Again, *Doctor of Doom* is outside the public domain, with only the briefest of clips included on the *Trick or Treat?* video.

LUAU (1982)

Creative Consultants: Harry Sabin, Randy Cartwright
Special Thanks: The Lauziseros, David Silverman, Sue
Mantle, Organs by Gismo, Tron Trailer Girl, Ron Clements
special process stage, APD. Parks Department, Casat-
aways Golf Course
Filmed Entirely in Hollywood, USA
Original Music by Kent Halliday, featuring Jan and Dave
Written, Directed and Produced by Tim Burton, Jerry Rees

CAST: Mike Gabriel (*Bob*), Susan Frankenberger (*Arlene*), Terrey Hamada (*Princess Yakamoshi*), Jow Raft, Jay Jackson, Brian McEntee, Harry Sabin, Jerry Rees, Cynthia Prince (*The Surfers*), John Musker, Ben Burgess, Dick Heinrichs, Brick Newton, George Sukara, Ed Sommert, Gale Muster, Sue Kroser (*The Businessmen*), Phil Young (*Kahuna*), Randy Cartwright (*IQ*), Tim Burton (*The Supreme Being/Mortie*), Louis Take, Rosalie Lauzisero, Kathleen A Sabin, Meredith Jackson, Rebecca LoDolo, Amy Sabin, Darrell Van Citters (*Unknown*)

TITLE SEQUENCE: Bright colours reveal themselves to be a spinning beach ball held up to the camera. The camera pulls back to reveal a girl in a red jumper, white boots and white miniskirt. She's dancing. As she does, the film's credits are projected onto her skirt and back, with her moving between each caption card to disguise the slide shifts. At the end of the sequence, she holds the spinning beach ball back up to the camera, and we cut to stock footage of a sun-kissed beach.

SUMMARY: A group of surfers are on the beach, checking out the girls and the waves. Arlene, the girlfriend of Bob the surfer, shows up with her house guest, the Princess Yakamoshi, who will be staying with her for the summer. Bob is attracted to the Princess, but tells Arlene that he hopes 'This gorgeous new girl doesn't disturb our great relationship.' Yakamoshi then gets into the swing of the beach atmosphere by removing her demure kimono to reveal a skimpy bikini beneath, and the surfers go mad at the sight. One is so impressed that he shouts 'This calls for a celebration! You're all invited to my house tonight for a big Luau!'

Arlene starts to tell Bob about what a great boyfriend he is, but he ignores her to ask the Princess to go to the Luau with him. Enraged by this action, Arlene slaps him, screaming, 'I'd rather French-kiss a leper than ever lay eyes on you again!'

We then cut to the Luau that night, where everybody is dancing. Once the party is well advanced, Bob and the Princess go outside together, and he attempts to seduce her. Meanwhile, 'the life of the party', Kahuna, suddenly has an existential crisis and goes outside. IQ, one of the surfers, follows him, and Kahuna replies, 'I'm not cut out for being the life of the party anymore, man. You know it's a big brain-fry man, is what it is. The whole thing – it's the Katzenjammer kids gone to the moon, man!' He then rejects his name, declaring 'I don't wanna be called Kahuna, I wanna be called by my right name: Vladimir Moonface *Junior*!'

As Kahuna continues to talk, a strange light appears in the sky, which apparently mesmerises IQ. He crosses to a flashing object that has landed on the sand. It appears to be some kind of small dustbin. He lifts up the lid, and in it is a disembodied head, which claims to be 'the Most Powerful Being in the Universe', and proudly announces that it has turned IQ into a zombie. This is clearly not the case, as IQ promptly throws him into the Luau, where he lands amongst piles of food laid out on a long table. For the rest of the party, he desperately tries to attract attention by muttering, 'Excuse me, I'm the Most Powerful Being in the Universe.'

After a series of misunderstandings based around her Oriental accent, Bob and the Princess head back to the Luau, where they bump into Arlene. Even angrier at seeing them together, she launches into a song and dance routine that involves the entire cast. Throughout the song and dance number, the head continues to try and attract the attention of the partygoers. This he finally achieves when he belches loudly. Turning to Bob, the apparent leader of the surfers, the head announces, 'Bob, as the Supreme Being, I challenge you to a surfing contest! . . . If I win, I receive your body.'

The next day, Bob and the head begin their surfing competition, and initially Bob is losing badly. Watching from the shore, Kahuna is getting increasingly upset: 'Oh man! Bob doesn't stand a chance out there today, man! I mean, we're just melted Eskimo Pies left outside the refrigerator of time, man!' As IQ ponders his friend's words of wisdom, Kahuna vanishes. At this point, for the first time, a voice-over intrudes: 'The Kahuna left the beach that day, never to be seen by his good friends again.'

Back in the surfing contest, the head notices a crab on his surfboard: 'Oh, it's my crab assistant Steve!' he exclaims. He orders the crab to 'go and kill Bob until he's defeated, and then bring him to me so I can kill him!' The head then erupts into maniacal laughter as the crab launches itself at Bob's throat. After a struggle, Bob emerges victorious (to which the head responds, 'Oh, oops!')

Meanwhile, back on the shore, a besuited man appears, and asks Bob's cheering friends, 'Hey, would you keep it down, we're trying to conduct a business meeting.' Indeed he is, as he returns to a table on the beach, surrounded by pinstriped businesspeople discussing the Gross National Product.

As everyone congratulates Bob on his victory, the head sneers at them ('I beg your pardon, but losing the contest means nothing. Being the Supreme Being, I can say anything I want to! Fools! Idiots! I hate you all! I can't stand you! You're such stupid idiots!') before politely introducing his crab assistant and telling them that 'At this very moment, I am sending telepathic waves into his crustacean mind. He will kill every one of you until I receive the body I so richly deserve!' To deal with this new problem, Bob, who has been quietly slipping on an American Football referee's shirt throughout this speech, blows a whistle, and a man in full gridiron trappings charges out of nowhere, and punts the disembodied head off into the distance.

There then follows a cat-fight between Arlene and the Princess over Bob's affections. The object of their scrap remains uninterested by their actions, as the voice-over tells us 'Bob was understandably concerned about the disappearance of his good friend, the Kahuna. He, not unlike the other kids, hadn't seen him in quite some time.' The voice-over then goes on to tell us that 'In other parts of the country, there have been several Kahuna sightings.' We then cut to a woman in a living room describing her late-night encounter with Kahuna, whom she lured out with catfood, and who has apparently taken to wearing a tatty straw hat. 'I don't care what anybody says,' she exclaims, 'he's really real, he really is.'

We then cut back to the cat-fight, which suddenly and abruptly stops as the girls and the surfers start backing away from the camera, screaming in terror at some off-screen horror. Then one of the surfers says, 'Hey, hey, hey – calm down! This is a celebrity – Ray Wonder Jr,' as the camera swings around to a gold jewellery-bedecked black man, who is clearly modelled on former Rat Packer, Sammy Davis Jr. The surfers happily go over to greet him, relieved: 'I'm sorry Mr Wonder,' says IQ. 'We thought you were a Negro.'

With this danger now passed, Wonder suggests that they all go to his house for another Luau. Even crazier dancing ensues, as the businessmen look on in disgust. 'Hey, those surfers, those kids look like they're having a lot of fun,' comments one of the pinstripes, to which another replies: 'Well let them have their fun – for now!' The businessmen begin to growl in a feral manner.

Back to Mr Wonder's Luau, where he is performing a song and dance routine, concluding with a Louis Armstrong-style scat. The voice-over ominously tells us that 'Everyone was having a wonderful time, but they all had wished that their good friend Kahuna was with them, so they could be having a better time than they were *actually* having!' The voice-over goes on: 'However, in other parts of the country, Kahuna sightings were reaching epidemic proportions!' We are then treated to more stock footage of people with binoculars, and a middle-aged man protesting, 'Why doesn't anybody believe me that the Kahuna's real?'

Back at Ray Wonder Jr's place, the Luau is interrupted by the arrival of the businessmen, one of whom announces, 'You kids can't have a party here, we're building an office building on this very spot.' The chief businessman's secretary then sets up a desk in the middle of the party, and refuses Bob a meeting with him, claiming he is not present, despite the fact he is standing in clear view right behind her. A brutal fight breaks out between the two sides, and in the middle of the battle Arlene and Bob stop attacking their enemies and start fighting each other. The voice-over explains, 'At this point, they had forgotten their quarrel with the businessmen, they had even forgotten the disappearance of their good friend, Kahuna. But there was one man who would never forget!' We cut to the middle-aged man, who has now been incarcerated. 'I've seen the Kahuna – I've seen it over there!' he says, vaguely gesticulating off to the left, as the other inmates wander aimlessly around in the background.

Back at the Luau, two surfers cut off a businessman's hand, place it between two pieces of bread, and IQ eats it. In a domestic kitchen we see a very fat woman (Rosalie) in a huge tent-like dress, and a snivelling, geeky man. She tells him, 'Mortie – I made this pie special, so don't you mess it up!' Lecturing him on how to conduct himself on leaving her kitchen, she warns him about fantasising about taking a train trip to Denver, claiming that if he does, 'You might bump into a businessman, who might hit you with a big fish, and send you careering into an innocent bystander with my pie!' All these events then ensue, exactly as she foresaw them, as Mortie staggers inelegantly through the ruck at the Luau. As the businessman who had been hit with Rosalie's pie collapses, the voice-over tells us, 'The pie had landed squarely in his face, and the heavy cream content blocked his breathing passages.' IQ staggers over to the (possibly dead) businessman, scrapes the pie from his face, and begins to eat it.

As the fight continues, there is a brief cross-cut to another man, screaming, 'My God! The Kahuna is here! What are we going to do?' At this point, Rosalie comes out of her house, and interrupts the fight. As Bob and Arlene begin to make up, Rosalie points out that the previously unmentioned local volcano is erupting (stock footage), and she invites everyone into her house to shelter from the molten lava. 'Considering the alternatives,' explains the voice-over, 'Rosalie's proposition seemed like a pretty good idea.'

The last of the combatants to enter the house is IQ. Rosalie force-feeds him a banana, and turns on the television for him to watch. After flicking through the channels, IQ catches a glimpse of Kahuna hiding behind a bar. Pointing at the screen, IQ bellows his friend's name. Kahuna stares out of the TV screen at IQ, and declares, 'I'm not Kahuna – I'm Vladimir Moonface Junior!' We then cut to the guy from the asylum ranting, 'I've seen the Kahuna!' as a cacophony of voices start singing 'Kahuna' over and over again.

Merry Luau dancing music begins over a close-up of Kahuna's face, and the end credits roll.

SOURCE MATERIAL: The film is basically a rummage through bad surfer movies, cheap horror films, schlock science fiction, Edward D Wood Jr's low-budget cult classics, and any number of other B-movies. There is also something of the work of Herschell Gordon Lewis about it, although this is more atmospheric and aesthetic, rather than the imitation of any specific film storylines or moments from the cult director's back catalogue.

REFERENCES: As the businessmen and surfers begin to fight, there is a very clear visual quotation from *Monty Python's Flying Circus*'s 'The Women's Institute recreates the Battle of Trafalgar' sketch.

Much of the early part of the film is a pastiche of such Elvis Presley film vehicles as *Blue Hawaii* and *Aloha From Hawaii*, a point which is reiterated when Bob performs a rock and roll number whilst miming badly that he is playing the Ukulele.

The voice-over at times seems to specifically parody the often infinitely bad dialogue from *Plan 9 From Outer Space* (Edward D Wood Jr, 1958), and whoever is reading it is attempting, with some success, an impersonation of Rod Serling, the writer/presenter of *The Twilight Zone*, who also wrote the screenplay for the 1968 film, *Planet of the Apes*.

Both the opening sequence's gratuitous close-ups on a girl in a miniskirt, and the long cat-fight between Arlene and Princess Yakamoshi, seem deliberate reference to bosom-fixated exploitation master, Russ Meyer.

The way the movie's credits are projected onto the moving body parts of a woman is similar to Robert Brownjohn's titles to *From Russia With Love* (Terence Young, 1963).

PRODUCTION: This independent, low-budget film was filmed during 1980, shortly after *Doctor of Doom*, before entering an editing process that lasted nearly two years. Rick Heinrichs elaborates that 'It was really just a pressure-relief valve for a lot of incredibly talented young animators at Disney, and a lot of CalArts grads – because a lot of people from there were working at Disney. There weren't any investors. It was people who went to a school for animation, funding it for their own entertainment.'

CASTING: Most of the cast and crew on *Luau* were friends and acquaintances of Burton's from either Disney or CalArts.

John Musker, playing one of the businessmen, is one of the most successful of the *Luau* cast besides Burton himself. Having worked on *The Fox and the Hound*, he also helped develop *The Black Cauldron* (Ted Burman and Richard Rich, 1985), before writing and co-directing *The Great Mouse Detective* (1986), which starred the vocal talents of Burton's hero Vincent Price. He then went on to write, co-direct and produce three of Disney's all-time biggest hits, *The Little Mermaid* (1989), *Aladdin* (1992) and *Hercules* (1997).

Mike Gabriel (Bob) was an animator on the 1982 Disney short, *Fun With Mr Future*, as well as the feature-length *The Great Mouse Detective*. Gabriel went on to direct *The Rescuers Down Under* (1990) and *Pocahontas* (1995) for the Disney Company.

Phil Young, (Kahuna), is another animator who worked on *The Fox and the Hound*, *The Great Mouse Detective*, *The Little Mermaid*, *The Lion King* (Roger Allers and Rob Minkoff, 1994), where he animated Musafa (voiced by *Aladdin and his Wonderful Lamp*'s James Earl Jones), as well as *The Emperor's New Groove* (Mark Dindal, 2000).

Randy Cartwright (IQ) has contributed to numerous films in various roles, mostly as an animator, notably *The Fox and the Hound*, Mike Gabriel's *The Rescuers Down Under*, *Mickey's Christmas Carol* (Bunny Mattinson, 1983), *Beauty and the Beast* (Gary Trousdale and Kirk Wise, 1991), *Aladdin*, *The Lion King* (Roger Allers and Rob Minkoff, 1994), *Hercules*, *Antz* (Eric Darnell and Tim Johnson, 1998) and *Shrek* (Andrew Adamson, Vicky Jenson and Scott Marshall, 2001).

Jay Jackson went on to help animate *The Little Mermaid* (Ron Clements and John Musker, 1989), was Directing Animator for the Scott Bakula-voiced 'Danny' on *Cats Don't Dance* (Mark

Dindal, 1997), and was the Supervising Animator for the Gorilla family on the hit feature-length cartoon, *Tarzan* (Chris Buck and Kevin Lima, 1999).

Brian McEntee was Layout Artist on *Fun With Mr Future*, and has since acted as Art Director on *Beauty and the Beast*.

Jerry Rees was also an animator on *The Fox and the Hound*, as well as producing storyboards, choreographing the computer imagery, and acting as Visual Effects Supervisor on the visually groundbreaking *Tron* (Steven Lisberger, 1982), to which it was rumoured in early 2002 that Burton would be directing a sequel. He also worked on *Space Jam*, and wrote and directed Disney's *The Brave Little Toaster* (1987).

BURTON REGULARS: Rick Heinrichs, here credited as 'Dick Heinrichs' and playing one of the businessmen, became Burton's most regular collaborator. He has worked in various behind the scenes capacities on almost every film Burton has made. He created the sculptures for and Co-Produced *Vincent*, did some more effects work on *Hansel and Gretel*, was credited as Associate Producer on *Frankenweenie*, did model work on *Aladdin and his Wonderful Lamp*, effects on *Pee-wee's Big Adventure*, designed the jar for *The Jar*, was credited as Visual Effects Consultant on *Beetlejuice*, was a Set Designer on *Edward Scissorhands*, Art Director on *Batman Returns*, Visual Consultant on *The Nightmare Before Christmas*, and Production Designer on *Sleepy Hollow* (for which he won an Oscar) and *Planet of the Apes*. He has been described by *The Nightmare Before Christmas* director Henry Selick as 'Tim's hidden partner'.[1] He has also worked with Terry Gilliam as Set Designer for *The Fisher King* (1991), and with the Coen brothers as Production Designer on *Fargo* (1996) and *The Big Lebowski* (1998).

Rosalie Lauzisero returned for *Frankenweenie*, where she appeared as Rose, the owner of Raymond the dog.

CRITICS: Because the film was never released, indeed was never intended for release, no one has ever reviewed it. But we like it.

MUSIC: Both the original compositions and stock pieces perfectly fit the film's schizophrenic style, while maintaining a vaguely Hawaiian air throughout. Arlene's song is particularly good.

CINEMATOGRAPHY: Surprisingly, given that it was apparently shot over some period of time, *Luau*'s visual style is highly imaginative. During the dance sequences there are close-ups of the participants' feet, and twisting camera moves from the floor up. The film also uses a number of extreme close-ups on characters' faces to emphasise important lines of dialogue. The editing technique of constantly cutting to and from the action via stock footage, *non-sequiters* and random shots of dancing toys, ensures that the film's visual interest never wanes. The Point of View shot as IQ enters Rosalie's house near the end gives a personal touch to the anarchy, whilst at the same time adding to the impression of the character's constant disorientation throughout the film.

LOVE TRIANGLES: There is a classic Burton love triangle between long-time partners Bob and Arlene, and nubile newcomer, Yakamoshi.

CLOWNS AND THE CIRCUS: The Supreme Being, with his black and white makeup, distinctly resembles a clown (it also bears a resemblance to Michael Keaton's Betelgeuse). There is an elaborate pie-in-the-face gag, the staple of circus 'humour' for the last several aeons.

CHECKS, STRIPES, DOTS: Having donned the black and white striped referee's shirt, Bob continues to wear it for the rest of the movie. Many of the other surfers also wear stripy shirts.

JUST PLAIN WEIRD: Everything. Particularly, however, Steve the crustacean minion, Kahuna's hat, and the moment when, having been asleep for the entire scene, IQ suddenly wakes up, screams 'Luau!' and then smashes a bottle over his own head.

DIALOGUE TO GO BACK FOR: Loads – see **SUMMARY**.
Man on TV: 'I just can't go on this way Marcia, so I'm going to go that way for a while, and see what happens.'
Marcia: 'Things can change!'
Man: 'I know for me they will – I'm leaving!'

Rosalie: 'Come on in kids, come on in. Oh – look at that. The volcano's erupting.'

ANALYSIS: *Luau* is a series of incidents joined only in that they are sequential. There's no pretence at plot or plotting. It's a heavily comic pastiche/parody of the state of popular culture in the decade before its production. Many of the visual trademarks of Tim Burton's later work are already present, as are such thematic concerns as a conflict between outsiders (the surfers) and the establishment (the businessmen), the alienation of young people, and a clear desire to indulge in genre subversion. It even manages to mock the casual racism of those who celebrated the undeniable talents of the likes of Sammy Davis Jr and Louis Armstrong, whilst simultaneously opposing the civil rights movement.

Bob should be the hero of *Luau* – he has the hero's role, but the film, the voice-over, and ultimately the audience, are far more concerned with the disappearance of the fascinating Kahuna (sorry – Vladimir Moonface Junior). Kahuna is an outsider amongst outsiders, perceived as 'the life of the party' by his friends, and as a near-mythical figure to the rest of society, he nonetheless is uncomfortable with his role, and feels the need to escape such social confinements. As such he could perhaps be considered Burton's first on-screen avatar, a precursor to Vincent Molloy, Edward Scissorhands *et al*.

Luau is an absurdist tract, pretending to be a surfer movie, in which things happen just because they are funny.

EXPERT WITNESS: Rick Heinrichs: 'It was a lot of fun to work on. It was mainly Tim's ... There were a lot of very talented people at Disney at the time, and they were finding it very hard to deal with the day to day requirements of producing the footage for those films, because of the way things were set up at Disney at the time. *Luau* was a great pressure relief valve for everybody, away from the factory line. It's a silly little film, but it was a lot of fun, it has a very peculiar energy to it, an entertaining thing.'

AVAILABILITY: Unavailable on any format, and never commercially released, either to cinemas or for home viewing, *Luau* is impossible to get hold of. Almost.

THE BOTTOM LINE: Frantic, cheap and utterly inspired, *Luau* is frequently hilarious. It is also hugely imaginative, relentlessly unorthodox, and somehow transcends the circumstances of its production to become a tremendous viewing experience. If only it were more readily available.

VINCENT (1982)

Distributed by Buena Vista Distribution Co, Inc
A film by Tim Burton and Rick Heinrichs
Narrated by Vincent Price
Written, designed and directed by Tim Burton
Produced by Rick Heinrichs
Technical Director: Stephen Chiodo
Director of Photography: Victor Abdalow
Music: Tom Hilton
Sculpture and Additional Design: Rick Heinrichs
Animation: Stephen Chiodo
With gratitude to Julie Hickson, Chris Roth, Dave Allen, Eric Brevig, Chas Smith, New Hollywood Inc

TITLE SEQUENCE: The opening credits run in white over simple, plain black backgrounds, which dissolve into a highly stylised black cat slinking past a greyish wall, on which the title of the short film appears.

SUMMARY: Vincent Molloy is a seven-year-old boy. Described as 'considerate and nice' we discover that he wishes to be 'just like Vincent Price'. Obsessed with Price, and with author Edgar Allan Poe, Vincent dreams of a life 'alone and tormented' that would take him away from the banalities of his suburban existence. Sent to his room for digging up his mother's flower bed whilst believing himself a character in a Poe story, Vincent convinces himself that all the horrors he has imagined in his life are attacking him, and tries to escape. He fails – falling, perhaps dying (perhaps merely fantasising that he is) to the floor. Lying alone in the dark he quotes the final lines from Poe's 'The Raven' (first published in *The Raven and other poems*, 1841): 'And my soul from out that shadow that lies floating on the floor, shall be lifted Nevermore.'

SOURCE MATERIAL: *Vincent* has numerous sources, including the poetry and prose of Edgar Allan Poe (1809–1849) and the life and film career of actor Vincent Price (1911–1993). These are covered in more detail in **REFERENCES**, below. However, the primary inspiration for the film appears to be Burton's recollections of his own childhood. As he would later explain, 'Vincent Price helped me get through childhood. I loved horror movies as a child. It was just sort of natural escapism. It encompassed everything – humour, psychology, darkness, emotion. They tapped into the way I feel about life.'[1] Later he would further confirm the impact that screen heroes had on his life, telling Mark Kermode in an interview at London's National Film Theatre in January 2000 that 'you see these people up on the screen going through torment and being on the outside and somehow you relate to them and it helps you get through life.'[2]

REFERENCES: Visually the film suggests aspects of Expressionism, with its continually shifting, shadow-enshrouded backgrounds, 'a film that might be termed '*The Cabinet of Dr Caligari* (Robert Wiene, 1920) meets Ray Harryhausen',[3] as one commentator put it. Most noticeably *M* (Fritz Lang, 1931) and *Nosferatu – a symphony in terror* (FW Murnau, 1922) provide visual cues. For example, the night-stalking form of Vincent's zombie dog, Abercrombie, casts a shadow that suggests Count Orlock in the latter picture. The twisted handrails and snaking black architecture do indeed recall *Das Kabinett des Doktor Caligari*. The 'Harryhausen' aspect is present only in as much as the animation is stop-motion. There is little or nothing to suggest the organic, Technicolor vibrancy of Harryhausen's best work in *Vincent*.

Vincent Molloy's obsession with Vincent Price leads to him wishing to dip his aunt in wax and display her in his wax museum, a clear reference to *House of Wax* (Andre de Toth, 1953).

The story that young Vincent reads, and which leads him to believe he has inadvertently buried his wife alive, is a conflation of 'The Fall of the House of Usher' (first published, incidentally, in *Burton's* in September 1839, and subsequently revised for Poe's collection *Tales of the Grotesque and Arabesque – volume 1* in 1840) and 'The Premature Burial' (published in *Dollar Newspaper*, 31 July 1844). 'Usher' was made into a film starring – yes, Vincent Price – by director Roger Corman in 1960. 'The

Premature Burial' was also adapted into a film by Corman in 1962, though Vincent Price did not feature.

The film also features a black cat, the titular nasty of 'The Black Cat', another Poe story first published in the *United States Saturday Post* on 19 August 1843. It too was later revised by the author for a collection, this time *Tales*, published in 1845. 'The Black Cat' was also filmed by Corman with a starring role for Price, this time as a segment of his *Tales of Terror* (1962).

Despite his Vincent Price moustache, Vincent's high-collared coat in the 'fantasy' sequences makes him look more like Henry Frankenstein in *Frankenstein* (James Whale, 1931). The electrical equipment strapped to Abercrombie's head is also reminiscent of laboratory equipment from that film.

PRODUCTION: *Vincent* was made for $60,000 while Burton and Heinrichs were at Disney, during the same period as *Luau*. They managed to get the studio's financial backing to make the picture – which was based on a children's story Burton had already written – thanks to the good-will of studio vice-president Tom Wilhite, who had spotted something unusual in Burton's rough sketches. As Heinrichs admitted at the time, 'To be quite honest, it's something of a fluke that this film was made at all, because it's very unusual for a studio the size of Disney to invest in a short film such as *Vincent*.'[4]

But these were unusual times at Disney. The company's animated films had been consistently poorly received since the release of 1967's *The Jungle Book*, the last full-length animated film to have been produced during the lifetime of studio founder, Walt Disney (1901–66).

Despite efforts to bring in fresh artistic blood throughout the 1970s *The Aristocats* (1970), *The Rescuers* (1977), *The Many Adventures of Winnie the Pooh* (1977), and *The Fox and the Hound* (1981) all failed to live up to the earlier high standards of the studio. Although the company was still doing well financially – largely due to the revenue generated by the newly opened theme park Disneyworld – executives realised that it might be time for a change.

One of the ideas they were toying with was a shift from traditional cel animation, with which Disney had for so long been associated, to a completely different style. The use of three-dimensional ball and socket models for the animation, combined with harsh black and white photography, certainly created something visually utterly different to the company's usual style for animated pictures. According to Heinrichs, although Disney had toyed with the idea of making a children's movie using three-dimensional animation in the past, they had been put off by their unfamiliarity with the process. Burton and Heinrichs felt that '. . . we could convince the hierarchy that a feature-length, model-animated film with the Disney logo on it could be commercially viable, and *Vincent* was our way of showing them.'[5]

The project was officially kept at 'off the lot' status – meaning that despite the company's financial support for it, Burton and Heinrichs had to provide all their own materials. This would enable Disney to distance themselves from the project should it turn out poorly. *Vincent* was thus shot in rented space with rented equipment at Dave Allen's studio across town, with little interference from the Disney hierarchy. Its production, therefore, more closely resembles that of an independent film like *Luau* than a regular studio picture.

Eventually, the hoped-for revolution at Disney would be ushered in by Michael Eisner, following his appointment in 1984 as the head of the company, and the release of the high-grossing *Oliver and Company* (George Scribner, 1988) and *Luau* cast-member John Musker's 1989 feature *The Little Mermaid*. These two films spearheaded a full decade of high grossing, critically acclaimed Disney features, many of which would have significant input from Burton's *Luau* partners.

CASTING: There is only one actor in the movie, the narrator. For the film to work effectively there could really only ever have been one man for the job – Vincent Price. Burton decided he might as well give it a shot: 'I remember sending it to him in little booklet form, and he wrote me back and it was such an amazing thing . . . [for] somebody who I'd idolised so much to be so nice.'[6]

Burton's hero lived up to his image. Nearly twenty years later, Burton was still hugely impressed with that first experience of meeting Price, and with the man himself: 'He was great . . . it was the first experience I'd had like that where somebody who you admired was also a great person . . . a real shining light.'[7] Heinrichs was equally impressed, 'one of the best things about making this was getting to meet Vincent Price . . . Vincent seemed quite pleased and flattered by the entire project.'[8]

Price's narration was recorded in one day in December 1981, before the animation had been developed. He too enjoyed the experience, not simply because 'it was very flattering to be the subject of a Disney film,' but also because 'it was a delightful film.'[9]

BURTON REGULARS: Vincent Price would return on *Edward Scissorhands*, where he acts as a mentor to another character often identified as a Burton alter-ego.

Stephen Chiodo would work on *Pee-wee's Big Adventure*, where he acted as Animated Effects Consultant, as well as on *Hansel and Gretel* and *Aladdin and his Wonderful Lamp*, where he provided Special Effects.

CRITICS: *Vincent* received little coverage on its initial limited release. *Cinefantastique* seemed impressed, stating that 'Although it's not the most publicised film from the Walt Disney studios, *Vincent* may certainly be the most unusual. *Bambi* it ain't.'[10] Years later, the same magazine would again sing its praises, arguing that the film was 'Brimming with feeling, brilliantly designed and executed . . . a mini-masterpiece deserving of the widest possible exposure,'[11] and bemoaning its unavailability.

MUSIC: Tom Hilton's score is hugely atmospheric, mostly consisting of melodic variations on 'In an Egyptian Marketplace' and JS Bach's 'Toccata and Fugue in D minor'. The movie's mood derives as much from Hilton's crashing chords as Burton's shadows.

CINEMATOGRAPHY: Much of the camerawork on *Vincent* is fairly basic, primarily employing static shots, as is often the case with stop-motion animation. Limited by both time and budget, the simple approach works especially well, particularly as much of the action is purely Vincent's imaginings. Thus, scenes shoot rapidly out of the darkness that surrounds the terrified boy at all times, grainy black and white nightmare images, half-glimpsed through the general air of gloom and darkness that permeates the entire film.

DEATH: No actual killing, but the topic is ever present as so much of the film is made up of Vincent's own morbid fantasies of murder and death. Equally, by the end of the film, 'the kid basically has the impression of not living ... even though it's in his own mind.'[12]

CHILDREN AND FAMILIES: The story is, of course, that of a seven-year-old with morbid pretensions. More than that it plays with the idea that children are alienated from their parents, and the notion that children often find it difficult to distinguish between fact and fantasy, the real and the unreal. 'These games that you play are all in your head,' says Vincent's disapproving mother at one point. It's hard not to note the similarities with the picture Burton has painted of himself as a child.

DOGS: Vincent wants to do Frankenstein-like electrical experiments on his dog, the wonderfully named Abercrombie. He hopes these experiments will turn it into a 'horrible zombie'. In Burton's next short film, Vincent's dreams would be realised.

AUTOBIOGRAPHY?: *Vincent* is one of the most – if not *the* most – autobiographical films Burton has yet made. 'I can't tell you what [Price] meant to me growing up. This sounds dramatic but he helped me live. When you're a child and a teenager it's not unusual to go through a melodramatic phase,' Burton explained. 'But by watching [Price's] films, there was a catharsis for me. I channelled my melodrama into that, as opposed to suicide probably.'[13]

AFTERLIFE: It has been reported that an executive asked that the film be given a more positive, upbeat ending. 'They wanted me to have him get up and walk around and have it be a happy ending, which was the exact opposite point on it,'[14] Burton later commented disdainfully.

Ultimately, *Vincent* was deemed too dark to be distributed as a support feature to any of Disney's other projects. Except for a brief run on the festival circuits it remained largely unseen. Its only real impact on Disney was that, having lent his voice to this, Disney's first foray into 3-D animation, Vincent Price would later play Professor Ratigan for the studio's *The Great Mouse Detective* (1986) the first feature-length film to feature computer animation.

AWARDS: *Vincent* received the prestigious 'Critic's Prize' at the Annecy Festival (France), as well as some favourable comments at film festivals in LA, Chicago and Seattle.

EXPERT WITNESS: Rick Heinrichs: 'Disney likes to make sculptures of the characters for its animated movies so that the animators can hold three-dimensional things in their hands. Tim and I learned that you can combine the graphic look that makes the most of the design elements of a two-dimensional picture with something three dimensional. It finally came to fruition in *Vincent* . . . showing us we could have the best of both. We loved that expressionistic approach then, and Tim still strives for it in all his work.'

ANALYSIS: Although Burton clearly identifies with Vincent (there is, after all, some physical resemblance) the child is obviously a sad figure, morbidly obsessed not just with death, but the idea that such an obsession makes him 'deeper' than the banal world inhabited by the other occupants of the house. Vincent's malaise is described by the narrator as a 'sad insanity', and in some ways the film seems designed as a warning to those who perceive themselves as 'outsiders' to avoid the trap of believing too strongly in their own superiority.

AVAILABILITY: *Vincent* is one of the many 'bonus materials' included on the Special Edition DVD of *Tim Burton's The Nightmare Before Christmas*. It's worth the price of the disc on its own.

THE BOTTOM LINE: *Vincent* is stark, compulsive and lyrical. It blends pop-psychology with mordant wit and frankly astounding visuals. Despite running at just over five minutes, it is a beautiful piece of film.

Hansel and Gretel

Despite considering *Vincent* too dark for their studio's image, executives at Disney still seem to have realised that Burton had something special. Soon afterwards, they gave him the chance to direct *Hansel and Gretel* for television. The 45 minute production, shot on 16mm film stock, was made for just $116,000 – less than twice the budget of *Vincent*, despite being nine times its length – and was once again an 'off-the-lot' project.

Taking a different approach to the fairy tale formula, as he would later do with his adaptation of *Aladdin and his Wonderful Lamp*, Burton relocated the story from the German Black Forest to a highly stylised world of his own concoction, one populated solely by Japanese people; a decision perhaps influenced by the director's declared love for Japanese culture, especially its 'chop socky' martial arts pictures, and the 'man in a suit' *Godzilla* series. As with *Luau*, none of the cast were professional actors.

Following the basic storyline of the fairy tale, there were only comparatively minor changes. In changing the profession of Hansel and Gretel's father (played by Jim Ishida) from a woodcutter to a toy maker, Burton was able to populate one set with Transformers and other Japanese toys, creating a kitsch-filled environment similar to the home of the titular character in *Pee-wee's Big Adventure*. Furthermore, following the traditions of Japanese theatre, in which women were not allowed on stage, both the children's step-mother and the wicked witch were played by a man, Michael Yama, the first part for which he appears in traditional Kabuki attire. Aside from that, the only major change was the climactic karate battle – 'Burton at his utmost crazed',[1] according to one of the few articles about the project.

Burton's first foray into professional live-action filmmaking was not a wholesale success story. His cast of amateurs, some of whom had a limited grasp of English, were not an ideal introduction to the world of serious directing. The experience at least taught him enough to know how he should approach the situation when he came to make his next project – hence his decision to approach highly experienced performers such as Shelley Duvall when it came to casting for *Frankenweenie*.

Hansel and Gretel's excessive running time may also have influenced *Frankenweenie*'s shorter length, as Burton surely realised that many scenes in the film are too stretched. This was an unfortunate necessity; the special was expected to fill a one-hour slot on the then newly created Disney Channel.

Furthermore, due to the meagre budget, Burton had to find innovative ways of producing the special effects he needed. From stop-motion, front projection, and forced perspective to any number of other on-set visual tricks he appears to have tried anything that was possible within his limited means, even a repulsive effect where the walls of the witch's house seem to ooze jam like a doughnut (visually undoubtedly a reference to Peter John Duffell's *The House that Dripped Blood* [1970]). The experience of working to create good-looking effects on a tiny budget would prove invaluable when Burton later came to *Beetlejuice*.

Like *Vincent* before it, and the later *Frankenweenie*, his employers seemed unsure of what to do with Burton's new production. When the Disney Channel eventually did show *Hansel and Gretel*, for the first and only time, it was – appropriately enough – buried in the 10.30 p.m. graveyard slot on 31 October – Halloween. When, a decade later, Touchstone video prepared to release *The Nightmare Before Christmas* on DVD they chose not to include this early Burton piece as a 'special feature' despite the much-touted presence of both *Vincent* and *Frankenweenie* on the disc. This seems odd given that, in terms of design at least, the landscape of *Hansel and Gretel* is more similar to the world of Jack Skellington than any other Burton production.

FRANKENWEENIE (1984)

Distributed by Buena Vista Distribution Co, Inc
Walt Disney Pictures presents
Screenplay by Lenny Ripps
Based on an original idea by Tim Burton
Director of Photography: Thomas Ackerman
Art Director: John B Mansbridge
Produced by Julie Hickson
Associate Producer: Rick Heinrichs
Production Supervisor: Tom Leech

Casting: Bill Shepard, CSA Joe Scully, CSA
Editor: Ernest Milano, ACE
Directed by Tim Burton

CAST: Shelley Duvall (*Susan Frankenstein*), Daniel Stern (*Ben Frankenstein*), Barret Oliver (*Victor Frankenstein*), Mr Chambers (*Joseph Maher*), Roz Braverman (*Mrs Epstein*), Paul Bartel (*Mr Walsh*), Domino (*Ann Chambers*), Jason Hervey (*Frank Dale*), Paul C Scott (*Mike Anderson*), Helen Boll (*Mrs Curtis*), Bob Herron (Street Player), Donna Hall (Street Player), Sparky (*Sparky*), Rusty James (*Raymond*).

TITLE SEQUENCE: A pre-credits sequence shows a contemporary suburban American family watching their son's home movies. Young Victor Frankenstein has shot a film entitled *Monsters From Long Ago*. This features his dog, Sparky, dressed up as some kind of dinosaur, battling plastic pterodactyls and a GI Joe doll, and encountering Victor's mother's oven gloves. The family are impressed by Victor's cinematic efforts and as the film finishes Victor basks in the admiration. But tragedy strikes as Sparky unexpectedly charges out of the house and into the road, where he is knocked down by a car and killed. Then we fade from young Victor's trauma to several still shots of a graveyard – as it turns out a pet cemetery – where Sparky will shortly be buried. Over this morbid backdrop a lush orchestral swell plays, and the captions come up.

SUMMARY: Following a surprising science lesson at school, Victor becomes convinced that he can revive his beloved pet using electric shocks. Cobbling together some laboratory equipment, using pieces from his father's garage, he successfully re-animates his pet during a lightning storm. Hiding the results of his scientific expertise from his parents and their neighbours proves more difficult than he anticipated when Sparky again escapes, prompting local citizens to believe that a monster, or at the very least a tiger, is on the loose in their neighbourhood.

Having been discovered with the revived Sparky by his father, Victor explains his experiments to his parents, who accept that despite the bolt through his neck and the thread holding his head on, this really is their beloved pet. Victor's dad arranges a meeting of local residents to explain everything, but thanks to the screaming of a loud, fat, obnoxious woman named Rose, Sparky is frightened into running away again. The residents then pursue him in mob formation, as Victor and his parents try desperately to find their beloved mutt before the screaming crowd. Victor tracks Sparky to a closed miniature golf course, and they sit together in the scale-model of a windmill, hiding from the mob.

Eventually the mob catches up with them and, more by accident than design, set light to the windmill. Sparky saves Victor, but at the cost of his own life. Impressed by the nobility of the dog's self-sacrifice, the locals relent and use their car batteries to revive the dog for a second time. Just when it looks like the ending can't get any happier, Sparky falls instantly in love with a pretty girl-dog. It seems very likely that they all live happily ever after.

SOURCE MATERIAL: Although the credits say 'Based on an original idea by Tim Burton', the principle source is the first-ever film adaptation of Mary Shelley's novel *Frankenstein* (James Whale, 1931) the style of which is emulated in everything from camera angles, to Victor's clothes, to the musical score, to the finale inside a blazing windmill. Incidentally, our hero retains the name *Victor* Frankenstein (like the character in Mary Shelley's novel) even though Whale's film re-named him Henry. This was partially because Burton wanted to make a few changes: 'This suburban family is the Frankenstein family and the little boy is Victor, but it's not a nudge in the ribs type of thing. We don't have the family watching the Universal original as a foreboding of things to come. At least to me, the more you went with a heh-heh-heh mad scientist kid, the less impact the film had.'[1] Almost every major set-piece from the picture, including the monster's encounter with an old man and the intervention of a torch-wielding mob, is represented at some point in *Franken-weenie* (although in this case the torches are not burning, but battery-powered). The finale, in which Sparky meets a lady dog with whom he instantly falls in love, is a sideways glance to Whale's own sequel *The Bride of Frankenstein* (1935), as the female dog's fur resembles the hair of Elsa Lanchester's eponymous bride.

When interviewed Burton discussed his bizarre synthesising of Universal horror classics with suburban dog trauma – 'I started thinking just how incredible the whole idea of . . . bringing something dead back to life [is]. But all the versions of it so far have just dealt with the horrible aspects of the idea.' Intrigued by the idea of putting a new spin on the concept Burton began looking for ideas, and 'at some point, the idea of my dog and *Frankenstein* just connected.'[2]

REFERENCES: Keeping up the Universal horror asides, young Victor's breakfast mug is in the shape of Lon Chaney Jr's head, as he appears in Universal's version of *The Wolf Man* (George Waggner, 1941).

There are several jokey references in the shots of the pet cemetery's gravestones. One is to a cat that looks suspiciously like the Japanese marketing extravaganza that is 'Hello Kitty' with the slogan 'Goodbye Kitty' underneath.

During the classroom sequence, the teacher refers to the frog on which he is experimenting as being 'an ex-frog' – raising his eyebrows to see if any of his class get the reference. They evidently haven't seen the 'Dead Parrot Sketch' from *Monty Python's Flying Circus*.

A Disney film would not be complete without some of the recognisable Disney icons, and this one of Burton's is no different, featuring as it does not only a Mickey Mouse toy in the attic, but also Donald Duck orange juice at the breakfast table.

Betraying his love for Dr Seuss, which had already become evident in the verse of *Vincent*, Victor has a toy Cat in the Hat, from Dr Seuss' book of the same name.

PRODUCTION: Having successfully pitched his storyboards to Disney production chief Richard Berger, Burton got together with writer Lenny Ripps to knock his ideas into narrative shape. They were on a tight schedule, as *Frankenweenie* was originally planned to be shot in early 1984 so it could be paired with that summer's re-release of *Jungle Book* (Wolfgang Reitherman, 1967). The Disney company later re-scheduled the film, allotting it a late summer shooting schedule – plans had changed and they now wished to pair the film with the Christmas re-release of *Pinocchio* (Hamilton Luske and Ben Sharpsteen, 1940). Judging by what he said at the time, the change seemed to please Burton, as '*Pinocchio* is Julie [Hickson]'s and my favourite Disney movie . . . one of the best colour movies ever made, so we're real happy about this.'[3]

There was a downside though – the stop-start nature of the production meant that the entire 30-minute featurette had to be shot in just two weeks. According to Hickson a lot of the rush was because 'Disney was trying to keep the production costs down. There [was] an enormous overload at the studio. The actual production was a 15-day shoot with a couple of months for post-production.'[4] 'We're really happy about being with *Pinocchio* because they'll be terrific together. They're both very primal stories. Ours is like a fairy tale, really.'[5]

Burton seemed happy with the production as a whole, saying, 'When I look at the stuff we asked them to make from the designs, I don't think we could have gotten it at any other studio. It's like Disneyland. When you look at Disneyland, there's a certain bent, it's subtle, but it really is different.'[6]

Something that greatly pleased both Burton and Hickson was their acquisition of some of the original laboratory set from Whale's *Frankenstein*, designed by the brilliant Kenneth Strickfadden. Having lain in storage for decades it had been found and used in Mel Brooks' magnificent sequel/parody *Young Frankenstein* (1974) only a decade earlier. Once acquired it was duly incorporated into young Victor's equipment. As Hickson put it, 'There was never any doubt in our minds that we wanted it [the Strickfadden equipment] but it was hard to get.'[7] It was apparently difficult for Disney's management to understand why two horror fans wanted the props so badly, until they finally saw it, and had to concur. When interviewed Burton found it hard to contain his enthusiasm for what were genuine pieces of Hollywood history: 'It's one of those things that's like a dream come true when you first see that stuff.'[8]

CASTING: Burton and Hickson tried to get a number of name-actors for *Frankenweenie* to ensure a high profile for the project. According to Hickson, 'I really believe that you can get anybody you want if you just get the kind of material that they can respond to ... I just had the feeling that [Shelley Duvall would] understand what we were trying to do.' Hickson wrote to Duvall, who read the script and liked it. 'Once I had her, it became easier to get people like Daniel Stern, because he wanted to work with her.' Paul Bartel agreed to take part because he 'loved the material and really believes in supporting short films. Basically, we got this cast for no money because they all wanted to do it.'[9]

BURTON REGULARS: Shelley Duvall would go on to executive produce and introduce *Aladdin and his Wonderful Lamp*.

Joseph Maher appeared as the Sultan in *Aladdin and his Wonderful Lamp*, and cameoed as the White House decorator in *Mars Attacks!*

Jason Hervey would appear as the spoiled brat actor, Kevin Morton, in *Pee-wee's Big Adventure*.

Bob Herron returned to do stunt work on *Pee-wee's Big Adventure*. Women's Costumer Sandy Berke Jordan would have the same role on *Pee-wee*. Animal trainer Christy Miele acted as Animal Co-ordinator on *Pee-wee*. Ed Nunnery, who here receives 'special thanks', later designed Delia's sculptures for *Beetlejuice*. Score Mixer Shawn Murphy acted in similar roles on *Batman*, *Batman Returns*, *Edward Scissorhands*, *Mars Attacks!* and *Sleepy Hollow*.

CRITICS: Contemporary reviews of *Frankenweenie* are rare, *Cinefantastique*, however, was impressed: 'Probably the last studio on earth you'd expect to do another version of the Frankenstein legend is Walt Disney Studios, but the ever-changing World of Walt has done just that ... designed and directed by mad genius Tim Burton with a sly but subtle eye for understated parody that may turn this 30-minute featurette into Disney's first modern cult classic.'[10]

CINEMATOGRAPHY: Despite Burton's complaints about the poor results of shooting in black and white on colour stock the picture remains surprisingly crisp, with good contrasts between the light and shadows.

There's something very, very odd about watching suburban America photographed like nineteenth-century Bavaria. The innovation of using typical suburban items like Venetian blinds and table lamps to provide long, dramatic shadows and stark uplighting effects, is one Burton would repeat in *Ed Wood*. Furthermore, the frequent use of low down, dog's-eye-view camera angles help to make something very familiar seem very distant, but without separating the audience from the story.

DEATH: The entire film is fuelled by a death – Sparky's first untimely demise, filmed from his perspective as he charges into the road. This short film is a wish-fulfilment fantasy come true, where death is never permanent for pets; they can always be revived. Here, death starts off as its usual depressing self, Victor Frankenstein sinking into fits of misery akin to those of Vincent Molloy, but by the end of the film death is no more than a temporary inconvenience – assuming there are car batteries handy.

CHILDREN AND FAMILIES: Victor's father is the perfect sitcom dad, who calls his son 'Sport' and 'Champ'. His mother is another supportive type, trying to cheer him up by cooking his favourite dinner. Unfortunately, they seem distant, Victor's mother gets his favourite meal wrong, and his father is slow to accept the positive results of his son's bizarre experiment.

CLOWNS AND THE CIRCUS: In the miniature golf course, aside from the windmill, there is a castle, a boat house, and an evil-looking clown's head with a ramp leading up to its gaping mouth for the ball to run up.

DOGS: The ultimate dog movie. Victor's love for his cute, yappy mutt is the spur on the entire story. And Sparky the dog, playing – erm – Sparky the dog, is the perfect mixture of cute and odd-looking to slot neatly into Burton's vision, just as his own dog, Poppy the chihuahua, would later fit nicely into *Mars Attacks!* Yet as in *Vincent*, and indeed in many of Burton's films in which dogs play a major role, he seems to take a perverse glee in experimenting on them, here turning the 'handsome' Sparky into a stitched-up, bolt-necked 'monster', just as Victor earlier dressed up the poor mutt to appear in his home-made movie.

CHECKS, STRIPES, DOTS: These appear absolutely everywhere: via shadows created by harsh lights diffused by Venetian blinds; on one of the supports on the roof contraption; spirals on the bicycle dynamo wheels; the black and white checked floor in the Frankensteins' house; even Sparky himself has black and white spots on his coat.

JUST PLAIN WEIRD: A dog called Raymond? Come on ...

AUTOBIOGRAPHY?: A suburban boy with nice but strangely distant parents who becomes involved in something untoward – says it all, really.

DIALOGUE TO SKIP BACK FOR:

Teacher: 'So that, class, is what is meant by the old adage "Rome wasn't built in a day".'

Rose: 'It was six foot tall, like a wolf – it tried to eat my Raymond!'

Neighbour: 'I heard they had a lion in there!'
Rose: 'I saw it, it's worse, and it's bigger!'

Victor: 'People are weird'

AFTERLIFE: Despite Disney's declared intentions *Frankenweenie* was not released with *Pinocchio* at the end of 1984. Two test screenings had been held in late September – the audience consisting of mothers and children in the six–nine age bracket. The Motion Pictures Association of America had given the short a PG rating and Disney wished to ascertain what parents thought before committing to a theatrical run. Apparently many parents from this sample were concerned that the picture would influence their children into playing with electricity, while many more felt the picture too 'intense' – and ultimately unsuitable for release with the ostensibly more family friendly *Pinocchio*.

Instead *Frankenweenie* ran in various LA art cinemas in December in order to qualify for the following year's Oscars.

By spring 1985 the company had found a more appropriate project to release Burton's film alongside, *My Science Project* (1985) directed by Steven L Schneider, who would later collaborate with Burton on the design for *Pee-wee's Big Adventure*. For no declared reason, this thematically sensible idea did not come to pass, and the December '85 art house run would become *Frankenweenie*'s only Stateside cinematic exposure. In Britain, though, *Frankenweenie* enjoyed more exposure, being added as a support feature to Disney's *Baby – Secret of the Lost Legend* (BWL Norton, 1985).

The reasons for the studio's lack of support were somewhat akin to their feelings about *Vincent*; there was something about the film and its approach to childhood, the kind of thing Disney should not associate itself with. Asked about this, Burton tried to explain the company's reaction with reference to what he had set out to do with the short: 'What interests me is trying to give things like *Vincent* and *Frankenweenie* real feelings and emotions . . . not just make them funny.'[11] This did not sit easily with his employers, who shied away from the film precisely because it tried to be 'powerful and full of real feelings that stay with you a long time'. Defending his picture against charges of being too intense, he said, 'I don't think this is a dark or macabre story, and we didn't try to make the dog something horrible. He brings the dog back to life because he really loves the dog.'[12]

The lack of support from Disney over *Frankenweenie*, following as it did their reluctance to promote *Vincent*, or to televise *Hansel and Gretel* more than once, was the final straw for Burton. He left the studio shortly afterwards.

TRIVIA: The actress playing Ann Chambers is credited as 'Domino' – a pseudonym for a then very young Sofia Coppola, the actress/director/fashion designer daughter of Francis Ford Coppola (later credited as Executive Producer on Burton's *Sleepy Hollow*). She is also a cousin of Nicolas Cage (who signed up to star as Clark Kent/Superman in Burton's abortive *Superman Lives* project).

ANALYSIS: For a long time *Frankenweenie* looks like it's going to be about the unforgiving, insular nature of suburbia – a fable about how middle America can't accept things that are beyond its understanding. But then the happy ending arrives and undoes all that. People can be brought round, opinions can be changed, people can become accepting – even suspicious Mr Chambers and hideous Rose. There is no evidence to suggest that this was anything other than Burton's intention from the start, yet it remains odd that Burton's most hopeful, idealistic picture would also be his last for Disney. Equally, as Burton himself has pointed out, it seems truly odd that it was considered unsuitable for release with *Pinocchio*, as that earlier Disney classic is, in places, much more disturbing than *Frankenweenie*.

AVAILABILITY: Like *Vincent*, *Frankenweenie* is included on the DVD of *The Nightmare Before Christmas*.

THE BOTTOM LINE: Whatever executives thought at the time, *Frankenweenie* is an effective cross-breeding of Burton's stylistic predilections with traditional Disney warmth. It is sweet, charming, has a happy ending, and shows great faith in people's ability to see the error of their ways. Shame about the dreadful title, though.

Aladdin and his Wonderful Lamp

Following his split with Disney, Burton was offered the chance to direct an episode of Showtime's *Faerie Tale Theatre* by Shelley Duvall. Duvall had originated the idea for the series, and both acted as Executive Producer on the programme and introduced each episode. For the young Burton to suddenly find himself working on a series, to which such big names as director Francis Ford Coppola had also contributed, ensured a lot of self-imposed pressure.

A straightforward re-telling of a well-known fairy tale, here Burton's quirky sense of design complements rather than detracts from the story, as written by Mark Curtiss and Rod Ash (who also penned Coppola's episode, 'Rip Van Winkle'). Shot on video and running at 47 minutes, it – like *Vincent* – featured an actor with a substantial cult following, Leonard Nimoy, as the Evil Magician.

Also, in the first of many examples where Burton has worked with members of the *Star Wars* films' cast and crew, James Earl Jones, the voice of Darth Vader, appeared in three roles – as the narrator, and as two different genies.

Unfortunately these two well-known actors rather overshadow the film's lead, Robert Carradine (son of John, brother of Keith, half-brother of David), with Nimoy soaring deliciously over the top in a performance akin to his turn as Galvatron in *Transformers The Movie* (Nelson Shin, 1986) – about as far as one can imagine from his famous Vulcan role.

Aladdin did feature other personnel, besides Shelley Duvall, with whom Burton had worked on *Frankenweenie*, including Joseph Maher (playing the Sultan), with David Newman and Michael Covertino again providing the score. Rick Heinrichs and Steven Chiodo provided models and special effects, which nicely complement the overall look, which is as if a ghost train collided with the *Arabian Nights*, but the budget was low, and it shows.

Burton found the experience rather daunting, not least because he only had one week to record the entire episode, as well as trying to direct, in Nimoy, one of the icons of his childhood. It was a tough shoot, and one that proved to Burton that he worked best when allowed control over his projects, as he had had on his previous directorial efforts, even if only due to Disney's desire to distance themselves.

Even with the accommodating encouragement of Shelley Duvall, Burton found it tricky to really personalise the film. Perhaps the closest thing to a trademark Burton sequence is as Nimoy's Evil Magician sends Carradine's Aladdin into a desert cave, filled with skeletons and creepy-crawlies, to find the lamp, which is held by a hand thrust out of the gaping mouth of a bronze fish. There are other touches too, the Sultan having filled his home with toys, and watching a truly odd television show; surreal, *Caligari* style tunnels lined with skulls, and even the odd topiary.

However, Burton has since gone on record to say that he neither enjoyed the experience, nor the finished product.

PEE-WEE'S BIG ADVENTURE (1985)

Warner Brothers presents
An Aspen Film Society/Robert Shapiro Production
Written by Phil Hartman and Paul Reubens and Michael Varhol
Director of Photography: Victor J Kemper, ASC
Production Designer: David L Snyder
Set Decorator: Thomas L Roysden
Produced by Robert Shapiro and Richard Gilbert Abramson
Executive Producer: William E McEuen
Casting by Wally Nicita
Music by Danny Elfman
Costume Designer: Aggie Guerard Rodgers
Edited by Billy Weber
Directed by Tim Burton

CAST: Paul Reubens (*Pee-wee Herman*), Elizabeth Daily (*Dottie*), Mark Holton (*Francis*), Diane Salinger (*Simone*), Mickey (*Judd Omen*), Irving Hellman (*Neighbour*), Monte Landis (*Mario*), Damon Martin (*Chip*), David Glasser, Gregory Brown, Mark Everett (*BMX Kids*), Daryl Roach (*Chuck*), Bill Cable (Policeman #1), Peter Looney (Policeman #2) Starletta DuPois (*Sgt Hunter*), Prof Toru Tanaka (*Butler*), Ed Herlihy (*Mr Buxton*), Ralph

Seymour (*Francis' accomplice*), Lou Cutell (*Amazing Larry*), Raymon Martino (*Gang Member*), Erica Yohng (*Madam Ruby*), Bill Richmond (*Highway Patrolman*), Alice Nunn (*Large Marge*), Ed Griffith (*Trucker*), Simmy Bow (*Man in Diner*), John Harris (*Andy*), Carmen Filip (*Hobo Jack*), Jan Hooks (*Tina*), John Moody (*Bus Clerk*), John O'Niell (*Cowboy #1*), Alex Sharp (*Cowboy #2*), Chester Grimes (*Biker #1*), Luis Contreras (*Biker #2*), Lonnie Parkinson (*Biker #3*), Howard Hirdler (*Biker #4*), Cassandra Peterson (*Biker Mama*), Jason Hervey (*Kevin Morton*), Bob McClurg (*Studio Guard*), John Paragaon (*Movie Lot Actor*), Susan Barnes (*Movie Lot Actress*), Zachary Hoffman (*Director*), Lynne Stewart (*Mother Superior*), George Sasakai (*Japanese Director*), Richard Brose (*Tarzan*), Drew Seward (*Kid #1*), Brett Fellman (*Kid #2*), Bob Drew (*Fireman*), John Gilgreen (*Policeman at pet shop*), Noreen Hennessy (*Reporter*), Phil Hartman (*Reporter*), Michael Varhol (*Photographer*), David Rothenberg, Pat Cranshaw, Sunshine Parker (*Bums*), Giles Savard (*Pierre*).

Special Appearances by James Brolin ('*P.W.*'), Morgan Fairchild ('*Dottie*'), Tony Bull (*Terry Hawthorne*), Twisted Sister.

TRAILER: The trailer for *Pee-wee*, cut as it was in the mid-80s, now seems crushingly slow and dated, and is therefore about as unlike the movie it's trailing as it's possible to be.

TITLE SEQUENCE: We begin with the usual Warner Brothers logo. Over this a swell of chaotic, circus-style music, laced with the sound of parping tubas, starts playing. The logo fades to black. The first few credits come up in plain white text on a black background. Then 'Pee-wee's Big Adventure' appears in multicoloured fridge-magnet style letters. 'We didn't have money for a big credits sequence,' commented Burton later on this simple but effective sequence, 'so we had to try and set the tone as best we could right from the beginning. The music certainly helps with that.'[1]

SUMMARY: Pee-wee Herman wakes from a dream of winning the Tour de France; it's another beautiful day. The day quickly goes wrong, however, when he discovers that his beloved bike has been stolen by rich kid Francis and then fenced. He chases his bike across the country, from one state to another. During this lengthy road trip he has a series of encounters with numerous bizarre individuals, including an escaped criminal called Mickey, a singing tramp, the ghost of a female trucker and a gang of Hell's Angels bikers. He eventually retrieves his bike from the Warner Brothers studio lot in Burbank, California, but is captured by security staff after he chooses to save numerous animals from a burning pet shop rather than make good his escape. Impressed by his story and his bravery Warner Brothers offers him a deal.

The film closes with the premier of *Pee-wee's Big Adventure*, a bad James Bond pastiche starring James Brolin as 'P.W. Herman', with all of the friends Pee-wee has made on his journey in attendance. Pee-wee and Dottie, a girl who is infatuated with him, ride off on bikes together – he points out that he doesn't have to see the rest of the movie as, 'I lived it.'

SOURCE MATERIAL: Pee-wee Herman was created in 1978 at the Groundlings, a Los Angeles comedy improvisation group founded in 1972 (as 'The Gary Austin Workshop'). Alumni include *Pee-wee* co-writer and *Simpsons* voice-over artist, the late Phil Hartman, the actress Lisa Kudrow, Jon Lovitz and numerous other *Saturday Night Live* stars. The Groundlings is one of the best places in the world to learn improvisational skills, working as it does on a schooling system, where lucky members progress up the levels to graduation. Despite its emphasis on improvisation, the group also teaches writing skills, getting each member to write sketches for other actors' characters, ensuring that Phil Hartman knew the Pee-wee character as well as his initial creator did by the time they came to write the film.

The besuited man-child that is Pee-wee Herman was the most successful of the many comic characters of one Paul Reubens. The native New Yorker had joined the group in 1978, after moving from his longtime Florida home to Southern California, in order to study acting at the California Institute of the Arts (Burton was also studying there, but the two never met).

Reubens once claimed, 'I just sort of flipped a switch and the character came out,'[2] and then apologised that he hadn't got a better story. He has, however, also elaborated that the name came from a combination of the brand of harmonica he owned, which he spliced with the surname of a 'weird kid' he grew up with in Florida. Reubens was also born in the New York district of Peekskill.

Reubens had developed the character's distinctively nasal voice during his time as the resident juvenile at the Sarasota repertory theatre company back East. Initially intending Pee-wee to be 'a really bad comic, somebody you would look at and go, "This guy's never going to make it",'[3] Reubens found instead that audiences responded so well to the character that it was worthwhile expanding his role.

Reubens narrowly missed out on joining the rep company of *Saturday Night Live* in 1980, having auditioned for a regular role in what was the series' first year without any of its original regular cast. After losing out to Gilbert Gottfried, Reubens began to worry that he had missed out on what should have been his big break so he borrowed money from his parents, and staged a show of his own at the Roxy Theatre on Sunset Strip.

Thus *The Pee-wee Herman Show* was born, a colourful parody of the children's television of the 50s and 60s. An adult-oriented revue, rife with sexual innuendo, it ran to packed houses for five months, and was eventually recorded as a TV special by cable channel HBO. This televised performance launched the character into the national consciousness, exposure that Reubens took advantage of by making several successful appearances on *Late Night with David Letterman*.

By this time, Reubens had effectively *become* Pee-wee Herman, ensuring he was never seen in public out of character. 'There was a higher likeability factor to Pee-wee Herman,' he once explained. 'This sounds really weird, but I was actually thinking of that musical number in *Gypsy* (Mervyn Le Roy, 1962) ["You Gotta Have a Gimmick"]. There's these three strippers singing a song, and I was . . . thinking, "A gimmick? Yes. That's good." '[4] Tim Burton, describing a slightly later period in Rubens' life summed it up thus: 'Pee-wee comes from a very real place. As crazy as he is he's rooted in a real man. And if anyone did Pee-wee 24 hours a day, they'd be dead. Paul Reubens is still alive.'[5]

REFERENCES: Pee-wee slides down a metal pole in his house, and his clothes change as he does so, clearly an allusion to the 1960s *Batman* television series.

Pee-wee's appearance, in the 'movie within the movie' as a hotel clerk is a reference to both Pee-wee's first big screen appearance in *Cheech & Chong's Next Movie* (Thomas Chong, 1980), and *The Bellboy* (Jerry Lewis, 1960) where Jerry Lewis (to whom many critics likened Reubens) is also employed as a bellboy.

As Francis plays with his toy ships in his huge sunken bath he is clearly imitating Godzilla, who later makes an appearance in the studio chase sequence.

The sequence of close-ups after Pee-wee's bike is stolen has more than a touch of Hitchcock about it. As if to reinforce the point, Elfman's music suddenly goes all Bernard Herrmann (Hitchcock's most regular composer). Later as Pee-wee exits the Alamo we have more Hitchcock pastiche, as Herman's anguished face and pose strongly suggest several moments in *Vertigo* (Alfred Hitchcock, 1958).

Burton points out on the DVD commentary that the music for the bicycle race echoes *Chariots of Fire* (Hugh Hudson, 1981).

PRODUCTION: Having reached a deal with Warners, Reubens found himself and the studio discussing who would direct the feature. Reubens has claimed that he 'made a list of at least a hundred directors, people whose movies I've liked, or who had a certain sensibility'[6] that he then submitted to the studio. On returning from a brief vacation he discovered the studio had compiled an alternative list, 'a list of one'.[7] Whilst he has diplomatically refused to name the – apparently highly experienced – director the studio wished to assign, Reubens remains adamant that he was 'not right for it'.[8] Risking the possibility that any delay could mean the movie not being made at all, he bargained with the studio, asking for an extra week to find a more suitable director. He re-started his search from scratch: 'I was willing to risk everything, it took me ten years to get to [the] point where I have a movie and it had to be directed by someone who's great.'[9] One of the people Reubens contacted was Shelley Duvall who told him about a project she had recently worked on, *Frankenweenie*. 'It's a great film,' she told him, 'and oh my god Paul, you would love the director.'[10] Reubens screened *Frankenweenie* for himself and his designated producers, and has claimed that he knew within seconds he was looking at the work of the right man to bring Pee-wee to the big screen.

Burton read the screenplay, which he has since described as 'a great script',[11] and went to meet Reubens. 'I had seen Pee-wee's show at the Roxy and was a real fan, but I was a little worried about going into a film with such an established character. I didn't see what I could add of my own'[12] (see **ANALYSIS**, below). Buoyed up by the idea that the script as written would allow him to 'get to try every genre'[13] he signed to direct the picture, his first feature-length film.

Burton threw himself into ascertaining the picture's visual style (a process carried out in conjunction with Reubens and Production Designer David L Schneider), suggesting the visual joke of Pee-wee's bedroom window actually being a fish tank, and designing both the breakfast-making machine and the elaborate series of bicycle wheels which spin behind Pee-wee's head after his bicycle is stolen. Schneider recalls Burton's motto during design stages to be 'If it ain't bright, it ain't right!'[14] a surprising mantra for someone now held to be Hollywood's darkest mainstream filmmaker.

Shooting began with the film's opening dream sequence of Pee-wee winning the Tour de France. Reubens' bike was pulled forward on wires attached to the back of a truck to ensure that he moved faster than those around him. The low budget meant that the crowds for Pee-wee's 'coronation' were not as thick as Burton would have liked, 'a cast of 35!'[15] he later said dismissively. At one point a passer-by was even cajoled into joining the crowd in an attempt to thicken the adoring throng around Reubens.

For the sequences set in Pee-wee's house both director and star remember 'raiding every thrift shop in town'.[16] Both also admit that large amounts of the kitsch littering Pee-wee's home came from their own private collections.

Filming continued at the Santa Monica Third St Mall. Schneider remembers that 'half of the mall was vacant. We needed a downtown, anywhere USA'[17] and in the Santa Monica Mall they found a block of shops that had been built immediately after the Second World War 'so it was the perfect architecture [for their purposes]. We got to revamp the existing shops . . . the Kinney Shoe Store revamped into the bicycle shop and the electronics store revamped into the magic shop.'[18]

Burton himself claims to have played the clown marionette that Reubens chains his bike near. Low traffic volume made the shooting run smoothly, despite Reubens being unwell during filming. 'We virtually had a street that was as good as the backlot,' says Schneider, 'but which had a lot more character than the backlot because it was real.'[19]

Despite the picture's wide variety of locations, the production team never moved more than 30 miles outside their central LA base. The scenes at the Alamo were shot at the nearby San Fernando Mission, 'similar in architecture'[20] to the Alamo and built in a similar period.

The film's finale, an epic chase through a movie studio, was shot at the Burbank Studios, once owned by Warners but at that time leased out to Columbia. Schneider found himself in the strange position of having to mock up Warner Brothers signs for a Warner Brothers picture, in order to position them on what had once been the Warners lot.

BURTON REGULARS: Paul Reubens provided the voice for the mischievous Lock in *The Nightmare Before Christmas*, as well as appearing as the Penguin's father at the start of *Batman Returns*, with Diane Salinger (Simone) as his wife.

Carmen Filipi, playing Hobo Jack, would return as Roadkill Man in *Beetlejuice*, and in a small role as the 'Old Crusty Man' in *Ed Wood*.

Simmy Bow, the Man in a Diner, would also appear as the Creepy Janitor in *Beetlejuice*.

Jan Hooks (Tina, the tour guide) cropped up briefly in *Batman Returns*, playing the Penguin's image consultant, Jen.

Danny Elfman would return to provide scores for every subsequent Burton project, bar *Ed Wood*. This even includes television's *The Jar*, the on-line *Stainboy*, the Burton-designed *Amazing Stories: Family Dog*, the Burton-produced *Beetlejuice* animated series and *The Nightmare Before Christmas*. He would also write dozens of other highly acclaimed movie scores.

Steve Bartek (who collaborated with Elfman in the band Oingo Boingo), here acting as Music Arranger, would return as Orchestrator on *Beetlejuice*, *Batman*, *Edward Scissorhands*, *Batman Returns* (where he was also Music Producer), *The Nightmare Before Christmas*, and *Sleepy Hollow* (as Additional Orchestrator). Another of Elfman's Oingo Boingo chums, Bob Badami, here acting as Music Editor, returned in the same capacity on *Beetlejuice*, *Batman*, *Edward Scissorhands*, *Batman Returns*, and *Mars Attacks!*

Costume Designer Aggie Guerard Rogers would also design costumes for *Beetlejuice*. Interestingly, four of the special effects crew – Chuck Gaspar, Elmer Hui, Joe Day, Thomas Mertz and Jeffrey A Wischnack – went on to work on *Beetlejuice*, which perhaps helps to explain the consistency of effects work in the two films.

CRITICS: Critical response to the film varied greatly at the time of its original release: 'The film's plot is episodic to the point of surreal juxtaposition,'[21] commented one critic, accurately reflecting the picture's road movie tone. He went on to commend the way the film offered audiences 'a unique ... Pee-wee-centered view of the world. There is a preternatural quality to the imagery, as if we – like [Reubens] himself – rediscover our capacity for ... wonder through our identification with Pee-wee's point of view.'[22] Other positive comments included, 'At its best, *Pee-Wee's Big Adventure* is surreal – and reminded me strongly of the best of *Blue Velvet*'[23] (David Lynch, 1986).

Other critics seemed unable to understand why they had enjoyed *Pee-wee*: 'Is this a great bad movie? It could be ... Is it funny? I think so. I laughed. I also spent a lot of time staring at the screen in disbelief. But ... I would like to see it again.'[24] Others were even less understanding: 'There are two funny things in *Pee-wee's Big Adventure*. One is a waitress who explains why her boyfriend doesn't want to go to Paris. "He flunked French in high school and now thinks everybody over there is out to make him look dumb." The other is a pretty, unstoppably gushy young woman named Tina (Jan Hooks) who acts as a tour guide at the Alamo in San Antonio ... *Pee-wee's Big Adventure* is otherwise the most barren comedy I've seen in years, maybe ever.'[25]

MUSIC: Composer Danny Elfman had played in show act The Mystic Knights, sung with the band Oingo Boingo and felt himself to be an odd choice for Burton and Reubens to entrust the scoring of their feature.

Burton called Elfman in for an interview, surprising the composer. 'I didn't know why. I don't know how someone could see this rock band and think, "This dude could do my orchestral film score." It defies logic, as far as I'm concerned.' For Elfman this leap of faith is 'one of the great mysteries of my life – I would never have had the guts to ask someone with my background to do that job.'[26] 'The first thing I asked them was, "Why me?" I told them I had no experience with orchestra and I didn't really know how to write music.'[27] 'It's not weird for a director to come out of the blue, be self-taught, and learn while doing films. But for a [film] composer to learn by instinct is unheard of.'[28]

Even after accepting the assignment, Elfman expected it all to go badly wrong. 'I was terrified when I started. I was really convinced that I was gonna destroy their movie.'[29] 'I'm gonna come limping back to rock 'n' roll with my tail between my legs, saying, "See? Rock 'n' rollers should never do orchestral film scores".[30]

Returning home, Elfman did a demo of what later became the film's main theme: 'I took a wild chance and did something which seemed outlandish and innappropate,' he's said. Discussing the score, he became convinced that *Pee-wee* should sound 'like a European film made in the 60s ... because there's something about the Pee-wee character that seems very un-contemporary.'[31] Elfman wanted to avoid the light orchestral or pop soundtracks that most comedies of the time used for scores, wanting to prove that someone from his background could do something unusual with film music.

Despite his reservations, Elfman soon realised he had found his calling: 'When I heard the first cue for Pee Wee's bike race, I became addicted for life ... I knew right at that moment that I was hooked to orchestral composition.'[32]

Response to Elfman's 'European-sounding' score was universally positive, Paul Reubens publicly labelled it 'phenomenal,'[33] and film reviewers agreed: 'composer Danny Elfman's Felliniesque score contributes the aural illusion of a circus,'[34] said one. Regarding the Fellini comparison, Elfman said that the 'Pee-wee [score] was very consciously [Fellini's regular composer] Nino Rota.'[35] 'A little bit of Bernard Herrmann, a little bit of Nino Rota ... those two were my two big film music influences. When I was younger, I dreamed of writing music in that style, but I didn't ever think I'd get a chance to do it.'[36]

CINEMATOGRAPHY: The episodic nature of the plot allowed cinematographer Victor J Kemper to introduce an eclectic mix of visual styles. Yet the camera and lighting here is largely workmanlike, with mostly static shots – except when deliberately imitating other film styles, from Hitchcock to film noir. In the dream sequences, red and green lighting predominates to separate them from the rest of the film, and there are a few extreme close-ups to heighten Pee-wee's terror. Yet most of the visual interest comes from the generally bright colour scheme – something Burton has rarely returned to, with the exception of *Mars Attacks!* The simplicity of the camera-work mirrors the simplistic view Pee-wee has of the world, keeping itself unobtrusive, so as not to detract from the situations in which he finds himself, and as such does its job perfectly.

PLOT PROBLEMS: The 'big adventure' that Pee-wee sets out on is a road movie. These all have certain inherent problems in terms of creating a coherent narrative – problems amplified in this case by only having one person on the trip, which allows for little in the way of the development of character relationships. Better examples of the genre, such as *Wild at Heart* (David Lynch, 1990), *Easy Rider* (Dennis Hopper, 1969), *The Grapes of Wrath* (John Ford, 1940), *It Happened One Night* (Frank Capra, 1934) etc. have all generally focused on two or more characters, and their developing relationship(s), brought about by their experiences on the road.

In the relatively few examples of the genre where a lone person takes the trip, their experiences on their physical journey usually lead to personal or psychological changes in the character, and it is this personal transformation that is the focus of the film. Even in the recent *Jay and Silent Bob Strike Back* (Kevin Smith, 2001), which in many ways imitates *Pee-wee* (right down to the chase through a movie studio, where many of the same gags crop up, along with a red bicycle), the titular Jay, a stoner who had appeared largely unaltered across Smith's previous four films, has noticeably changed by the end of the movie.

Yet Pee-wee seems to have been unaffected by his experiences, except in having widened his eclectic array of friends; even the idea that he is now 'a movie star' leaves him unfazed. Although he may end up at the drive-in with Dottie there is no indication that Pee-wee has decided to allow their relationship to progress in the way she hopes it will. After all, it is his bike that he is most pleased to see. His journey has simply provided him with a bit more excitement – something he hardly needs in his life, considering the joy he gets out of his breakfast routine. For Pee-wee, life appears to be just a series of largely unconnected events, and as his over-the-top analysis of his bike's disappearance demonstrates, he can't determine what's important and what isn't. Just like this film, in fact.

The road trip is an ideal way to present as many different situations for a character to tackle as possible, especially one born in improvisational comedy, and as such is a perfect formula for Pee-wee Herman.

DEATH: Unusually for a Burton film, no one actually dies. However, death remains a conceptual presence, most notably in the form of the menacing ghost of a grandma trucker, Large Marge.

Although fully scripted, the look of the scene in which her face contorts in a hideous piece of stop-motion, animated by *Vincent* alumnus Stephen Chiodo, was based on rough sketches by Burton. The thirty-six frames (one and a half seconds) of the facial transformation took eleven hours to animate, following four weeks of preparation for the facial moulds, creating one of the most effective sight gags in the movie. A similar joke would later be used in *Beetlejuice* (much of the visual style of which seems to be based on this short sequence of *Pee-wee*).

CHILDREN: Pee-wee Herman *is* a child. That, in this incarnation at least, is the point of the character. Innocent, chaotic, periodically brilliant, easily bored, selfish, sweet and kind. There's something about Reubens' extraordinary performance that isn't simply childlike, it's a perfect synthesis of actually being a child. Francis, of course, is an overgrown, spoilt brat. There is also the *real* child, the stuck-up actor kid Kevin Morton, who gets given Pee-wee's bike by Warners, despite obviously not appreciating anything so fantastic.

CLOWNS AND THE CIRCUS: Clowns are an ever-present threat throughout the film, from the moment Pee-wee's bike is stolen after being chained to one. They crop up continually in his various dreams, chasing him and destroying his bike over and over again, often shot at skewed angles with harsh lighting to heighten their inherent scariness.

DOGS: Pee-wee has a pet, the charming Speck, who does very little except yap and be cute. There are also dogs among the many animals Pee-wee rescues from the pet shop at the end of the movie.

LOVE TRIANGLES: For a film so utterly sexless, there's plenty of love triangle action. Pee-wee is only interested in his bike, but Dottie certainly has more than a passing interest in him. Pee-wee's non-erotic flirtation with Simone arouses the anger and indignation of her boyfriend, the rough (and tall) Andy.

JUST PLAIN WEIRD: There are several dream sequences with very high levels of strangeness. That and Pee-wee Herman himself, of course.

DIALOGUE TO SKIP BACK FOR:

Pee-wee: (shouting at someone who appears not to be listening) 'Is this something you can share with the rest of us, Amazing Larry?'

Simone: 'Do you have any dreams?'
Pee-wee: 'Yes. I'm all alone, I'm rolling this big donut and there's this snake wearing a vest.'

Tour Guide: 'There are thousands and thousands of uses for corn, all of which I will tell you about right now!'

Cowboy: 'Do you remember anything?'
Pee-wee: 'I remember the Alamo.'
Cowboys: 'Yee-ha!'

Policewoman: (After Pee-wee has reported his bike stolen, and explained who he believes to be responsible) 'What exactly leads you to believe the Soviets were involved?'

AFTERLIFE: Reubens knew that the film would make-or-break both him and the character. As he told a contemporary interviewer, 'everything . . . hinges on the success of *Big Adventure*. If it's a smash, it will be a Pee-wee world!'[39] After the film unexpectedly grossed $45 million, CBS offered Reubens the chance to take his stage show to its logical conclusion – an actual children's TV series – *Pee-wee's Playhouse*, which debuted in the 1986 autumn season to instant critical acclaim. Very different from the movie, but similar in some ways to the stage show, it showed Pee-wee living in a twisted, yet cheerful, psychedelic madhouse full of talking furniture (Chairry), windows (Mr Window), and even a talking floor (Floory), where he was visited by an assortment of bizarre characters, who ranged from Laurence Fishburne's Cowboy Curtis and Phil Hartman's Captain Karl (who had appeared in the stage show) to ex-Groundling/*Big Adventure* Guest Star John Paragon's Jambi the Genie.

The series eventually won a total of 22 Emmys, including two for Reubens himself, who, as well as playing Pee-wee, composed the theme, helped decorate the set, wrote, produced and directed the show. However, each episode cost as much as $425,000 to $535,000 (high for a prime-time slot, let alone a Saturday morning series), Reubens' production company steadily lost money on the show, hoping instead for profit through syndication sales and merchandising. It ran until 1991.

Pee-wee became such a phenomenon that, two years after the film's release, one commentator felt able to argue that 'An examination of contemporary issues of comedy would be incomplete without taking into consideration the meaning behind Pee Wee Herman.'[38] Reubens appeared as his favourite character for what many believed would be the last time at 1991's MTV Music Video Awards. Other work soon followed, with impressive roles in Burton's *Batman Returns*, and the initial *Buffy the Vampire Slayer* feature film (Fran Rubel Kuzi, 1992), on which the TV series is based. Reubens returned to television as Andrew J Lansing III, a major character in the drama *Murphy Brown*, but continued to work in films including *Dunston Checks In* (Ken Kwapis, 1996), *Matilda* (Danny DeVito, 1996), *Buddy* (David Nichols and Daniel Lomino, 1997) and *Mystery Men* (Kinka Usher, 1999). In April 2001, Reubens appeared on *Late Night With Conan O'Brien* where he confirmed that he plans to bring back the character of Pee-wee Herman, although what form the revival will take is as yet unknown.

ANALYSIS: Critical summaries of Tim Burton's contribution to *Pee-wee* have generally fallen into one of two categories. Initially, no one seemed to consider the impact of the young director from Burbank. Why should they? He was then unknown. Few contemporary reviews of *Pee-wee* even mentioned Burton. One critic, Petr Kral in the usually remarkable French film journal *Postif*, even got his name wrong, calling him 'Tom Burton'. Ironically, *Postif* later became one of Burton's most ardent admirers, devoting several long articles to each of his films, and interviewing the director on numerous occasions.

The second 'phase' of appraisal came later, after Burton had become an established Hollywood name with several box office successes behind him. With hindsight, many felt they could identify aspects of Burton's cinematic personality in his first feature. 'During Herman's comedic quest to retrieve his stolen bicycle, he takes a cross-country road-trip stopping at Burtonland almost every step of the way,'[39] said one critic, seemingly unaware that practically all of Pee-wee's stops were comprehensively scripted before Burton was even brought on board. The unfavourable response to the Reubens-penned sequel, *Big Top Pee-wee* (Randal Kleiser, 1988), further cemented the idea of Burton as the driving force behind *Pee-wee's Big Adventure*. As one commentator argued, 'To stress the importance of Burton's contribution to *Pee-wee's Big Adventure* one only need look at *Big Top Pee-wee*, the dismal follow-up in which director Randal Kleiser clearly failed to jibe with Herman's sensibilities.'[40] Whilst this is true to an extent, one could also point to the fact that *Big Adventure* co-screenwriter and Groundlings alumnus Phil Hartman was also absent from the project, and that the sequel's linear narrative and overtly sexual nature may have been less well suited to a character whose appeal is, in many ways, his endearing simplicity.

The truth of the nature of Burton's involvement is, of course, somewhere between these two extreme positions. Yes, many of the things that critics have come to associate with Burton are in evidence, but not simply because they are some of Burton's defining passions (clowns, Godzilla, dogs, Christmas, children, love triangles, etc.). It is because they are things in which Burton and Reubens have a shared interest. Burton's home is full of kitsch knick-knacks and 'junk', as is Reubens'. During production, the two men became good friends, and have remained so ever since. As a director, Burton has been in a better position to express his interests through his work, but Reubens' later projects have also displayed many of the same fascinations.

Paul Reubens is unequivocal about Burton's contribution to the picture, saying at one point to his friend, 'Thank you, Tim, for directing this movie – no one could have directed this movie half as good as you.'[41]

A later collaborator described the driving force behind the film thus: 'He's a very personal artist, who naturally wants to control everything that represents him or his image. It must have been a difficult position to be in – to try and keep track of all that, while trying to let people have the creative freedom they need.'[42] Whilst many commentators would doubtless agree that this is a fine description of Tim Burton, the man under discussion in this instance was Paul Reubens.

TRIVIA: Several of the items Pee-wee looks at in the magic shop seem to come up in other, later, Burton films. The squirting flower

The Jar

In 1985, NBC resurrected the *Alfred Hitchcock Presents* television series, which originally aired from 1955, remaking some of the episodes. Burton signed on to direct a remake of *The Jar*, based on a Ray Bradbury short story.

The original episode actually aired as part of the later *The Alfred Hitchcock Hour* (1962–1964), airing on 14 February 1964. It was written by James Bridges (the co-writer/director of *The China Syndrome*, 1979) and starred Pat Buttram (who voiced the Sheriff of Nottingham in Disney's *Robin Hood* (Wolfgang Reitherman, 1973)) as a country bumpkin who buys a jar from a carnival sideshow. The jar's contents seem different to everyone who looks at it, mesmerising them.

Burton's version was written by Michael McDowell, whose *Beetlejuice* script would shortly afterwards be offered to Burton to direct, and who would go on to help adapt *The Nightmare Before Christmas* for the screen. Danny Elfman returned to provide the score. The score for the original was written by his idol Bernard Herrmann (Elfman would later rewrite Herrmann's score for *Psycho* on Gus van Sant's 1998 cover version of Hitchcock's original).

Starring Griffin Dunne (who had just played the lead in Martin Scorsese's *After Hours*, 1985) as the jar's owner, with former Hammer Horror actress Fiona Lewis as his wife, McDowell's script shifted the action to the world of art exhibitions, where Dunne presents the jar as his latest creation (the contents were actually designed by Rick Heinrichs). Amongst the other cast, many of whom become enchanted by the jar's strange effects, are *Saturday Night Live*'s Laraine Newman, and *Frankenweenie*'s Paul Bartel.

It aired on 6 April 1986, and is currently unavailable on video or DVD.

is like the one utilised by the Joker in *Batman*, the shrunken head echoes the ending of *Beetlejuice* and the extendable spectacles are reminiscent of Ichabod's extraordinary eyeglasses in *Sleepy Hollow*.

James Brolin, who plays PW Herman as pseudo James Bond in the film-within-the-film, had been asked to play Bond himself in *Octopussy* (John Glen, 1983) before Roger Moore agreed to return to the role at the last minute.

A clip from the sequence of Pee-wee dancing to The Champs' 'Tequila' was included, much to Reubens' delight, in the 'summary of a century' sequence shown at the White House on the night of 31 December 1999.

AVAILABILITY: *Pee-wee's Big Adventure* is available on R1 (US) DVD, with two commentary tracks, a handful of deleted scenes, a gallery of production sketches presented with a narration by production designer David L Schneider, plus a copy of the trailer for the movie.

THE BOTTOM LINE: *Pee-wee's Big Adventure* is not a deep or complex masterpiece. What it is is fresh, engaging, colourful and funny, with several inspired sequences, and occasional unfortunate misses. In many ways radically different to any other American comedy of the 80s, it is easy to see why it became a hit, and how it catapulted its writer/star to extraordinary levels of mainstream success.

BEETLEJUICE (1988)

The Geffen Company presents
A Tim Burton Film
Story by Michael McDowell and Larry Wilson
Screenplay by Michael McDowell and Warren Skaaren
Director of Photography: Thomas Ackerman
Production Designer: Bo Welch
Art Director: Tom Duffield
Produced by Michael Bender, Larry Wilson and Richard Hasimoto
Casting by Jan Jenkins and Janet Hirshenson CSA
Music by Danny Elfman
Costume Designer: Affie Guerard Rodgers
Edited by Jane Kurson
Visual Effects Supervisor: Alan Munro
Visual Effects Consultant: Rick Heinrichs
Directed by Tim Burton

NOTE: On the posters and the DVD box the film is called *Beetlejuice* (one word) but on the credits of the movie itself it's called *Beetle Juice*. On the shooting draft of the script (dated 4 August 1986) the title is given as one word. According to many in-camera props (the gravestone *et al*) Michael Keaton's character is called Betelgeuse (spelled like the star) even though his name is spelled Beetle Juice on the opening credits. This has understandably caused some confusion in the past. For this chapter we're going for *Beetlejuice* for the film's title, and Betelgeuse for the character's name. We just thought we'd clear that up.

CAST: Michael Keaton (*Betelgeuse*), Alec Baldwin (*Adam Maitland*), Geena Davis (*Barbara Maitland*), Jeffrey Jones (*Charles Deitz*), Catherine O'Hara, (*Delia Deitz*), Winona Ryder (*Lydia Deitz*), Sylvia Sidney (*Juno*), Robert Goulet (*Maxie Dean*), Glenn Shadix (*Otho*), Dick Cavett (*Bernard*), Annie McEnroe (*Jane Butterfield*), Maurice Page (*Ernie*), Hugo Stanger (*Old Bill*), Rachel Mittleman (*Little Jane*), J Jay Saunders (*Moving Man #1*), Mark Ettlinger (*Moving Man #2*), Patrice Martinez (*Receptionist*), Cynthia Daily (*3-fingered typist*), Douglas Turner (*Charred Man*), Carmen Filip (*Messenger*), Simmy Bow (*Janitor*), Susan Kellerman (*Grace*), Adelle Lutz (*Beryl*), Gary Jochimsen (*Stupid Football Player*), Bob Pettersen (*Dumb Football Player*), Duane Davis (*Very Dumb Football Player*), Marie Cheatham (*Sarah Dean*), Tony Cox (*Preacher*), Jack Angel (*Voice of Preacher*).

TAGLINE: 'The name in laughter from the hereafter' and 'Guaranteed to put some life in your afterlife'.

TRAILER: A suitable scene-setter of a trailer – evocative of the movie's tone without blowing its best jokes; unsurprisingly Keaton features prominently. The trailer's voiceover tells us that the picture is 'from the director of *Pee-wee's Big Adventure*', but doesn't tell us his name. A clear indication that *Pee-wee* was a big enough hit for Geffen/Warners to want to cash in on it, but that they were not confident of the brand-recognition factor of its director's name. Not yet. (Although the film itself does have the credit 'A Tim Burton Film' for the first time.)

TITLE SEQUENCE: 'Day-oh!' – a faint, echoing variation of Harry Belafonte drifts over the Geffen Pictures logo, and then we're into the title sequence proper. The camera races above a wood and over a small rural town, taking in the very little that the distinctly genteel environment has to show – we race up a dusty road towards a white house, and as we reach it an apparently huge spider crawls over the top of the building, only to be stopped by two human hands. It becomes clear that the town was a model.

Director Burton and FX guy Alan Munro had initially planned for the sequence to be more spectacular. The original concept was to show the camera progress over an upstate New York town (as happens in the finished film). The hope was that it would be possible to invisibly dissolve from helicopter shots taken on location (which incorporated shots of the frontage for the Maitlands' house erected on location by Production Designer Bo Welch and his team) to a seventy-eighth scale model of the house. The spell that we were watching an uninterrupted stream of real footage was only to be broken by the introduction of the two out-of-scale elements, the spider and Adam Maitland's hands. Unfortunately, spiders are not the easiest of beasts to train, Munro complaining that 'We shot miles of footage – about 70 takes – trying to get the spider to crawl up the miniature house and move towards the actor's hands.' A usable take was finally obtained, but the shot of the model itself was deemed unacceptable. It had been filmed with a locked off camera, which rendered the invisible dissolve from the (moving) helicopter footage impossible. The solution was to build a larger model of the town and initiate the dissolve earlier. If the sequence was to be kept in, Munro was presented with several problems. How was he to achieve a long overhead shot of a model town on this incredibly small scale – without the audience realising that they were no longer looking at the real town – and then have the camera naturally come to rest on the house just as the spider crawled over the roof? Munro finally solved his problem. He got crew members Rick Kess, Jim Belohovek and Tom Conti to build a forty-eighth scale section of the town for the overhead part of the move to ensure maximum detail, and then did 'a short, forced perspective blend from the forty-eighth scale miniature to the eighty-seventh scale house.' The house of course still had to be forty-eighth scale because of the intervention of real human hands. The new models were then shot with a motion control camera at Peter Kuran's Visual Concepts Engineering (VCE), based in Sylmar, California, a facility that 'enabled us to have a camera move end at a point where we could then sit and shoot endless takes of spiders doing whatever they damn well pleased until we got a usable take.'[1] After all this effort the sequence was completed, and whilst it goes some way to fulfilling Munro's intentions the dissolves are both obvious, even if you don't have an eye for such things. Nice try, though.

SUMMARY: Connecticut couple Adam and Barbara Maitland are killed in a road accident. Returning to their house as ghosts, they become trapped inside it – every time they try to leave they find themselves in a strange Technicolor desert populated by huge carnivorous worms. The Maitlands are informed by their afterlife counsellor, Juno, that they have been sentenced to a further 125 years on Earth as spirits, before they are allowed to pass through to eternity.

More horrifying than this revelation is the discovery that New Yorker Alan Deitz along with his 'Goth' daughter Lydia, and his second wife, Delia, have moved into their home. Delia is, with the assistance of her interior decorator Otho, in the process of refitting it to her own specifications.

Adam and Barbara try to scare the newcomers away, but the Manhattanites aren't frightened. In fact they're impressed by the fact that they have ghosts in their home, and invite several of their friends to come and develop business opportunities incorporating the late Maitlands.

Driven to distraction by the intruders, and having been given little help by the bureaucratic world of the afterlife, the Maitlands eventually stoop to employing 'bio-exorcist' Betelgeuse, who promises to rid them of their unwanted house guests. However, they soon realise they have made a terrible mistake, especially when Betelgeuse attempts to marry the Deitzes' teenage daughter. Having disposed of Betelgeuse, and some of the Deitzes' more exploitative friends, the Maitlands agree to see out the remainder of their century-long exile with the Deitzes in the same house, indulging in such wholesome activities as doing DIY and aiding Lydia with her schoolwork.

SOURCE MATERIAL: Unusually for a Tim Burton film, *Beetlejuice* was an original screenplay, and not based on any previously existing material. The main writer, novelist Michael

McDowell, was at the time best known as an author of horror fiction (such as the *Blackwater* sequence, *The Elementals* and *Cold Moon Over Babylon*) but had recently shifted towards more comic material. McDowell always credited Producer Larry Wilson with the very basic idea for the movie, which he worked up into a full screen story and then later scripted.

The screenplay was offered to Burton to direct by Geffen Films, the company headed by mogul David Geffen (now the G in Dreamworks SKG). Burton said, 'It was totally opposite from everything else I'd read. It had no structure, no plot – it just had a weird quality that I loved.'[2]

REFERENCES: The film's plot shares some incidental similarities with *Topper* (Norman Z McLeod,1937) in which a couple who die in a car accident return to haunt a straight-laced friend, bank manager Mr Topper (Cary Grant).

The opening scene resembles that of *The Shining* (Stanley Kubrick, 1980). The sequences on the sand planet owe more than a little to the Sea of Time section of The Beatles' *Yellow Submarine* (George Dunning, 1968). The sandworms were described in the screenplay as 'out of *Dune*', yet have a striped pattern that doesn't come from either Frank Herbert's novel or David Lynch's compromised, yet intriguing, 1985 film adaptation.

The expressionistic corridors of the afterlife again reference *M* (Fritz Lang, 1930) and look more than a little like the nightmarish hallways of Pee-wee's dreams in Burton's first feature and some of the backgrounds in *Vincent*.

PRODUCTION: *Beetlejuice*'s principal studio photography took place between March and early June 1987, primarily at Culver Studios in Culver City – the same lot, incidentally, as that used for *Gone With the Wind* (Victor Fleming, 1939). An additional ten days of location shooting in the town of East Corinth, Vermont, was also completed within this period. East Corinth was chosen even though the script specified Connecticut as the state the Maitlands resided in – Production Designer Bo Welch felt that East Corinth better represented the town of Winter River as described in the script than any of the Connecticut locations he had scouted.

It was, by all accounts, a very happy production for all concerned. Actor Glenn Shadix, who played the eye-rolling Otho, remembers that 'the set of *Beetlejuice* – and I think anybody who was on that set would agree with me – was one of the most exciting and fun and hilarious sets that any of us had ever been on. There was a real chemistry between the actors – we all thoroughly enjoyed one another . . . For me it was just like going to the circus, I was just dropped down into an ideal situation, and so I had a *lot* of fun, as everyone else did too.'

Unusually for a film made in the late 80s, Burton and his crew were required to shoot a great deal more than just the actors during the principal photography stage. It had always been apparent from the script that a large number of special effects would be required of the production. One of Geffen's then most recent productions was the tonally similar spoof horror musical remake of *Little Shop of Horrors* (Frank Oz, 1986) which had featured a wide variety of *Saturday Night Live* stars. It had overspent considerably, and the company were keen to avoid a similar situation occurring with Burton's film. *Beetlejuice*'s budget of $13 million was average for a movie at the time, but not for one with such a huge number of special effects. Bearing in mind both the recent overspend and the tight budget, a decision was made to avoid expensive post-production wherever possible, and produce effects live on set.

Storyboards put together by Burton and Special Effects Supervisor Alan Munro reflected this, detailing camera angles that could minimise overbuilding and therefore save money (e.g. the sequence where Betelgeuse demonstrates that he's scary to the Maitlands by distorting his face is specified as being shot from behind). The first few weeks of production were spent shooting test footage 'to show everybody that you really could do these shots using all sorts of cheap, stupid, easy methods'.[3]

Munro formed an immediate bond with the director. 'Tim and I really hit it off,' he says, adding that they were 'of a single mind, always going for the straightforward, quick-and-dirty approach'.[4] ('I like effects that have a little humanity to them,'[5] was the director's comment.)

It sometimes wasn't easy to convince the more traditionally minded principal photography crew that it was for the best to do so many of the movie's effects during production, rather than in post-production. Munro recalled that 'The crew on principle photography was very uncomfortable a lot of times with our approach to certain shots and with what we'd show up with on the set. There weren't a lot of believers when we were actually working on the film. The big advantage was that most of us came from that same school of low-low-budget filmmaking, so everybody had a lot of experience throwing stuff together on the fly.' Burton, too, had had some experience creating low-budget effects whilst making *Hansel and Gretel* for Disney, as well as his intervening projects – especially *Frankenweenie* (with its $1 million budget) and *Aladdin* (with its ultra-short shooting time). 'There are a lot of shots where the backgrounds are fiddled together with little shapes, little pieces of paper, a little spraypaint, a little cardboard, and a little glue,' explained Munro. 'We'd just stick it up and go with it. None of us had any fear, but occasionally people on the production would come over to where we were shooting and give us that "you-gotta-be-kidding" look when they'd see how unbelievably wanky some of this stuff looked on the set.'[6] Visual Effects Consultant Rick Heinrichs, a veteran of all Burton's previous productions, felt the same: 'It was hair-raising, exhausting and frustrating. I remember the assistant cameraman telling me it was a gag-a-day script. There was loads of effects stuff and it worked fine. However, sometimes production seemed to screech to a halt and hold its breath because of an uncooperative cable mechanism or motor.'

Peter Kuran of VCE, who had been initially drafted in to assist with the opening fly-by sequence, understood the difficulties the production faced: 'They needed somebody like me, who's willing to figure out the most effective *and* least expensive way to do something to keep the price down . . . The movie could easily have turned into a $40 million picture. They needed people like us to do the work and not charge an arm and a leg.'[7] Munro was impressed that 'Some of the techniques we've used in the film have been used in motion pictures since the earliest days of moviemaking. For instance, there are a couple of scenes we shot using old-style mirror effects, rather than the more readily accepted and standard Blue Screen.'[8]

The makeup team were given three weeks preparation time for Michael Keaton's elaborate Betelgeuse visage. Makeup artist Ve Neill claims credit for his look: 'I came up with the idea of the moss and mould growing on his face and hands. We also did acrylic nails to make him look really nasty.' Keaton had no problems with performing under such heavy makeup: 'In fact, he actually loved it because he had never really done anything where he didn't look like himself, so he was really excited about doing it.'[9] On set, Glenn Shadix found that the opportunity of working under such heavy makeup 'just gave [Keaton] licence to go anywhere. It was just so wonderfully perverse that it freed him to do things that Michael would not normally have been able to do as easily.'

One of many alterations made to the script during production concerned the landscape the Maitlands encountered each time they tried to leave their home. Originally Adam and Barbara encountered a different surreal environment every time they attempted to leave the house, until Burton objected, citing audience incomprehension: 'I dislike the tendency of fantasy films to have so many story points that you can't remember them all. I think we would have totally lost people if Adam and Barbara had been in a different place every time they walked out of the house. It would have been too much of a distraction.'[10]

Having decided that the single background to face Adam and Barbara as they emerged from the house would be the sand planet, director and team then had to achieve it. All the sand planet sequences were achieved without opticals, crewmember Steve Burg constructing a forced perspective set with a 40-foot blue skyscape and painted planets. At the front the set was fifteen feet wide, at the back twenty-two feet across, and it was twelve feet deep. Munro explained the technique: 'all we did was build rocks in seven scales ranging from eight feet tall down to about an inch and a half and arrange them in diminishing perspective.'[11] The set incorporated eight tonnes of yellow aquarium sand. The garish, almost psychedelic colour scheme was something insisted on by Burton. 'It was like Walt Disney had thrown up on you,'[12] is Munro's fairly accurate description.

Burton also produced initial designs for the sand worm (described by Rick Heinrichs as a 'scary shark with no eyes'[13]). Heinrichs built a maquette based on Burton's design. Shots of the worm diving through the sand were achieved through live action. The model was six feet long with rods underneath, allowing it to be puppeteered from beneath the dunes. Also produced was a large-scale, five feet long, fully mechanised head, for close-ups. Controlled by cables, it had the ability to pull out of its outer shell, snap its jaws and roll its eyes. However, it was not quite up to the job, and some shots in the finished film were achieved by assistant Doug Beswick, who stop-motion animated a smaller puppet. (Interestingly, one effect that most viewers have identified as being stop-motion – the fly in the graveyard consumed by Keaton – was in fact a fibreglass rod and cable puppet shot at four frames per second to give it fast, jerky movement reminiscent of stop motion.)

The Betelgeuse snake was also initially planned as a live effect. Short had built a full size prop to a design by Heinrichs even before Keaton was cast. It was, according to Heinrichs, 'more reptilian, more snake-like, but still cartoony, with a big grin on its face and great big, dilating eyes. Its mouth opened and closed and its fangs snapped out like switchblades. It was one bad mother.'[14] There were unexpected problems when the creature got on set, however, and it was dropped after two days' shooting. Burton again opted for stop-motion, plus a redesign to make the creature look more like Michael Keaton.

The sequence in which Adam and Barbara stretch their faces was storyboarded by Rick Heinrichs, who did a rough 2-D pencil sketch, detailing the exact number of frames to be used in each sequence. The animation process took twenty weeks.

Rick Heinrichs remains quick to credit Burton with establishing the film's distinctive visual feel, of turning someone else's material into something so distinctly him: 'Tim was the style setter. He's the one who found his material in the script in the first place and it conjured up a lot of stuff for him.'[15] Short agrees, 'The movie really owes a great debt to Tim Burton for being the one who had the overall vision . . . to say, "Well, I have the vision of this film and now it's up to you guys. Break the rules and make a film that nobody's ever seen before".'[16]

For his part, Burton was complimentary about the screenplay, and how easily it had become the kind of film he wanted to make. 'I felt very in sync with this material. It had the kind of abstract and unusual imagery that I like to develop on my own. All of its strange images and characters and the way they float in and out of the story really clicked with me. I felt comfortable with them.'[17]

In the end the film's total of nearly 300 effects was completed – with nearly every technique imaginable used except front-projection – and all for $1 million.

CASTING: Given that this was such an unusual project, with a relatively unknown director, the casting process was unsurprisingly difficult. According to Jeffrey Jones, initially he 'turned it down . . . I don't think Tim hired anybody who didn't turn him down first.'[18]

Burton wanted to cast Sammy Davis Jr as Betelgeuse. After some studio resistance to utilising the undoubted talents of the then 62-year-old former Rat Packer, David Geffen recommended Michael Keaton. Although Burton had never seen Keaton in anything, after meeting him he realised that Keaton was perfect for the role.

Anjelica Huston was initially cast as Delia, but had to pull out due to illness. As a replacement Burton cast SCTV comedy troupe regular Catherine O'Hara (dubbed 'the funniest woman in television'). Burton said of O'Hara, 'Catherine's so good, maybe too good. She works on levels that people don't even know. I think she scares people because she operates at such high levels.'[19]

Glenn Shadix was the first of the cast to be selected, although as a relative newcomer to film work he was the last to receive his official contract. He was asked to play Otho after Burton saw him – on the recommendation of screenwriter Michael McDowell, a friend of the actor – in the play *Dr Faustus Lights the Lights* at the LA Ensemble Studio Theatre. Shadix was playing Gertrude Stein. ('You're going to corner the market in ageing expatriate lesbian writers but I'm trying to sell you as a character man!' Shadix recalls his agent saying when he accepted the role.)

BURTON REGULARS: *Beetlejuice* began a number of ongoing relationships for its director: Michael Keaton, of course, worked with Burton twice more as Bruce Wayne/Batman. He left the series when Burton did. Winona Ryder would play the rather less 'strange and unusual' Kim in *Edward Scissorhands*. The next year she would star in *Ed Wood* Executive Producer Michael Lehmann's *Heathers*, which was written by *Batman Returns* scribe Daniel Waters, and also featured *Beetlejuice* actor Glenn Shadix. Shadix voiced the Mayor in *The Nightmare Before Christmas*, as well as Sgt Glen Dale and others in *Stainboy* before appearing (almost unrecognisable) as Senator Nado in *Planet of the Apes*. Catherine O'Hara voiced both Sally and Shock in *The Nightmare Before Christmas*. Jeffrey Jones came back as Criswell in *Ed Wood* and as the Reverend Steenwyck in *Sleepy Hollow*. Sylvia Sidney rejoined Burton for *Mars Attacks!*, her last film, playing Grandma Florence Norris.

Production Designer Bo Welch, with his Art Director Tom Duffield, also designed *Edward Scissorhands* and *Batman Returns*; Duffield also acted as Production Designer on *Ed Wood*. Makeup Department Head Ve Neil, who had previously worked alongside Welch and Duffield on *The Lost Boys* (Joel Schumacher, 1987) also did makeup duties on *Edward Scissorhands*, *Batman Returns*, *Ed Wood* and *Mars Attacks!* Co-Screenwriter Warren Skaaren, who had contributed to *Beverley Hills Cop II* (Tony Scott, 1987) and who had been a producer on *Top Gun* (Tony Scott, 1986), would also co-write Burton's *Batman* before succumbing to cancer in December 1989. Producer Richard Hashimoto co-produced *Edward Scissorhands*, as well as acting as Unit Production Manager on Cameron Crowe's *Singles* (1992), in which Burton has a cameo role.

CRITICS: The reviews of *Pee-wee's Big Adventure*, both positive and negative, had largely ignored the director's contribution, with writer/star Paul Reubens being identified as the main creative force behind the film. With *Beetlejuice* however, Burton's name and approach finally became noticed by the critics, with some seeking to compensate for what they saw as their earlier error. 'It becomes apparent that much of what was admirable in [*Pee-wee*] was down to the director rather than the star,' wrote British critic Kim Newman, himself a novelist in something close to the McDowell mode. 'The director doesn't yet have the discipline to structure a movie as more than a series of individual skits . . . And yet, the film keeps pulling itself together.' Newman concluded that '*Beetlejuice* confirms Burton's promise as a combination Frank Tashlin and David Lynch, and establishes McDowell as a screenwriter to watch.'[20]

Most critics mentioned 'talented young director Tim Burton'[21] in their reactions, with some reviewers both going out of their way to praise the picture, and seeing the director as the main man behind it all: 'some of the funniest moments and most inspired visual humour and design we may expect to experience at the movies all year . . . a dazzling display of director Tim Burton's unique pop culture sensibility . . . There's a distinctive feel to *Beetlejuice* . . . a deliberate Brecht–Weill jerkiness that allows satire and just plain silliness to play off each other most successfully.'[22] Another review which laid all their praise for the picture at the director's feet appeared in the *Washington Post*:

'Tim Burton . . . is the mind behind this stylish screwball blend of Capraesque fantasy, Marx Brothers anarchy and horror parody. And Michael Keaton is the juice that makes it go.'[23]

Others damned with the kind of faint praise which indicates that, whilst they can find nothing in particular to dislike about the film, they can find little to actually like about it either: 'technically sophisticated and so amiable and well meaning that it seems rude to point out that, like some of our public figures, it is more of a bore to watch than to describe.'[24] Some saw little of interest in the picture at all, arguing that Burton 'shows a keen grasp of preadolescent tastes in special effects (the weirder the better), pacing (illogical but busy) and comic constructs (only something incongruous . . . is funnier than something rude).' The same critic also felt that 'there really isn't much plot here, only a parade of arbitrary visual tricks to hold the film together . . . [Burton] only occasionally manages something marginally funny . . . His actors, not surprisingly, are limited by the stupidity of their material.'[25]

In the final analysis, *Beetlejuice* got more good reviews than bad, and did such business that Burton's future as a director of distinctive, A-list pictures was assured. 'The thing that *Beetlejuice* did for me was, it made me feel really great about audiences,' said Burton later. 'I felt great that people could get into seeing something that random. Anything that fucks up the system and doesn't prove itself part of their plan, I think is positive.'[26]

MUSIC: Danny Elfman's occasionally riotous score bears more resemblance to *Pee-wee* than it does to his more 'signature' work like the later *Batman* theme. Although, at moments of tension, there are rumbles of the strong chords of his next Burton project, more frequently Elfman's pacing is fast and frantic, with rumbling cymbals and parping brass, sometimes slipping into gentler variations or the occasional Bernard Herrmann-style stabbing of violins, all the while maintaining a slightly sinister air. In amongst this, Harry Belafonte is jarringly different, yet remains largely unnoticeable while the Maitlands are alive, ensuring that its later introduction at the dinner party is even more unexpected and amusing.

CINEMATOGRAPHY: Much as with *Pee-Wee*, the cinematography here is, for the most part, functional, adding to the air of normality of the Maitlands' lives to begin with, and managing to remain unobtrusive once the effects kick in. In fact, due to the large number of effects shots in the film, Director of Photography Thomas Ackerman was rather constrained by the necessity of framing many shots so that they would disguise the mechanics of the visual tricks. As such, his work here seems somewhat less adventurous than that he did for Burton on *Frankenweenie* a few years earlier.

Having said that, the afterlife sequences are frequently shot at slightly skewed angles, with unusual lighting schemes of harsh primary colours, casting strong shadows that successfully add to the general sense of weirdness. This use of jutting shadows also begins to cross over into the real world as the film progresses. Added to Otho's redesign of the house, this successfully increases the hideous similarity between life and death (hence the Maitlands' inability to recognise their own home for a moment on first meeting Juno). However, this appears to have been more down to the designs of Burton and Welch than to Ackerman, Tom Duffield explaining that part of the thinking behind the film was that 'at the beginning it was two different worlds . . . they sort of became one . . . it got more ethereal as it went on.'

PLOT PROBLEMS: At several points in the film it is confirmed that when you die, you enter the afterlife looking as you did on your death (hence all the grotesques in the waiting room). If the Maitlands died when their car plunged off the bridge, presumably they drowned. So, how come their corpses aren't bloated?

Betelgeuse at one point states that he is already dead, and yet after he is eaten by the sandworm he goes to the waiting room for the dead. Does this mean he's now twice dead? Surely as somebody already deceased he's been processed once before? As it has been established that 'death for the dead' has an entirely different effect, what precisely is going on here?

The Maitlands never find out how to pronounce 'Betelgeuse' yet still manage to call him up.

After being asked by Juno how they're going to scare the Deitzes, the Maitlands contort their faces and Juno seems to approve of the tactic, yet it has already been made clear (and is later confirmed) that the Deitzes can't actually see them . . . so how is this scaring thing going to work, exactly?

DEATH: Death, in *Beetlejuice*, is a huge inconvenience – something that gets in the way of whatever you're planning. Although your personality, and indeed your appearance (see **PLOT PROB-LEMS**) survive the final curtain unchanged, your problems don't go away. Death is not so much a release, or an ending, as a changing of state from one irritatingly petty level of existence to another. 'When Adam and Barbara die things only change marginally for them,' says Burton. 'After death, they simply have to deal with a more extreme version of what they would encounter in . . . life.'[27]

CHILDREN AND FAMILIES: Lydia, the only character under 30 in the film, is the beginning of an ongoing Burton archetype, the 'Goth' girl. Although consistently portrayed as less irritating than the adults on show (including the absurdly twee Adam and Barbara Maitland) she is rather self-indulgent, as adolescents are wont to be, and her decision to throw herself out of the window to join the Maitlands in death is rather strange. She also seems to believe that by wearing black and sighing a lot she's rebelling against her father and stepmother, when surely the most accurate and complete way to rebel against the ridiculously baroque Delia is to be as strait-laced as possible?

By the end of the picture Lydia has abandoned her pretensions, started wearing her school uniform and worrying about her grades. In many ways she has become a picture of teenage conformity – it probably annoys the hell out of her stepmother.

CLOWNS AND THE CIRCUS: Betelgeuse's fairground costume, prefiguring one of the Joker's less traditional suits. This outfit was originally going to be an octopus-like carnival-ride, with seats mounted on the end of each tentacle. However, after Burton viewed *Time Bandits* (Terry Gilliam, 1985), where David Warner's 'Evil' spins a bunch of cowboys around on ropes, it was decided that the effect would be too similar.

In addition to this, Charles Deitz makes a brief reference to a popular 'talking Marcel Marceau statue'. Marceau, of course, is one of the best-known mime artists of all time, and mimes are a type of (mute) clown.

DOGS: The dog who causes the Maitlands' fatal crash is really the only example. Furthermore, it actually features a lot less in the finished film than it did in the screenplay, where it was to be seen wandering around the town more extensively before causing the crash, and walking off with Juno at the very end.

CHECKS, STRIPES, DOTS: In approximate order, there's Adam's shirt (which Betelgeuse later imitates), a cushion on a chair by the front door before the house is redecorated, the sandworms (including their tongues), Delia's dress at the first Deitz family meal, black and white stripes on the house itself after its redesign by Otho, the chequered floor of the waiting-room and corridor in the afterlife, Betelgeuse's suit (on the poster/cover and when Lydia calls him to save the Maitlands), one of the little beasties dangling from Betelgeuse's rotating hat, and the snakes given to Charles as 'dowry'.

AUTOBIOGRAPHY?: Some critics have suggested that Lydia is the Burton figure here, with Ken Hanke asserting that, 'There can be no doubt that she is Burton's on-screen self – she dresses all in black . . . and her black hair is pulled upward in a version of Burton's own unruly mop.' However, she is a decidedly reactive figure, and clearly based on the stereotypical death-obsessed teenagers that can be seen hanging around, dressed in black, in almost any small town. (Furthermore, Burton's hairstyle at the time of *Beetlejuice*'s filming was not the 'unruly mop' that he later adopted, but a much neater cut). Hanke also mentions her photographic hobby, likening it to Burton's adolescent interests, and goes as far as to claim that she is 'more a portrait of Burton than any offered so far'[28] onscreen – apparently even more so than Vincent Molloy. However, unlike Vincent, Lydia is ultimately persuaded to come out of her interiorised world and act more like a regular child by the exceptionally 'normal' (if dead) Maitlands, and it is clear that the audience is supposed to feel pleased that she does so. Added to this is Hanke's assumption that Lydia's aversion to hearing her parents having sex relates to Burton's own discomfort with the subject – it apparently has little to do with the fact that, as she puts it, 'I'm a child!', or that the scene was included in McDowell's original screenplay, as were all her other character traits.

JUST PLAIN WEIRD: Perhaps the film's most striking concept, both personally and visually, is the waiting room – a place where the recently deceased sit and await smug counter service from the bureaucratic dead – filled with the grotesque, ghostly forms of people calmly sitting around in the physical state in which they died. In designing both the waiting room and the other areas of the world of the dead, Bo Welch set out to create 'something vague and evasive enough to defy categorising and invite disorientation, yet specific enough to invoke the fear that the afterlife might not be much different than real life.'[29] The afterlife is a *Brazil*-style (Terry Gilliam, 1985) bureaucratic nightmare, based (according to Tom Duffield) on the Johnson's Wax building, designed by Frank Lloyd Wright as the ultimate office space. 'We took that and gave it a really hard, hard take,' Duffield explained. 'Those little columns that are like tornados were basically a variation on a theme of Frank Lloyd Wright – he has these columns that go straight up and then they umbrella at the top. And also because the afterlife may not be on the same plane as the human one we gave it an angled floor. We just took the Frank Lloyd Wright thing and just gave it the Tim Burton punch to it, and made it weird, with mountains of paper – the vast number of people going through the afterlife, the total chaos.'

The 'waiting room' was one area that the script did little to specify. Burton did sketches of the woman who had been sawn-in-half, and the cigarette-smoking burns victim, which set the tone for the piece. The director had a brainstorming session with Munro and Heinrichs in order to decide what else would be trapped in the room, awaiting service. Munro and Heinrichs had the idea of a phone booth stuffed full of college students with their faces, feet and hands squashed against the glass and the muffled sound of the phone ringing. Other unused ideas from this session included a scientist holding two vials of liquid who had had his head blown clean off, an actor in a Godzilla suit with a miniature plane stuck through his head. Munro lamented their absence: 'There were tons of others . . . A lot of it just got dumped by the wayside for a pared-down, spare version. It's ironic, too, because a lot of people have singled it out as one of the highlights of the film.'[30]

The dinner party scene, with its shrimp-shaped fists and floating ventriloquist karaoke, is probably the strangest thing in the picture. Glenn Shadix recalls the genesis of this celebrated sequence: 'With the dinner party scene we were all given an hour after lunch for several days to work with the choreographer, and we gathered up a lot of our own props, and just began to play.

Originally we were going to dance to an old Ink Spots song but Catherine O'Hara and Jeffrey Jones suggested something calypso might be more fun. We had a little cassette of "Day-O" ["The Banana Boat Song"], the Harry Belafonte song, and we just laughed ourselves silly after lunch for a few days, and then showed it to Tim, and he and his producer were quick to agree. Our shrimp dinners were really just hand puppets controlled by a group of puppeteers who were all under the dinner table – they worked them through holes in the table's surface. It was a bit crowded under there and we all got very familiar with the people pretending to be our dinners.'

Let's face it, everything about the film is pretty strange: the colours, the design, some of the performances. The great thing about *Beetlejuice* is that the whole film is utterly unlike anything that mainstream Hollywood was producing at the time, as if from some parallel movie-making universe.

DIALOGUE TO SKIP BACK FOR:
Lydia: 'I myself am strange and unusual.'
Barbara: 'You look like a regular girl to me.'

Delia: 'They're dead – it's a little late to be neurotic.'

Otho: 'Don't worry about her. She's still upset because somebody dropped a house on her sister.' (This line was suggested by Shadix, who felt his character should respond to being insulted.)

AFTERLIFE: The film, as originally shot, was to end with Betelgeuse, who had become trapped in the Maitlands' house after being eaten by the sand worm, trying to escape from the sand planet and failing. But Burton was never happy with this as a conclusion for either the picture or the character: 'I wasn't sure until the end of the project how we were going to end the film. I had felt that the original ending was not very strong.'[31] When preview screenings suggested that audiences reacted very positively to Keaton's performance, money and time were made available to shoot extra scenes with the character (Keaton had worked for just two weeks of the movie's original shoot). Burton took the opportunity offered by this to alter the ending, as well as add the character's first scene where he's reading the paper looking for work. In addition to the 'shrunken head' ending used on the released film, another alternative version was shot. This featured Betelgeuse being incessantly talked to by Old Bill until his head leapt two feet above his body, screaming as his hair flailed around. Both versions were tested out on preview audiences, with the shrunken head finale being judged to be the more effective.

The previews also offered some less welcome opportunities to change the film, or more precisely, to change its title. As Burton remembers it the studio held a meeting to tell him, ' "See, *Beetlejuice* doesn't test, but *House Ghosts* here is going through the roof." I remember going, "House Ghosts?" Then I said, as a joke, "Why don't we call it *Scared Sheetless*?" And they consider-ed it, until I threatened to jump out of a window.'[32]

The picture was well marketed by Warners, earning over $33 million in the US and Canada alone. The grosses from *Beetlejuice* finally gave Warner Bros the confidence they needed to give the go ahead to the (potentially extraordinarily expensive) *Batman*, which, by 1988, had been in development for nearly a decade.

The waiting room character with the shrunken head became so popular he began making guest appearances on *Entertainment Tonight*, amongst other TV shows. Operated by puppeteer Mark Wilson, the Warners Publicity Department dubbed him 'Harry the Haunted Hunter'.

Beetlejuice's Rockin' Graveyard Revue, a combination of live stage show and theme park attraction was, for several years, a popular part of the tour at Universal Studios, Hollywood. The Hollywood *Revue* has now closed, although the equivalent show at Universal Studios, Florida, is still going strong. Universal Studios, Japan has the similar *Beetlejuice's Rockin' Midnight Monsterfest*.

AWARDS: The first Oscars for a Burton film were justifiably given out to makeup artists Ve Neill, Steve LaPorte and Bob Short. The visual effects work was down to the last four films to be considered for Oscar nomination, but didn't make it to the final three nominees.

TRIVIA: Well, not trivial for those involved. Having been introduced by Glenn Shadix on the set, Catherine O'Hara and Production Designer Bo Welch eventually married. They are still happily together, and have two children.

Geffen Pictures, as a fairly small production company, did not have the resources to handle the distribution of their own pictures. Instead they had arranged a long-term deal with Warner Brothers that gave Warners distribution rights to the film both theatrically and on video, whilst Geffen retained ownership of the film. This is why the DVD and Video releases are on Warners' own label. Ownership of Geffen passed to Universal some years ago, hence the attractions being at Universal's theme parks.

In the background when Juno is berating the Maitlands after Betelgeuse first attacks the Deitzes, there is a pair of skeletons, one red, one green – like those left behind by the Martian rayguns in *Mars Attacks!* Also, the skull on top of Betelgeuse's hat as he rises out of the model looks very much like Jack Skellington's. Betelgeuse also has bat wings for ears, and his merry-go-round hat is much like one of the Penguin's umbrellas in *Batman Returns*. The skull and bat wings at least may have been deliberate, as the idea of *The Nightmare Before Christmas* had first come about in the late 70s, and as Burton had begun developing *Batman* for Warners even before making *Beetlejuice*.

EXPERT WITNESS: Glenn Shadix: 'there was very much a spirit of openness, and the welcoming of improvisation when we wanted to try to experiment a little bit. And Tim's always open to what he likes to call the "happy accident" – you know in other words you don't want to be too rigid. He has an instinctive respect and feel for actors, and was amazingly easy going and calm. He doesn't make your choices for you; I mean some directors will tell you almost too specifically what they want. He knew what he wanted and brought everyone else into line with his vision. I never saw him lose his temper. Not ever. Though he was certainly frustrated at times. He always managed to work his way through any delays and accomplish his goal somehow. He would be set on getting the precise effect he wanted, and was not inclined to settle for anything less than magic. I was really impressed . . . What he does, and still does, is try and make you as comfortable as possible, give you some parameters, but then let you go at it, and then he shapes, through rehearsal, and with his cinemato-grapher, they choose what they really like about a performance, and then when we set it, of course, it's Tim's ball-game what he shoots.'

Alan Munro: 'Tim was a perfectionist in every way, and he definitely had a strong sense of how he wanted things to look and move. It always helps to have that sense of collaboration on a film. Some of the best ideas came from people who had what you would otherwise consider small, peripheral involvement. That air of "Everybody's suggestion is welcome" was always there. It was really amazing.'[33]

ANALYSIS: *Beetlejuice* is a scattershot comedy of manners, continually riffing on the subject of death in any way it can come up with. It mocks everyone and everything in it and whilst no one is evil (not even Betelgeuse) there aren't any genuinely sympathetic characters either. The Maitlands are twee, the Deitzes are ghastly, and Lydia is just a pompous adolescent obsessed with her own 'depth'. Like *Frankenweenie*, and unlike *Edward Scissorhands*, *Beetlejuice* seems to believe in compromise as a solution to people's problems. The Deitzes are made to come round to something closer to the Maitlands' way of thinking, Lydia becomes more 'normal' but without having to give up her individuality, and the Maitlands get to make their afterlives as much like their earthly existence as possible. Everything works out in the end.

AVAILABILITY: A vanilla DVD edition is available in both Britain and America. An isolated music and a theatrical trailer are the only special features. It's also a flipper, with the 1.85.1 wide screen edition of the film on one side and 1.33.1 panned and scanned edition on the other. Please don't watch the 1.33.1 edition, it looks horrible.

THE BOTTOM LINE: Episodic, but both effortlessly funny and continually visually inventive, *Beetlejuice* is like an absurdist sketch show that only pretends to have an ongoing plot. Michael Keaton's performance is brilliant, but Jeffrey Jones' deadpan Charles Deitz and Glenn Shadix's eyebrow-raising polymath Otho give him a run for his money. We're not sure if *Beetlejuice* was ever meant to have any genuine frights in it, but frankly the scariest thing in the entire movie is Geena Davis' hair.

BATMAN (1989)

Warner Brothers Presents
A Tim Burton Film
Story by Sam Hamm
Screenplay by Sam Hamm and Warren Skarren
Director of Photography: Roger Pratt
Production Designer: Anton Furst
Art Director: Les Tomkins
Executive Producers: Michael E Uslan and Benjamin Melniker
Produced by Jon Peters and Peter Guber
Associate Producer: Barbara Kalish
Co-Producer: Chris Kenny
Casting by Marion Doughery, Owen Hill
Music by Danny Elfman
Songs by Prince
Costumes designed by Bob Ringwood, Linda Henrikson
Editor: Ray Lovejoy
Based on characters appearing in magazines published by DC Comics
Batman created by Bob Kane
Directed by Tim Burton

CAST: Jack Nicholson (*Jack Napier/The Joker*), Michael Keaton (*Batman/Bruce Wayne*), Kim Basinger (*Vicki Vale*), Jack Palance (*Carl Grissom*), Robert Wuhl (*Alexander Knox*), Michael Gough (*Alfred*), Billy Dee Williams (*District Attorney Harvey Dent*), Pat Hingle (*Police Commissioner Gordon*), Jerry Hall (*Alicia*), Lee Wallace (*Mayor Borg*), Tracey Walter (*Bob – The Joker's Goon*), William Hootkins (*Lieutenant Eckhardt*), John Dair (*Rotelli*), Steve Plytas (*Doctor*), Hugo E Black (*Young Jack Napier*), Charles Roskilly (*Young Bruce Wayne*), George Roth (*Eddie*), Christopher Fairbank (*Nick*), David Baxt (*Dr Thomas Wayne*), Sharon Holm (*Mrs Wayne*), Denis Lill (*Bob Kane*), Liza Ross (*Mom*), Garrick Hagon (*Dad*), Adrian Meyers (*Jimmy*), John Sterland (*Accountant*), Edwin Craig (*Antoine Rotelli*), John Dair

(*Vinnie Ricorso*), Kate Harper (*Anchorwoman*), Bruce McGuire (*Anchorman*), Richard Durden (*TV Director*), Kit Hollerbach (*Becky Narita*), Lachelle Carl (*TV Technician*), Keith Edwards (*Reporter*), Leon Herbert (*Reporter*), Anthony Wellington (*Patrolman at Party*), Amir M Korangy (*Wine Steward*), Philip O'Brien (*Maitre d'*), Michael Balfour (*Scientist*).

TRAILER: Frequently reported to have been put together to try and assuage the controversy surrounding the film's production, *Batman*'s trailer is far from inspired. Rapidly cut-together sequences try and give some indication of the picture's tone, but don't really manage it. There are a number of bad edits, and an almost total lack of music. Shots of the Batwing swooping through the streets as if they are a canyon and opening fire on the Joker cut to Vicki Vale shaking hands with Bruce in Wayne Manor and introducing herself, then asking Wayne, 'What do you do for a living?' This then switches to a montage of Batman fighting and then Knox asking 'is there a six-foot bat in Gotham city?' We see Jack Napier looking at Batman and saying 'nice outfit' – highlighting the fact that the trailer was put out in part to show it was indeed a nice outfit. There is also a shot of Bruce kissing Vicki, probably to convince people that Bruce Wayne is not a wimp. We also see sequences of Batman's assault on Axis Chemicals, shots of Nicholson as Napier and Nicholson as the Joker, more quick cuts of Batman beating people up, another tiny clip of Keaton as Wayne, plus the Joker's line, 'Where does he get those wonderful toys?' which was mutilated in the film itself. The trailer ends with the Joker saying, 'Winged freak terrorises? Wait until they get a load of me?' It sounds far better on paper than it is in reality.

TITLE SEQUENCE: The camera moves slowly through a labyrinth of what appear to be city streets. Over this credits are overlaid in very simple lettering, which is an unfortunate sickly yellow-gold colour (presumably chosen to match the yellow oval around the Bat emblem on Batman's costume in both this film and some comic book interpretations). It is only as the credits end that we are shown that what we have been travelling through is in fact an entirely grey rendering of that Bat emblem, which looks as if it has been carved out of stone. This then dissolves to a wide shot of a dark and cloudy cityscape, accompanied by the caption 'Gotham City'.

SUMMARY: Gotham City, USA – a place of police corruption and governmental incompetence. Billionaire playboy Bruce Wayne, whose parents were murdered before his eyes at the age of eight, stalks the night as the Batman, taking brutal, sometimes murderous, revenge on criminals. Mob enforcer Jack Napier falls into a vat of toxic waste after a fight with Batman and re-emerges, physically scarred and utterly insane, calling himself the Joker.

He wages war against the people of the city, indulging in surreal acts of terrorism that include the destruction of an art gallery and the poisoning of household products. Batman and the Joker engage in a series of encounters across town until the Joker dies after falling from the roof of the cathedral. Gotham police realise they can trust Batman and he gives them a searchlight sized 'signal' to summon him whenever they need his help.

SOURCE MATERIAL: Created by Bob Kane, Batman is, of course, a popular comic-book character. He appears in periodicals published by DC Comics Ltd, starring in several monthly books, including *Detective Comics* and the eponymous *Batman*.

Making his initial appearance in *Detective Comics* #27 (May 1939), the character has never been out of print, and this film was intended to celebrate the fiftieth anniversary of that first appearance. The Joker, also a creation of Kane's (although some accounts give credit to Kane's art assistant Jerry Robinson) first appeared in *Batman* #1 (Spring 1940). Aspects of the movie's plot, such as the Joker's 'Smilex' venom and his primary costume of a purple suit and yellow shirt, can be traced right back to this first appearance.

Earlier scripts for the Batman film project were specifically based on one year's worth of *Detective Comics* (see **PRODUCTION**), and traces of their plots remain in the final film, with such elements as a murderous confrontation in a chemical factory and Batman's romance with a beautiful woman who works out his secret, directly linked to those issues.

A pronounced influence on the film is the Batman story *The Killing Joke*, written by Alan Moore and drawn by Brian Bolland, which was first published whilst the film was in preproduction. As well as exerting a visual influence, *The Killing Joke* impacts the film's versions of its central characters – as one critic put it, 'the retro 40s look and Batman/Joker relationship [come] from Moore's *The Killing Joke*.'[1] Moore's story sets out that Batman and the Joker are each, in their own ways, equally insane. Its central premise, that one bad day can send anyone over the edge, is very clearly an influence on *Batman*'s storytelling, which spends a lot of screen time examining the way in which the characters come to be. Moore himself had discussions with both Burton and screenwriter Sam Hamm about the project: 'I told [them] to make it dark and serious and exorcise the ghost of Adam West . . . Sam Hamm . . . said it was largely based on *Killing Joke*.'[2]

During advanced preproduction on *Batman* many commentators referred to it as if it were in some way an adaptation of Frank Miller's colossally praised *Batman – The Dark Knight Returns*. Miller was writer/artist on *Dark Knight*, which made its debut in March 1986 and ran for four months, setting off 'industry shockwaves that would continue to be felt a decade later.'[3] The story, which sought to place an aged Batman in a realistic political context and which satirised Reagan's America, was an extreme take on the Batman mythos, one which although widely praised and strongly influential on many aspects of contemporary comics, strangely did not have much impact on the portrayal of the comics' Batman himself. Given that Miller saw his central figure as not so much a man, but more 'the god of vengeance',[4] it was not an approach sustainable in monthly comic books aimed at teenagers as well as older readers. This is not to criticise Miller's extraordinary work, but to point out that Hamm and Burton owe, in truth, far more to Moore than they could to Miller.

Aside from the comics, the previous filmed adaptations of the Batman character had to be taken somewhat into account. He first appeared on screen in 1943 in a fifteen-part serial produced by Columbia Pictures. Lewis Wilson was cast as a laid-back, slightly chubby Bruce Wayne, with Douglas Croft as Robin, as the crime fighters battled against the wartime foe of Dr Daka (J Carrol Naish), the head of a group of saboteurs. The characters returned to the screen six years later in another fifteen-part serial, *The Adventures of Batman and Robin*, laden with stock footage. This time Batman was pitted against The Wizard, a black-robed figure who was stealing top-secret remote-controlled devices. The character then vanished from the big screen until 1966, when a feature-length version of the popular Adam West-starring ABC television show, *Batman*, hit the screens. It was this camp 60s version of the character, full of jolly wise-cracks, bright colours, and with a Batman who usually operated during the day, that was still the best-known incarnation of the character to the non-comic-reading public at large by the late 80s. As Burton put it, 'The people who remember the TV series don't know the comic.'[5]

Although aware of all these different versions of the character, Burton 'decided to take the movie in the direction I thought was right and remain unshaken by anything that would eventually happen ... Like all larger-than-life images, [the Joker and Batman] can be explored any number of different ways,' as, after all, 'There is just as much room for the TV show and *Dark Knight* as there is for my movie. Why shouldn't there be?'[6] On another occasion, he argued more definitely that 'My tone fell somewhere between the TV series and the new dark comics ... I grew up with the TV series, and I love the new comics because they blow apart the conventions of comics ... Batman has a history that goes all over the place.'[7] Indeed, there are aspects of almost every version of the Batman character within Burton's film – arguably his portrayal of Batman as a straight-up grotesque in a caricatured noir world is much closer to Adam West's histrionics than it is to Miller's earnest political brutality.

REFERENCES: As Dent gives his first speech there is a visual quotation from *Citizen Kane* (Orson Welles, 1941). Additionally, before becoming the Joker Jack Napier's dress sense is obviously indebted to that of Harry Lime, the monstrous anti-hero of *The Third Man* (Carol Reed, 1949). Lime was played, of course, by *Citizen Kane*'s director.

During the sequence in which Batman follows the Joker up the inside of the Cathedral there are numerous visual references to *Vertigo* (Alfred Hitchcock, 1958), as well as to various filmed adaptations of Victor Hugo's *The Hunchback of Notre Dame*.

The mugger who points a gun at the young family in the very first scene is visually patterned after Joseph Chill, the murderer of Bruce Wayne's parents in the Batman comics. This deliberately and subtly assists the suggestion that the assault we are witnessing is the robbery in which Wayne's parents died – which would be an obvious place to begin a Batman film. Chill can be seen in *Batman Year Two* written by Mike W Barr, originally published in *Detective Comics* #575–578 (June–September 1987).

The casting of glamour model Jerry Hall as Jack Napier's glamour model girlfriend Alicia leads to inevitable comparisons between Hall's character and her real life persona. In fact, Hall's own portfolio shots are displayed on the walls of her apartment. The Joker's disfiguring of Alicia's face is all the more disturbing because of the connection to reality by Hall's appearance; the act reaches out of the fiction at the audience.

Corrupt cop Lieutenant Eckhardt is, visually and in terms of personality, reminiscent of the popular comics supporting character, Sergeant Harvey Bullock. It has often been speculated that the character was meant to be Bullock, but was changed after consideration of the effect the screen character's corruption might have on the (resolutely loyal and indeed still popular) comics character's portrayal.

Gotham's Mayor, as played by Lee Wallace, is obviously modelled on the then Mayor of New York, Ed Koch. Koch was the Mayor from 1978 to 1990, serving three full elected terms of office. Now a political commentator, he is the author of no less than twelve books and countless book, film and restaurant reviews. Credited with restoring financial stability to NYC during his administration, he is widely revered by the people of New York City. In addition, Burton's version of Harvey Dent has been seen by some as being based partially on Koch's successor as New York's Mayor (and Manhattan borough president 1986–89), David Dinkins – the first African American to hold the post.

The story 'The Joker's Utility Belt' from *Batman* #73 (October/November 1952) by Bob Kane, Dick Sprang and Charles Paris probably provided the basis for the scene where the Joker and his gang deface several artworks in the museum.

CASTING: Surprisingly, given Keaton and Burton's collaboration on *Beetlejuice*, it was producer Jon Peters, not Burton, who suggested him to portray Batman/Bruce Wayne. Once the casting was made public, severe criticism followed, with denunciations of Keaton's appointment appearing in the *Wall Street Journal*, *Newsweek* and *Comics Scene Magazine*.

Buffeted by criticisms, Warners hastily released colour stills of Keaton in his Batman costume to *Newsweek* and the *Los Angeles Times* to try to calm sweaty comics fanboys across the nation, as well as allowing some scenes to be shown on *Entertainment Tonight*. Despite this public angst, Keaton's casting did have some public supporters – people more clued up on the versatile performer's career to date. Dann Gire, writing in *Cinefantastique*, rightly pointed out that people perceived as comedians had demonstrated unexpected range before, such as Jerry Lewis in *The King of Comedy* (Martin Scorsese, 1983) and, for an encore, went on to list the Keaton performances that proved him ideal for the role. *Clean and Sober* (Glen Gordon Caron, 1988) was singled out for praise, with Keaton's award-winning performance described as a 'gritty, realistic portrait of a yuppie alcoholic and coke-head, trying to work out how a one-night-stand died of an overdose . . . serious drama.'[8] Also talked up was *Touch and Go* (Robert Mandel, 1986) which featured Keaton indulging in extensive physical action, proof in Gire's eyes that he was 'tough enough'[9] to play Batman. Writing in the same issue, Joseph Reboy was unconvinced, demanding, 'Why choose somebody so physically unlike the character?'[10]

Burton, however, had an excellent answer. Whilst he conceded that Michael Keaton was not the most obvious choice for the role, the director argued that his casting grew out of the psychology of the character – if Bruce Wayne were seven feet tall and built like a tank he wouldn't need to dress as an armoured Man-Bat when out avenging the deaths of his parents. In finding a psychological basis for the way Batman dressed, Burton felt that it didn't work to say, 'Oh!, a bat's flown in through the window. Yes, that's it. I'll become a Batman! That's all stupid comic book stuff.'[11] For Burton, 'With Michael, the bottom line is, I could see him putting on a bat suit [precisely because] he's not a square-jawed hulk.'[12] After considering some of the more traditional action hero actors, Burton also felt that would be far less interesting, and that taking someone like Michael Keaton and making him Batman supported the character's schizophrenia. 'Michael's personality tunes into those differences, making him the perfect choice. He has a lot going on inside him, there's an explosive side; he has a temper and a great amount of anger – that was exactly the Bruce Wayne character, not some unknown, handsome, strong hunk.'[13]

Despite initially wanting an unknown for the title role, screen-writer Sam Hamm thoroughly approved of Keaton after seeing the finished movie. 'I think Keaton is extraordinary . . . a wild gamble that paid off absolutely.'[14]

If Keaton was a less obvious choice to portray Bruce Wayne, then the casting of Jack Nicholson as the Joker delighted most and surprised none. In the very early 80s Batman creator Bob Kane himself had sent a photograph of Nicholson in *The Shining* (Stanley Kubrick, 1980), doctored to give the actor green hair and a pale face, to Warners' executives. Other actors had been suggested for the role, including Christian Slater (whom many critics have likened to a young Jack Nicholson), Willem Dafoe (whose trademark odd smile would certainly have cut down the makeup costs), *Once Upon a Time in America* (Sergio Leone, 1984) star James Woods, and Glam idol David Bowie, who had some experience of pretending to be a clown. However, Nicholson was always the ideal choice – as Hamm put it, 'It was so fucking obvious. I don't think there was ever a part more tailor made for him.'[15] To appear in the film, Nicholson allegedly struck a deal with Warner Brothers in which he was entitled to an undisclosed percentage of the film's *gross* takings, *including* the merchandising, on top of his initial fee. The precise figure he earned on this picture remains unknown even today, except maybe to Nicholson, and he isn't telling. Some of the figures suggested in the press are as mad as the Joker himself – but even conservative estimates have suggested that he may well have earned as much as $1 million for every minute that he appears on screen.

After this casting choice had been confirmed, Burton explained that, 'We hired [Jack] Palance [to play Grissom] because we could not otherwise answer the question, "Who can be Jack Nicholson's boss?" I mean, Palance even today makes Nicholson look like a kid.'[16]

Cast as Vicki Vale, a Lois Lane-type character created in 1948 and quickly dropped, was Sean Young. She was subsequently forced to pull out of the picture at the last moment after sustaining an injury whilst out horse riding with Michael Keaton to prepare for a scene in the picture (later cut from the script). In her place came model and actress Kim Basinger.

Batman's butler, Alfred (who first appeared in *Batman* #16, April–May, 1943), was to be played by English actor Michael Gough. A Hammer veteran whose work was known to Burton, Gough was pleased to portray Batman's longest-standing ally: 'Alan Napier, who played Alfred on TV, was a great friend of mine hundreds of years ago. I lost touch with him when he went to America,'[17] he recalled. Gough was unaware that he had been cast until rather late in the day. 'When Tim Burton came to Britain, he saw me and said, "I just wanted to meet you before we start work." Until then, I didn't know that I'd actually got the job. Nobody had said anything final about it.'[18]

Another actor potentially signing on for a number of appearances was *The Empire Strikes Back* (Irvin Kershner, 1980) and *Return of the Jedi* (Richard Marquand, 1983) veteran Billy Dee Williams, cast as District Attorney Harvey Dent, a friend of Bruce Wayne's destined to become Batman villain Two-Face, who made his debut in *Detective Comics* #66 (August 1942). When Two-Face did eventually appear in *Batman Forever* (Joel Schumacher, 1995) Williams, along with the character's subtlety and appeal, had gone.

Robert Wuhl, best known for his appearance in *Good Morning, Vietnam* (Barry Levinson, 1987), was hired by Burton to portray reporter Alexander Knox. Wuhl, with dry humour, attributed his acquisition of the role to 'Tim Burton's momentary loss of his senses.'[19]

PRODUCTION: *Batman* originated as a project a long time before Tim Burton was mooted as director. The rights to produce a cinematic *Batman* feature were acquired by producers Michael Uslan and Benjamin Melniker in 1979. Uslan was thoroughly familiar with the character, having worked for DC in the early 70s on a programme that taught children to read using comic books, and had also written Batman stories for DC while a law student at Indiana University.

After a few months of shopping around, Melniker arranged a deal with Peter Guber's Casablanca Film Works, who were linked with Warners. Uslan and Melniker hired James Bond series screenwriter Tom Mankiewicz to write a screenplay. The Mankiewicz screenplay took a similar approach to Richard Donner's 1978 *Superman* feature, taking a long-term and linear, chronological approach to the long-running character's history. Although based on many different aspects of the Batman mythos as presented in the comic books, the screenplay avoided the campest excesses of the 60s television series (and indeed comics), concentrating instead on a portrayal far closer to that envisaged by the character's creator before the Second World War. In plot terms it drew heavily on a particular series of issues of *Detective Comics*, which were then very much in vogue amongst more literate comics readers. Written by Steve Englehart, *Detective Comics* #469–476 (May 1977 to March–April 1978) were pencilled by Walt Simonson (#469–470) and Marshall Rogers (#471–476) with inks by Al Milgrom (#469–470) and Terry Austin (#471–476). Widely celebrated at time of publication, by the early 80s they had begun to be seen as the 'definitive' comic book interpretation of the Batman character. The Mankiewicz script took many elements from the stories, including a strong subplot featuring Gotham City crime boss Rupert Thorne and the romantic figure of a beautiful, white-haired young woman, Silver St Cloud.

Announced in 1981, with a projected budget of $15 million, all seemed to be well with the project. But then it stalled. By 1983 the budget had expanded to $20 million, not solely because of inflation, and the picture was projected for a summer 1985 release. Directors suggested for the picture included Joe Dante (*Piranha*, 1978) and Ivan Reitman (*Ghostbusters*, 1984). Uslan wanted an unknown to play Bruce Wayne, William Holden for his ally Police Commissioner James Gordon, with David Niven as his loyal Gentleman's Gentleman, Alfred Pennyworth.

Again the project floundered due to budget, and was once again pushed back. Enter Burton, assigned to assist in developing the project after the huge success of *Pee-wee's Big Adventure*. Burton was not particularly enamoured of the Mankiewicz script which, based as it was on the *Superman* formula of seven years earlier, seemed rather dated: 'The very first *Batman* treatment I read was remarkably similar to *Superman*.' This chronological approach seemed completely inappropriate to Burton because: 'While that was probably fine in the case of *Superman*, there was absolutely no exploration or acknowledgement of the character's psychological structure and why he would dress up in a bat suit. In *that* respect, it was very much like the television series.'[20]

To solve these problems Burton brought in a new screenwriter, Sam Hamm. They had met in (executive) Bonnie Lee's offices at Warner some time before. 'We talked, goofed around and hit it off,' remembers Hamm. The next time he met Burton, the director asked if he had any interest in working on the script to Batman. Hamm was keen, although the 'project was just sort of lying around wounded and I think they were basically getting ready to unload it . . . nobody could quite figure out what to do.' They decided to treat the scripting process as a last try at an already failed project, and so to just do what they wanted to do, which was to write a story 'about a guy who is obviously extremely fucked up and what happens to him as a result of it . . . the basic story is about a guy who has a sick hobby that fucks up his love life.'[21] Although Burton has since described Sam Hamm as a comics fan, the writer himself insists that he stopped reading comics as a teenager, whilst conceding that he was more familiar with the minutiae of the subject matter than Burton.

During this period director and screenwriter would meet up at weekends to discuss the picture (a collaborative process Hamm has often described as 'freakishly smooth') while Burton worked on other things. Burton felt that 'We knocked it into good shape while I directed *Beetlejuice*, but as a "go" project it was only greenlighted by Warners when the opening figures for *Beetlejuice* surprised everybody – including myself!'[22]

Once the film had finally been cleared for production there was only the small matter of making it. Anton First was hired as Production Designer. He had worked on Stanley Kubrick's *Full Metal Jacket* (1987). Keen to create a Gotham distinct both from the comics' portrayal of the city, and far away from cinema's two much celebrated fictional cities, the worlds of *Metropolis* (Fritz Lang, 1926) and *Blade Runner* (Ridley Scott, 1982), Furst based his city on the script's suggestion that it should look 'like hell had erupted out of the pavement and kept going'. Furst outlined his take on Gotham thus: 'Imagine what could have happened to New York had it all gone wrong . . . for example the zoning they did in New York, stepping back the buildings to get light in . . . we thought we would do the opposite. As you cantilever forward, you get these oppressive canyons.'[23] Furst was working on Burton's insistence that Gotham be unlike anything that had gone before: 'If people say Gotham City looks like *Blade Runner*, I'll be furious,' the director explained. 'So few great movie cities have been built, *Metropolis* and *Blade Runner* seem to be the accepted spectrum. We tried so hard to do something different although people tend to lump things in categories.'[24] Furst and his 14-strong department, plus 200 construction workers, worked for five months to construct the $5.5 million Gotham on a studio backlot, with Furst enthusiastically commenting that with 'a main street which is a quarter of a mile long . . . it's the biggest set since *Cleopatra* (Rouben Mamoulian, Joseph L Mankiewicz and Darryl F Zanuck, 1963).'[25]

The decision to shoot the picture in England was made early on, at least partially because Burton wanted to escape from the hype surrounding the production. Pinewood Studios, a facility outside London, was set up in the 1930s as a British answer to Hollywood. By the 1980s, however, it was principally known as a production base for American pictures wishing to make use of

British talent (either in front of or behind the camera) and advantageous dollar/sterling exchange rates.

Principal photography began at the end of summer 1988. Many of the minor roles were filled out by British actors adept at American accents, including William Hootkins (who had featured in *Star Wars*) and Christopher Fairbank, at the time something of a star on British television thanks to his role in the popular comedy-drama *Auf Wiedersehen, Pet*. Several of the crew were based in Britain too, including key personnel such as Costume Designer Bob Ringwood, who was hired after a chance meeting at Pinewood during scouting.

Once shooting began in October 1988 there was still work to be done on the script. In addition to Warren Skaaren, who had been brought onto the project after the conclusion of the 1988 writers' strike, the unaccredited Charles McKeown was present during much of the shooting, providing daily rewrites on set. This aspect of production was one thing that Burton found especially frustrating: 'We started out with a script by Sam [Hamm] that everyone liked, although we all recognised that there were a few little things which needed changing, and – zoom – we were suddenly shooting. In certain scenes the actors and myself were blocking out new lines on the day we had to film them. A couple of days near the end of production I was close to death over this insane situation.[26] Hamm, however, simply argued, 'I mean, shit happens . . . I frankly couldn't care less. If they want to substitute punchlines, jokes are basically interchangeable. The rhythm, the basic thrust of the characters, how the story fits together, all that is more important than any one localised element.'[27]

Nobody, even today, can confidently put a figure to how much *Batman* ultimately cost. Estimates at the time varied, with most commentators settling on around $35 million. This is, frankly, unbelievable. If you put together the salaries for the film's stars and director, never mind the singer Prince, you don't have enough money left to buy a medium-sized round of drinks, let alone make two hours of lavishly shot sets and special effects, packed with extras, and promoted with one of the most aggressively sizeable marketing campaigns in history.

BURTON REGULARS: Jack Nicholson enthusiastically came back to work with Burton on *Mars Attacks!*, having been in talks to co-star in Burton's abortive project, *The Hawkline Monster*.

Michael Gough returned as Alfred for *Batman Returns* (as well as playing the role in both *Batman Forever* and *Batman and Robin*). He came out of retirement in 1999 to play Notary Hardenbrook in *Sleepy Hollow*. Pat Hingle also returned, as Commissioner Gordon, in the next three Batman films.

Bob Ringwood also designed costumes for *Batman Returns*. Paul Barrett-Brown, who designed the Batsuit, worked on costume effects for Burton's sequel.

Philip Tan, here playing a Goon, played both the '2nd Ape Teenager' and 'Gossiping Ape' in *Planet of the Apes*.

CRITICS: After all the fears of *Batman* being a comedy, most reviewers were quick to point out that 'Director Burton has sensibly turned his back on the camp of the 60s *Batman* TV series, and has drawn his menacing atmosphere from the Gotham City of *Batman*'s creator, Bob Kane,'[28] lending the film 'precisely the sort of grimness, violence and believably eerie atmosphere that fans always wished for.'[29] *Newsweek* applauded the picture's approach as 'hip, post-modern, noir, a swooping dive into the tangled recesses of the contemporary psyche,' and singled out the director as 'one of the most original moviemakers to come along in years'. The players, too, were appreciated: 'The cast is first-rate. Nicholson is a one-man theatre of evil . . . Michael Keaton plays his underwritten part with a brooding style and charm that suggests much more than meets the eye.'[30]

Despite their initial fears on his casting, Keaton's approach was appreciated by pretty much every critic, one commentator writing that, 'When he sheds his armour, the emotional barrier remains. There isn't much shading to Keaton's superhero. That's the point. His psyche is scarred almost beyond repair. He's a vacuum, in danger of imploding. It is a riveting, understated performance.'[31]

However, some were more critical, the *Los Angeles Times* bemoaning in turn the film's fitful interesting moments, lack of fun and wit, unfocussed screenplay and inability to explain why Batman takes bats as his motif, as well as the fact that the similarities between Batman and the Joker are not played up enough (a common complaint). Even Nicholson was criticised for a 'performance of such draining intensity and so few really quotable lines, most of which have been packed into the trailer, that it has us on the ropes begging for mercy long before the Joker waltzes into his climax.'[32]

But most found more positive than negative in the movie, the *Washington Post* labelling *Batman* 'a masterpiece of pulp, the work of a true artist,'[33] before asserting that it is 'dark, haunting and poetic . . . a violent urban fairy tale. And it's as rich and satisfying a movie as you're likely to see all year.'[34] Jay Carr in the *Boston Globe*, despite identifying some flaws, also fell in love with Burton's work: '*Batman* will take its place alongside the small handful of film's visionary apocalyptic cityscapes.'[35]

Not really a critic *per se*, but one man with opinions on the movie which many people were interested in hearing was the former occupant of cape and cowl, Adam West: 'How can the audience be confused between my Batman and the one in the leather and rubber suit?' West predicted, that 'they can polish up the franchise, they can enhance it, they can make it healthier if they become more family-friendly . . . make it more light-hearted, with more wit; not so nihilistic and dark and sinister and violent.'[36] With the light, inconsequential box office disaster that was 1997's *Batman & Robin*, he was almost right.

MUSIC: Nobody had anything but praise for Danny Elfman's 'darkly enveloping score,'[37] with many noting its Wagnerian sound. Elfman himself, though, was having none of it – 'I'm extremely illiterate when it comes to my classical music background,'[38] he commented, and suggested that people who heard echoes of Wagner in his work were noticing things he had inherited second-hand from great movie composers like Erich Korngold. Elfman's *Batman* theme would set a new standard for superhero work, continuing to be profoundly influential for more than a decade, see *X-Men* (Bryan Singer, 2000).

Also providing music for the picture was the artist still then, and now once more, known as Prince. The acquisition of Prince to write several songs for the movie is something that, in retrospect, seems rather strange. Of those that appear in the finished film only 'Crush' – played during the Joker's demolition of the Flugelheim museum – really works. Nevertheless the involvement of Prince invited yet more publicity to the project, and led some people to overlook Elfman's contribution, amidst press reports that Prince had written 'the score'. Faced with this misapprehension Elfman wrote to the *Los Angeles Times* to set the record straight: 'None of this is Prince's fault. People heard Prince was writing songs for the movie and assumed he was doing the score. But the score is all that music that underscores the action. I did that . . . I just spent three months, working night and day on this score. I'm proud of it. I want people to realise that I wrote it.'[39]

In truth there's not as much Elfman in the picture as many people would like, with too many scenes under-scored, or simply devoid of music. It's when Elfman really lets rip, such as when Batman and Vicki take a ride in the Batmobile, that the picture's best moments arrive.

CINEMATOGRAPHY: Cinematographer Roger Pratt had experience of shooting depressingly stylised urban chaos thanks to his work on Terry Gilliam's 1985 masterpiece, *Brazil*. A few critics compared the look of Burton's Gotham with the (unnamed) city in Gilliam's twisted take on George Orwell's *Nineteen Eighty-Four*. To people who know both films well, it is apparent that pretty much the only reason for this is Pratt's camerawork, as Anton Furst's sets are utterly different to those created by Norman Garwood for the earlier film. Pratt's other work for Terry Gilliam, to whom Burton was compared early in his career, has included *The Fisher King* (1991), on which some sets were designed by Rick Heinrichs, and *Twelve Monkeys* (1995), as well as Gilliam's 'The Crimson Permanent Assurance' segment of *Monty Python's The Meaning of Life* (Terry Gilliam and Terry Jones, 1983). All of these have involved the melding together of modelwork and sets in creating the impression of vast, slightly odd-looking cityscapes. Pratt has an innate ability to make model buildings appear an immense part of the background in which the characters are moving, and to make sets glisten with a dark reality. *Batman* is amongst his best work.

PLOT PROBLEMS: Not so much 'plot' problems, as a few difficulties with the characters' progressions according to the screenplay. In the scene where Jack Napier falls into the vat of toxic ooze there are visual suggestions that Batman suddenly recognises him (a double-take close-up as Wayne seems to contemplate his enemy's visage, for example). This presumably means that, though Jack Napier is a fairly public figure, Wayne has only just realised that it was a young Napier who murdered his parents. The rest of the scene is ambiguous as to whether Batman drops Napier, lets him fall or simply fails to save him. Either of the first two is a deliberate act of murder (see **DEATH**).

Vicki Vale never seems to work out that Bruce Wayne is Batman. In one scene she doesn't know, and in the next Alfred is showing her into the Batcave (see **Batman Returns**). In a similar vein, during the confrontation between Batman and the Joker in the cathedral the Joker suddenly seems to know that a) Bruce Wayne is Batman b) that he killed Wayne's parents. As Wayne himself doesn't appear to know the latter at some points in the film, it's all rather confused. Speaking of the Joker, why does no one other than Batman and the GCPD seem to equate Jack Napier with the Joker at any point in the film? (Napier is a public figure, and when the Joker comes on TV he's got flesh tone makeup on).

Finally, why do the people of Gotham attend the Joker's parade and believe his pleas of innocence when he's gone on television and publicly claimed responsibility for the 'Smilex' related acts of terrorism?

DEATH: This Batman kills. That may not seem a big deal in the world of blockbuster movies, where all screen heroes from James Bond onwards rack up enormous body counts, but it's a major departure for Batman, who since the early 1940s has been styled as a figure who never, ever kills. This aspect of the character has been extensively explored over the years, and stated more times than can be counted. Long-time Batman writer/editor Denny O'Neil has repeatedly said that he sees Bruce Wayne's refusal to take life as the very cornerstone of the character. Burton and/or Hamm must have made a conscious decision to make this Batman a murderer – it emphasises the interiorised nature of this Bruce Wayne. He kills because, unlike his comic book counterpart, he doesn't empathise with everyone in Gotham, and isn't *constantly* disturbed by the notion that someone somewhere is going through what he went through on the night his parents were killed. It's a subtle but substantial shift in the character, as both previously and subsequently presented.

CHILDREN AND FAMILIES: We have the two family units of the Waynes and their clear analogues, Jimmy's family (who appear in the opening scene). Both run into brutal situations on a night in Gotham City, although for one the night does not end as badly as for the other, at least partially because of Batman's existence.

The Joker gets Alicia to call him 'Daddy' – which is a touch Freudian, to say the least.

CLOWNS AND THE CIRCUS: 'I am the world's first, fully functioning homicidal artist,' exults the Joker at one point, explaining his 'motivation'. 'I love the idea of a man dressed up like a bat versus a man who has literally turned into a clown,'[40] said Burton during production, and it's clear from the finished product that the villain of the piece is of as much interest to him as the hero. Nicholson's Joker doesn't really have any motivation at all. He simply seems to enjoy killing people in bizarre ways and have a crush on Vicki Vale. The only objective he seems to have is a desire to stop the Batman getting all his press. He's genuinely irrational, truly insane, unlike most 'mad' movie villains who are often little more than vaguely eccentric and badly dressed.

LOVE TRIANGLES: 'You know how people have different sides to their personalities?' Bruce asks Vicki, as he tries to explain to her that he and Batman are one and the same. Vale/Bruce/Batman form a love triangle with two people, and thanks to the Joker's single-minded pursuit of Vicki, Bruce/Joker/Vicki form a more conventional triangle. There's also Alex Knox, who looks a bit like Bruce Wayne himself, and who clearly has eyes for Vicki. Both Grissom and Napier are sleeping with Alicia in the early parts of the film, and when Napier (now the Joker) finally has her to himself, he starts pursuing Vicki. 'Sometimes I don't understand all this,' mutters Bruce at one point. Understandable really, when people insist on having multiple personalities and lusting after each other's girlfriends.

CHECKS, STRIPES, DOTS: The Joker's black suit has white checked trousers, and his clown gang are covered in various black and white striped items of clothing. Some of the floors in Wayne Manor are checked too.

DIALOGUE TO SKIP BACK FOR:
Knox: 'Lieutenant, is there a six foot bat in Gotham City, and if so is he on the police payroll? And if so, what's he pulling down? After taxes.'

Napier on Harvey Dent: 'If this clown could touch Grissom I'd have handed him his lungs by now.'

DIALOGUE TO SKIP PAST:

'Oh my God, you're married,' pouts Vale as Bruce Wayne tries to tell her his big secret. 'That wasn't just another night for either of us was it?' she says at another point, and caps it off with, 'Are we going to try and love each other?' You'd think that given that they were rewriting right up through shooting they'd have got rid of thoroughly rotten dialogue like this.

AUTOBIOGRAPHY?: It is only in retrospect that anyone has attempted to find autobiographical elements in *Batman* – a trend that started with Burton's next, more blatantly autobiographical film, *Edward Scissorhands*. Most suggestions were that Burton could perhaps identify with the lonely man, separated from society, yet doing great things for it, rather than accusing him of having a fetish for leather and crimefighting – those accusations would come with *Batman Returns*. There might well be some truth to these theories, but it is retroactive and self-applied – the Batman character had been around for nearly 50 years in very similar forms when Burton got involved. If Burton *identified* with Bruce Wayne, it's not the same as the film being autobiographical, and the director has stated that he always tries to find *something* to identify with in his characters.

JUST PLAIN WEIRD: Batman is a very, very weird idea. It is only the fact that it has gradually permeated mainstream Western culture over the last half century that everyone has come to accept it. Think about it for a moment. A man, dressed as a bat, fighting insane, garish criminals at night, and the police don't really mind?

AFTERLIFE: Well let's put it this way, *The Economist* described Burton's Batman as 'The most financially successful film in the most successful summer in Hollywood history.'[41] It was the first movie in motion picture history to make $100 million in ten days. It seems insane, a decade on, that not just Hollywood but mainstream America as a whole questioned so loudly if Burton and Keaton were the right combination of director and star to bring the Dark Knight detective to the big screen; presumably they had either not seen *Beetlejuice*, or had not paid attention to it.

Expectation for the film before release was enormous, reaching heights not surpassed until *Star Wars: Episode I – The Phantom Menace* in 1999. Whether *Batman* would have equalled *Star Wars* if it too had been released in the age of the Internet will never be known. Reflecting on the anticipation for the movie, Burton said, 'Hype is a funny thing because *true* hype is something that happens culturally and you don't have any control over it – you may not like it, but you don't have any control over that. But when [the studios] are hyping it *themselves*, that was a big, big mistake.'[42] Warners to an extent concurred, as Head of Marketing Rob Friedman admitted, 'Too much hype can be potentially negative to any product. We've tried to manage the publicity flow to preclude that ... but to some extent it's become a feeding frenzy.' However he felt that 'The film does deliver, so we have no real concerns.'[43]

Towards the end of 1989, when *Batman* was still making money in movie theatres, Warners withdrew the film in order to have the VHS release ready for Christmas. Burton felt 'They cut off their own noses, they actually took the film *out of release* ... so that they could release it on video, and then they didn't make as much on video ... it was sort of frightening to see that.'[44] Having a studio determine one of his film's releases based solely on perceived commercial benefits was something Burton would later experience again with *Planet of the Apes*.

Of the finished film itself Burton initially had this to say: 'The tone is more consistent than in any other film I've made,'[45] also asserting that 'it was finished, contrary to rumours, as I intended ... given all the possible pitfalls, this movie still has its personality, its style,'[46] although later interviews would see him revise his opinion. Nonetheless, he still felt at the time that it 'was the toughest job I've ever had to do ... I always felt like I was catching up. I worked six days a week and exhausted myself because I feared I wasn't doing a good job. I was afraid my mental condition wasn't right for me to be making this movie, and even now I have amnesia about certain times during the shooting.'[47] This is almost identical to comments he made twelve years later on completion of *Planet of the Apes*. Two years after its release he went on record to say that 'Of all the films I've made, *Batman* is the one I've liked least. Of course there are aspects about it I'm happy with, but because it was such a big movie, and the first of its type for me, I felt it kind of got away from the vision I wanted.'[48] He would soon restate this: 'I think if you ask most directors, the first big movie you do is a bit shocking – it's hard to even describe. Everything's heightened, and it's harder to get it up on the screen. So I just feel that there are some images that I don't feel I got as strongly as I'd like to have done.'[49]

Whatever the director's concerns about the finished product, and the studio's approach to it, Burton's *Batman* is unquestionably the most influential superhero film of all time. It started a trend for 'dark' blockbusters that, whilst soon descending into self-parody with movies such as *The Crow* (Alex Pyroas, 1994), defined how fantastical motion pictures were approached for a decade. The hugely successful *Batman – The Animated Series* is a direct result of the style, tone and success of Burton's film. Its spin-off and successor series such as *Superman*, *The Adventures of Batman and Robin* and *Batman Beyond*, not to mention *Justice League*, owe an enormous amount to this film. They simply would not have existed without it, and these cartoon series across the 90s and beyond have shaped how Warner Brothers/Time Warner AOL have treated and responded to some of the most financially and culturally valuable properties they own. *That's* impact.

AWARDS: The film won the 1990 US People's Choice Awards for both Favourite Dramatic Motion Picture and Favourite All-Round Motion Picture. Anton Furst and Peter Young won the 1990 Academy Award for Best Art Direction-Set Design. The film also won a Brit Award for Best Soundtrack, and was (oddly, considering its violent and depressing nature) nominated as Best Family Motion Picture at the Young Artist Awards. Jack Nicholson was nominated for both a Golden Globe and a BAFTA. Also at the BAFTAS, Bob Ringwood and Anton Furst were nominated for Costume Design and Production Design respectively, and the film received additional nominations for Makeup, Sound, and Special Effects.

ANALYSIS: One reviewer called Keaton's Bruce Wayne 'the Hamlet of millionaire socialite philanthropists',[50] and as a description of Burton's reinvention of Batman's alter ego, it's spot on. Scottish comics writer Grant Morrison, who has written for the character on more than one occasion, has frequently argued that Bruce Wayne is simply an aggressive aristocrat who gets his kicks in a strange way, and that all the psychoanalysis is an unimportant side issue.

Keaton/Hamm/Burton's Batman is, whatever the publicity surrounding the film tried to say, a new interpretation. Batman as an outsider, Batman is lonely recluse; a man who should be, indeed appears to be, one of the highest ranking members of the metropolitan establishment but who is, in the end, just a broken man trying to work out his problems. It's a portrayal that is simultaneously comforting and disturbing. It makes Bruce Wayne more understandable, but it makes him a hero with feet of clay.

TRIVIA: Keaton's Bruce Wayne wears glasses. This is not a characteristic exhibited by any other version of the character, but does help emphasise the geeky, outsider nature of the man.

In the beginning of the movie at the *Gotham Globe* offices, when everyone is making fun of Knox's Batman obsession, one guy hands Knox a drawing of a bat creature, signed by Batman creator, Bob Kane.

According to producer Jon Peters, he toyed with the idea of casting Bill Murray and Eddie Murphy as Batman and Robin.

The comic book Joker was originally based on the actor Conrad Veidt – particularly his image as Gwynplaine in the silent movie, *The Man Who Laughs* (Paul Leni, 1928), adapted from the Victor Hugo novel, *L'Homme Qui Rit*. Veidt is perhaps best known for playing Jaffar in *The Thief of Baghdad* (Ludwig Berger, Alexander Korda, Zoltan Korda, William Cameron Menzies, Michael Powell and Tim Whelan, 1940), on which André de Toth, the director of the Vincent Price-starring *House of Wax* (1953), worked. *House of Wax* was referenced in Burton's homage to Price, *Vincent*. How's that for six degrees of separation?

Bob Kane gave Batman a cape thanks to the look of Bela Lugosi in *Dracula* (Tod Browning, 1930). *The Bat Whispers* (Roland West, 1930), a remake of silent movie *The Bat* (Roland West, 1926) also helped inspire the original Batman costume.

EXPERT WITNESS: Michael Gough: 'Tim Burton's one of those directors who ... casts you for what you *are*, or what he's seen you do. Then, very sweetly, he pushes you along the line you're on, or holds you back. Tim's very wild. He looks totally undisciplined. His hair is everywhere ... But I think he's totally single-minded when he's working. He has an amazing imagination.'[51]

Glenn Shadix: '*Batman* was the first time he did a *big* movie. When he was in London, I visited him for two weeks near the end of the shoot. He would come home in the evenings and say, "Jon Peters is shaking my tree just to shake my tree!" What he really meant was that sometimes producers and executives, they deliberately stir up tension just because they somehow think that by stirring up tension they will "improve" the product, or that they will have some impact.'

AVAILABILTY: Batman is available on DVD in pan and scanned formats, with effectively no extra features. It is also available as part of a *Batman* boxed set on both DVD and VHS, with the other three Warners Batman movies. There hasn't yet been a 'special edition' DVD.

THE BOTTOM LINE: An inspired pairing of director and material, *Batman*'s plot inconsistencies are relatively minor and skated over with considerable visual flair. Nicholson is astonishing as the Joker, and for many Michael Keaton will be forever the very epitome of Bruce Wayne, playboy, superhero and freak. There are scenes, such as the Bruce Wayne/Joker confrontation in Vicki's apartment, the murder of Bruce Wayne's parents and the sequences at the Flugelheim museum, which are as impressive and involving as anything that Burton has ever put on screen.

In the year of its release *Batman* was a phenomenon, accompanied by a cavalcade of tie-ins. 'There's nobody more tired of seeing the stuff than me,' said Burton. 'I'm very afraid of this kind of marketing stuff. It kind of destroys the movie sometimes.'[52] Produced under these conditions it isn't *admirable* that *Batman* is such a good movie, it's a miracle.

EDWARD SCISSORHANDS (1990)

Twentieth Century Fox
A Tim Burton Film
Story by Tim Burton and Caroline Thompson
Screenplay by Caroline Thompson

Director of Photography: Stefan Czapsky
Production Designer: Bo Welch
Art Director: Tom Duffield
Produced by Denise Di Novi and Tim Burton
Executive Producer: Richard Hashimoto
Casting by Victoria Thomas
Music by Danny Elfman
Costume Designer: Colleen Attwood
Makeup effects created by Stan Winston
Directed by Tim Burton

CAST: Johnny Depp (*Edward*), Winona Ryder (*Kim Boggs*), Diane Wiest (*Pegg Boggs*), Anthony Michael Hall (*Jim*), Alan Arkin (*Bill Boggs*), Vincent Price (*The Inventor*), Kathy Baker (*Joyce Monroe*), Robert Oliveri (*Kevin Boggs*), Conchata Ferrell (*Helen*), Caroline Aaron (*Marge*), Dick Anthony Williams (*Officer Allen*), O-Lan Jones (*Esmeralda*), Susan J Blommaert (*Tinka*), Linda Perri (*Cissy*), John Davidson (*Host-TV*), Biff Yeager (*George*), Marti Greenberg (*Suzanne*), Bryan Larkin (*Max*), John McMahon (*Denny*), Victoria Price (*TV Newswoman*), Stuart Lancaster (*Retired Man*), Gina Gallagher (*Granddaughter*) Aaron Lustig (*Psychologist*), Alan Fudge (*Loan Officer*), Steven Brill (*Dishwasher Man*), Peter Palmer (*Editor*), Marc Macaulay (*Reporter*), Carmen J Alexander (*Reporter*), Brett Rice (*Reporter*), Andrew B Clark (*Beefy Man*), Kelli Crofton (*Pink Girl*), Linda Jean Hess (*Older Woman/TV*), Rosalyn Thomson (*Young Woman/TV*), Lee Ralls (*Red-Haired Woman/TV*), Eileen Meurer (*Teenage Girl/TV*), Bea Albano (*Rich Widow/TV*), Donna Pieroni (*Blonde/TV*), Ken De Vaul (*Policeman*), Michael Gaughan (*Policeman*), Tricia Lloyd (*Teenage Girl*), Kathy Dombo (*Other Teen*), Rex Fox (*Police Sergeant*), Sherry Ferguson (*Max's Mother*), Tabetha Thomas (*Little Girl on Bike*).

TRAILER: There are two trailers. The first one is pretty awful; the second is rather effective. The first follows the film's plot more or less exactly in order, giving the entire plot away while failing to indicate the film's tone thanks to an unfortunate choice of clips, which make it appear like a wacky comedy. The second, specially scored by Danny Elfman, mixes pieces of the title sequence with moody shots of Edward and occasional moments of levity. The ending of this trailer, as the music soars over a version of the logo never used on the finished film, is strikingly beautiful and uplifting.

TITLE SEQUENCE: After a snow-covered version of the 20th Century Fox logo we enter a sequence that owes more than a little to Alfred Hitchcock's regular title designer, Saul Bass, accompanied by music in waltz time. As we move up stairs, which evoke the climax of *Vertigo* (1958) and indeed that of Burton's recently completed *Batman*, the credits arrive in a slanted white font reminiscent of several Hitchcock movies. A pair of human hands, shot from above, although doubtlessly thematically relevant to this picture, provides another link with Bass and *Vertigo*, but this time to Jimmy Stewart's vertiginous dream/panic sequences. The camera strolls through laboratory equipment which owes a sizeable debt to Kenneth Strickfadden's designs for James Whale's 1931 *Frankenstein*, before ending on a long shot of a castle which seems designed to remind the audience of the home of Lugosi's *Dracula* (Tod Browning, 1930). It's an extremely effective sequence, and one which contextualises *Edward Scissorhands* both in the traditions of Universal's horror series, and Burton's own work so far. It's also, of course, the elaborate setup for the punch line of the first shot, a bright, shiny Middle American neighbourhood displaying no signs of the shadows the titles exhibit.

SUMMARY: An old woman settles down to recount to her granddaughter the story of how snow is made . . . She tells her of a suburban America, in an era of pastel-painted houses, twin sets and Bakelite telephones, where Avon cosmetics lady Pegg Boggs, desperate to make a sale, goes to a castle on a hill and meets a man called Edward who has scissors instead of hands. Taking pity on the boy, she takes him into her home where he meets her husband Jim and her children Kevin, who's about ten, and Kim, a popular senior in High School. After some resistance from the neighbours, Edward becomes a part of the local community – especially after he proves to have talents for sculpting hedges, trimming dogs and cutting hair.

Soon he finds himself at the centre of a media circus, even appearing on television to answer questions about his life. Unfortunately, thanks to the actions of a woman (Joyce) with a sexual fascination for Edward who is angered by his rejection of her, and Kim's macho boyfriend Jim, Edward is gradually alienated from the only community he has ever known.

On Christmas Eve, Edward sculpts an angel out of ice on the Boggs' lawn, creating shards of snow-like ice as he does so. Kim is enchanted, and goes to Edward, before Jim startles him, and Edward accidentally slices her hand. Jim chases him off, and in a rage Edward terrorises the neighbourhood, before calming down in time to save Kevin from being run over by a van being driven by a drunken Jim. Yet the neighbours mistake his actions for an attack, and a mob forms that chases him back to his creator's castle.

Both Kim and Jim follow Edward back to the mansion, Kim to tell him she loves him, Jim to kill him for stealing his girlfriend. A fight breaks out, and when Jim attacks Kim, Edward stabs him and then pushes him out of a window. Understanding why he did this, and knowing what the approaching mob will do to him if they find out he has killed Jim, Kim goes outside and tells the assembled populace that Jim and Edward killed each other, and that they should all go home, offering a spare scissorhand as proof of Edward's death.

The grandmother finishes her story, and the audience realises that she is Kim. When the child asks how her grandmother knows if Edward is still alive, Kim explains that each Christmas it snows, something that never happened before Edward arrived, and that she believes the snow is the shards of ice drifting away from his many sculptures and down towards the town. The film ends with Edward doing just this, 'snow' blowing out of a high window in the castle in one of the most beautiful images of the entire film.

SOURCE MATERIAL: *Edward Scissorhands* was a creation of Burton's own. As he was later to explain, 'I'd liked to draw since I was younger . . . and oftentimes images would come up that would stay with you and you would keep drawing them.'[1] One of the images to which he would frequently return was that of a man with long scissor blades for fingers. It was basically a doodle, and one that 'came before I had any real sort of application in mind.'[2]

After pondering this image, others soon came to the young Burton, whose love of drawing was, after all, what led him to Disney and into his filmmaking career. Some of these would later emerge in *Vincent* and *Frankenweenie*, many more in *The Nightmare Before Christmas*, and eventually a number of them, with accompanying verse, would appear in book form as *The Melancholy Death of Oyster Boy and Other Stories* in 1997. Like 'The Boy With Nails in his Eyes' or 'Jimmy, the Hideous Penguin Boy', 'Edward Scissorhands' could just as easily have ended up as one of the half-formed ideas in Burton's little book for children, especially as the image first appeared long before he became a director. Nonetheless, other images soon joined his initial vision of a lone man with hands that were scissors: 'I wanted to make a story involving scissors, coiffeur-ed dogs and snow. Forming the narrative around those . . . images was always my intention, I just didn't know how to do it at the time.'[3]

Unlike both *Vincent* and *The Nightmare Before Christmas*, both of which were initially conceived of as simple Dr Seuss/ Charles Addams-style children's books, akin to what *Oyster Boy* became, Burton seems to have sensed the potential for a more ambitious project within *Edward* from an early stage. With many of the *Oyster Boy* characters, such as 'James' or 'Char Boy', the image itself seems to be the point of the character, with no deeper meaning than that obvious from a surface reading. With *Edward*, however, as Caroline Thompson, the writer who developed the idea into a narrative, explained, 'The metaphor was immediately apparent to me. It seemed both really brilliant and really dumb at the same time.'[4]

For Burton, Edward 'somewhat represented those years as a teenager when you were feeling quite intense and misperceived . . . growing up in Burbank as well heightened those feelings for me, so this is very representative of a lot of feelings and perceptions of that time, that place . . . it was a story that I had in my mind for a long time.'[5] In looking for applications, he told one interviewer that 'At one point I wanted to make it into an opera because I felt the imagery was so strongly related to singing.'[6] But Burton had little musical inclination, making the writing of an opera a near impossibility. He decided instead to stick with what he knew – the fairy tale. As he explained, 'I've always had a love of fairy tales, like "Little Red Riding Hood" or "Hansel and Gretel", and the idea of them was wonderful, but the psychological connection wasn't there for me.'[7] He has also stated on various occasions that he sees the *Batman* comics characters, and even Washington Irving's *Sleepy Hollow*, as modern fairy tales.

Some time after he started pondering the nature of myth, Burton recalls having 'this conversation with somebody that made a lot of sense for me. They said, "Imagine how 'Little Red Riding Hood' was received in the world in which it was written – it probably made complete sense".[8] He began to realise that as much as he loved fairy tales, in his home country they had all but lost their power and meaning. 'Disney have been guilty in sanitising them to a great degree. I don't know how it happened, but people use the term fairy tale now to mean something good or something just for children . . . The term is so loosely bandied about.'[9]

Like Roald Dahl (whose *James and the Giant Peach* Burton would help see turned into a film) before him, Burton began to consider the possibilities of retelling old, and creating new, fairy tales for the more cynical world of the late twentieth century. Reducing the stories to their essential elements allowed Burton to realise that 'what I love about fairy tales is something very simple and emotional in them which is shown on a much broader symbolic scale.' His sketch of a man with scissors for hands fulfilled all his criteria for the basis of a good fairy tale: 'it's in the inability to communicate, the inability to touch, being at odds with yourself. How you are perceived as opposed to what you are.' Something Burton has often stated he felt whilst growing up, was an isolation and vague sense of being different. But he realised his image had a much wider application: 'Everybody's felt they've wanted something in life and not been able to get it. Everybody has a couple of sides to their personality. And in a very quick, visual way, he encapsulates all that.'[10]

Despite the relative failure of both his initial attempts to bring fairy tales to screen (*Hansel and Gretel* and *Aladdin and his Wonderful Lamp*), Burton still wanted to make 'a movie that expressed my affection for, and the feelings I get out of, fairy tales.'[11] Edward looked like an obvious choice for this, and Burton began to tailor the idea for the screen, all the while aware that if it was to be filmed in the manner he intended, it would have to wait until he had sufficient influence in the industry to ensure that no one interfered.

After the success of *Pee-wee*, but before pre-production work began on *Beetlejuice*, Burton found himself in a limbo, often spending his days visiting his agent in order to read yet another script which he knew he had no interest in directing. On one such visit he met Caroline Thompson, who had been picked up by the same agency purely on the strength of her screenplay, *First Born*, which was based upon a novel she had also written. Its subject matter – an aborted foetus that comes back to haunt its mother – was as weird as many of Burton's own ideas. It sounds gruesome, but Thompson insists, 'It's not meant to be taken seriously. It's a spirited, angry black comedy about being raised in suburbia. *Edward Scissorhands* was, in some sense, the warmer, gentler version of the same story ... which is what it feels like to look in from the outside.'[12]

Burton and Thompson were introduced by agency staff. 'Quite honestly, they didn't know what to do with either of us,' Thompson explained. 'He had just made *Pee-Wee's Big Adventure*, and I had just done this strange screenplay.'[13] Their shared predicament soon led to a growing friendship. Thompson felt that there was an instant connection between the two of them. Burton read her novel, and they discussed projects with each other. Their friendship quickly developed into a working partnership when, after a chat over lunch one day, he told her of his sketch. As Thompson told one interviewer, 'The attraction of all stories for me is the metaphor ... to me my work is more realistic than so-called realist movies because life is about what things feel like, not the clock ticking. It is metaphors that express what things feel like: the metaphor in *Edward Scissorhands* of a man who cannot touch or be touched, cannot hold or participate – that's what life feels like.'[14] 'I never even saw the drawing, but [Tim] just said, "Well, it's a picture of a guy whose got scissors instead of hands." I said, "Stop. That's it." It was one of those miraculous things where the story came to me in a flash. The story would never have existed but for the brilliance of Tim's image. I consider it one of the greatest gifts that anyone's ever given me.'[15]

REFERENCES: Burton was aware from the start that his idea was hardly mind-blowingly original; but then that was never the point, the idea was to revitalise extant formulas for a modern audience. As he tried to explain, the film is 'not a new story. It's *Frankenstein*. It's *Phantom of the Opera*. It's *Hunchback of Notre Dame*, *King Kong*, *Creature From the Black Lagoon*, and countless fairy tales.'[16] Relocating these classic tales to a more suburban setting came largely due to the fact that the suburbs were what he knew, but also because 'I remember watching *Frankenstein* ... the angry villagers reminded me of certain things in the neighbourhood ... never really getting a sense of individuality about anything.'[17] Thus, the most obvious references in *Edward* are from almost every film version of *Frankenstein* – including Burton's own *Frankenweenie* in the bizarre looking, yet very 'normal' neighbours.

Aside from the multitude of thematic and visual quotations in the title sequence (see **TITLE SEQUENCE**) and the obvious *Frankenstein* riffs, there are more than a few references in the film itself. The Inventor has a machine that automatically produces food on a production line, and it looks more than a little like both the breakfast machine from *Pee-wee's Big Adventure*, and a similar device from its contemporary, *Back to The Future* (Robert Zemeckis, 1985). Some of the Inventor's robots bear a passing resemblance to the 'Smash'-advertising Martians of 70s TV commercials, of which Burton must have been aware.

In some ways the ending, a fight in a castle which leads to the death of the villain and the abandonment of the hero, is like a re-run of the finale of *Batman*, except there the hero emerges triumphant from the battle to become revered by society. Burton would later, after the *Superman* experience, use ideas abounding in superhero storytelling in a more personal, less optimistic way in *Stainboy*.

PRODUCTION: After the difficulties of shooting *Batman*, and having been unable to put as personal a stamp on the film as he would have liked, Burton was at once disillusioned with Holly-wood while being one of its biggest directorial stars. Finally he appeared to have the clout to get one of his own projects made. And yet, *Edward Scissorhands* had actually gone quite far into development before *Batman* had even been given the go-ahead for production.

Having found a kindred spirit in Caroline Thompson, Burton began paying her himself to develop a script for the film while he was busy making *Beetlejuice*. As he later explained, 'It was a great working relationship. I'm not the most verbal of people, especially when it's an idea coming from my subconscious, so I was lucky to meet her. She was very in tune with my ideas and we connected almost psychically. I'd give her a little money and we'd work secretly on the script which she eventually wrote.'[18] At the same time, they attempted to figure out the budget, estimating it at about $8–$9 million, and were soon in a position to start submitting it to studios.

Naturally enough, Warner Brothers were the first studio Burton approached; he'd successfully worked with them on his previous two films, and was still being paid to help develop *Batman* for them. According to Burton he and Thompson 'gave them two weeks only to say yes or no ... This was the route I was determined to take so no one could force changes on me.' Warners didn't want to force any changes – they didn't want to make *Edward Scissorhands* at all, choosing to pass on this weird idea from their resident prodigy. Looking back at this decision, Burton realised 'I was glad they didn't do it in some ways. I didn't want a studio making *Edward* specifically based on my previous successes ... They would still have had to distribute it had they taken the hands-off policy. And that was a little worrisome. If they didn't understand it while I was pitching it, what hope would the marketing people have had?'[19]

Instead it was Twentieth Century Fox who picked up the film. The studio's production chief, Scott Rudin, had enjoyed Burton's previous work, and decided that he wanted to work with the young director. Rudin picked up the project, giving Burton and Thompson complete creative control, and began financing further development of the screenplay. Burton was overjoyed: 'Fox understood what I wanted to achieve far better.'[20] He even felt comfortable leaving the project to develop at Fox whilst he went off to England to make *Batman*.

But whilst Burton was at Shepperton there was a management overhaul at Fox. For a while, there were fears that the new executives might not be so keen on a film based around such an apparently peculiar character. Yet the success of *Beetlejuice* (and the hype surrounding *Batman*) had made Burton Hollywood's latest *wünderkind*, and the new team at Fox realised that they had a potential goldmine in development.

Fox chairman Joe Roth likened *Edward* to two previous rather odd commercial successes: 'Like a lot of things – *Pinocchio*, *E.T.* – it's both very new and very familiar. It takes something that's very odd and lets it show what's right about us and what's wrong about us.'[21] More importantly, however, and as Roth's comments suggest, the studio still seemed to understand the picture – they were, in fact, prepared to invest much more than the miserly $8 million Burton had originally anticipated requiring for its production. *Edward Scissorhands* was one of the first films Roth green-lit after he took over. Burton had already publicly expressed misgivings about the negative effect of the publicity for *Batman*, and Roth's faith in both Burton and the film was such that he determined, 'We have to let it find its place, we want to be careful not to hype the movie out of the universe.'[22] Thus, very few publicity shots were released prior to the film's release and the look of the film remained a closely guarded secret throughout.

Filming lasted for three months, largely on location in the distinctly un-showbiz Carpenters Run district of Pasco County, Florida, and then on the same Fox soundstages on which the more typically Hollywood *Die Hard II: Die Harder* (Renny Harlin, 1990) had just wrapped. Florida seemed like a perfect choice due to the stable, sunny weather. However, there were some downsides to shooting in the intense Florida heat, with temperatures often reaching highs of 110 degrees Fahrenheit. Swarms of insects, another typical Florida problem, also made the shoot more difficult. Johnny Depp, who spent much of the shoot strapped into a costume consisting largely of black leather and rubber, at one point complained, 'This is the most uncomfortable I've ever been in a movie. I'm strapped and buckled into this . . . I feel like I'm in an old sailor's trunk, no way to get out of it.'[23] To keep him from perspiring to death, cooling fluid had to be pumped through tubes in his costume, and even then he found himself fainting and vomiting from the heat on more than one occasion. This was only made worse by the scissorhands themselves, with which Depp began practising months before shooting began: 'Normal things like working the remote control on the television set were just impossible . . . Going to the bathroom is something I don't want to talk about. I went to sleep with the hands on. I nicked myself a few times.'[24]

The Saddlebrook Golf and Tennis Resort in Pasco County was the base of operations for the hundred plus cast and crew, with the principal locations situated a short drive away, on Platt Road (the mansion) and Tinsmith Circle (the suburbs), on the outskirts of Dade City. According to Production Designer Bo Welch, they were looking for 'a kind of generic, plain-wrap suburb', which they then 'made even more characterless by painting all the houses in faded pastels, and reducing the window sizes to make it look a little more paranoid.'[25] Other than this basic cosmetic work on the local houses (and the addition of plastic topiaries), an 80-foot-high two-sided mansion façade, fashioned out of plaster and cement, and its grounds landscaped with 15,000 zinnias, marigolds and other flowers, was constructed nearby.

Burton and his design team managed to mould the locations to fit the fairy tale vision perfectly, surprising even screenwriter Caroline Thompson in the process. As she put it, 'To us it was like a memory of childhood. I had described suburbia, but Tim Burton realised it in such a way that it was of no time and no place, as if it was our memories.'[26] Burton was determined to express his love of the suburbs, as 'it's a very fascinating place, suburbia. It is a funny place, very strange and bizarre, but not totally negative. So in the film I hope it's presented in a way that is extreme and kind of crazy, but not judgemental and laughing at people ... I just wanted to put images out there; hopefully people can make up their own minds about it.'[27]

Art Director Tom Duffield remembers that 'The concept behind suburbia was that we wanted a playground. We wanted it to be very graphic – it was like if Stalingrad or Leningrad had a suburb it would sort of be like this. We took all the detail out, we took out all the round-headed windows, all the brick trim. We covered up almost any feature detail with just a flat wall, then we painted it the colours of Neco Wafer candy – they have all these pastel colours. That was Bo [Welch]'s call.'

The pastel paint-jobs were combined with skewed takes on classic 50s and 60s designs, with many of the props being bought in the local Salvation Army charity store, and costume designer Colleen Atwood carried the concept over into her creations, creating 'a feeling of timeless polyester'[28] that fitted ideally with Bo Welch's refitting of the neighbourhood.

The film's most unusual set, yet the one most like the public's now entrenched perception of Burton, was the mansion in which the Inventor created Edward, and to which he returned at the film's end. Tom Duffield describes it as, 'Kooky, spooky – a slanted look on the old fairy castle, old and abandoned.' The film's entire design dynamic was felt by him and Welch to be 'a take on Americana. We looked at a lot of books on Americana, one called *Suburbia* by Bill Owens was a very strong influence in this movie. We wanted to do a spin, and extremely accentuate some of the monotony of suburban life – we wanted to create the most severe portrayal of mundane suburban life. That was kind of the point of it. Then here was this other character who lived in this almost alternate world up on this mountain, and there was a very strong contrast definitely between the two.'

Unusually for a Burton film, but largely due to the fact that he had directly supervised the writing process, there was little improvisation on set, perhaps also partly due to the stress of the daily rewrites on *Batman*. The only feature film Burton has made which kept more to the dialogue as written than *Edward Scissorhands* remains *Ed Wood*. However, as Burton explained, 'because ... it was a fantasy we wanted to make sure that everything sounded real even if it was heightened, so I think everybody was sensitive throughout to finding the right tone and maybe changing a word or two here and there just to make it more real.'[29]

CASTING: According to Burton, 'Dianne [Wiest] was the first actress to read *Edward* who supported it completely. She was our first signing and, because she's so well respected in the industry, once she endorsed the project it got others interested. She was my guardian angel.'[30] Following her Best Supporting Actress Oscar for Woody Allen's *Hannah and her Sisters* (1986), Wiest had switched to less esoteric fare with Joel Schumacher's *The Lost Boys* (1986, and designed by Bo Welch), and Ron Howard's comedy/drama *Parenthood* (1989), for which she was again nominated by the Academy. She found Caroline Thompson's script 'very strange and wonderful ... I hadn't seen any of Tim's movies, but I went out and saw *Batman* immediately. I was as taken with the man as I was with his work.'[31] She would later admit 'I haven't felt this strongly about a director since Woody [Allen].'[32]

For such an odd, mostly silent lead character, an immensely skilled physical actor was essential to get across the subtle shifts in emotion that Edward experiences throughout the film. It was also important to maintain the character's endearing air of innocence and wonder. Twentieth Century Fox spent months trying to get Tom Cruise to play Edward, hoping that a star name would help the film's Box Office chances, even though Burton had told them that, 'He was never my image of the character.'[33] They continued to pursue the pretty-boy star, with back-up choices of William Hurt, Tom Hanks (who passed in favour of Brian de Palma's *The Bonfire of the Vanities*), and (perhaps the most sensible choice on the list) Robert Downey Jr. Supposedly (and unsurprisingly, if one thinks of his *Bad*-era look, not to mention his continuing alienation from mainstream American society) musician Michael Jackson was eager to play the role, but he was never formally approached. Cruise eventually decided not to participate, allegedly because the character wasn't masculine enough for the star of *Top Gun* (Tony Scott, 1986) but also as he was due to start shooting the massively high concept '*Top Gun* with cars', *Days of Thunder* (Tony Scott, 1990). Burton, for one, was relieved: 'I knew he wouldn't do it and I'm glad he didn't . . . [but] we had to go through the pretence . . . I simply went along with their suggestions to get my bearings, knowing it would work out the way I wanted it to anyway.'[34]

At the time, Johnny Depp seemed like one of the oddest casting decisions Burton had ever made – even more so than asking Michael Keaton to play Bruce Wayne. Depp, best known as an undercover policeman who spies on delinquent High Schoolers in the often blatantly right-wing TV series *21 Jump Street*, was primarily thought of as a pretty-boy teen idol, a younger Tom Cruise with no real suggestion of actual talent. Although that sounds ridiculous now, at that point in his career Depp hadn't been given opportunities to demonstrate the range, depth and character with which he is now automatically associated. Depp himself was painfully aware of this: 'America has been sold this perception of me . . . [Fox] had this product . . . and in order to sell it they had to generate heat, so they sold this character I played on TV as if it were me.'[35]

Burton, however, had never seen *21 Jump Street*, and as such had no preconceptions about the actor. Depp had got hold of a script via his agent, and decided it 'was one of the two or three best things I've ever read.'[36] He immediately 'had a feeling about the story and the character that I can't describe . . . I knew I had to do it.'[37] Determined to get the part, Depp managed to set up a meeting with Burton, in part facilitated by the fact that his then girlfriend and *Beetlejuice* star Winona Ryder had already been cast as Kim. The director 'knew right away from meeting him that he had that kind of quality, you could just see it in his eyes, and that was an important aspect to the character in terms of not having to say anything and just being able to project something simply, much like a silent movie actor.'[38] Depp felt the same: 'When I first met with Tim, we talked for two or three hours – me and Tim and Denise Di Novi, the producer. I think we had similar images of the character. I saw Tim's drawings, and everything just clicked.'[39] Burton, however, was left with some small reservations at the time: 'My worry was that, being relatively new to the business, he'd take Edward over the top and make him flamboyant.'[40]

Yet thanks in part to his 'teen idol' status, Depp knew instinctively what was required: 'I started thinking about the character right away. I kept thinking of the faces of dogs I had owned. The eyes of new-born babies. *Pinocchio.* . . . Dogs have that unconditional love. If you scold a dog, he cowers in a corner. As soon as you call him back, he's there, and all is forgotten.'[41] As Burton explained, 'he . . . understood the dynamic of misperception'[42] that was central to the character, as 'his own life mirrors the theme of the movie. He's supposed to be this sexy teen idol and he's so far from that. There's a sadness about being perceived as something quite different from what you are inside. It gives Johnny a sense of isolation, and he used that in his performance.'[43] Dianne Wiest later told of her thoughts on Depp, 'It's embarrassing to admit these things. People said he's a teen idol. I thought, "Oh, great." Then I met him . . . what a depth of talent. I'd look at him some days and I thought he's like Chaplin. He's got a walk and a sweetness of manner. He's just an angel.'[44]

Vincent Price's brief, in fact nearly wordless, cameo as Edward's Father/Creator meant a great deal to Burton: 'His cameo had a real emotional context. He was in the first film I ever made [*Vincent*] and was so supportive of it and me. He's an amazing guy and I got through my childhood watching his horror movies. That he agreed to appear in *Edward* gave it the strongest personal feeling for me.'[45] Rounding out the main cast were Alan Arkin, as Kim's father ('Nothing really made sense to me until I saw the sets. Burton's visual imagination is extraordinary'[46]), and Anthony Michael Hall as Kim's abusive boyfriend, Jim. Crispin Glover (of *Back To The Future* and *Platoon* [Oliver Stone, 1986] fame, the latter also featured Depp) also read for the part, but wasn't hired because Burton saw something of himself in Glover – he couldn't cast someone he felt he could identify with in such a negative role.

As a final note, it is worth mentioning that Depp was not the only person to be cast against type. Winona Ryder was, at this stage of her career, best known for playing quirky, rebellious characters, and for being the goddaughter of hippie guru Dr Timothy Leary, and yet Burton cast her as the all-American cheerleader. Also Anthony Michael Hall was best known for playing the nerdy Brian in John Hughes' *The Breakfast Club* (1985), yet Burton decided he would be ideal as the vicious, brain-dead bully for his film. These apparently odd decisions were deliberate, ensuring that there was a deeper understanding among the young leads of the 'dynamic of misperception' that permeates the film.

BURTON REGULARS: *Edward Scissorhands* was Vincent Price's last film. He succumbed to lung cancer on 23 October 1993, while filming a documentary about his life, *Conversations With Vincent* (see **Unrealised Projects**).

Johnny Depp would return to work with Burton in both *Ed Wood* and *Sleepy Hollow*, where he again turned in magnificent (and utterly different) performances. In these two films, not to mention his diverse roles in *Benny & Joon* (Jeremiah S Chechik, 1993), *Dead Man* (Jim Jarmusch, 1995), *Donnie Brasco* (Mike Newell, 1997), and *Fear and Loathing in Las Vegas* (Terry Gilliam, 1998), Burton's faith in the actor has been more than justified.

O-Lan Jones, (Esmeralda, crazy religious zealot neighbour lady), returned as Richie Norris' trailer trash mother, Sue Ann, in *Mars Attacks!* Biff Yeager, playing George, appeared again in small roles in *Batman Returns* (as one of the security guards in the department store) and *Ed Wood* (as 'Rude Boss'). Steven Brill, the unfortunate dishwasher repairman targeted by the neighbourhood nymphomaniac, had a very small role in *Batman Returns*. Russ Meyer stalwart Stuart Lancaster (*Faster, Pussycat! Kill! Kill!* [1965], *Mudhoney* [1965], *Good Morning . . . and Goodbye!* [1967], *The Seven Minutes* [1971], *Supervixens* [1975], and *Beneath the Valley of the Ultravixens* [1979]), playing the retired man sitting on a lawn chair in his garage, briefly surfaced as Mrs Cobblepot's doctor at the very start of *Batman Returns*.

Edward also began a number of important behind the scenes relationships for Burton. Costume Designer Colleen Atwood has since created fantastically diverse creations on *Ed Wood*, *Mars Attacks!*, *Sleepy Hollow* and *Planet of the Apes*. Producer Denise Di Novi also helped bring *Batman Returns* and *Ed Wood* to the screen. This was also the first occasion Burton acted as Producer for one of his own directorial efforts, doing so again on *Batman Returns*, *Ed Wood* and *Mars Attacks!* Cinematographer Stefan

Czapsky turned in two very different styles for Burton on *Batman Returns* and *Ed Wood*. Caroline Thompson helped script *The Nightmare Before Christmas*, before branching out as a director in her own right. Robert Dawson, who designed the main title sequence, also designed the titles for *Batman Returns*, *Ed Wood*, *Mars Attacks!* and *Sleepy Hollow*.

Casting Director Victoria Thomas was called back for *Ed Wood* and *Mars Attacks!* In the Makeup Department, Stan Winston deserves a special mention for designing Edward's hands, and also helped design much of Danny DeVito's makeup for *Batman Returns*. On top of this, he was the initial makeup man on *Planet of the Apes*, even before Burton became involved with the project.

CRITICS: Most critics saw something special but slightly flawed in *Edward* (much like the character himself), and as Burton's fourth feature film there was now nearly enough of a back catalogue to start making generalisations. Roger Ebert liked the way all Burton films looked, but started wondering if there was something missing: 'All of the central characters in a Burton film ... exist in personality vacuums; they're self-contained oddities with no connection to the real world. It's saying something about a director's work when the most well-rounded and socialized hero in any of his films is Pee-wee Herman.'[47] Derek Malcolm was more generous, arguing in the *Guardian* that the film was 'often beautifully stylised' and that 'the whole is a refreshing change from any current Hollywood norm. Burton is a real film-maker, equipped with imagination and the technical means to display it properly.'[48] His fourth feature seemed finally to have gained his talent the recognition it arguably deserved (although whether anyone would have noticed, or even distributed, *Edward* without *Batman* on Burton's resumé is questionable).

Alan Jones in *Starburst* concluded that 'this delicate, timeless fable must not be missed on any account ... a slice of sheer unbridled magnificence and one of the most beautiful movies it has been my pleasure to view.'[49] Yet most critics argued that the film, although very good, still had a few flaws, *Rolling Stone* suggesting that 'Burton's flamboyant style courts disaster and sometimes achieves it. A few scenes are clumsily staged; a few others are fussy beyond endurance. But Burton is a true movie visionary with uncommon insights into hearts in torment ...

Edward Scissorhands isn't perfect. It's something better: Pure Magic.'[50]

Most who pointed out flaws generally concluded that the film was well worth seeing. *Empire* posited, '*Edward Scissorhands* certainly has its flaws, dwelling too long on Edward's talent for scissorwork and leaving a number of characters too thinly sketched for comfort. What remains, however, is an ambitious and quite beautifully conceived fairy tale for the 90s.'[51] It was very rare that a review would be as negative as the *Nation*'s succinct 'all premise and no payoff'[52] or the *San Francisco Chronicle*'s judgement that 'Its satire of suburban life is strictly routine, and when the movie turns sentimental, it's all so obvious, insincere and clichéd that it's hard to care at all ... [an] emotionally uncommitted picture that's smirky and mawkish, by turns, and at heart, empty.'[53]

As is often the case with the press, the bad puns flowed left, right and centre, with few sub-editors missing the fact that this film had something to do with sharp blades. The *Boston Globe* headed its review 'A Shear Delight',[54] whereas *Time* decided the film was 'Shear Heaven'.[55] The *Seattle Times* evidently felt that this pun was too subtle not to highlight with inverted commas, labelling their review 'A Fairy Tale of "Shear" Purity'.[56] *Rolling Stone* thought it was 'A Cut Above the Rest'[57] and the *San Diego Union-Tribune* opting for the long-winded headline ' "Edward Scissorhands" Rises Several Cuts Above Usual Holiday Fare',[58] although the *San Francisco Chronicle* took a different line, arguing instead that ' "Scissorhands" Just Doesn't Cut It'.[59] *USA Today* took an alternate approach, playing up the autobiographical elements of the film with ' "Scissorhands" Cuts To Tim Burton's Core'[60] (three days later, in a different article by the same writer, witty subs opted for 'Shear Geniuses'[61] instead). The Louisville, Kentucky *Courier-Journal* felt 'Johnny Depp Turns Cutup'[62] was the best description, whereas the *Daily Yomiuri* opted for 'Cutting Up, Burton Style,'[63] and *Premier* for 'Tim Burton Cuts Up.'[64] Slightly more originally, both the *New York Times* and the *St Louis Post-Dispatch* pointed out how 'Handy'[65] Edward was, and more subtly, the *Sunday Times* went for 'Fantasy With A Familiar Edge'[66] with its sister paper *The Times* settling for the brief 'Pointed, Poignant'[67] on the film's UK video release a few years later. Finally, the *Toronto Star* had one of the better puns, labelling it 'A Fantastic Slice Of Suburban Life.'[68]

The press generally seemed to agree that *Edward* was a pretty good, even excellent film, but half the time they seemed more concerned with making bad jokes about the titular character's handicap. Handicap – get it?

MUSIC: 'I've always loved Danny,' commented Burton of *Edward Scissorhands*' composer ten years after the film's release, 'because, although I like music, I'm not musically inclined and he would always explain things and involve me right from the beginning.'[69] Looking back, Elfman himself remains hugely pleased with his *Edward Scissorhands* score – one of his favourites because of the number of levels to it. It 'taps into my love of the really old, old movie scoring, back to the 30s and 40s, which is the stuff that kind of inspired me,' and the score coincided with the time in his career where he was beginning to feel more confident. Though normally relieved at the end of a film because of the physical effort, with *Edward* Elfman 'was sad it was over when I finished I wished it was longer, that there'd be an addendum or something more, I wanted to do more little variations, I think I just wanted to keep doing it forever.'[70] In a sense, there have been variations on Elfman's score cropping up forever – it must surely rank as his most imitated, with similar-sounding music cropping up in films and advertisements for the last decade – including the Chanel perfume adverts with future Burton actress Estella Warren as Little Red Riding Hood.

Aside from Elfman's celebrated score, *Edward* also featured a surprisingly large amount of music from the greatest living Welshman, singer Tom Jones. Burton explains that he decided to use Tom Jones because 'growing up . . . everybody liked Tom Jones . . . so it was like the music of the neighbourhood.' The director remains at pains to point out that, despite Burton's sometimes apparent contempt for suburbia, this comment is not any kind of criticism of Jones or his work: 'He's great. He's a great guy and a great musician, and a great voice, so if they picked one thing, they picked something pretty good.'[71] Six years later, Burton would cast Jones in *Mars Attacks!*

CINEMATOGRAPHY: Burton at the time praised Director of Photography Stefan Czapsky: 'He's great to work with . . . able to capture a real fairy tale quality that you're trying to get. For some reason we ended up using a lot of wide lenses . . . to capture the starkness and wonder of suburbia.'[72] Indeed, the wide lenses do add to the general sense of sameness, especially in the interiors of the houses, where the sparsity of the rooms creates a sense of immense isolation when the camera magnifies their pokiness. With the suburban exteriors, the crisp, clear, brightly lit, low-contrast shots emphasise further the uniformity of the neighbourhood, and the oddness of Edward in comparison. The mansion is a huge shift in style – much more expressionistic, with stark shadows, deep contrasts, and a blue-grey tint that further separates these sequences from the gaudy colour-scheme of the neighbourhood below. Furthermore, as Pegg first approaches the mansion, the static camera shots previously seen in the suburbs shift to a gently floating series of camera movements, expertly portraying her shock and wonder at the garden Edward has crafted in the mansion's grounds. It is thus hardly surprising that Czapsky would be called back to work with Burton again on his next two directorial outings, although he provided very different styles for each.

PLOT PROBLEMS: *Edward Scissorhands*, lest we forget, is introduced as a fairy tale being told by an ageing woman. Although it is indeed suggested that there is some truth to the tale, by the glimpse of Edward at the beginning, and by the shots of him creating his ice sculptures and the snow at the end, the vast majority of the film is simply the pictorial depiction of a tale told to a young child by her grandmother. As such, most inconsistencies can be forgiven as the narrator's fault. As Burton puts it, 'it's abstract, it's certainly not a *literal* movie, and for those people who go to see it and ask questions like, "Where'd he get the ice?" I mean, forget it, don't go see it, because ... just *forget* it.'[73] In general, the plot holds together well.

DEATH: There are only two deaths in *Edward*. The first is the sad, touching demise of Edward's inventor/father, displayed perfectly on the face of Vincent Price as his smile fixes, his eyes glaze, his face slackens, and he keels over to the floor, leaving Edward clutching desperately at the proper hands he was about to be given, and in the process slicing off the fingers with his blades. As Edward crouches to work out what's wrong, shocked and confused, he slices Price's cheek, unable to help the man who made him.

The other death, that of Kim's former beau, Jim, at Edward's blades is somewhat more controversial. Some critics and viewers felt that this climactic death was 'miscalculated, introducing a kind of violence for which we haven't been adequately prepared',[74] as well as detracting from Edward's innocence, his most endearing quality. Burton attempted to answer these criticisms in an interview to promote the film's European release: 'Many people lost the meaning there a little bit ... Fairy tales are symbolic, the violence is abstract, and I don't think it's gratuitous at all ... I have my own rules on excessive violence and I don't think anything like that. Edward's character needs that catharsis because he's been tortured and abused throughout the whole movie. It was his necessary emotional response.'[75] Certainly Burton's view holds some artistic weight. The film has earlier gone out of its way to argue that Edward cannot be expected to understand society's contrary rules whilst they refuse to let him be a part of it. And besides which, has anyone actually told him that killing people is wrong? The only example he has is Jim himself, whose multiple attempts to harm, and later outright murder, him surely indicate to Edward that in these situations killing is simply what is done?

Either way, a few seconds of Edward's fight with Jim were cut out of the UK print to ensure a PG (Parental Guidance) certificate. The effect is to make Jim's death seem far less intentional on Edward's part, and thus, for this sequence's critics, perhaps keep the ending more in tune with their understanding of Edward as a being of near infinite patience.

CHILDREN AND FAMILIES: The whole film revolves around the man/robot/child Edward's quest to find himself a family and home in which he can fit in and be loved. The fact that it doesn't work out for him isn't actually his fault, or the fault of the family, who remain loyal and loving to the end.

CLOWNS AND THE CIRCUS: There's a clown doll on Kim's bed the first time Edward goes to sleep on it. Later when Kim and her friends are discussing Edward's topiary carvings, and one claims they find them disturbing, another responds, 'You should see the clown in Mrs Peters' yard.'

One of the suburban houses is covered by a blue and orange striped fumigation tent resembling a circus big top.

The ultimate circus scene is where Edward is put on the modern equivalent of a freak show, the Jerry Springer-style daytime TV chat show, and subjected to moronic questions from a gasping audience.

DOGS: Most obviously, there is the abundance of canines queuing for coiffures, whose coats Edward trims into various truly hideous, but at the same time, spectacular, creations. There is also the shaggy mutt that sits with Edward after Jim has chased him away for cutting Kim's hand.

Edward himself is rather like many dog-lovers' idea of the species. As Johnny Depp explained, 'It was strange because it's not like there was anything to base [the character] on. Edward is not a human being, he's not an android, he's not an alien. To me he was like a newborn baby, with that kind of innocence . . . or like a dog that gives unconditional love.'[76] Caroline Thompson confirmed this insight from Depp, elaborating that she specifically based Edward's personality on her own pet dog, Ariel: 'She had this preternaturally alert quality . . . but no way to communicate it. But for the physical constraints, I always felt she could speak.'[77]

Edward's puppy-dog eyes, unconditional adoration and waggy-tailed devotion to Kim and Pegg, plus his repressed, but real, ability to cause them physical harm, all combine to create the impression of a dog in human form.

On a completely different level, the reason we infer that Joyce is 'all bad' is that she audibly kicks her pet dog off-screen.

LOVE TRIANGLES: Fairly simply, Kim has a boyfriend – Jim – who she becomes disillusioned with as she grows closer, personally and romantically, to Edward – a situation to which Jim reacts very badly.

CHECKS, STRIPES, DOTS: Most of these are in the mansion, notably its floor, but only in the flashback sequences to when Vincent Price's Inventor was alive – in the later scenes, the floor is covered with dust. The Inventor's jacket also has thin black and white stripes. There is also the shadow of bars on the wall in the police station, and the horizontal stripes on Jim's T-shirt right at the end.

AUTOBIOGRAPHY?: '*Edward Scissorhands* was almost a veiled autobiography of Tim, I think he saw a lot of himself in that character,' commented Art Director Tom Duffield when asked about the nature of the film, and that's certainly how most commentators have chosen to see it. The only film that Burton has made that could be seen as more explicitly personal and autobiographical than *Edward Scissorhands* (according to the limited information about his early life that the director has revealed) is *Vincent*. Yet whereas few people would have shared Burton's experience of idolising Vincent Price as a child, many can find themselves identifying with Edward's predicament.

The character of Edward is almost certainly derived from emotions that Burton experienced whilst growing up. As he has admitted, 'it contains themes that I can relate to more than any other movie I've made,'[78] 'with the scissors, there's something in the theme of somebody not being able to touch that I love. I just wanted a character that – visually, there he is, internally, externally. It's a visual representation of what's inside . . . there's something about it that rings very true for me.'[79] More specifically, Burton elaborated that '*Edward* delves into personal memories and all manner of emotional, cultural and social themes that have always interested me . . . Life is a mix of everything: the good, the bad, the dark, the light, the funny and the sad. It's this big mass of conflicting emotions and it's never that straightforward . . . Those contradictions are very much a part of what makes me, well, me, and how I think and cope with it on a day to day basis.'[80]

Burton and Thompson, in a little in-joke demonstrating their awareness of this aspect of the film, even included a line that could well have been lifted from one of the reviews of Burton's films, as the police psychologist delivers his assessment of Edward's character: 'His work, the garden sculptures, the hair styles and so forth, indicate that he's a highly imaginative character. It seems clear that his awareness of what we call reality is radically underdeveloped.' On the 10th Anniversary DVD of *Edward*, Burton's comment on this piece of dialogue is simply that it was 'for those people who think my films don't have any psychological foundation to them. It's a very deep movie.'[81]

When asked about the autobiographical elements of the film, Burton responded (in his usual eloquent manner) with, 'That freaks me out too much . . . I wouldn't have approached a film like that. I don't want to get so interiorised that it's just . . . I'm hoping the feelings are fairly universal.'[82] According to Caroline

Thompson, during the making of the film, 'People were always telling Tim he looked like Edward and I really felt for him . . . It seemed so awkward.'[83] When asked on a different occasion whether he ever identified with his lead character, or saw similarities, his response was more certain: 'I shy away from that. I did so during the film because I had to. I would have been too interiorized . . . I would have needed years of therapy if I did.'[84] However, most of the rest of the film's cast and crew seemed to feel, like Danny Elfman, that 'There's so much of Tim in Edward,'[85] with Denise Di Novi elaborating that 'In a way Edward really is the metaphor for the artist who does not fit into the world . . . It was a hard movie . . . Every detail was important to Tim, because it is so personal.'[86]

Few critics missed the fact that there were elements of Burton's life (which had become much better known thanks to the publicity for and success of *Batman*) on screen. The *Boston Globe* rightly suggested that 'You don't need dazzling interpretive skills to recognize Burton's self-portrait in Depp's android.'[87] Burton played this element up more often than he tried to deny it, often stating categorically that 'This is the movie that I feel closest to,'[88] and that 'there's just more meaning to this than anything else I've ever done before. I've never had the opportunity to express how I feel completely before. This is an image that I identify with.'[89] More explicitly, he stated, 'I went through a time where I wasn't making any kind of connection . . . I feel better now. That was in my teens and early 20s. I don't feel quite as dramatic now . . . I'm a happy depressive,'[90] and later added that 'A lot of characters in this are either fantasy or represented on some people I actually knew. A lot of times a combination of people.'[91]

The suburban setting adds further layers of personal experience to the film, as it was similar to Burton's own upbringing. 'I remember there was no real communication, but if there was ever a tragedy, if there was a car accident out front, people would come out from their houses, and it would be like a block party. It's not something I can relate to really – this blood lust. It's like a way to make yourself feel alive. It's very strange . . . I just find it fascinating.'[92] More explicitly, he tried to explain to another interviewer that, in suburbia, 'There's no sense of culture, no sense of history, no sense of real passion, no strong displays of emotion, no sense of connection . . . How else are you supposed to feel? . . . So I got a strange ambivalent feeling – something felt weird, something's not right, I don't feel right here.'[93]

As Burton's most personal film, it's received some knocks for being his most self-indulgent as well. '*Edward Scissorhands* can be read as a paranoid, undoubtedly autobiographical teen fantasy, about a misfit who is incapable of finding his place in the adult world. As such, it may seem thin and self-pitying,'[94] concluded the *Seattle Times*, somewhat churlishly.

JUST PLAIN WEIRD: The mascot for the *Edward Scissorhands* crew, Uncle Billy, was in fact a 100-year-old mummified head of an Ecuadorian tribesman, owned by Danny Elfman.

DIALOGUE TO SKIP BACK FOR:
Mr Boggs: 'You've got to learn not to take things so literally.'

Mr Boggs on women: 'I don't know what it is. They reach a certain age, they develop these gland things. They go crazy.'

Mr Boggs: 'We're not talking nice, we're talking right and wrong.'

Kim: 'Hold me.'
Edward: 'I can't.'

AFTERLIFE: Danny Elfman has stated 'I think it was really one of Tim's purest works . . . I'll really be forever grateful that I was able to write the score to this movie.'[95] In fact the entire cast and crew appear to have come away from the film satisfied.

On first viewing the movie Burton also knew he had created something special and wonderful: 'I saw the first rough cut and burst into tears myself. From that moment on I decided I didn't care what anyone else thought of it and I've never felt that way before.'[96]

The film was rigorously mocked on popular British comedy series *The Mary Whitehouse Experience* (ironically named after a right-wing Christian TV campaigner that the show's stars professed to loathe) with Rob Newman using a combination of his physical resemblance to Edward and scathing irony to mock the film's gentle-hearted sincerity. Unfair, but funny.

AWARDS: The film won Best Fantasy Film at the 1991 Saturn Awards as well as Best Dramatic Presentation at the Hugos. Bo Welch also won a BAFTA for his Production Design. In addition, Johnny Depp was nominated as Best Actor at the Golden Globes,

Ve Neil and Stan Winston were nominated for an Oscar for Makeup, with both receiving individual nominations from BAFTA (for Best Makeup Artist and Best Special Visual Effects respectively), where Colleen Atwood was also nominated for Best Costume Design.

TRIVIA: Depp's first film role was in *A Nightmare on Elm Street* (Wes Craven, 1984), which featured Robert Englund as the razor-gloved dream killer, Freddy Kruger, to whose appearance many critics compared Edward's.

During shooting of the sequence where Jim smashes Edward's face into the ground after he has saved Kevin from the van, Johnny Depp did accidentally stab Anthony Michael Hall in the arm with his scissors, drawing blood.

EXPERT WITNESS: Caroline Thompson: 'David [Lynch]'s obsessions are the obsessions of a nineteen-year-old, and Tim's are the obsessions of a twelve-year-old. And this is much more of a twelve-year-old's culture.'[97] (Hence Burton's greater box office success.)

Why scissors? Burton: 'They're an interesting invention; they cut through things . . . I mean scissors are both simple and complicated. They're a very simple design. But I remember as a kid I could never figure out how they worked.'[98]

Describing the process of creating her screenplay, Thompson confessed to an unusual way of working: 'I'm totally instinctive . . . I've watched so many movies in my life that the rhythm is inside me. I don't do anything consciously: I don't outline; I don't do index cards. I just sit down and go at it, and it seems to work out.'[99]

ANALYSIS: 'There was a long period of time when I just hadn't been able to connect with anybody or have a relationship,' Burton once said. 'Everybody goes through periods like that – the feeling that you can't connect, you can't touch.'[100]

Although the idea for *Edward* originated in autobiography, the finished result manages to touch on the rarest of all artistic values – universality. Burton is far from alone in growing up in the suburbs, or in feeling isolated as an adolescent. He certainly isn't alone in having experienced difficulty in approaching members of the opposite sex (as Edward has with Kim), and he's far from the only teenage male to be appalled by 'normal' definitions of masculinity as represented by Jim. By tapping into feelings that lie dormant in the contemporary western psyche, he achieved his aim of creating anew, not pastiching, a fairy tale.

Burton himself perhaps put it best when trying to explain why people had latched onto the so-called autobiographical aspects of the film: 'People are always looking for clear-cut explanations to everything in real life aren't they?'[101]

AVAILABILITY: In the US a DVD edition was released for the movie's tenth anniversary, featuring trailers, two commentary tracks (one from Elfman, one from Burton), concept art, a new documentary and gorgeous 3-D menus. Get it.

THE BOTTOM LINE: *Edward Scissorhands* encapsulates practically all of Burton's trademarks and obsessions, from alienation in suburbia through Vincent Price as a father-figure, to dogs as faithful companions. It may not have shattered any film-making formulas, but at the same time it remains a beautiful movie that deserves to be watched time and again. What's more, its pleas for understanding and tolerance, and outright condemnation of the stupidity of mob-rule, seem even more relevant now than they did at the time of its release.

BATMAN RETURNS (1992)

Warner Brothers presents
A Tim Burton Film
Screenplay by Daniel Waters
Story by Daniel Waters and Sam Hamm
Director of Photography: Stefan Czapsky
Production Designer: Bo Welch
Supervising Art Director: Tom Duffield
Art Director: Rick Heinrichs

Produced by Tim Burton and Denise Di Novi

Co-Producer: Larry Franco

Associate Producer: Ian Bryce

Executive Producer: Peter Guber

Executive Producer: Benjamin Melniker

Executive Producer: Jon Peters

Executive Producer: Michael E Uslan

Casting by Marion Dougherty

Music by Danny Elfman

Costumes Designed by Bob Ringwood, Mary Vogt

Edited by Bob Badami, Chris Lebenzon

Based on characters appearing in magazines published by
DC Comics

Batman created by Bob Kane

Directed by Tim Burton

CAST: Michael Keaton (*Batman/Bruce Wayne*), Danny DeVito (*Oswald Cobblepot/The Penguin*), Michelle Pfeiffer (*Selina Kyle/ Catwoman*), Christopher Walken, (*Maximillian Shreck*), Michael Gough (*Alfred*), Michael Murphy (*The Mayor*), Cristi Conaway (*Ice Princess*), Andrew Bryniarski (*Charles 'Chip' Shreck*), Pat Hingle (*Commissioner Gordon*), Vincent Schiavelli (*Organ Grinder*), Steve Witting (*Josh*), Jan Hooks (*Jen*), John Strong (*Sword Swallower*), Rick Zumwalt (*Tattooed Strongman*), Anna Katerina (*Poodle Lady*), Gregory Scott Cummins (*Acrobat Thug One*), Erika Andersch (*Knifethrower Dame*), Travis McKenna (*Fat Clown*), Doug Jones (*Thin Clown*), Branscombe Richmond (*Terrifying Clown 1*), Paul Reubens (*Tucker Cobblepot*), Diane Salinger (*Esther Cobblepot*), Stuart Lancaster (*Mrs Cobblepot's Doctor*), Cal Hoffman (*Happy Man*), Joan Jurige (*Happy Woman*), Rosie O'Connor (*Adorable Little Girl*), Sean M Whalen (*Paperboy*), Erik Onate (*Aggressive Reporter*), Joey DePinto (*Shreck Security Guard*), Steven Brill (*Gothamite #1*), Neal Lerner (*Gothamite #2*), Ashley Tillman (*Gothamite #3*), Elizabeth Sanders (*Gothamite #4*), Henry Kingi (*Mugger #4*), Joan Giammarco (*Female Victim*), Lisa Coles (*Volunteer Bimbo*), Frank DiElsi (*Security #1*), Biff Yeager (*Security #2*), Robert Gossett (*TV Anchorman*), Adam Drescher (*Crowd Member*).

TAGLINE: The Bat, the Cat and the Penguin.

TRAILER: The trailer focuses more on the relationship between Catwoman and Batman than any of the Penguin's machinations, with numerous shots of Pfeiffer, skulking around, or sitting astride Batman and licking his face. DeVito's Penguin only really makes his entrance towards the end as an apparently motiveless villain set on mass destruction.

OPENING SEQUENCE: The blue cloudy sky fades to night, with wafting snow. The camera pans over a wrought-iron gate, emblazoned with a monogrammed 'C' and the name 'Cobblepot', before moving in on an overly tall window in the giant building beyond, at which stands a silhouetted figure. From the inside, we see Mr Cobblepot looking out on the snowscape as the screams of his wife echo down the long corridors of the mansion. As he turns to the room in which his wife is in labour, a harsh infant's cry can be heard, and he dashes to see his child as a doctor and nurse run out, evidently deeply disturbed. The camera fades as we hear his anguished cry, cutting to the Cobblepots standing together at the window, drinking and smoking, in deep thought. It is now Christmas, and their child's apparent deformity has led to its imprisonment within a sturdy box, from which it reaches out to grab and kill the family cat. Downing their drinks, the Cobblepots determine a solution. Hurrying out to a Gotham City park, in the shadow of an abandoned zoo, they take their baby in a pram, and throw it off a bridge into the icy waters of a stream, shocked and amazed at their own actions. The camera then follows the pram as it drifts with the current into the city's sewers, the child screaming as it falls. The main credits then begin, as we continue to follow the floating pram through the immense, elliptical underground waterways of Gotham, the title of the film unfurling as if a scroll, as shrieking bats dash towards the camera, prompting a resurgence of Danny Elfman's powerful score from the first movie, with subtle, more sinister variations. As the credits come to a close, with 'Directed by Tim Burton', the pram comes ashore and is greeted by a group of penguins.

SUMMARY: Batman takes on the Penguin (a hideously deformed criminal mastermind) and Catwoman (with whom he falls in love). Also see **PLOT PROBLEMS**.

SOURCE MATERIAL: *Batman* had earned $406 million in worldwide ticket sales, $150 million on video, and $750 million in merchandising revenues. It was inevitable that Warner Brothers would want a follow-up to their gigantic summer hit, and as far as they were concerned there was only one man suitable to bring a second Batman picture to the screen. So for the first, and thus far only, time in his career Tim Burton took on one of the great traditions of modern mainstream cinema – the sequel.

Burton, when asked about the project he had initially expressed no enthusiasm for, said, 'Oftentimes with sequels, they're like the same movie except everything gets jacked up a little. I didn't feel I could *do* that.' The solution then, was obvious – to approach any further Batman film not as a sequel to the 1989 feature but as a new, independent take on the Batman mythos, or as its director put it, 'I wanted to treat this like it was another Batman . . . altogether.'[1] Burton often repeated that he simply 'didn't want to do the same thing . . . So the dilemma is, how do you remain true to the spirit of it and still do something different? I like this stuff better, in a way . . . It was an emotional choice. I just wanted a coolness.'[2] More explicitly still, making *Batman Returns* was 'a way of getting the images that I *really* wanted in the first one on the screen.' Of the finished film he would say, 'It's more personal . . . it's another movie with that character and some new characters . . . with some new images.'[3] Burton expressly told the studio and his crew that he 'was not interested in jacking up "Okay, another Batman backstory" kind of thing. We chose to treat him as "He's that character, and he's in this movie".'[4] Returning star Michael Keaton was more succinct, 'It's *Batman*, but it's also a completely different movie.'[5]

One 'new' character for *Batman Returns* was to be the Penguin, another old-time comic-book villain, who had also been invented by Batman's own creator, Bob Kane, in *Detective Comics* #58 (December, 1941). The design for Kane's Penguin came from the illustration of an actual penguin shown on packets of Kool Cigarettes, the brand Kane smoked at the time. Kane: 'I thought, "This penguin looks kind of like a little fat man in a tuxedo" [so] why not have a villain called the Penguin?'[6]

Played with some success by Burgess Meredith in the 60s TV series, the Penguin is not one of the comic book's more complex villains, and has been dismissed by Burton as 'one of my least favourite characters in the comic. Just a guy in a tuxedo.'[7] Variously represented as either a largely humorous criminal armed with a series of increasingly outlandish 'trick' umbrellas, or (more recently) as a cunning crime lord with a complex about his height, the Penguin is also one of the few Batman villains who isn't, by some definition, insane. The Penguin of Waters' script shares only the name, height and rotund appearance of Kane's character; other than that he is a new creation entirely.

More faithful to the comics, up to a point, is the movie's Catwoman, who had first appeared in *Batman* #1 (Spring 1940), and a 'kitten with a whip'[8] in Burton's view. She too retained the comic-book character's name, Selina Kyle, and her adversarial yet sexually charged relationship with Batman. Some Batman comics had shown Bruce Wayne and Selina Kyle as eventually putting aside their differences, marrying and having children – one of whom, Helena, grows up to be crime-fighter The Huntress. However, the comics' Catwoman is, in most interpretations, a sophisticated jewel thief, in crime for the love of the chase. She doesn't demonstrate the psychosis or the seemingly real 'nine lives' powers afforded the movie version.

This playing around with the source material, in a more extreme way than Sam Hamm, was all part of the game as far as primary screenwriter Daniel Waters was concerned: 'The only rule going into *Batman Returns* was that there were no rules.'[9]

REFERENCES: Selina's question about whether he's 'The Batman' or just 'Batman' was actually a big issue amongst comics readers in the mid-80s. Most immediate post-Crisis adverts call him 'The Batman', presumably to separate this Dark Knight Detective from public perception of the TV character. This was being dropped in the early 90s. Waters (or someone) seems to be aware of this. (By the way, if you don't know what the 'Crisis' was, ask in your local comic shop – they'll be more than happy to give you the abridged, six-hour explanation of this ridiculously complex event in comics' history, where a villain called the Anti-monitor gradually destroyed an infinite number of alternate earths [most of which had their own versions of characters like Batman and Superman] reformatting the 50-year-old 'DC Universe' in the process.)

The 'Shreck Collection' logo inside the department store looks rather too much like the then contemporary 'French Connection' one to be a coincidence.

At Shreck's party, there is a figure in a red mask just like the one that comes to meet Vincent Price at the party he throws in Roger Corman's *The Masque of the Red Death* (1964).

His plans having been thwarted, Oswald screams, 'I am not a human being, I am an animal!' – a parody of John Merrick's statement 'I am not an animal, I am a human being' in *The Elephant Man* (David Lynch, 1980).

As Bruce tries to explain his unsuccessful relationship with Vicky Vale to Selina, he worries that she may take him 'as a Norman Bates/Ted Bundy type' – the first is of course the titular maniac in Alfred Hitchcock's *Psycho* (1960) and its various sequels, the second is the real-life serial-killer who confessed to 28 murders between 1965 and the late 1970s, and was himself killed by the State on 24 January 1989.

There are yet more visual references to *Citizen Kane* here, especially in the political scenes, but also in the opening tracking shot over the gates to the Cobblepot estate.

Batman pulling the sword out of the sword-swallower's mouth appears to be a riff on a similar scene in the James Bond film *Octopussy* (John Glen, 1983).

As the Penguin approaches his parents' grave, he brushes past a tombstone which noticeably wobbles. It has been suggested that this is in homage to Edward D Wood's *Plan 9 From Outer Space* (1958), in which a more obvious gravestone wobble occurs, as recreated in Burton's biopic of the director. However, it remains unclear whether this was intentional.

On top of these pop-cultural references (and the usual Expressionist and Universal horror influences), *Batman Returns* was more than aware that its release was set for the year of a presidential election. There are asides to the attempt to impeach President Nixon, and suggestions of the possibility of political corruption run rife throughout. Nixon's mention is also the only indication in Burton's *Batman* films that Gotham exists within a wider world similar to our own.

PRODUCTION: Seemingly as part of his desire to place distance between *Batman* and *Returns*, Burton elected not to return to England to shoot the film. This meant abandoning Anton Furst's Gotham City set which had lain idle, at enormous cost, since the original film had wrapped.

Interviewed, Burton stated that he was making *Batman Returns* 'for myself, and I want to infuse it with new ideas. Being back in Pinewood would seem like going over old territory in many ways.'[10] It was thus decided that *Batman Returns* would be shot on the Warners lot in Burbank, and on a new Gotham set which would be the responsibility of Production Designer Bo Welch.

Art Director Tom Duffield recalls the production's approach to building a new, highly stylised Gotham: 'The first movie established a look. But we didn't really like it. To me it was in the middle of the road. I never got the impression of pressure to conform to the look of that first film. We were meeting with some of the executives and they said basically "*Carte Blanche*, do what you want, go for it." We didn't get "Oh, we want this and this to match" – we knew from the get-go that the Batmobile was going to be the Batmobile, although we made a few changes to it, but for the most part that was the only thing that was really carried over from the first one. Bo [Welch] and I didn't even really want to look at a lot of the things from the first movie, like the Batcave and things like that – it was a total clean take. You can get your mind kind of polluted sometimes by looking at the previous stuff – even if you try not to do it, it's always in there. Sometimes it helps not to look too closely at the original so you don't have these preconceived images in your head. Even though you think you're going around them, sometimes they just pop up and you don't even know it.' As with the first movie though, there were some things that the design team wanted to avoid: 'Obviously we didn't want the *Blade Runner* look – I worked on *Blade Runner*, but we didn't want that because it was too futuristic,' Duffield revealed, adding that, unlike the conscious decision to avoid Fritz Lang's city on the first movie, 'Some of the interiors of the Shreck building did have a *Metropolis* influence.'

Other influences for the architecture of Welch's Gotham set were unusual for a big budget Hollywood production. Burton claimed that 'I'm not interested in good-looking sets and what-a-great-shot. I'm interested in all of that reflecting and being symbolic of something, that's all.'[11] To aid the symbolism, Welch designed the movie to be 'very vertical ... It goes from the Penguin in the sewers to a flying rodent. So these are aggressive sets, not passive backdrops incidental to the action.'[12] Duffield underlined the symbolism inherent in the stylised Gotham sets, as designed by Bo Welch: 'It was based on a neo-fascist look. We figured that for this Gotham we were going to take fascist architecture and give it an edge that fitted the Burton look. Fascist architecture has a strangely sterile, yet monumental look, so we went back and we looked at all the WPA stuff, and we looked at

German fascist architecture, the Albert Speer stuff. If you look at the fascist architecture they have these huge sculptures, so we decided to have these huge gear-pullers, and everywhere you looked there would be these monumental sculptures. There were a couple of buildings that had a more international style, but the stuff in the square is fascist and monumental – stone and concrete.' This style of architecture further underlined the depressingly gloomy nature of Gotham, the buildings themselves adding to the sense of fear amongst the populace as a whole, who are mostly seen running and screaming in terror from various bizarrely-clad characters. By the time filming on *Batman Returns* had concluded Welch's sets not only occupied all of the Warners stage space, but had spread to the neighbouring Universal lot as well.

Costume Designer Bob Ringwood was one of the few members of the *Batman* production team to return. Like Burton he seemed to consider the sequel a chance to achieve that which time and money had prevented on the first picture. 'Batman's new costume is much closer to the original concept we had for the first film,' he said when discussing Bruce Wayne's restyled Bat-togs, 'It's much more like armour now, rather than a muscle suit.'[13] (The costume would return to being a simple muscle suit for the third film, even gaining nipples for 1997's *Batman and Robin*.) A retro-40s look was decided on for many of the costumes in *Returns*, with this providing perhaps the film's strongest visual link to *Batman*. Actively archaically-styled suits, often with hats, were prevalent for the male characters and knee-length two-pieces common for the women. 'I like the late 40s, especially 1947,'[14] said Ringwood by way of explanation.

Before principal photography commenced, however, there were rewrites on the script to be done. Daniel Waters, the screenwriter of *Heathers* (Michael Lehmann, 1988) had turned in a draft which was very nearly what was required. Most of the pieces of the finished film, such as the characterisation of the Penguin, and the presentation of Catwoman, were already present. But something was missing. Wesley Strick was brought in to do touch up work on the screenplay (dubbed 'normalisation' by the studio), and add the plot strand concerning the Penguin's attempt to kidnap then kill all the first-born sons of Gotham. Several earlier scenes were also altered to accommodate this aspect of the storyline. However, Strick's script-doctoring was not judged sufficient to merit an on-screen credit.

With design, construction and script-doctoring out of the way, filming began on 2 September 1991, wrapping late in February the next year.

Early on in the shoot old hand Michael Keaton found great amusement in Pfeiffer and DeVito's reaction to filmmaking of a kind neither of them had been involved in before. 'It was kind of sadistically funny to watch [Michelle] and Danny's faces all the time – everyone gets this similar lost look on their face for the first week.'[15]

During production Danny DeVito apparently stayed in character almost the whole time he was on set, talking to Burton and the crew in his Penguin voice, and doing several of his own stunts, even refusing a stand-in for the scene where the Penguin is pelted with rotten fruit. Burton expressed a perverse glee at witnessing such an extreme form of Method acting for such an unusual character: 'Danny became the Penguin. If people got close to him on set, he would bite them. He chased around after Michelle a few times and would fix all his on-screen enemies with an evil eye whenever they weren't working.'[16] 'After wearing [the makeup] for . . . 12 to 15 hours a day, I've been looking at myself more as the Penguin than as Danny,' DeVito later explained. 'When the makeup's put on, it's so organic that it just becomes part of you.'[17] One occasion on which he did break character was to perform an impromptu half-hour stand-up routine for the cast and crew in full Penguin getup. DeVito's costume and makeup eventually weighed as much as 60 pounds, and took four hours to get into each day.

Added to this were the difficulties inherent in such an unusual film, Burton revealing that for some shots 'we'd have two species of live penguins, puppets, people in costumes, 30 people under the floor, 30 across the way with radios, and here we're trying to treat the shot like it was normal . . . you couldn't even tell the actors that. If I said to them, "We've got this live penguin, your life is being ruled by it . . ." I felt so bad for the actors . . . this is getting in the way of their acting.'[18]

As with the first *Batman* film, the final budget for the film remains somewhat of a mystery even to those who made it.

CASTING: Danny DeVito had been mentioned in trade papers as playing the Penguin in a potential Batman sequel as early as June 1989, so the eventual announcement of his appointment came as no surprise to anyone. DeVito had seen Burgess Meredith's performance as Penguin in the TV series, and didn't feel it was appropriate for his version of the character. 'I didn't see myself playing a weird Nick Charles with a martini glass and a tuxedo,' he said. 'It just didn't tickle my fancy.' Instead his Penguin was based on a picture by Burton, which was later to be printed in the director's *The Melancholy Death of Oyster Boy and Other Stories*. DeVito's described it as 'a toddler with a big round head and big eyes and a protrusion in the nose and mouth and a bulbous body with little appendages. And there was a caption that said, "My name is Jimmy, but they call me the hideous penguin boy." And I got this weird chill.'[19]

Thanks to the success of *Batman*, there was little – if any – of the kind of rage that had greeted the casting decisions for Burton's first Batman feature. This was not a relief to returning Batman Michael Keaton: 'There was something in that negative response that stirred in me what I'm going to call a healthy "attitude" ... I secretly liked the challenge, and was determined to prove that I could nail it,'[20] he said. He was initially reluctant to return to the part, wanting to see the script first. He was told there wasn't one at the time, and then that Burton was definitely on board. He again requested a script – and still didn't get to see one. Burton understood his star's reluctance: 'I think this part drives him crazy.' In *Beetlejuice* Burton had noticed Keaton's 'caged energy' but 'For this part, he's got to keep a lid on it. Face it, the villains are the ones that get to eat up most of the sets.'[21] However, now that he'd proved himself in the complex dual role, and received excellent notices for doing so, Keaton found that the sequel had its own intrigues, as 'I've never played the same character twice, which is a challenge [but] I had to be careful that I wasn't doing an imitation of Michael Keaton playing Batman and Bruce Wayne ... I had to *become* those characters once again, without anything else getting in the way.'[22] As well as this challenge, 'it was so clear that [Burton] felt good about having this in his own hands, whereas in the first one, the bat was – no pun intended – taken out of his hands a few times.' Furthermore, the director had now been told *Returns* would be pretty much his vision, so 'I just decided, "I trust him, so I'm going down with him if it doesn't work".'[23]

To play secretary turned leather-clad vigilante Catwoman, Burton cast actress Annette Bening, after a long search. According to Producer Denise Di Novi, 'every major movie star from 17 through the late 40s'[24] got in touch about the role. Sigourney Weaver went as far as to send a photograph of herself pinned to a Catwoman book and actress Sean Young, who had lost out on the part of Vicki Vale in *Batman* due to injury, also tried to land the part. Some of the more unorthodox methods she used to garner the role included gate-crashing a meeting between Warners exec Mark Canton and Michael Keaton, and crafting her own amateur Catwoman costume. She also made television appearances, including on *The Joan Rivers Show*, demanding the role.

However, the decision had already been made. 'Annette is a really exciting actress. I'm so glad we've got her,'[25] said Burton at the time. Apparently also considered were Jennifer Jason Leigh, Lena Olin, and Ellen Barkin, but it was to none of these that Burton and Di Novi turned when Bening pulled out of the production shortly before filming – she was pregnant. There wasn't much time to recast. 'It was later than I would have liked,'[26] stated Burton diplomatically. Denise Di Novi is somewhat more forthright on the matter: 'We were very freaked about it. When Tim called me with the news, we sat in silence on the phone for, like, three minutes. Michelle was the only other natural choice.'[27]

Pfeiffer, for her part, was delighted to have been cast. A huge fan of Julie Newmar's sensual Catwoman from the *Batman* television series, Pfeiffer had had mutual friends suggest to Burton that she could cameo as Catwoman on the first *Batman* picture. Recalling her adolescent enthusiasm for Newmar, Pfeiffer explained, 'I guess she just broke all of the stereotypes of what it meant to be a woman. I found that shocking and titillating and forbidden . . . I was probably at the age where I was really coming into my own sexuality, and I just found Catwoman thrilling to watch.'[28]

Cast as Max Shreck, an original corporate villain named for the star of *Nosferatu* (FW Murnau, 1922), was Christopher Walken. Walken, who had won a Best Supporting Actor Oscar and numerous other awards for his performance in *The Deer Hunter*, had had an eccentric career in film, incorporating everything from *The King of New York* (Abel Ferrera, 1990) to *A View to a Kill* (John Glen, 1985), the fourteenth James Bond adventure.

BURTON REGULARS: Danny DeVito came back to the Burton fold for a small role in *Mars Attacks!*, as well as casting his on-screen father and Burton regular, Paul Reubens, as hapless FBI Agent Bob in his filmed adaptation of Roald Dahl's *Matilda* (1996). Christopher Walken returned in yet another sinister role as the Hessian Horseman in *Sleepy Hollow*.

Editor Chris Lebenzon has performed the same task on all of Burton's subsequent directorial outings, whilst enjoying a similar relationship with Director Tony Scott on *Top Gun* (1986), *Beverly Hills Cop II* (1987), *Days of Thunder* (1990), *Revenge* (1990), *Crimson Tide* (1995) and *Enemy of the State* (1998). He also edited the Jerry Bruckheimer-produced, Michael Bay-directed *Armageddon* (1998) and *Pearl Harbor* (2001). That he has formed such close relationships with filmmakers of such vastly different visual styles attests to his strong editing skill.

CRITICS: Contrary to popular myth, initial press response to *Batman Returns* was primarily positive. Furthermore, it was not merely the grudging praise impressive popcorn films receive, but rather a torrent of considered criticism, which usually emphasised both its 'magisterial'[29] visuals and emotional depth.

Newsweek was enamoured of Tim Burton's 'wild, imaginative sequel', which they felt took Batman 'down even stranger streets than before.' The film was labelled, 'eccentric, surreal, childlike', and said to be one of a series of Burton 'nightmares that taste like candy.' Danny DeVito's performance as the Penguin was described as 'indelible' and the whole picture summarised as 'a moody, grotesque, perversely funny $50 million art film.' The reviewer, David Ansen, identified some flaws: 'This demented toyshop of a movie is a bit of a mess . . . [but] it's a visionary mess. Of how many sequels can that be said?'[30]

Time went even further, saying that *Batman Returns* was 'a lesson on how pop entertainment can soar into the realm of poetry.' The Penguin was 'a creature of Dickensian rhetoric, proportions and comic depth,' that managed to live up to the high expectations for Batman's opponents set up by Jack Nicholson in the previous film. Daniel Waters' script was also picked out as a delight for its 'elaborate wordplay and complex characters,' though other critics were to disagree (see **PLOT PROBLEMS**). The magazine further took the opportunity to criticise the literal, pseudo-realist sensibility that it felt Hollywood had been propagating for the last 65 years, and argued that Burton understood that it was simply not the way to make art: 'to go deeper, you must fly higher, to liberation from plot into poetry. Here he's done it. This Batman soars.'[31]

Films in Review admired the way *Returns* had dealt with election year and praised Burton for bravely taking on 'contemporary state-of-the-union concerns that the government and media ought to be taking more seriously, such as corporate and political corruption, urban blight and warfare [and] feminism.' It also recognised that the film was at its most compelling neither with the scenery or special effects, but with 'the consummately unconsummated exchanges' between the two main characters – 'Keaton has never seemed more attractive nor Pfeiffer more ravishing . . . the screen sizzles when they're together.'[32]

Other positive reviews include the *Columbus Despatch*: '*Batman Returns* is a satirical, disturbing, gruesome fable, much more original than any sequel deserves to be.' It went on to praise Burton and Keaton's take on Bruce Wayne for daring to 'bring out the neuroses of a man who dresses up as a bat to fight crime.'[33] *Maclean's* lauded Keaton's Batman as 'perversely spartan and introspective, more antihero than superhero' and the film as 'above all a spectacle of visual design – an operatic costume drama by a director who worships weirdness.' It concluded that Michelle Pfeiffer, by virtue of playing 'a multiple personality who finds manic liberation in a cat suit,'[34] stole the movie from under the noses of everyone else involved.

The *Toronto Star*'s Dave Kehr wasn't going to forget that this was an action movie: 'There are flashes of commercially oriented action and humour,' but was impressed that the picture's overall mood was 'one of a languid depression sprung straight from the heart of its author.' The chief difference between *Batman Returns* and Burton's previous film, was, in Kehr's mind, the triumvirate of social outcasts afforded by *Returns* over *Edward Scissorhands*' simple one. Even 'the tattered leather costumes, the exaggerated, expressionistic set design, the swelling, highly emotional score by Danny Elfman' were considered to be surprisingly consistent. The concluding Penguin battle was described as an 'hallucinatory finale' and the film in total was considered 'the most expensive mood piece ever made,' adept at 'moving smoothly between visual epiphanies.'[35] He did, however, have some concerns (see **PLOT PROBLEMS**).

Writing in the *National Review*, critic John Simon clearly felt that this silly Bat-film was getting far too much positive press. In a piece that exudes a palpable irritation at the picture's critical lauding, he laid into every reviewer who dared disagree with him, Burton, Batman as a concept, and the medium of comic books itself. Simon called Burton 'loutish' and dismissed both strip cartoons and sequels as 'queasy genres'. Queasy is of course a highly subjective term, but neither sequels nor comics could really be considered a genre, no matter how far you try to stretch the definition of the word. The director was derided for 'specialising in films for children (Backwards ones, at that),' although whether Simon meant backwards films or backwards children the reader is left to guess. Seemingly offended on his gender's behalf by Catwoman's faintly 'anti-male' attitude, he goes on to simultaneously berate the picture for having a confusingly large number of villains, (it 'cries out for one good knock-down, drag-out contest,' apparently) and knock it as 'simplistic'. Apparently the Penguin should be charming, too. Most nonsensical is, 'This Catwoman, moreover, has literally nine lives, when even James Bond only had 007.'[36] Any attempts to make logical sense of this sentence are likely to fail. Whilst it may seem unfair to single out Simon's review for particular scorn, every critic from Pauline Kael downwards (Kael had by this stage retired) is insulted both personally and professionally during the piece; the whole gang of them furiously labelled 'well-fed [and] bourgeois,'[37] and mocked for apparently misunderstanding what good popular art *should* be. If only it were parody.

Yet other critics also found flaws in Burton's film. The *New Republic* attested that 'Welch's work is less impressive [than Anton Furst's],' arguing, 'the new picture seems a collection of bizarre sets rather than a whole weird city in the toils of a miasma ... it's as if high school kids had made a film – talented, financed by big banks rather than piggy banks, but nonetheless kids.'[38] By the time the film reached the UK, the *Guardian*'s Derek Malcolm in particular seemed to resent the waves of positive noise about this blockbuster. He dismissed it as too like its predecessor, and stated that both missed 'their true mark by something like a mile, buried by extravagance and covered in hype'. The performers were also picked out for scorn, DeVito described as having 'one acting hand tied around his back', and Keaton's edgy psychosis being dismissed as 'robot-like disengagement'. Whilst conceding that Burton's film was 'Better, perhaps, than ... *Hook*' (Steven Spielberg, 1992) which had itself received a (largely justified) critical mauling, Malcolm asserted that *Batman Returns* was simply 'a blacker, spikier but less focused version of a Disney animation feature made flesh.'[39]

These negative views are not representative of the picture's general press, so perhaps the final word should go to *Rolling Stone*'s considered analysis. Here, after praising all concerned, Peter Travers concluded that Bruce Wayne and Selina Kyle were 'a dysfunctional Romeo and Juliet', clearly feeling this could only be taken as praise. The director's accomplishment was summed up more poetically than anywhere else when Travers finished, 'Burton uses the summer's most explosively entertaining movie to lead us . . . into the liberating darkness of dreams.'[40]

MUSIC: At Max's party we hear an elaborate orchestral version of MC Hammer's #1 hit, *U Can't Touch This*. This is very, very funny. Siouxsie and the Banshees' specially composed *Face to Face* makes more thematic sense as a theme song to the deeply troubled yet beautiful *Batman Returns* than any Bond theme does to its respective picture, and underscores Bruce and Selina's sobbing dance, one of the film's best scenes.

Danny Elfman's music is an evolution of *Edward Scissorhands*, which itself contained some elements of the original *Batman* score. It heightens the melancholy feel of the three main characters, while adding a layer of charm to the entire film. Some of the best passages are the three-quarter time waltz Christmas music pieces, which are deeply sinister, as well as the Bernard Herrmann-style shrieking violins which are used to herald both Catwoman and other felines. Unlike the first film, where Warners seemed reluctant to use Elfman's music to its full effect, here his score reverberates throughout, and fully justifies its place as one of the most evocative and recognisable movie themes of the last 20 years. However, Elfman has publicly expressed unhappiness with the way the sound and music are mixed in this film, and finds the movie difficult to watch for this reason.

CINEMATOGRAPHY: Director of Photography Stefan Czapsky, returning from his work on *Edward Scissorhands*, stated, 'I just try to listen to the director and satisfy his needs for what is best for the movie . . . I try not to be too intellectual about film. For me, film is simply an emotional and visual experience.'[41] Evidently Burton and Czapsky decided that a metallic blue tint would most effectively evoke the wintery atmosphere of this vision of Gotham.

Added to this general colour tone is the occasional reddish contrast, perhaps to maintain the spirit of the festive Christmas season, even though the film was released at the height of summer.

At its most basic level Czapsky's cinematography has little to do other than show off Bo Welch's elaborately stylised sets, and was criticised by one commentator for rarely taking flight: 'there's a difference between something looking good and being used effectively.'[42] Yet the numerous wide-angle shots, often at slightly skewed angles, manage to take in large sections of the stages without emphasising the artificiality of the setting. This is actually very effective, and fits perfectly with the style and tone of the film itself. The numerous harsh contrasts produced by Czapsky's lighting, frequently using water effects in the sewer sequences, are especially effective in keeping both Batman and Catwoman largely silhouetted, whereas many would have been tempted to show off their kinky costumes (especially Pfeiffer's) in brighter environments. The fact that Burton and Czapsky were able to avoid any lingering, overly exploitative close-ups on an attractive actress clad in such a revealingly skin-tight outfit is one of the major counters to any accusations of overt fetishisation of the sadomasochistic elements in the film.

PLOT PROBLEMS: The one consistent complaint about the film in the Press was about the scripting and plotting. Some had come to expect this from the director by now, admitting that 'As always in a Burton film, the story is the weakest link. It sputters along on conventional threads that are soon abandoned,' but these usually concluded that 'In the end, it doesn't much matter. Burton is after stylish moments that add up to haunting characters, not conventional stories.'[43] Others were less kind, claiming, as Dave Kehr put it, 'As narrative, *Batman Returns* barely functions.'[44] These criticisms sometimes got more specific, such as *Films in Review*'s complaint that 'the movie seems like a long run-on sentence, full of sound and furiously overloaded action that doesn't make much sense for at least half of its over two-hour running time. One explanation for the often-incomprehensible morass might be the muddied Waters' plot – or lack of one.'[45]

Yet despite these comments, *Batman Returns* really does hang together. Honestly. At times it doesn't explain itself as clearly as it might, and often the big plot revelations are submerged under witty one-liners, but it does make sense.

What's not to understand? Oswald Cobblepott is sent into the sewers by his parents. Some time later the Red Triangle Circus finds him, and he joins their Freak Show as the 'Penguin Boy', named so because of his bizarre physical appearance, and because he was found in the Penguin section of the abandoned Gotham Zoo where many of the creatures still live. This circus is actually partially a cover for a criminal gang, who continue to exist after the circus is shut down. The Penguin takes control of this gang. (This is discussed when Bruce is seen checking newspaper reports on the computer in the Batcave).

The Penguin formulates a plan to murder all the first-born sons of Gotham, as some kind of psychotic pseudo-Biblical revenge for his parent's abandonment of him (just as the Joker planned to massacre half of Gotham for 'performance art' in the first film). To this end he sets out to recover the names of all of Gotham's eldest sons from the public record office, and this he does, using a media circus and the quest to discover his name as a cover.

After emerging from the sewer he becomes sidetracked from this plan by industrialist Max Shreck, who wishes to use Oswald's popularity to recall the Mayor, who is opposing his plan to build a giant capacitor in the city. Attracted by the idea of becoming Mayor, Oswald puts the slaughter of the first-born on hold and runs for office. He tries to get rid of Batman, whose popularity threatens his own, and who suspects him of foul play (no pun intended), by besmirching his name. He fails. Oswald is then thwarted in his political ambitions by Batman, and runs back to the sewers, putting his 'first-born slaughter' plan back into motion. When Batman also thwarts this, he tries to destroy the city using bombs mounted on penguins that are attracted to an ultrasonic homing source in Gotham Square. Batman provides an alternative homing device for the penguins to lock on to, and leads them back to Oswald's lair. Oswald is killed.

In parallel to this, Shreck employee Selina Kyle seeks revenge on her boss as 'Catwoman', a rubber-clad avenger. She fights Batman even though she is attracted to him, and briefly allies herself with the Penguin when it appears that their interests coincide. During daylight hours she dates Bruce Wayne, unaware that he is Batman. She decides to kill and humiliate Shreck publicly once and for all, but is interrupted by the Penguin's kidnap of Max. She follows them to the Penguin's lair and kills Max with a huge electric shock. The End.

The reason that Shreck's capacitor is not mentioned again after the film reaches the halfway mark is because it's a Hitchcockian Maguffin, a red herring. A way of setting up enmity between Max Shreck and Bruce Wayne, a way of creating a reason for Max to despise the Mayor, and a motivation for Max to try to kill Selina. Clear?

Some have quibbled with the seemingly supernatural nature of Selina Kyle's 'nine lives' powers, and her unexpected athleticism following her decision to become Catwoman. The film actually offers two explanations for Catwoman's ability to fight Batman to a standstill on a rooftop whilst wearing four-inch heels. You can accept, should you choose (and the movie seems to want you to) that Selina Kyle dies when pushed out of the Shreck building by Max, and is reborn as Catwoman – some kind of spirit of revenge empowered with nine lives, extraordinary athletic abilities and a desire to kick some ass. Alternatively you can believe that the emotionally repressed, but physically powerful (she's just been dumped by a guy she kept beating at racketball, remember?) Selina Kyle survives a murder attempt with some brain damage. She then constructs a new personality for herself out of the Shreck company's cat-shaped logo, her own pre-existing love of felines, and the large number of alley cats surrounding her. She doesn't have nine lives, she only believes she does. She doesn't die when she's attacked by either Batman, the Penguin or Max, and the reason Max can't shoot her dead in the final scene is because, inspired by Batman, she has bullet-proofed her costume. Even without the bullet-proofing, the only wound that is visible is just below her left shoulder, and thus not fatal – the other bullets could have hit other non-fatal areas. As she electrocutes Max, she decides not to die herself, and rather than placing the electro-shock handset in both their mouths, she puts it solely into his. She is insulated against the electric cable she pulls down into the top of his head by the fact that she's wearing a rubber suit. Before Bruce Wayne stands up, she manages to leave, her exit disguised by the smoke emerging from Shreck's corpse. Bruce finds no trace of her body, and the audience catches a glimpse of her at the very end of the film – it is safe to assume she got away quite happily.

Batman Returns also takes some time to explain a plot problem in the first film. Burton had realised some of the problems with *Batman*, later confessing, 'Believe it or not, in the first movie I was trying to make a coherent plot,'[46] and determined to try to fix some of the more glaring inconsistencies in the semi-sequel. This decision provides one of the most understated lines of dialogue in the entire film, as Bruce chides Alfred for revealing his secret identity: 'Security? Who let Vicky Vale into the Batcave? I'm sitting there working, I turn around, and there she is – "Oh, hi Vic! Come on in . . ." '

In other words, everything that happens in the film is explained, albeit often a bit too briefly to necessarily grasp amongst all the excitement and luscious visuals. The only thing that remains unexplained, as in the first film, is precisely why Bruce Wayne decided to adopt the mantle of the bat, and let's face it, who cares? If the films had been about a more obscure comics character, such as Ralph ('the Elongated Man') Dibney, Hourman, the Shining Knight or the Red Bee, perhaps an origin-story would have been more necessary. However, Batman's origins are not relevant to the stories Burton wanted to tell, and the character was an icon before Burton became involved with him. No explanation was really necessary.

DEATH: Although less murderous than last time, Batman is still prepared to kill when he feels he needs to. He sets fire to a circus performer using the jets on the back of the Batmobile, and plants a bomb on another. He also punches Selina Kyle off a rooftop for stabbing him, an action that, if it weren't for the convenient presence of a moving truck full of cat litter below, would have resulted in her death.

CHILDREN AND FAMILIES: The Penguin's entire motivation, and indeed the exact nature of his plan, comes out of his mistreatment and abandonment as a child, with strong parallels being drawn between him and Bruce Wayne. Rumours during production suggested that the film would see the Penguin revealed to be Bruce Wayne's older brother, abandoned by the parents Bruce himself venerates. Other rumours stated that it was Max who was the Penguin's younger brother in some drafts of the script. The Penguin also has a family-like relationship with his penguin army, referring to them as 'My babies'.

The only human trait Max demonstrates is a compassion and concern for his moronic, preppy son. He offers himself in Chip's place when the Penguin sets out to kill the first-born of Gotham, and is willing to die so that his son might live. This love is reciprocated: witness the scene at the beginning of the film where Chip protects Max from the Triangle gang, and allows his father to escape.

It is again suggested (as in *Batman*) that Alfred is the closest Bruce Wayne has to family. In addition, Selina Kyle has a distant, whining mother whom she clearly dislikes, and whom we never see. She did not want to spend Christmas with her, even before becoming Catwoman. It is also the iconography of her childhood, such as her stuffed toys and dolls, which Selina is keenest to destroy after Max tries to kill her.

CLOWNS AND THE CIRCUS: In keeping with the Burton notion of clowns and circuses being evil, the Penguin's henchmen all work for the Red Triangle Circus, who are involved in both child kidnappings and extortion. They also stage a mean riot.

DOGS: Brilliantly and inexplicably Max has a stuffed Chihuahua called 'Geraldo', whose name is the password on all his most secret computer files. There's also the evil Poodle Lady of the circus and her grubby, bomb-dropping and Batarang-stealing Poodle who enables the Penguin to booby trap the Batmobile.

LOVE TRIANGLES: Not just love triangles but situations far more complex. Even leaving aside the romance between two schizophrenics, that is the Selina Kyle/Bruce Wayne affair, there's plenty more to look at. The Penguin's lust for Catwoman, although it never gets him anywhere, is a mirror of Batman's. Also, notice how disturbed Bruce is at the party when it occurs to him that Selina and Max may have a secret thing going.

CHECKS, STRIPES, DOTS: These abound throughout, from Max Shreck's office to the various accessories of the Red Triangle Gang, and the Penguin's dapper neckerchief.

AUTOBIOGRAPHY? Critic Dave Kehr determined that '*Batman Returns* is so personal that it owes much more to *Edward Scissorhands* ... than it does to the comic-book hero created by Bob Kane ... the misunderstood man-boy, whose knowledge of the dark side of life has made him unlovable, he fears, to other human beings.'[47] Yet although there is a strong sense of alienation in all three main characters, here Batman seems rather more grounded than in the previous film. Selina's decision to turn her back on a comfortable life with Bruce Wayne is portrayed as a bit mad, and the Penguin, though a sad figure, is at the same time a hideous failed mass-murderer. There is nothing more to indicate autobiographical elements here than there was in the first Batman film. The personal touches simply derive from Burton's complete creative control over the project, which ensured that his own visual style and interests dominated much more.

AFTERLIFE: As McDonald's had bought up some of the merchandising rights before its release, many expected *Batman Returns* also to be a children's film. Its star, Michael Keaton, expressed concerns about some of the content, telling reporters that 'There's a couple of things in it [my son] doesn't need to see . . . and it's a tad too twisted for young, young kids – five- or six-year-olds.' Burton responded to these criticisms in his usual manner: 'I think children have their own barometers. Kids are not necessarily these pure little everything-is-beautiful creatures. I was always grateful for heavier subject matter when I was growing up.'[48]

Batman Returns made less money than its predecessor, as is usual for sequels. Yet the studio appeared to be expecting a rather larger profit-margin and, over the next few years, *Batman Returns* picked up the unjustifiable reputation of having been a critical and commercial underperformer.

In any case, Burton seemed pleased with what he had achieved. 'I believe this movie is better and different and surprising, but that's just me,' he later told *Premier*, continuing, 'Look, I don't even have to pay to go see it, so what do I count in all of this?'[49] Although with the first Batman movie, 'There's *parts* I liked,' Burton had come to feel that 'it was a little boring at times.'[50] With *Batman Returns* Burton appeared much more satisfied, and felt 'like it's got a little piece of every movie I've ever done, so I kind of feel like I'm done with something, in a way.'[51]

TRIVIA: George Barris, who designed the Batmobile for the 60s Batman television series, built the Red Triangle Circus' Train seen in *Batman Returns*.

The Shreck company logo of a grinning cathead came about, according to Tom Duffield, because of plot concerns. 'It was all to do with Catwoman . . . that was kind of why she became Catwoman – when she was thrown out of the building she had all these images of cats in her head that were originally from the Shreck Cat logo.' Corporate concerns also played a part in the final design. 'They were worried about it looking like Felix the Cat – we had the lawyers at Warners review the cat face to make sure there were some substantial differences between that and Felix the Cat and some other famous cats – Fritz the Cat and Sylvester the cat, or whatever.'

AWARDS: The film was nominated for two Academy Awards, for Best Effects and Best Makeup, also receiving nods for the same two categories at the BAFTAs. Other nominations included Best Villain for Danny DeVito at the MTV Movie Awards, where Michelle Pfeiffer was also nominated for 'Most Desirable Female' and, along with Michael Keaton, for 'Best Kiss'.

Although the film was nominated for a Hugo Award for Best Dramatic Presentation, it lost out to an episode of *Star Trek: The Next Generation*. To add insult to injury, Danny DeVito received a nomination for Worst Supporting Actor at the Razzie Awards.

The only award the film received was for Ve Neill and Stan Winston for Best Makeup at the American Academy of Science Fiction, Fantasy and Horror Films' Saturn Awards.

EXPERT WITNESS: Denise Di Novi: 'Tim is unique in that he's a commercially successful director who doesn't make mainstream movies. There's a simplicity and underlying sweetness to his work that embraces the outcast and differences in people. I think that's why his films are so accessible to moviegoers'[52]

Pfeiffer: 'Tim has a very unusual way of viewing the world. There's just no getting around it. He's very definite about what he wants, and he refuses to compromise.'[53]

Keaton: 'For some reason during the discussions and making of *Beetlejuice*, he and I really connected. I could see how he expressed himself and he has a tremendous sense of humour. The films he makes could fall apart if he was hesitant, not trusting, or one of those directors who have pretty hands-on agenda. He is always wide open to what the actor wants to do.'[58]

ANALYSIS: It could be fatuously suggested that the moral of *Batman Returns* is 'Just because you're ugly doesn't mean you're evil. Oops, sorry it does.' But the film is a bit more complex than that.

At the heart of *Batman Returns* are masks. Particularly the masks people used to hide themselves and their internal divisions from others, especially from the opposite sex. Keaton's rendition of the Batman character was always a borderline schizophrenic, and here he gets paired with an equally unsettled love interest in the broken and scarred Selina Kyle. She's far more Bruce Wayne's kinda girl than the forthright, stable Vicki Vale could ever be, as his spluttering attempts to explain his relationship with the photojournalist in the first film demonstrate.

What Catwoman/Selina shares with Batman/Bruce is the physical distilling of separate personality traits into two distinct personas. That and a seemingly insatiable desire for vengeance; he wants to get his own back on the kind of criminality that took his parents from him, she wants revenge on the *man* specific and the *men* generic that mistreated, belittled and ultimately killed her. Result? They both stalk Gotham's rooftops at night clad in leather and looking for people to beat unconscious. When they meet, sparks inevitably fly as they each recognise something of themselves in the black-clad figure opposite them. Both are drawn to the other's combination of furious, visible aggression and barely concealed emotional wounds. Despite, or maybe because of their attraction, there's a fear of what they might find out about themselves and each other from any coupling. It is the similarity between them that creates the chemistry. Notice how Batman's first meeting with a pre-accident Selina, when he rescues her from the circus freak, is uneventful and sexual-tension free. Compare and contrast that with Bruce Wayne's reaction the first time he meets the damaged Selina in Max's office. He can't take his eyes off her, and she takes every chance she gets to touch him. They make moves towards arranging a date before he's even entered the lift. As Batman and Catwoman the two can fight, fondle, lick and try to kill each other. As Bruce and Selina they have trouble looking each other in the eyes. It's when the masks come on that, ironically, true feelings are revealed.

All this reaches a climax in the final confrontation in the Penguin's lair, when Bruce Wayne is finally able to bring himself to be Batman without the mask, ripping away his protective barrier whilst remaining heroic and strong. Seeing someone as damaged as he, and wanting to be rescued from this situation, actually helps Bruce Wayne begin to reconcile his personalities. Here we begin to see him acting like Batman when dressed as Bruce and like Bruce when dressed as a bat. Had Burton and Keaton made a third Batman film together it could have been very interesting indeed . . .

AVAILABILITY: *Batman Returns* is available on both sides of the Atlantic in both DVD and VHS formats, although quite why there isn't a deluxe DVD special edition yet is anyone's guess. The current DVD version, although available in widescreen, has nothing extra on the disc, and some VHS versions have been cut in seemingly random places.

THE BOTTOM LINE: *Batman Returns* is not just complex, involving and visually mouth-watering, it is exquisitely detailed in every conceivable sense. It's the little things that conspire to make the film what it is. Bruce Wayne sitting silent and alone waiting for the Bat-signal to be lit; Batman ripping his mask off to convince Catwoman of his sincerity; Bruce and Selina's dance where they're the only unmasked people at the costume party; the way Max jokes with Selina just before pushing her out of the window; Selina's head ducking into shot in the last frame. The only blatantly psychoanalytical, pseudo-expressionist S&M art film that anybody has ever sold to McDonald's as a summer blockbuster for the kids, *Batman Returns* is magnificent.

TIM BURTON'S THE NIGHTMARE BEFORE CHRISTMAS (1993)

Touchstone Pictures
Story and Characters by Tim Burton
Adaptation by Michael McDowell
Screenplay by Caroline Thompson
Director of Photography: Peter Kozachik
Co-Producer: Kathleen Gavinco
Associate Producer: Danny Elfman

Associate Producer: Jill Jacobs
Associate Producer: Diane Minter
Associate Producer: Philip Lofaro
Produced by Tim Burton and Denise DiNovi
Music and lyrics by Danny Elfman
Visual Consultant: Rick Heinrichs
Edited by Stan Webb
Directed by Henry Selick

VOICE CAST: Danny Elfman (Jack Skellington/Clown with Tearaway Face/Barrel), Catherine O'Hara (Sally/Shock), Glenn Shadix (The Mayor), William Hickey (Dr Finklestein), Paul Reubens (Lock), Ken Page (Oogie Boogie), Ed Ivory (Santa), Susan McBride (Big Witch), Debi Durst (Corpse Kid/Corpse Mother/Small Witch), Greg Proops (Harlequin Demon/Devil/Sax Player), Kerry Katz (Man Under Stairs/Vampire/Corpse Father), Randy Crenshaw (Mr Hyde/Behemoth/Vampire), Sherwood Ball (Mummy/Vampire), Carmen Twillie (Undersea Gal/Man Under the Stairs), Glenn Walters (Wolfman), Chris Sarandon (Jack Skellington – Non singing), Mia Brown, L Peter Callender, Ann Fraser, Jesse McClurg, Robert Olague, Jennifer Levey, Elena Praskin, Judi M Durand, John Morris, Daamen J Krall, Bobbi Page, David McCharen, David Randolph, Trampas Warman, Doris Hess, Christina MacGregor, Gary Raff, Gary Schwartz (Additional Voices).

TRAILER: Of the two trailers for *The Nightmare Before Christmas*, the first is the most interesting because it was clearly made before it was decided that *Nightmare* would not be distributed as a Disney film 'proper'. The trailer has the then-standard pale blue Disney logo, and places the teaser in the context of the company's history of animated features and technical innovation. The second trailer is far more standard, and has the Touchstone logo attached to it. It deals with the film's plot, characters and songs in a straightforward way.

TITLE SEQUENCE: The film begins within a circle of trees, each of which has upon it a single iconic image representing some festival or holiday. As a voice-over asks us if we have considered where holidays come from, the camera zooms through the pumpkin shaped door on the Halloween tree and into Halloween-town. Here begins the first musical number. The camera sweeps through the town in a series of arcs as the iconography of Halloween flies past it.

SUMMARY: Halloweentown is a kind of magical kingdom, which is responsible for all the fun and frights of Halloween. Its ruler is one Jack Skellington, a tall white-boned figure who delights in the grotesque and the macabre. But as yet another Halloween comes to an end Jack grows increasingly melancholy. He is bored. Wandering alone one night, he accidentally discovers another kingdom similar to his own. It is called Christmastown. The next morning Jack returns to Halloweentown full of excite-ment, desperate to explain to his fellow citizens what Christmas means. He has a plan: just as he is bored of organising Halloween every year, perhaps the ruler of Christmastown, one 'Sandy Claws', is also bored of being in charge of Christmas. Jack will take over Christmas for that year, meaning that Claws will be able to have a year off.

He sets about organising his workforce so that they can take over Christmas, and sends three children Lock, Shock and Barrel to fetch Santa Claus (as the ruler of Christmastown is of course actually known) and bring him to him. Before they go he warns them to not involve Oogie Boogie, a monstrous wraith figure who lives on the peripheries of Halloweentown and whom he does not trust. Ignoring this advice Lock, Shock and Barrel turn Santa over to Oogie, who chains the King of Christmastown up and plans to tip him into a bubbling vat of some kind of ooze for his own amusement.

Jack sets out on his Christmas trip, but it does not go well, as he has misjudged the kind of presents children wish to receive, and ends up terrifying them. The army fires upon his coffin-shaped sleigh and skeletal reindeer, and brings his flying craft down. Meanwhile Sally, a young resident of Halloweentown who is in love with Jack and realises that his plan is doomed to failure, sets out to rescue Santa from Oogie, but is herself captured for her pains.

Returning to his world, Jack frees Sally and Santa from Oogie, who drops into his pit himself during the fight. Santa rushes off to save Christmas in time, but returns later to cover Halloween-town in snow, and wish Jack a Happy Halloween and a Merry

Christmas. The other residents of Halloweentown begin to realise how wonderful Christmas can be, and the songs 'This is Halloween' and 'What's This?' which symbolise the two holidays, are sung together, fitting perfectly, suggesting a compatibility to the two worlds. Jack and Sally realise they are made for each other, and the film ends with them kissing.

SOURCE MATERIAL: *Tim Burton's The Nightmare Before Christmas* (to give it the full title) was, like *Edward Scissorhands*, an original idea from Burton, as opposed to a reworking of existing material. However there were several inspirations, both direct and indirect, which contributed greatly to Burton's vision for the picture. As he explains, 'Growing up ... I always loved [Dr Seuss's] *The Grinch Who Stole Christmas*, and *Rudolph* [*the Red-Nosed Reindeer*, Kizo Nagashima and Larry Roemer, 1964] and I loved Halloween [so] I wanted to do a story that would put the two of them together. I thought about Halloweentown, and took images, and sort of twisted them together.'[1]

The idea originated whilst Burton was still at Disney. It was fresh and original, but nobody at the then relatively troubled entertainment giant showed any interest in producing anything based on the character designs and poem outline the young Burton had put together. 'You couldn't give it away,'[2] he ruefully reflected years later. 'I pitched it around, and people seemed to like it, but it never went anywhere.'[3]

Because *Nightmare* had been developed whilst Burton was a Disney employee, once he left Disney (see **Early Life and Disney Times**) he effectively lost control of the property. Whilst he didn't expect his former employers to do anything with his creation, it was frustrating to not own something that was so wholly his. His later overly-Biblical impression of the copyright situation was simply that 'You signed your soul away in blood when you worked there. They owned your firstborn.'[4]

Although after *Pee-wee* he would occasionally refer to the abandoned project in interviews, the sketches and poetry for *Nightmare* languished, forgotten, in Disney's archives for the best part of a decade.

REFERENCES: *The Nightmare Before Christmas* doesn't strongly resemble any one thing, and there are fewer visual quotations than in most of the films Burton directs himself. Nevertheless, one of the statues in the background in Halloweentown is clearly based on Edvard Munch's classic painting of adolescent angst, *The Scream* (1893), whilst another resembles (as had a gravestone in Burton's *Vincent*) the Japanese icon, Hello Kitty.

Dr Finkelstein, unsurprisingly, wears a lab coat reminiscent of Henry Frankenstein's in James Whale's 1931 film.

Many of the film's crew agree that the visual style was consciously moulded on *The Night of the Hunter* (Charles Laughton, 1955). Other reported influences are the illustrations of Edward Gorey and Charles Addams for Halloweentown, with Dr Seuss's view of Christmas providing inspiration for Christmastown.

During production Visual Consultant Rick Heinrichs introduced the animation team to the films of obscure Russian animator Starevich, who used real fur and live insects in his stop-motion films. Although few of his techniques were adopted, similar styles are visible in some sequences. There were also a few homages to Lotte Reiniger, a German animator who frequently worked with silhouettes to depict classic fairy tales. More conventionally the team paid some attention to Wilfred Jackson's 'Night on Bald Mountain' sequence from Disney's own *Fantasia* (1940).

PRODUCTION: Following *Batman*, when his star was very much in the ascendant, Burton began to make tentative enquires as to how he could recover the idea of his that had lain useless for so long: 'I quietly looked into it, not trying to make too much noise.'[5] In response, David Hoberman, then the President of Disney/ Touchstone, recalls that he 'sent researchers down into the files to see what we had and they came back with *Nightmare before Christmas*.'[6]

Burton's request was simple – 'I kind of gently said "Could I just have it back?"'[7] Disney, now fully aware of having lost Burton once, weren't going to just give away a project which they owned outright, and which bore the unique stamp of one of the most financially successful directors in the world.

Furthermore they certainly weren't prepared to let their former employee take a project such as *Nightmare* to a rival studio. Jeffrey Katzenberg, then head of Walt Disney Studios (and now the K in DreamWorks SKG) made the company's position clear: 'When it comes to animation, we believe in and enjoy the notion of a monopoly.'[8] Disney, it was obvious, wanted to produce *Nightmare* themselves.

Although pleased by the opportunity to finally realise his project, Burton did not want *Nightmare* to 'fit in to the type of cartoon movies [Disney] have been having so much success with,'[9] just as Burton's earlier *Vincent* had been planned to break away from the normal Disney mould. *Nightmare*, like *Vincent*, was planned for stop-motion, yet Disney at this stage had still failed to give the 1982 short any proper release. Burton was well aware of this, and wanted to ensure that no major stylistic changes were to be enforced.

Perhaps surprisingly, Hoberman understood this, and was unconcerned. The picture's 'completely unique' nature was, for him, part of the project's appeal, although his comments reveal that Burton himself was probably the main interest for the company: 'This was an opportunity for us to do business with Tim Burton and to say, "We can think outside the envelope. We can do different and unusual things".' He went on: 'I hope it goes out and makes a fortune. If it doesn't, that doesn't negate the validity of the process.'[10] It is unclear whether the 'process' mentioned here was stop-motion, or working with an established name director. However, Disney have yet to produce any more stop-motion features (although this could in part be put down to the advances in three-dimensional computer technology following the huge success of 1995's *Toy Story*, directed by Burton's CalArts friend, John Lasseter).

During discussions with Disney Burton contacted Danny Elfman – a great fan of musicals, as *Nightmare* was now intended to be – and Elfman wrote several songs for the feature. 'We actually went through a process, after I'd written the ten songs that laid out the story,' remembers Elfman, laughing, '[where] Tim and I went into the studio and we did demos of every song. Me actually singing every part. It was an all-night session.'[11]

Costing around $18 million, *Nightmare* would be far cheaper than the average Disney animated feature, and so it was not essential that it grossed especially highly. So keen was the studio to recapture its escaped *wünderkind* that it contractually granted Burton full creative autonomy on the project, and green-lit *Nightmare* for production based only on Burton's original materials and ten of Elfman's compositions. There wasn't even a finished script.

With contracts signed *The Nightmare Before Christmas* was announced as Disney's first stop-motion animated feature.

Designated Producer Denise Di Novi felt that Disney were 'very smart in saying, "We'll get the best ... if we don't tamper too much." All his movies have been hits ... what reason does anyone have not to listen to Tim's instincts?'[12]

Burton's announcement that this, certainly one of his more personal projects, was something he was not choosing to direct surprised many. The reason lay with the stop-motion nature of the film: 'If I had [directed it], I'd be dead before I ever saw the final version ... the reason I originally got out of animation is because I didn't have the patience for it.'[13] Instead he asked Henry Selick, a contemporary from his Disney days who'd also left the company, to fill the directorial post.

Like Burton, Selick was incapable of drawing cute foxes, and was thus an ideal choice as a stand-in director. He had started at CalArts in Jules Engel's experimental animation programme, from which he produced early films like *Phases* (1978) and *Seepage* (1981), both of which used multiple animation techniques, such as a melding of stop-motion and cel animation, and displayed his tendency towards visual abstraction. After leaving Disney Selick had animated shorts for MTV, *Sesame Street* and adverts for Ritz crackers, as well as second-unit directing and storyboarding some live action films, such as *Return to Oz* (Walter Murch, 1985). However, he decided to return to full-time animation in 1989 with *Slow Bob in the Lower Dimensions* (released 1990) for MTV. Selick reported that, 'My MTV work, from 1987 to 1990, was what convinced Tim that I should direct,'[14] adding that, 'Everything that I've done before seems to have prepared me to do *The Nightmare Before Christmas*.'[15]

Because of the prerecorded nature of Elfman's demos, and the extensive storyboards that had already been prepared under Burton's supervision, it wasn't necessary to have a completed script until very late in the day. Caroline Thompson, who had written Burton's equally personal *Edward Scissorhands*, was brought in to supply the characters' dialogue for the scenes where they weren't singing. Yet Selick has claimed that 'there are very few lines of dialogue in the movie that are Caroline's. We worked with her, but ... we were constantly rewriting, reconfiguring, developing the film visually.'[16]

In assembling his team for what would inevitably be a long shoot, director Selick picked people he had worked with before – including Animation Supervisor Eric Leighton, Director of Photography Pete Kozachik, Chief Armature Designer Tom St Amand, Puppet Reproduction Supervisor John Reed, Puppet Fabricator Bonita De Carlo, and Miniature Set Builder Bo Henry. Selick set up Skellington Productions to produce the film, and moved the operation to a warehouse in San Francisco's South of Market district in July 1991. The initial 25,000 square feet of the building weren't enough for the 230 sets, so the crew had to colonise a further 15,000 by the time production began the following October. The schedule was tight – a crew of 110 aimed to get 70 seconds of film finished per week, which by stop motion standards is a *lot* of work. Selick later commented, only half-jokingly, that the reason the production decamped to San Francisco was so 'the execs could visit and get nervous maybe once a month instead of every day.'[17]

Nightmare was the most complex and longest stop-motion project in history. Although most stop-motion shots used between 40 and 100 frames, in *Nightmare* it was often as many as 540, with many scenes requiring numerous characters, special lighting effects, and intricate camera moves more common to ambitiously visual live action features than animation. At 24 frames per second (1,440 per minute) *Nightmare* contains approximately 106,560 individual frames across its running time of 74 minutes. In comparison, *Vincent* used only about 8,500 frames, the most complex of which featured six different moving elements, compared to the huge number of animated characters in many of *Nightmare*'s shots. Every single one of these frames was shot individually, with every single movement painstakingly made by hand.

Furthermore, the elaborate camera movements planned required huge amounts of coordination between the camera operators and animators, as, if either was out by just a fraction of an inch, the entire shot would be ruined. A reshoot from scratch would lose several days' work. Added to this, unlike most stop-motion projects, where access to the puppets was considered the single most important factor in building the sets, Eric Leighton explained, 'On this film ... the animators and camera crews constantly found themselves having to crawl around the top of the sets just to reach the puppets,' thanks to the elaborate visual look. This meant that 'the physical labour aspect of this project challenged even the best of our animators. We went through a lot of kneepads, and hired a staff masseuse midway through production to deal with all the sore backs.'[18]

The feature contained 74 characters, requiring several hundred fully armatured puppets. Oogie Boogie, for example, needed 173 separate parts – nearly 80 just from the neck up, and all had to be built strong enough to withstand the incredibly long and arduous shooting process. Most of the puppets were 12–15 inches tall, much larger than is normal for stop-motion, and Oogie Boogie was two feet tall. The extra scale made the models extra heavy, necessitating the construction of the sets from reinforced, three-quarter inch thick medite as, if the sets were made out of wood, the heavier models would severely dent them. On top of this, the natural wear and tear of the shooting schedule meant the foam coverings for each character had to be rebuilt several times. For example, Jack's love-interest, Sally, had to be stripped back down to the skeleton armature and remoulded from scratch 35 times. If this sounds extreme, Jack had 800 different replacement heads due to the need for different mouth shapes and minor expression variations. Only the nostrils remained unchanged to maintain some kind of consistency.

Whilst all this was going on in San Francisco, Burton was busy in LA working on *Batman Returns*. This separation left him unconcerned, as 'I could still affect things as I needed to. I felt very comfortable with my role, and I knew Henry and how talented he is. I stayed involved and knew what was going on.'[19] That Burton could exert creative control whenever he chose is backed up by the fact that most people involved on *Nightmare* recall an occasion when production ground to a halt for a week because Burton wanted Halloweentown to be darker. In any case, before animation started properly, Selick put together sequences of detailed storyboards to run to the prerecorded soundtrack for Burton to view, ensuring that he would know roughly what the finished product would look like.

In August 1993 the production was finally completed. The last sequence to be shot was the scene of Oogie Boogie coming apart at the seams (one of the most complicated, thanks to the numerous moving insect parts). All that was left to be done was the post-production touch-up, such as optical and digital work to remove wires, fix scratches and smooth out camera bumps. In comparison to the arduous shoot, this was nothing.

CASTING: In his casting role, Burton mostly turned to actors with whom he had previously worked and who could be trusted to deliver performances he was happy with. One such old collaborator was Glenn Shadix, who recalls how he gained the role of Halloweentown's schizophrenic Mayor: 'There was a Sunday pool gathering over at Tim's, and I turned up early. Tim was in the Jacuzzi and he just said, "Glenn, you've got a big voice, do you want to play the Mayor?" It really was as simple as that!' Aside from Shadix, Burton engaged another *Beetlejuice* cast member, Catherine O' Hara, to voice Sally and Shock. Paul Reubens (Pee-wee Herman) came in as Lock, and the key figure of Jack Skellington was to be portrayed by composer Danny Elfman. 'I have a lot in common with Jack,' Elfman has said. 'I made demos of all the songs, but I felt with Jack's character I had nailed it, and no one else would be able to do a better job than I had.'[20]

The actors recorded their lines in advance, working with Dan Mason, the track reader. They often did as many as 50 different takes, before Selick and editor Stan Webb picked the ones they wanted. For Shadix, the Mayor's two faces provided an unusual sort of challenge: 'I had to come up with a very specific voice for the anxiety-ridden face, the terrified Mayor face. What I couldn't get out of my head was, when I was trying to come up with a voice I saw Karen Black on television in a movie called *Airport 1975* [Jack Smight, 1974], and she's in the cockpit, and the pilot's dead, and she's trying to fly the plane, and she kind of crossed her eyes and went, "I can't fly a plane!" I tell you, I had to cross my eyes and repeat that line out loud to myself every time I did the anxiety face!'

Eventually it was decided that whilst Elfman would sing for Jack Skellington, a professional actor would be engaged to provide his speaking voice. 'We basically had to find an actor who matched my voice,' remembers Elfman, as all the songs had already been recorded. 'Normally, it's the other way around, but this is the reverse . . . Jack sings more than he speaks. Usually they'd find the actor and then someone to sing . . . the dilemma was for him – it was no sweat for me.'[21] Eventually chosen was Chris Sarandon, who as an actor is perhaps best known for his role as drug-addled transsexual Leon, Al Pacino's 'wife', in *Dog Day Afternoon* (Sidney Lumet, 1975). His greater claim to fame is starting the career of and lending his surname to former spouse, Susan Sarandon.

CRITICS: *Nightmare* received mixed notices, with some critics praising it to the skies and others doing equally detailed demolition jobs. *Newsweek* were very firmly in the former category: 'giddily imaginative ... so stuffed with visual delights you won't want to blink,'[22] it exclaimed. The *St Louis Post-Dispatch* was more inclined to side with the latter grouping, albeit with some caveats: 'There is no question that *The Nightmare Before Christmas* is an astonishing visual accomplishment. Unfortunately, it is not a very good movie ... decidedly uncheerful ... a charmless and muddled tale that aims at a target somewhere in the vast gulf between Franz Kafka and Walt Disney and hits nothing ... there is a lot less to *The Nightmare Before Christmas* than meets the eye.'[23]

Other positive reviews came from the the *Boston Globe* ('the black diamond of family films, brilliantly conceived, touchingly pure of heart, much more endearing than scary'[24]) and Roger Ebert, who enthused that Burton and Selick's vision was of a world 'as completely new as the worlds we saw for the first time in such films as *Metropolis*, *The Cabinet of Dr Caligari* and *Star Wars*.'[25]

British newspaper the *Independent* lent more qualified praise: 'director Henry Selick's camera swoops and swirls, as if it were on loan from Brian De Palma ... All this is magical – but not quite pure magic. The charm is rather calculated.' This wasn't enough, however, to stop it recommending the movie: 'It is beautifully detailed (worth seeing more than once), elegantly scored by Danny Elfman ... and stamped throughout with the vision of Tim Burton.'[26]

MUSIC: One critic at the time noted that Elfman's songs were, 'reminiscent of Kurt Weill',[27] whilst another noted how their rich inventiveness showed 'just how inadequate the trite pseudo-Broadway muzak of Menken, Ashman and Rice had become.'[28] Audible influences in the songs and their singing include the works of Noel Coward and those of Broadway genius Stephen Sondheim. 'I wanted to turn the clock backward and forward at the same time,' claimed Elfman, 'so that musically it feels fresh but is rooted in certain traditional styles.'[29] The melodies are simple in the best sense, in that they are instantly memorable and easy to hum, but the whole film also works on a symphonic level and phrases from one song recur in another, and key musical phrases (such as that which accompanies Jack's 'And I'm Jack the Pumpkin King') reappear at appropriate moments.

CINEMATOGRAPHY: The swirling camera movements perfectly echo many of the designs of the twisted Halloween world, and create a truly alive feeling that is missing in most stop-motion animation, even Selick's follow-up, *James and the Giant Peach*. The distinct colour-schemes of each world are perfectly amplified by Director of Photography Peter Kozachik's atmospheric in-camera lighting, often created with several dozen distinct miniature light-sources. Most of this can be put down to the extensive design crew, after all, it is not so much 'cinematography' as a collection of individual still photographs, albeit beautifully shot and lit ones.

DEATH: Early on Jack states that he is already dead as, presumably, are the other inhabitants of Halloweentown. The iconography of death is everywhere in this movie, with tombstones and corpses littering Halloweentown's streets and gardens. Even so, the citizens fear that Jack has been 'killed' after he is shot down on his Christmas run – presumably if he had been, it would be a death along the same lines as Betelgeuse's demise at the end of *Beetlejuice*. No one actually dies in the film, although Oogie's disintegration might count.

CHILDREN AND FAMILIES: Lock, Shock and Barrel are three particularly mischievous children, played with immaculate relish by Catherine O'Hara, Danny Elfman and a particularly hyper Paul Reubens. Several children are somewhat disturbed by Jack's gifts to them and run to their parents for comfort.

CLOWNS AND THE CIRCUS: Fitting in with the Burton belief that clowns are fundamentally terrifying, one of the scariest denizens of Halloweentown is a clown 'with a tearaway face'.

DOGS: Zero, Jack's ghostly mutt who follows him wherever he asks. Zero's glowing nose provides the Rudolph-style light at the front of Jack's sleigh. In addition, one of the children traumatised by Jack's unorthodox gifts is given a puppy by Santa as a replacement.

LOVE TRIANGLES: Jack's split of affection between Halloween and Christmas is a love triangle. Also Sally is bound to Dr Finkelstein, which prevents her from revealing her affection for Jack.

CHECKS, STRIPES, DOTS: They're everywhere, all over Halloweentown, and even Christmastown (although there they are red and white as opposed to black and white). Just a few examples of Burton's favoured recurring patterns as presented in this movie include on Jack Skellington's suit, on monsters' antennae, on ghost boy's T-shirts and across bandages.

AUTOBIOGRAPHY?: Kim Newman, an astute critic and enthusiastic fan of Burton's, felt *Nightmare* to be yet 'another of Burton's veiled experiments in autobiography (cf. *Edward Scissorhands*, *Ed Wood*), as it deals with the frustrations of a one-note creature who wants to break out and do something else, only to learn that he should stick to what he does best.'[30] The *Boston Globe* also felt this way, arguing that it was 'possible to read *The Nightmare Before Christmas* as an allegory of the public's recoil from Burton's *Batman* sequel because it was perceived as too dark and scary.'[31] Further to this, Ken Hanke suggests that Jack's failure to run Christmas echoes Burton's alleged failure to direct *Batman* successfully, especially as they both tried their best.

Thanks to the sheer diversity of the many characters, *Nightmare* is one of those projects into which one can read anything. There are certainly elements of Burton's public personality in Jack (everyone expecting so much of him despite his own self-doubt), and various themes to which Burton constantly returns are again in evidence, yet the considerable influence of Henry Selick, plus the contribution of Danny Elfman and scripters Michael McDowell and Caroline Thompson to both the characters and story, ensure that the overall feeling is as summed up by Kim Newman, that '*Nightmare* seems like a film *about* rather than *by* Tim Burton.'[32]

DIALOGUE TO SKIP BACK FOR:
Jack: 'There's got to be a logical way to explain this Christmas thing.'

Jack: 'Just because I cannot see it doesn't mean I can't believe it.'

The Mayor: 'I'm only an elected official, I can't make decisions on my own.'

AFTERLIFE: Burton's reaction on finally getting to see *Nightmare* after such a long period of gestation was simply, 'I'm very happy with the way it worked out.'[33] Shortly afterwards, *Nightmare* was first released into three theatres, then 400 – far less than the 2,000 + that housed *Luau* alumnus John Musker's *Aladdin* at a similar time.

For some critics the film's treatment of America's minorities was less than thoughtful, with one protesting that by having the picture's arch-villain speak in 'a constructed black dialect' the filmmakers were planting racist suggestions for their audience. She went on to argue that this 'singular and particularized instance of "blackspeak" has the narrative intent of invoking already circulating notions of black male criminality' and that this combined with jazz-like music made it worse. Although Oogie Boogie was not black in colour, 'his speech, his environment, and his function as narrative obstacle clearly deploy socially recognizable codifications of racial blackness and thus racial undesirability.'[34]

When these ideas were put to him, director Henry Selick confessed that the validity of these complaints had occurred to him as he knew that a 'boogie man' was characterised as a monstrous black person in some parts of America, but he insisted that the presentation of Oogie really came from Cab Calloway's dance numbers in old Betty Boop cartoons, where Calloway would dance his jazz dance while singing songs like 'Old Man of the Mountain' 'and they would rotoscope him [turn him into a cartoon character]. I think those are some of the most inventive moments in cartoon history, in no way racist, even though he was sometimes a villain.'[35]

Nevertheless doubt remains for Selick. 'It's controversial and I've got a slight twinge of guilt. But in the end we went with Ken Page, who is a black singer, because he was the best guy to sing the song. He had no problem with it.'[36]

Steven Spielberg's *Jurassic Park* (1993), the first live action feature with large amounts of computer-generated effect modelled to look 'real', was released just as *Nightmare* concluded production. Armature designer Tom St Armand, who worked on both, reflected on whether the emergence of GGI would lead to the death of stop-motion: 'For *Jurassic Park*, the idea was to create something that looked absolutely real; but that wasn't the point on *Nightmare* . . . you can appreciate the characters for what they are – outlandish and definitely *not* real.' Comparing the idea that CGI would kill stop-motion to the erroneous belief people once had that camera would replace the art of painting he concluded, 'the point is to see a person's *interpretation* of reality . . . if it means using a computer, use a computer. But I think there will always be a place for personal craftsmanship.'[37] Although he has maintained a love for more traditional effects techniques, four years after *Nightmare*'s release Burton would opt for CGI over stop-motion on *Mars Attacks!*, having realised the benefits.

AWARDS: Given its startling technical excellence, it is surprising that *Nightmare* wasn't nominated for more awards. As it is it won Saturn Awards for 'Best Fantasy Film' and 'Best Musical Score' at the awards from the Academy of Science Fiction, Fantasy and Horror Films, and whilst it was nominated for the Visual Effects Oscar, the 'Best Original Score' Golden Globe and 'Best Dramatic Presentation' Hugo, it didn't pick up any of them on the night.

TRIVIA: The vampires playing ice hockey with a Jack o' Lantern, were originally intended to be playing with a severed human head, modelled to look like Burton. It was decided this might be deemed a bit too gruesome for family audiences. The cut scene is included on the DVD.

ANALYSIS: During *Nightmare*'s original release period, the *New York Times* reported that Disney executives were trying to distance themselves from the project, or 'struggling to point out the difference without diluting the distinctiveness of the film. This effort . . . included attaching the Touchstone label rather than the Walt Disney Pictures stamp accorded all of its previous animated features and identifying the film as Tim Burton's, in case anyone was confused as to just whose *Nightmare* it was.'[39] Despite this glib comment, there was soon to be substantial controversy on the matter of to whom the film actually 'belonged'.

British magazine *Sight and Sound* confidently asserted that although the film was based on Burton's poem, 'It was shaped as much by the interpretation of its director, Henry Selick, as *Apocalypse Now* was by Coppola's reading of *Heart of Darkness*. It was Selick who put flesh on Burton's original, literally skeletal concept.'[40] Respected Stateside critic Roger Ebert concurred: 'The Nightmare Before Christmas is a Tim Burton film in the sense that the story, its world and its look first took shape in Burton's mind, and he supervised their filming. But the director of the film, a veteran stop-action master named Henry Selick, is the person who has made it all work. And his achievement is enormous.'[41]

The Los Angeles Times went for the opposite option – 'Tim Burton's The Nightmare Before Christmas is the movie this decidedly quirky filmmaker was fated to make . . . what may be the most personal piece of animation – and one of the most personal films, period – ever to come out of that studio . . . Nightmare's sensibility is clearly all Burton.'[42] This controversy clearly affected Henry Selick, who stated shortly afterwards in an interview that 'I don't want to take away from Tim, but he was not in San Francisco when we made it. He came [over] five times [in] two years . . . spent no more than . . . ten days here in total.' Comparing the process of making the film to that of adapting a book which Burton had once written, Selick concluded, 'the bottom line is that Tim Burton's name before the title is going to bring in more people than mine would.'[43]

Glenn Shadix sees things differently: 'Tim oversaw every detail of that film . . . Henry Selick was wonderful as a hands-on director of the stop-motion and an incredible group of animators, but the heart and soul of that movie is Tim Burton . . . He was hands-on in the sense that he made decisions all along the way. He wasn't at Skellington Productions in San Francisco all that often . . . but Tim was certainly at the helm creatively, and in on all the decisions.'

The Nightmare Before Christmas is, visually, one of the cornerstones of Tim Burton's filmic 'canon', but it is true that Henry Selick's contribution is massive, and cannot be overlooked. The groundbreakingly imaginative sweeping camera movements and beautiful framing are Selick's, of that there is no question. The day to day work of bringing the landscape of Halloweentown to such vivid life was Selick's and he should be celebrated for it; but the designs, the characters, the sensibility, the essential aesthetic of the film are Tim Burton's. There are more Burton designs in this than in many (all?) of the films he actually directed. This is a Tim Burton world. In order to ascertain whose film this truly is you only have to ask yourself one question. What does Nightmare more strongly resemble, James and the Giant Peach or Batman Returns?

EXPERT WITNESS: Glenn Shadix: 'I will never forget the first time I saw the film. Tim had Catherine [O'Hara] and Bo Welch, Jeffrey Jones and myself come to a little private screening, just for our little group. And I cried, because I knew how much of Tim's heart was in it, and I felt blessed to be a part of it.'

AVAILABILITY: A dynamic and featured-packed Touchstone DVD is available in both Britain and America. The packaging differs, and the UK one has more advertisements on it, but apart from that they're exactly the same.

THE BOTTOM LINE: *The Nightmare Before Christmas* is an astounding technical achievement and the simple statistics of the production make mind-boggling reading. The care and attention put into every single frame of the picture are very clearly visible onscreen. Between them, the film's creators managed to fashion an utterly original alternate reality, which looks unlike anything seen on screen before or since. This charming, beautifully designed feature is the very apotheosis of stop-motion as an art form; not even Selick's own adorable follow up *James and the Giant Peach* comes close.

ED WOOD (1994)

Touchstone Pictures
A Tim Burton Film
Written by Scott Alexander and Larry Karaszewski
Director of Photography: Stefan Czapsky
Production Designer: Tom Duffield
Art Director: [Michael] Okowita
Produced by Denise Di Novi and Tim Burton
Executive Producer: Michael Lehmann
Co-Producer: Michael Flynn
Casting by Victoria Thomas
Music by Howard Shore
Costume Designer: Coleen Attwood

Edited by Chris Lebenzon
Directed by Tim Burton

CAST: Johnny Depp (*Edward D Wood, Jr*), Martin Landau (*Bela Lugosi*), Sarah Jessica Parker (*Dolores Fuller*), Patricia Arquette (*Kathy O'Hara*), Jeffery Jones (*Criswell*), CP Spradlin (*Reverend Lemon*), Vincent D'Onofrio (*Orson Welles*), Lisa Marie (*Vampira*), Bill Murray (*Bunny Beckridge*), Mike Starr (*George Weiss*), Max Casell (*Paul Marco*), Brent Hinkley, (*Conrad Brooks*), George 'The Animal' Steele (*Tor Johnson*), Juliet Landau (*Loretta King*), Clive Rosengren (*Ed Reynolds*), Norman Alden (*Cameraman Bill*), Leonard Termo (*Makeup Man Harry*), Ned Bellamy (*Dr Tom Mason*), Danny Dayton (*Soundman*), John Ross (*Camera Assistant*), Bill Cusack (*Tony McCoy*), Aaron Nelms (*Teenage Kid*), Biff Yeager (*Rude Boss*), Joseph R Gannascoli (*Security Guard*), Carmen Filpi (*Old Crusty Man*), Lisa Malkiewicz (*Secretary #1*), Melora Walters (*Secretary #2*), Conrad Brooks (*Bartender*), Don Amendolia (*Salesman*), Tommy Bertelsen (*Tough Boy*), Reid Cruickshanks (*Stage Guard*), Stanley DeSantis (*Mr Feldman*), Lionel Decker (*Executive #1*), Edmund L Shaff (*Executive #2*), Gene LeBell (*Ring Announcer*), Jesse Hernandez (*Wrestling Opponent*), Bobby Slayton (*TV Show Host*), Gretchen Becker (*TV Host's Assistant*), John Rice (*Conservative Man*), Catherine Butterfield (*Conservative Wife*), Mary Portser (*Backer's Wife*), King Cotton (*Hick Backer*), Don Hood (*Southern Backer*), Frank Echols (*Doorman*), Matthew Barry (*Valet*), Ralph Monaco (*Waiter*), Anthony Russell (*Busboy*), Tommy Bush (*Stage Manager*), Gregory Walcott (*Potential Backer*), Charles C Stevenson Jr (*Backer*), Rance Howard (*Old Man McCoy*), Vasek Simek (*Professor Strowski*), Alan Martin (*Vampira's Assistant*), Salwa Ali (*Vampira's Girlfriend*), Rodney Kizziah (*Vampira's Friend*), Korla Pandit (*Indian Musician*), Hannah Eckstein (*Greta Johnson*), Luc De Schepper (*Karl Johnson*), Vinny Argiro (*TV Horror Show Director*), Patti Tippo (*Nurse*), Ray Baker (*Doctor*), Louis Lombardi (*Rental House Manager*), James Reid Boyce (*Theatre Manager*), Ben Ryan Ganger (*Angry Kid*), Ryan Holihan (*Frantic Usher*), Marc Revivo (*High School Punk*), Charlie Holliday (*Tourist*), Adam Drescher (*Photographer #1*), Ric Mancini (*Photographer #2*), Daniel Riordan (*Pilot/Strapping Young Man*), Mickey Cottrell (*Hammy Alien*), Christopher George Simpson (*Organist*).

TAGLINE: Movies were his passion. Women were his inspiration. Angora sweaters were his weakness.

TITLE SEQUENCE: The Touchstone logo appears, looking rather odd in monochrome. Suddenly a lightning bolt crackles from one side of the screen to the other, striking the circle at the end of the logo. Then we're straight into a pre-credits sequence, a pastiche of the opening of Wood's own *Bride of the Monster* (1953), his only picture to make money during his lifetime. The camera moves slowly up to a large, wooden house. Going in we see a coffin by a set of French windows. It opens from the inside, and a man sits up. It's Criswell who intones the following extraordinary monologue: 'Greetings, my friends. You are interested in the unknown, the mysterious, the unexplainable . . . now, for the first time, we are giving you all the evidence, based only on the secret testimony of the miserable souls who survived this terrifying ordeal. Can your hearts stand the shocking facts of the true story of Edward D Wood Jr?'

Criswell then closes his coffin, and the camera zooms out of the window behind it and through a graveyard in a sequence evocative of the (still) beginning of *Plan 9 From Outer Space*. We are then shown several Woodian moments, including an appearance by *Plan 9*'s saucers and a killer octopus which appears as both a stop motion maquette and in stock footage actually used by Wood himself. We finish with a long pan across a stylised Hollywood sky.

For the end of this sequence, Production Designer Tom Duffield had the crew build a model of Hollywood including a replica of the famous sign, and numerous recognisable buildings such as the Griffith Park Observatory. It wasn't, however, an accurate or even to-scale representation of the Tinseltown of the period, or indeed any period, as Duffield realised that 'All the landmarks and icons of Hollywood that we wanted in the shot were too far apart.' Instead, 'I just compressed them into one or two blocks, so you see the Max Factor building, you see the old Warner cinema, all the old Hollywood icon buildings, and they're all squeezed together, because I wanted to get more into that one shot. The old Warner building had these big antennae on them in the old photographs and I thought those would be great goalposts to bring the camera through, so that's what we did – we came over the Hollywood sign, across all the buildings, and through those antennae, and down the side of that, and then it blended into the side of the theatre at the bottom.' There were also stylistic, as well as geographical concerns when it came to the sequence, as special effects man Paul Boyington explains: 'We very much tried to copy the Woodian style by using cardboard cut-outs, Christmas tree lights, wood miniatures and windows that were just holes cut in the side of buildings [and] all done on a totally incongruent scale. Ed Wood was a practical filmmaker who worked with whatever he had at hand.'[1]

SUMMARY: Studio flunkey Edward D Wood Jr spots an ad in *Variety*, announcing the production of a feature film entitled *I Changed My Sex* and calls the producer, George Weiss, to request a meeting.

Once in Weiss's office, Wood informs the producer that he's a transvestite and has been for as long as he can remember.

Later Ed has a chance encounter with actor Bela Lugosi. Lugosi misses his bus, and Ed offers to drive him home. By the end of the journey the two men have established a rapport.

Returning to Weiss's office Ed tells him that he can get him a star for his picture. Although Weiss is surprised that Lugosi is still alive, he ultimately agrees to Wood shooting his picture, providing he can bring it in on time and within budget. Lugosi works one day, playing a God-like figure, and is paid $1,000.

Ed sets out to make another film, also to star Lugosi: *Bride of the Atom*, an atomic age SF horror picture. A round of funding parties begin, during which Ed's circle acquires a new round of misfits, including wrestler Tor Johnson, TV hostess Vampira and fake psychic mystic Criswell. Eventually, thanks to a local meat baron, Ed is able to get *Bride* completed but, as soon as he does, his loyal girlfriend Dolores leaves him. She was only staying with him until the end of the picture. She's sick of his constant fantasy world, and his esoteric friends.

After a suicide attempt, Bela commits himself into a local sanatorium, hoping he can receive help for his decades-long morphine addiction, acquired after the narcotic was prescribed to ease the pain of a war wound. Bela's health improves, but he is soon asked to leave the hospital because he cannot afford to pay for his treatment. Once on the outside Lugosi's health seems to improve a little, but all he wants to do is work. Wood sets up a camera and shoots a small amount of silent footage with the actor, ostensibly to form the basis of a new picture, but largely it seems to keep the old man happy.

Ed meets a girl called Kathy. They get on so well that he tells her about his transvestism on their first date. After a few moments' consideration she says she has no problem with Ed's hobby, and after this the relationship seems to go from strength to strength.

At home Ed receives a phone call telling him that Bela has died. After his funeral Ed sets about making a picture to feature Bela's last film footage – a science fiction epic concerning alien attempts to invade planet Earth. With financial backing from a local church, which hopes to use *Plan 9 From Outer Space* to finance a series of films on the lives of Jesus' apostles, Ed manages to begin making his film. Unfortunately the local churchmen try to interfere with Ed's 'vision' for the picture, and one afternoon during shooting, he cracks. Walking out he hails a cab and demands the driver take him to the nearest bar.

In the bar Wood is astonished to meet Orson Welles, who is himself depressed because of production problems with the studio over his own *A Touch of Evil*. Welles instantly treats the other director with courtesy and professional respect despite the fact that he's dressed entirely in women's clothing and the moment is a turning point for Ed. He returns to the lot and tells his backers that they cannot expect him to compromise his vision – they will simply have to sit back and let him make his movie.

The first night of *Plan 9* seems to go well, with the audience applauding the title cards. Confident of his picture's success Ed quietly states that this is the movie he'll be remembered for. Outside the theatre, he and Kathy climb into his convertible and head off to Las Vegas to get married.

SOURCE MATERIAL: This is a biopic – the life and works of Edward D Wood Jr are the source. Burton had long been acquainted with the filmmaker's much maligned *oeuvre*: 'I was about ten years old when I first saw *Plan 9 From Outer Space* on television; some of the action takes place at the airport and the cemetery in Burbank, right near where I lived then.'[2] He has even risen to Wood's defence when it has been suggested that his movies are 'so bad that they're good' or that the writer/director/ star of *Glen or Glenda* deserves his often used epitaph of 'The worst director of all time'. 'The film didn't strike me as bad . . . it had great presence . . . personality. It wasn't until much later that I saw [Wood's other movies] and although those films don't have similar settings you can see in them the marks of a very personal universe.'[3] Furthermore, defending the filmmaker's unique style Burton has stated, 'I've always felt that if anybody shows a style and their own belief, then it's not a bad movie.'[4]

Burton has drawn parallels between Wood's suburban upbringing and his own, and others have pointed to Wood's friendship with faded horror legend Bela Lugosi, and Burton's own collaborations with the equally legendary, but less faded, Vincent Price. Filmmaker Michael Lehmann, director of *Heathers*, summed up Burton's feelings on Wood perhaps more concisely than Burton himself ever has, 'It's amazing to me that Tim, with his sensibility, has been so successful in Hollywood, because he could just as easily have ended up like Ed Wood.'[5] Even before Burton's professional directorial career began, he had produced a number of surreal, low-budget films like those Wood produced, including 1980's *Doctor of Doom*, and especially *Luau*, with its mixture of filmmaking techniques, poor (but funny) dialogue, frequent use of stock footage, cheap sets, and location work filmed on the sly.

This makes it all the more surprising that the impetus for *Ed Wood* came not from Burton, but from screenwriters Scott Alexander and Larry Karaszewski. The two were also aware of Wood thanks to the Golden Turkey Awards of the late 1970s. Alexander says, 'The Medved brothers can really take the credit for putting [Ed] on the map, by electing him worst director of all time at their Golden Turkey awards. I guess I became aware of him when they put together a sort of travelling dog and pony show with *Glen or Glenda*, *Bride of the Monster* and *Plan 9*. They toured the revival houses with this triple feature, and then they'd go on stage in between the films and make fun of Ed Wood and point out all the mistakes in the movies, and everyone in the audience would laugh and hoot and sneer at Ed – that was basically the tone of things.'

Scott Alexander first started developing the idea of a film about Ed Wood in the early 1980s when he and Karaszewski were at the University of Southern California Film School together, writing and budgeting a hypothetical proposal for a documentary feature about Wood as a class project.

Alexander recalls that 'My film was going to be called *The Man in the Angora Sweater*, a sort of fake film project I did in my sophomore year at USC. This would have been in 1982. It was a class on putting together proposals to get grants for movies. You'd put together a fraudulent film proposal with fraudulent material. So mine was *The Man in the Angora Sweater* – I just found Ed Wood so interesting, and there was really absolutely nothing on him at that time, so I made up this presentation with fake letters to and from Vampira and Lyle Talbot, saying they would be delighted to cooperate with my production and please stay in touch, and they have fond memories of working with Mr Wood. It was all pretty nonsensical. I don't think anybody in the class, including the teacher, knew who Lyle Talbot was.'

As the 80s progressed the pair moved into screenwriting together, initiating the John Ritter-starring series of *Problem Child*. Alexander again: 'We wrote a couple of scripts, and our second script became the movie *Problem Child*. We set out to write this sophisticated black comedy about raising children, and it turned out to be this junky kid comedy ... We kind of got type-cast writing kiddie films after that.'

Despite their commercial success, albeit with material that they were unhappy with ('We knew it was a miserable piece of dreck,' Karaszewski says. 'Scott cried at the cast-and-crew screening.'[6]) the Ed Wood biopic remained a cherished potential project for both of them. Karaszewski again: 'We'd got to kind of a stalemate in our careers and we couldn't really get work, and we started talking about Ed Wood again – talking about Ed Wood sympathetically, because we had a very different take on him than everyone else in the world. Whenever we hated our lives we'd say, "We really should write that Ed Wood movie."'[7]

The release in 1992 of Rudolph Gray's biography/memoir *Nightmare of Ecstasy – The Life and Art of Edward D Wood Jr*, made the idea of a Wood biopic less of a pipe dream. 'We started talking about Ed Wood hypothetically, saying well, gee, he directed six feature films, and that's more than most people who come to Hollywood to break into movies, and he had a pretty good time doing it, and he made a lot of friends, and you know, maybe his life had value, maybe he was worth something,' Alexander elaborates. 'So we said, what if you treat Ed Wood sympathetically, would that be an interesting movie? That was sort of where we were coming from.' They approached director Michael Lehmann, who had been a friend of both of theirs at film school, about the project. He had just finished the critically derided *Hudson Hawk* (1991) and wanted to work on something smaller. Alexander and Karaszewski 'thought it was kind of funny that the three of us would team up and make a movie about the "Worst Director of All Time". We could talk from experience, so to speak.'[7] Michael Lehmann also felt that 'Part of the joke with Scott and Larry was: "Wouldn't it be funny for the guys who wrote *Problem Child* and the guy who made *Hudson Hawk* to make a movie about Ed Wood, because our movies had *also* been called the worst movies of all time." '[8] Scott Alexander picks up the story: 'We had done a treatment, and we were looking at this as a super-low-budget movie that we would just go off and make as an art film.' Larry Karaszewski: 'Michael had made a couple of movies that were just two or three million dollars, and we thought it would be on that kind of scale.'

Lehmann gave Alexander and Karaszewski's ten-page treatment, plus a copy of *Nightmare of Ecstasy* to Producer Denise Di Novi (who had overseen his own *Heathers*). Scott Alexander elaborates: 'Denise Di Novi had gone on to be Tim's producing partner, and Michael got the idea that if we got Tim Burton to put his name on the project, like "Tim Burton Presents" or something, it would make it easier to find the funding. Then Tim read our treatment and totally flipped out over it and got extremely passionate. Tim said if he read a script, and liked it, he'd make it. So we did an incredible rush job and wrote it in six weeks ... we turned in 147 pages on 20 November 1992. We hadn't even had the time to cut it down. And on the following Monday Tim called and said, "Let's go make the movie." And we said, "What about rewrites?" Because we never thought that the 147-page draft would be the shooting script. And Tim responded, "I have no notes."'

Seeing Burton's enthusiasm for the project, and having received an alternative offer to helm *Airheads* (1994), Lehmann bowed out as director, first making the stipulation that Burton did it as his very next film. For the work he had done Lehmann received an executive producer credit. As a consequence Burton jumped ship from Columbia/Sony's *Mary Reilly* (a retelling of Robert Louis Stevenson's *Jekyll and Hyde* told from the perspective of Jekyll's maid), which after some delay went to British director and *Comic Strip Presents* alumnus Stephen Frears.

The onscreen credits for *Ed Wood* have the script as being adapted from Gray's *Nightmare of Ecstasy*, but whilst Alexander and Karaszewski freely admit to having used it, the book's anecdotal and self-contradictory nature make it almost worse than useless as a relation of a linear sequence-of-events. According to Burton, 'Nightmare of Ecstasy has a very Rashomon-style of explaining what happened. Everyone has a different story,'[9] or as Karaszewski put it, 'whose version do you believe? As writers we were baffled at all times, because all these stories change and twist around. We just picked the version that helped tell our story.'[10]

Burton, who had a substantial connection to Wood and his work, already felt a still greater affinity with the source material as presented in Gray's book: 'It reminds me of my own memory, which is somewhat revisionist and foggy. I can definitely relate to that kind of denial and reinvention. I get the impression, and I don't mean this disrespectfully, because I feel this way myself, that everybody [in Nightmare of Ecstasy] is a little out of it.'[11]

CASTING: Heading up the cast was Johnny Depp – given Depp's much stated position as Burton's onscreen alter ego, and the director's own identification with Ed Wood, there could never really be any other choice.

Although the writers had initially suggested both Max Von Sydow and British theatrical giant John Neville for the role of Bela Lugosi, for Burton the shortlist consisted of one name – Martin Landau. Landau had attended Lee Strasberg's Actors' Studio, the much celebrated home of Method acting during the 50s, gaining one of just two places available to the 2,000 applicants that year. The other went to a young man called Steve McQueen.

Landau first appeared onscreen in Hitchcock's North by Northwest (1959), and went on to a career that would embrace many projects of varying quality. 'I've led many lives as an actor,' he himself has said. 'I've had somewhat of a rollercoaster career.' For many years he was arguably best known to the public at large for his television work, including several seasons of the original Mission: Impossible, and two years' worth of beautifully produced UK space opera Space 1999. But by the early 90s his movie career had experienced an overdue renaissance, with roles in Francis Ford Coppola's Tucker: The Man and His Dream (1988) and Woody Allen's Crimes and Misdemeanours (1989), both earning him well-deserved Oscar nominations.

'I got a telephone call saying there'd be a script on its way, and that I should check out the part of Bela,' remembers Landau.

'Within half an hour a messenger came to my home with a script. When I read it, I just loved it. I met with Tim shortly after that, and basically he told me that I was his first and only choice, which was very flattering. After I accepted the role I asked him how he came to me, and he said, "Well, you've worked in some wonderful movies, with some great directors and you've worked, in essence, on some films which should be turned into guitar picks." well, he didn't say exactly that, but *I'm* saying that. What he meant was that I've had some career ups and downs, and I was familiar with the vagaries of Hollywood, over then nearly 40 years in films.'

'He's done so much,' enthuses Burton when asked about Landau, 'I think he understands Hollywood [and] so was able to bring a certain amount of experience and feeling to Lugosi.'[12] 'He knows all about the highs and lows of an acting career and I believe he understood emotionally what Bela Lugosi went through. Martin did an incredible transformation – playing a real person, yet somebody who was so weird and out of it at that time of his life.'[13]

Screenwriter Scott Alexander thoroughly approved of the director's choice: 'Tim came up with Landau. He was looking for somebody who he felt had sympathy for the career highs and lows that Bela had. I think really that Tim thought that Martin had worked with Hitchcock, and helped set up the Actor's Studio, and all these other important things, and then by the mid-70s was doing things like *The Harlem Globetrotters on Gilligan's Island*, only to go through a renaissance and make more great movies. Tim thought, Here's a guy who could really feel the inside of Bela's soul.'

'It was a very complicated part, because everybody knows who Bela Lugosi is,' recalls Landau. 'His screen persona is so well known and all of his movies are still out there. Lugosi was probably better known in the mid-90s than he would have been ten, twenty years prior to that time. Then to see a Lugosi film you'd have to stay up late at night or go to some out of the way theatre. Whereas [by 1993] all of Lugosi's films, virtually, could be acquired at any video store.'

Bearing Lugosi's high public profile in mind, Landau undertook 'a lot of research. A lot. When I first talked to Tim I said, "This is a 74-year-old Hungarian alcoholic morphine-addict who has mood-swings – that alone would be hard enough, but he has to be *Bela Lugosi*, an icon, a very, very familiar person." Tim kept sending me Lugosi movies and interviews he did over the years. I watched 35 Lugosi films, and I watched his interviews.'

Of particular interest to the actor were 'the differences between Lugosi on film and Lugosi in life. He didn't do many on-camera interviews – there were four or five of them at different stages in his career. One was from the early 30s, when he was at the top of his game and one of the last ones was the film of him being released from hospital after going through detoxification, and saying formal goodbyes to all the medical staff. In that he's interviewed by a reporter where he says, "I'm going to go to work on a movie with Eddie Wood." At that point very sickly, wizened, very withered and weak-looking. I noticed that his voice was deeper when he wasn't acting, and I used that.' All this preparation was essential for an actor as committed as Landau, who 'wanted to take on his essence. I basically felt that I wanted to be able to juggle or tap-dance like Lugosi, if I was asked. I wanted us to be seamless, I wanted to behave like Lugosi, and to react like Lugosi without any extra thought.'

Landau was keen to capture Lugosi's physicality, feeling it to be essential to portraying, on film, a man known to millions *through* film. 'I began to notice the differences between us. I open my eyes wide when I become emotional, he closed his down. I have a lot of teeth when I smile or grimace, and you never saw his teeth – there was a sort of black hole. My energy goes right to my fingertips, his stopped at his knuckles, so he had a much softer hand than I did . . . he used his hands differently, and he walked differently. I started dealing with all that, so I wanted that to become organic, and not stuck on. I wanted to assume those things, so that I didn't have to think about that.'

Another challenge was the acquisition of Lugosi's Hungarian accent, an accent the actor had himself tried so hard to lose. 'I couldn't find Hungarian dialect tapes, so I bought a bunch of Hungarian language tapes, and began to see where the tongue went. It's a very odd accent. There they are in the middle of Europe, and yet they're not affected by the Romance languages or the Slavic languages. I did my research and discovered the closest accents to Hungarian were Finnish and Turkish, because of historical contacts between the countries. I wanted to have that accent down, then once I got it down, I did something which is a little unusual, which is I tried *not* to have the accent, which is what *he* wanted . . . the only person to pick up on that was Peter Medak, who is Hungarian. He called me after he saw the film, and he said, "Martin, you must be Hungarian!" And I said, "No, no I'm not actually," and he said, "That's the best Hungarian accent I've heard outside of Budapest!" And I said, "Why do you say that?" And he said, "Because you are not an actor trying to do a Hungarian accent, you are a character trying not to!" '

As the first of Wood's two onscreen love interests, Burton cast Sarah Jessica Parker. A TV and stage star since the age of eight, who had played Annie on Broadway at the age of thirteen, Parker had had little difficulty transferring to adult roles; working with Harold Pinter on stage and appearing in movies such as *LA Story* (Mick Jackson, 1991). Playing Dolores Fuller, a recognisably dreadful actress, was an interesting experience for Parker. 'Being deliberately bad is not easy. I watched *Glen or Glenda* a lot, I watched how bad she was over and over again and then in doing it I just didn't comment on it. She was totally self-conscious, totally uncomfortable in front of the camera, totally tight and not creative at all; nothing instinctual about her. It was great fun, I have to say.'[14] Parker's own performance is fantastic – after over 50 episodes of *Sex and the City* it should be difficult to think of Parker as anyone other than Carrie Bradshaw, yet every movement, word and glance is utterly divorced from Parker's later multiple Golden Globe-winning TV role.

The part of Kathy Wood went to Patricia of the immense Arquette clan.

Landau's actress daughter Juliet, later to find fame as calmly evil Vampirette Drusilla in TV's hugely successful *Buffy the Vampire Slayer* and its spin-off series *Angel*, gained the relatively small role of actress Loretta King.

Finally, the part of Wood confidant and wannabe transsexual Bunny Beckenbridge went to *Saturday Night Live* legend and *Ghostbusters* (Ivan Reitman, 1984) star Bill Murray (who was at one point mooted for the role of Batman).

PRODUCTION: Setting about the film, Burton described his feelings on approaching a biopic, a genre for which he normally had little enthusiasm, because of the need to stick close to the facts: 'Ed Wood died without an obituary. Nobody knew him from nothing! That allowed us a certain amount of freedom in telling the story.' For Burton the object of the exercise was 'to do it in the spirit of Ed Wood. We're not making fun of him, because I love all of these characters. There's a beauty to them and a passion.'[15] 'When I read Ed Wood's letters, I was very taken with how he perceived himself. He wrote about his films as if he was making *Citizen Kane* . . . however good or bad Ed Wood's films were, the fact is that he did what he did with a passion that is lacking in a lot of people in America.'[16]

Before production could begin, Burton had a major obstacle to overcome. He had decided to shoot *Ed Wood* in black and white. This commercially disadvantageous decision had not been taken lightly. Not wanting his picture to appear pretentious, or be considered 'an art film', Burton was torn between his filmic and commercial instincts. Eventually he went with monochrome for a number of reasons, as Scott Alexander explains: 'It really was a decision made by Tim. We were doing makeup tests on Martin Landau, and basically he looked great, but there always seemed to be something wrong. We were looking at him on the video, and saying, "This piece looks good, that piece looks good, when he turns his eyes this way he looks like him," and Tim walked over to the television set and turned off the colour, and all of a sudden it just popped, and we all realised that we'd never seen a colour photograph of Bela Lugosi. I think from pretty much that moment on, Tim was determined to shoot in black and white.'

Leaving aside that Lugosi had never made a colour picture, Wood's own films were in black and white. This made Burton reluctant to recreate their production in full colour. Then there were Burton's own preferences. 'Any period movie I see,' he later said, 'especially period movies that take place in Hollywood, I just don't like the way they look in colour.'[17] Both of the project's screenwriters agreed with Burton's instincts. Larry Karaszewski said, 'Aesthetically it was an amazing, amazing decision – I think that we're all happy that we're some of the few people who have managed to make a black and white film in the modern Hollywood era.' Scott Alexander concurs: 'Tim did take our pulse on it – kind of like, "Hey guys, I've got a sort of a funny idea, I'm thinking about maybe, what would you think if I shot the movie in black and white?" We always knew that it would be artistically great, and that commercially it would be a problem, because it's a weird movie. The story is about a transvestite and Dracula. It's got a strange subject matter, it's got a crazy cast, it's got a weird look, and then you put it in black and white – I mean, I don't know a studio that even wants to buy *commercials* for a black and white movie, it would just scare people. It would make a strange film look stranger. But it probably made it more memorable. At the end of the day, it's cool that we got to make a black and white movie.'

This combination of enthusiasm and intelligent reasoning didn't wash with Columbia, the studio that had green-lit the project. The studio claimed it couldn't sell a black-and-white picture in ancillary markets such as other countries (unconvincing) and video (plausible). As a bizarre compromise, it was suggested that Burton shoot in black and white on colour stock. 'I went through that ten years ago on *Frankenweenie*,' Burton said later. 'It looks like shit. If you're going to make a decision, make a decision. You don't hedge it. There's enough of that.'[18] When Burton turned down this compromise Columbia withdrew from the project. 'I'll never forget these meetings . . . They're sitting talking to me about my black-and-white movie that hardly costs anything.' He was told that people didn't go to see black-and-white movies, and that certain things were *too* weird. 'Who can predict? I can't predict. I don't pretend to. You only go by what you think. I like to deal with people that accept the fact that it's not a science.'[19]

With no funding for the picture available, the situation looked bleak, but help was at hand in the form of an unlikely saviour – the Disney Company.

'I felt a little like Ed Wood,' commented Burton. 'It was a weird time, trying to get the movie made, and I felt like I was in some sort of weird parallel universe in a way, because the only people who would do my projects were at Disney . . . they were really into it, and they got the whole issue of how I wanted to do it. It's just a little strange.'[20]

Martin Landau recalls being told that it had been decided that the picture should be made in black and white: 'I was sitting at home with a couple of Polaroids of me with the makeup, and I looked at them and then I ran them though my fax machine, and they came out black and white. I said to myself, "My God, I look so much more like Lugosi in black and white," then the phone rang, and it was Tim. He said, "Martin, I've run into a snag, we're not going to start production for another month, is that a problem for you?" And I said, "Why?" And he said, "Well, Columbia doesn't want to do the picture in black and white, which I want to do." And I had literally just gone through that same thought process, and I hadn't yet told Tim that this picture should be made in black and white. I said "Yes!" very quickly at that point, because I felt that Tim and I were virtually on the same path. What he said basically was that Disney were willing to do it in black and white, and that we were going over there, but it would take at least another month before we could get started because of the change in studio. I was really happy about it – I mean, whoever saw Lugosi in a colour film?'

It has been speculated that the Disney Corporation's interest in *Ed Wood* was not solely because they 'got' the nature of the project. Simply it appears that having let the now superstar director slip through their fingers once, they were keen to get him back permanently. Negotiations did go on during production, both about possible future movies and, it has been suggested, the use of Burton-originated characters at the company's various theme parks. Eventually Burton would decide to return to Warners, in many ways his spiritual home, for his next project. (Because of this, it has further been suggested that the prominence of the old Warner Brothers movie theatre in the opening sequence was a deliberate dig by Burton at Disney. Production Designer Tom Duffield, who was in charge of the sequence, refutes this utterly – the Warner theatre was simply a recognisable period landmark: 'It wasn't anything deliberate; there were no ulterior motives. That's what was there – there were a lot of people still around who would remember what that place looked like. I wanted people who would remember those towers and the Warners sign to say, "Yeah, yeah – I remember that!" ')

Once shooting of the 72-day schedule was underway there were other problems to overcome. Original Production Designer Richard Hoover, who had designed some sets, and picked some locations, left the project. He and Burton may have clashed over his recreation of the monologue shot from *Plan 9 From Outer Space* featuring Jeffrey Jones as Criswell. Hoover's set apparently had only six points of light behind Jones, whereas in Wood's film Criswell had seven. Remembering this sequence Scott Alexander recalls, 'That particular recreation was absurdly literal. In *Plan 9* there's a bump in the dolly shot up to Criswell's face, and Tim insisted that they put a bump in exactly the same place. The timing had to be identical. Recreating incompetence can be very difficult.' In Hoover's place Burton appointed Tom Duffield, with whom he had worked on several previous occasions.

Duffield remembers 'I had to take a running leap at it. I had to come up to speed in a matter of a week or two, as opposed to months.' This late start wasn't as much of a problem as might be expected though, as Duffield explains: 'I'd been lucky enough to work with Tim several times before as Art Director. I'd learned a lot about Tim as we came through *Beetlejuice*, *Edward Scissorhands* and *Batman Returns*, so on *Ed Wood* I was familiar with his vocabulary, his image vocabulary, it made it a lot easier.'

Duffield was delighted when informed that the picture was being shot in black and white. 'I thought that was cool. Some of my favourite movies are black and white, so I knew going in what problems were going to be involved with black and white filmmaking. I had to make some quick decisions: do I make the sets in greys or do I do the sets in colour? I thought about it for a long time, and researched into how it was done in the past, and my decision was I wanted to do the sets in colour, but I had a black and white Polaroid camera on my hip 24 hours a day. Whenever we'd pick colours and samples and paint I'd take some black and white pictures of it, because contrast is *everything* in black and white. So every decision was made with my black and white camera. For the actors, I just felt it was better for them to come into a set that looked cool, not just black and white. Also it gave a little better tonal control for me, because colours can go anywhere – greys you know what you're getting pretty much straight off the bat. Sometimes the camera helps you along with the colours. The only colour you had to be careful of was red – I used no red in the movie, because you don't know with black and white film if it's gonna go dark or light – depending on the film it can go either way. I saw it as a challenge. I really enjoyed that aspect. I saw it as a black and white movie of a colour reality.'

Duffield also saw no real difficulties with designing for what was arguably Burton's first 'period' film – 'I had all the reference I needed – that's a pretty easy period to refer to. There's a lot of pictures of it, the films are all there, the books, and we talked to people who had stills and stuff, so it was really easy to maintain the look of the movie.' Recreating Wood's own work provided the cast and crew with some of the shoot's most enjoyable moments. 'One of the funniest sets, and it was totally Tim's call, was the one with the guy standing in front of the cockpit of the airplane and they throw it together in about ten seconds. We had a picture of the original set, and we thought it would be really cool to have them build the sets there – they're just standing there talking, and in two seconds, all of a sudden the set's there – shunt in, drop the curtain, throw in the chairs, and it was done. That was one of my favourite moments.'

On one occasion Kathy Wood, the director's widow, visited the lot, and was introduced to many of the cast. 'Johnny was nervous,' remembers Patricia Arquette, 'but she loved Johnny. She gave him Eddie's wallet with his phone book and everything.'[21] 'I don't know what prompted me to do it,' said Kathy later, 'but I just felt Eddie would have wanted that.'[22] It wasn't just Depp Mrs Wood was impressed with. Flattered at being portrayed by an actress as accomplished and attractive as Patricia Arquette she also presented her with a gift, a zirconia ring Ed had given to her.

BURTON REGULARS: Lisa Marie appeared in Burton's next three films: *Mars Attacks!*, *Sleepy Hollow* and *Planet of the Apes*. Martin Landau appeared in a dialogue-free, uncredited cameo at the very start of *Sleepy Hollow*, as the hapless Peter Van Garrett.

A number of the cast and crew returned for *Mars Attacks!* These include Sarah Jessica Parker, Scott Alexander and Larry Karaszewski (who did some unaccredited script work on the project), Vinny Argiro, Tommy Bush, Rance Howard, Michelle Skoby (Colleen Atwood's assistant), and Illustrator James Carson.

Rick Baker's next outing with Burton was to design all the monkey makeup for *Planet of the Apes*.

CRITICS: The press were generally favourable to this decidedly non-commercial project, as the numerous critics' awards and nominations the project received testify (see **AWARDS**). *Films in Review* concluded that '*Ed Wood* is one of the best-conceived, most entertaining movies in many a year ... Martin Landau is unforgettable'[23]; *Rolling Stone* that 'In a career that spans five decades, these are Landau's finest two hours on screen.'[24] His Oscar came as little surprise to (almost) anyone who had seen the film.

Of the few dissenting voices, some singled out Johnny Depp's deliciously over-the-top performance for scorn, with one reviewer churlishly suggesting that 'The only misfire ... is Depp ... he tends to throw his head back and deliver his lines with an ironic, eager-beaver snap. He seems to be doing a Jon Lovitz impersonation.'[25] Kim Newman, writing in the British *Sight and Sound* (with the benefit of knowing the film's reception on its earlier release in the States), disagreed – praising Depp's 'hyperactive monomania and peculiar high voice'[26] at some length. Most other reviewers agreed.

One disappointed critic felt that 'Ed Wood, for all its charm, is ample proof that Burton can't shape a story to any real dramatic purpose.'[27] Again, Newman countered, stating instead that the film was 'Burton's most successful piece of proper storytelling.'[28] *Films in Review* rather more wordily agreed that 'Burton, Alexander and Karaszewski ... have brilliantly recreated a significant but largely undiscussed period in American life ... *Ed Wood* is an artistic triumph because it replicates the tone, look and emotions of the cultural players of that time without creating a false hindsight sensibility. Wood, a true artistic primitive, was voted the Worst Director of All Time, Tim Burton may become one of our finest.'[29]

Newsweek too was overwhelmingly positive, praising the movie as 'a valentine to the tenacious spirit of an artist who will do anything to see his vision realised on screen.'[30] Ultimately most critics were in enthusiastic agreement with *Rolling Stone*'s analysis of the picture as 'Burton's most ... provocative movie to date ... outrageously entertaining, the picture stands as a successful outsider's tribute to a failed kindred spirit.'[31]

MUSIC: *Ed Wood* was the first Tim Burton feature without a Danny Elfman score. At the time Burton was, understandably, somewhat disingenuous about his recent split with Elfman: 'I think Danny just got tired of working with me. He wanted to do other things maybe. I don't really know.'[32] Although a full explanation of their creative break-up has never been offered by Elfman or Burton, both men, entirely fairly, seeing it as nobody's business but their own, a more complex picture would emerge following the duo's decision to work together again. (see **Mars Attacks!**)

Howard Shore's lavish and often romantic-sounding score is very different from anything Elfman has produced, being more in the vein of the sweeping melodies of black and white romances than Elfman's (undeniably brilliant) moody, frequently waltz-time contributions to Burton films of this period. It is also very different to Shore's own work for director David Cronenberg, with whom he has shared a relationship similar to that of Burton and Elfman since *The Brood* (1979), and to his rousing, heroic work on Peter Jackson's *The Fellowship of the Ring* (2001). Shore occasionally makes use of the melodies of stock music from Ed Wood's own movies, most noticeably in his effective appropriation of the 'love theme' from *Glen or Glenda* to score the escalating romance between Ed and his future wife, Kathy.

CINEMATOGRAPHY: Director of Photography Stefan Czapsky leapt at the opportunity of being responsible for a black and white film. Scott Alexander confirms this: 'Stefan said something to the effect that he realised that this was probably the only time in his lifetime that a studio would let him make a movie in black and white. He knew this was a privileged position to be in. He took hours lighting every little detail of the scenes.'

'I wanted to get a crisp high-contrast look,' states Czapsky, 'like in *A Touch of Evil* (Orson Welles, 1958) or *The Third Man* (Carol Reed, 1949). It was great trying to combine great photography with crummy photography and make it fit together in one homogenous movie.'[33] Czapsky and Burton may also have been influenced by the look of *The Bad and the Beautiful* (Vincente Minnelli, 1952), the seminal story of Hollywood production politics, made at around the time Wood was himself working.

One of the reasons *Ed Wood* looks so beautiful is that it is genuinely a black and white movie, one designed and lit for monochrome and then shot in black and white for purely artistic reasons. Shot on actual black and white stock, rather than in black and white on colour stock, and then processed at monochromatic specialists DuArt Labs in New York (responsible for, amongst other things, printing Woody Allen's black and white movies), it looks splendid. Rich, inky blacks with silvery highlights dominate the non-filmmaking scenes, especially those involving Bela Lugosi. Sympathetic lighting picks out long shadows without ever dispelling the illusion of Hollywood weather. 'Stefan shot it *beautifully*,' enthused Tom Duffield, years later. Watching *Ed Wood* you begin to realise how Burton's suggested *Beetlejuice* sequel, a pseudo-expressionist surfer movie, would work.

Aside from the pleasures of shooting in black and white, there were other challenges unique to *Ed Wood* that needed to be dealt with by the camera crew. That Landau, and briefly Vincent D'Onofrio, would be required to recreate cinematic icons on screen presented its own problems. Larry Karaszewski felt: 'It was sort of fun when we were doing the make-up tests with Landau – as you'd watch him turning his head from side to side he would go in and out of Lugosi. And we'd watch him and it'd be like, "He looks like Lugosi, he looks like Lugosi – oh! He doesn't look like Lugosi – oh! He looks like Lugosi again." Tim became very aware that there were key angles that worked. If you watch the movie, the camera tends to stay full frontal.' In fact, Rick Baker, who designed Lugosi's makeup, even gave Burton a list of angles from which he felt it was advisable to shoot.

The film's conceptual finale, in which Wood meets his idol, Orson Welles, presented similar shooting problems. Scott Alexander recalls that director Burton was 'afraid of that scene, really, because we had to recreate Orson Welles spot on. I mean, it's one thing to recreate Criswell and Paul Marco, but when you're recreating an icon, and just casually tossing him into a scene late in a movie, that's asking a lot of the casting. I remember Tim really worrying, because basically there were two shots on Vincent D'Onofrio, and one angle worked and one angle didn't. On the close-up he thought it looked spot-on perfect, but in the wide shot he did not think it worked. The first half of the scene was only covered on the wide shot – Tim was so worried about the audience believing that this was really Orson Welles that he was going to cut out the first half of the scene, just so he wouldn't have to linger on the shot where the actor's resemblance wasn't perfect. Whereas I felt, that it was a good scene, and that the audience would forgive us if it's not exactly a doppelgänger!'

DELETED SCENES: A few sequences contained in Alexander and Karaszewski's original draft were trimmed before filming began, and a small number of scenes were shot but not included in the finished film. Scott Alexander confirms this: 'there was a section where Ed had basically a quickie marriage, a rebound marriage after Dolores Fuller. The only other revising we did was to accommodate Bill Murray's schedule.' Karaszewski says, 'A few pages got ripped out during production. I think when they got behind schedule one week some things got yanked. Alexander continues: 'Of the scenes that got shot, the poor DVD guys just spent a month, a very fruitless month looking through the Disney vault for cut scenes, and they couldn't find them. There was a sequence with Bill Murray singing "Que Sera Sera" with the

Mexican mariachis, which was a real crack up. There was a scene with Ed and Dolores moving into their apartment, and then there was a scene with her throwing him out of the apartment, and he's lying there sort of dishevelled and drunk in the alley, and she's yelling at him "Get out of here!" He ends up moving into Bela's, and there's a sequence of him at Bela's house, and he's sleeping over, and Bela talking about his faded dreams from when he was in Hungary, and he's unsure whether he can ever go back. They were all sort of pretty nice, really personal things that were all in the middle of the film.'

DEATH: Lugosi's death is beautifully and tastefully handled. It occurs off-screen immediately after one of Landau's most bravura scenes, in which he repeats his final speech from *Bride of the Monster* on a street corner to a crowd of admirers. Ed is at home, reading to Kathy, when the phone rings. We don't hear what is said to him – Depp's face does all the work. The succeeding scenes showing Bela's funeral are silent, carried only by the music. In a horrid case of life imitating art, Burton's own 'Lugosi' – Vincent Price – died during production of the movie, before Burton and his crew had shot these funeral scenes, making them an intense experience for all concerned.

CHILDREN AND FAMILIES: With their insular quality and unquestionable loyalty to each other, the idea appears to be that Wood's group form a family unit, protecting each other from the world. The only children that turn up are the trick or treating Halloweeners, whom Lugosi takes great delight in giving candy to, and frightening with his Dracula cape.

CLOWNS AND THE CIRCUS: Ed and Kathy go to a funfair on their first date, a sequence visually reminiscent of elements of Orson Welles' compromised *The Lady From Shanghai* (1948). It is while riding on a Ghost Train at the fair that Ed tells Kathy of his transvestism. One of the 'scary' things in this Spook House are skeletal arms reaching from the walls, just like in little Vincent Molloy's nightmarish fantasies in *Vincent*.

DOGS: Lugosi has a number of dogs, which he refers to alternatively as 'children of the night' (a line from *Dracula*) and his 'darlings'. After Bela's death Ed seems to inherit his army of mutts. Whilst this did happen in reality, Bela's dogs weren't the chihuahuas as seen in the film, but a Doberman (named Dracula after his most famous role) and a white German Shepherd called Bodri. The substitution was presumably made because of Burton's own fondness for chihuahuas.

LOVE TRIANGLES: Wood's own *Glen or Glenda* makes a great deal of play out of the idea of the two sides of its transvestite hero's personality forming a love triangle with the woman that he loves, but *Ed Wood* largely ignores this interpretation – quite sensibly given how heavy-handed and overdone it is in Wood's own film. Ed and Bela both admire Vampira from afar, but that's about it.

CHECKS, STRIPES, DOTS: Very few. There's a black and white striped Arabian-style tent in the background as Ed admires the camels in the Universal studio lot, stripes on the Spook House frontage, spiral 'eyes' on the carriages, and some use of shadowy stripes from Venetian blinds as in *Frankenweenie*.

AUTOBIOGRAPHY?: Many critics referred to *Ed Wood* as Burton's 'most personal film to date',[34] with Burton's unauthorised biographer Ken Hanke going beyond the obvious Bela Lugosi/Vincent Price analogy to draw parallels between Kathy O'Hara and Burton's then girlfriend Lisa Marie. Certainly Burton had an affinity with, and liking for, the work of Ed Wood, but it is important not to push the comparison too far.

Burton has claimed in one instance that Wood, through his work, 'was sort of my psychologist, I always felt like he got me through the abstractions of my early life with those movies. They helped me understand the drama of my life in a sort of abstract, fairy-tale way. For some people John Wayne does it. But that was mine.'[35] He has further stated, 'I understand what Ed went through, and I feel close to it ... I think every filmmaker thinks they're making the greatest film in the world. I know that's the way I feel all the time. That's kind of beautiful and tragic at the same time. Your passion can keep you going, but it can also blind you. You get too caught up in what you're doing ... That was perhaps Ed Wood's biggest flaw. He never realized he wasn't the talented filmmaker he saw himself as.'[36] The link, then, is fairly simple – Burton and Wood can both be seen as directors who believe passionately in their own work, something that can surely be said about any filmmaker worth mentioning.

Yet these connections do not confuse the boundaries between the two men – how could they? They never met, and their careers achieved wildly different degrees of success in Hollywoods separated by over a quarter of a century. Even though Burton has expressed a belief that he could easily have had a career as derided as Wood's own, this has never been the case. Burton's first film – a studio feature – made an enormous amount of money for its investors, and placed the director in an enviable position compared to many similar talents of his age. Wood is not an analogue for Burton, but someone he is interested in, someone he admires. He is not a fiction constructed to act as an avatar for him, but a real man who actually lived.

Furthermore, the apparent parallels between the two men, although partially real, were present in the screenplay as written – a screenplay specifically tailored to the director by the screenwriters. Burton had, after all, expressed an interest in the picture at the outline stage, and it is unsurprising that experienced screenwriters should deliberately create material suitable to be filmed by the projected director. 'As we wrote it, occasionally we would come to things and we would say, "Oh my God, this is a real Tim Burton kind of scene," and we would make it maybe a little more Gothic than really suited the description,' says Scott Alexander. 'And we also knew about Tim's relationship with Vincent Price, and we obviously saw parallels between Ed and Bela.' This deliberate tailoring to parallel aspects of Burton's own life and films evidently worked, as Burton later stated, 'I'd say 50 to 70 percent' of his final decision to direct 'had to do with that.'[37]

Even so, this deliberate approach did not interfere with the writers' own vision for the picture, as Alexander insists: 'All along, our purpose with this movie was to make it a love story between these two guys. When Tim became involved, it just became clearer. You know, it's funny that people consider it Tim's most autobiographical film, and he had nothing to do with the development of the script. It's sort of comical. I mean, we really wanted Tim to make the movie, and we would look at his body of work and say, "Oh, we can walk into the building, and we can put a gargoyle in the architecture . . . " The scene where we were really trying to kiss up to Tim, Tim sort of got back at us by cutting it from the movie, which was funny, was the scene where they're running through the cemetery at night – I can't remember the descriptions from the screenplay, but they're very self-consciously "Burtonesque" descriptions of tombstones and the night air and the moon shining down, and we felt "Oh my God, Tim's going to go crazy over this scene!" I remember I went down to the set that night, and I thought this was going to be a huge set-piece with the two men running through the cemetery, and Lugosi's cape flying in the wind, and – this was going to be a magical set-piece! Tim did, like, two set-ups, and said, "OK, we're done." That's what happens when people try and second-guess Tim, I guess.'

In other words, Burton deliberately avoided certain aspects of the screenplay which he felt echoed too closely those aspects of his work commonly identified by critics and commentators, further expanding the already existing gap between the life and art of Edward D Wood Jr and himself. *Ed Wood* is a film *directed by* Tim Burton, but it is *about* Ed Wood – how could it be anything else?

JUST PLAIN WEIRD: Surprisingly little – although Ed and his friends are not exactly the kind of people you bump into every day, there's no actual surrealism, mad dream sequences, drug-crazed murders or real-life monsters. Unlike in many of Ed's own films.

DIALOGUE TO SKIP BACK FOR:
Bela (on why he's buying a coffin): 'I'm planning on dying soon.'

Ed on Bela: 'He's very much alive . . . well, sort of.'

Bela (on how to do his wobbling hand trick): 'You must be double-jointed and you must be Hungarian.'

Ed: 'What is the one thing if you put it in a movie it'll be successful?'
Weiss: 'Tits.'

Ed is asked if he knows anything about the art of motion pictures, and indignantly replies: 'I like to think so.'

Ed: 'You're the ruler of the galaxy – show a little taste!'

Ed: 'All I want to do is tell stories.'

AFTERLIFE: During and shortly after production Dolores Fuller publicly expressed unhappiness with the portrayal of her in the film. Scott Alexander explained that 'Dolores ran really hot and cold on the movie. We rang her a number of times, and sometimes she'd say, "Oh my God, you made me look terrible," and sometimes she'd say, "Hey, you know what? Today I think the movie's pretty good." Dolores is a smart lady, and she's the savviest person to come out of that group. I think she probably resented the fact that she wasn't consulted up front. She probably would have considered it more respectful if we had called her up before we wrote the movie.' The fact that Dolores is given the line 'You people are insane – you're wasting your lives making shit! These movies are terrible!' – echoing the sentiments of most people who have watched Wood's movies – plus that her success in her future career as a songwriter is mentioned at the end of the film, is a further indication that she was not intended as a figure for ridicule.

Another member of Wood's circle, Maila Nurmi, the erstwhile Vampira, was unimpressed at the film's portrayal of Bela Lugosi as a man who frequently, perhaps excessively, swore – claiming that the real-life Lugosi would never have done such things. Scott Alexander simply felt that Lugosi's repeated cussing 'was funny. And it makes Lugosi charming. I think that comes down to John Andrews, who's an old crony of Ed's, who tells a lot of stories about basically going out and hanging out with Ed and Bela, and I think John Andrews is the person who uses a lot of swear-words. So when he's telling the story he says things like, "So Bela says, 'Fuck you! You get out of my house!'" He's swearing up a storm – the storyteller's swearing, and we interpreted that as Bela swearing.' Larry Karaszewski also counters, 'Some of [Wood's] gang said Bela did swear, but only around the guys. He wouldn't swear around ladies, but he would swear when he was in a bar with four men. We did it because we thought it would be a great character trait to have Bela go off whenever someone mentions Karloff.' This decision led to such delicious lines of dialogue as Lugosi's 'Karloff doesn't deserve to smell my shit!' adding an extra air of humour to a character who could otherwise have ended up simply morose and pathetic. The (occasional) swearing gives Lugosi vigour, and emphasises that despite his misfortunes, he still cares about *something*. Without it he could have ended up appearing simply as a sad old man, well past his prime, something all involved in the film evidently wanted to avoid.

However, Vampira's complaints were a small matter compared to the initial disapproval of Bela Lugosi Jr, who thoroughly objected to the onscreen portrayal of his late father, despite never having seen the picture. Alexander explained that 'Bela Jr said for many years that he read half the script and threw it down in disgust, and then he refused to see the movie. Martin [Landau] kept sending him letters and saying "Come on down, let's meet, let's shake hands, let's watch the movie together." This is probably the closest Lugosi will ever come to a biopic himself, and we fixate on the worst part of his life. I think that was really Bela Jr's problem with it – he justifiably looked at his father as a great man, yet for some reason when people come up to him on the street all they do is talk to him about those lousy drug-addicted five years he was with Ed Wood. It's like somebody making a Chaplin biopic, and the whole movie is about *A Countess From Hong Kong*! (Charles Chaplin, 1967).'

Landau recalls Bela Jr's opposition to the movie, thus: 'He had said some things about it, because although he hadn't seen the movie he had apparently read the script. He was in his early teens when Lugosi died, and said, "My father didn't use profanities, my father didn't have small dogs, my father this, my father that." He took exception to the script. He had been interviewed a number of times and said that he was against the film, and that it was an insult to his father's name and so on.'

Once Bela Jr finally saw the film, his attitude changed utterly, as Landau explains: 'I got a letter delivered to my home on his personal stationary apologising, and asking me to have lunch with him downtown at the Los Angeles Club ... We then became friends, and he basically told me that *Ed Wood* was an homage to his father, that in fact I had dignified his father ... I can understand if one reads the script that it may seem a little harsh, the fact that he was an alcoholic, the fact that he was a morphine addict, the fact that he was down on his luck and used profanity. My intention for the movie was to keep the dignity of the man and the talent of the man, and the humour of the man, and the pathos and sadness and disappointment of the man had to be there. Because I felt this was a love letter not only to Lugosi, but to all actors who've had difficult times over the years. I think he recognised that when he saw the movie.'

Burton's film ultimately led to a raised commercial profile for its eponymous hero, as well as some critical reappraisal of Wood's own pictures (the production of a lavish DVD edition of *Plan 9 From Outer Space* is largely due to this film's critical success), although as yet his heirs have not profited from the renewed interest in his work because of the intricacies of US copyright law.

AWARDS: Martin Landau justifiably won an Academy Award for his startling, poignant, complex portrayal of Bela Lugosi, despite stiff competition from, amongst others, Samuel L Jackson, nominated for his performance in Quentin Tarantino's *Pulp Fiction*. After receiving his statuette Landau intended to pay tribute to the man he had been honoured for portraying, but was interrupted: 'I had got through my entire [thank you] list and then I paused right at the very end, because there was one more person I wanted to thank, and the music started . . . they cut me off, and there was a big brouhaha because of it, and I wanted to thank Bela Lugosi, that was the last "Thank you". I never got to do it on the air.' Later, backstage, Landau made up for the television company's mistake, telling reporters, 'I managed to come back from a career in the doldrums, not much better than the Ed Wood movies. I managed to get out of it, but he [Lugosi] never did. This was for both of us.'[38]

Landau's performance also won, amongst others, Best Actor at the Saturn Awards, Funniest Supporting Actor at the American Comedy Awards, Best Supporting Actor at the Boston Society of Film Critics Awards, the BAFTAs, the Chicago Film Critics Association Awards, the Golden Globes, the Los Angeles Film Critics Association Awards (LAFCA), the National Society of Film Critics Awards, the New York Film Critics Circle Awards (NYFCC), the Southeastern Film Critics Association Awards, and the Screen Actors' Guild Awards.

Scott Alexander and Larry Karaszewski won the Writers Guild of America Award for Best Screenplay Written Directly for the Screen. Rick Baker, Ve Neil and Yolanda Toussieng won both Oscar and BAFTA for Best Makeup. Howard Shore won Best Music at the Saturn Awards and the LAFC Awards, Stefan Czapsky won Best Cinematography at the NYFCC Awards, LAFC Awards, and BFSC Awards. The film was nominated as Best Motion Picture at the 1995 Golden Globes, where Johnny Depp was also nominated for Best Actor – he won the London Film Critics Circle Award for Actor of the Year in 1996, partially in recognition of his work on *Ed Wood*, which was released in the

UK in 1995. The film was also nominated for the Palme D'Or at the 1995 Cannes Film Festival, and won the Silver Condor for Best Foreign Film at the 1996 Argentinean Film Critics Association Awards.

EXPERT WITNESS: Martin Landau: 'I think 90 percent of directing actors is in the casting . . . Tim hardly said anything to me, but all directors work like that. Hitchcock never said a word to you. Woody [Allen] didn't say anything, either. Good directors generally create a playground and let creative actors play. I basically haven't been directed in 25 years, I mean I haven't been given any direction – I come in with stuff, and I figure if they don't like what I'm doing, they'll tell me. Tim really enjoys what he's doing, and there were many times when he would actually ruin a take because he was laughing so loud – the soundman would say "Someone's laughing" and it was Tim. Tim and I have a shorthand. The thing that's amazing is after the first rehearsal of a scene, Tim will come over and say "You know?" and I say "Yeah I do." He doesn't finish a sentence, and I know what he means, because I know what's missing from the rehearsal, and then I'll do it again, and he'll come up and say "Exactly." He'd say "I want this, you know?" I'd say "Yeah, yeah". He'd say "You know, ah . . . you know, ah . . . " I'd say "Right! Right! – Bing! Bing! Bing! Bing! Bing!" And he'd say "Yeah, exactly!" Anyone watching us would think we were talking in Sanskrit or something!'

Tom Duffield: 'Tim is a great visual director, there's no two ways about it. He's great to work with, and he respects the art department. Some directors, they just want to go and shoot this. They're all dialogue – dialogue and action. He's great with the art department – that's almost as key an issue as storytelling. The visual element of the movie is really important to him. Comparing him with Ed Wood, I think the passion is there. Obviously he's much better schooled, he knows much more what to do, he knows much more what he's doing – it's really an unfair comparison. I think really the passion for filmmaking is what links them.'

TRIVIA: Maurice LaMarche (who provided, without credit, the voice of Orson Welles) is best known as the voice of evil genius lab mouse 'Brain' in the 'Pinky and the Brain' segments of the cartoon series *Animaniacs*.

There's no historical precedent for Wood's meeting with Orson Welles, but thematically it reaches to the heart of the movie. Larry Karaszewski explains: 'Basically Scott and I invented the whole meeting with Orson Welles at the end, because we looked at these guys' lives, and we thought that in the same time-period you've got the world's greatest director and the world's worst director, sort of in the exact same spot, and wouldn't it be funny if they just met up?'

ANALYSIS: *Ed Wood* manages to treat an assortment of unusual and insular characters with sympathy and respect, never patronising them or mocking their endeavours. It is a warm and very human tale about people working very hard at something they enjoy and believe in, and achieving results that they are enamoured of, no matter what anyone else may think. In ending on a high note, it avoids its subject's tragic decline – frozen out and perhaps broken by the very system he clearly loved, dying young, unrecognised, and far from a wealthy man.

If *Edward Scissorhands* is fundamentally about an artist misunderstood and rejected, *Ed Wood*, by ending when it docs, seems to be about an artist who is finally granted acceptance in reward for all his dedication, enthusiasm and hard work. It is a beautiful irony that, simply by existing, this film finally grants Wood the acceptance he never achieved. The only sadness is that it should happen posthumously, as his widow pointed out at the time of the film's release: 'All this publicity and fanfare – why didn't it happen before? He would have loved it.'[39]

AVAILABILITY: At the time of writing, *Ed Wood* is unavailable; the VHS has been discontinued in the US, and is very hard to come by in the UK. However, at the time of writing, Touchstone Home Video were planning a comprehensive DVD edition – featuring commentaries and new material – for simultaneous release on both sides of the Atlantic during spring 2002.

THE BOTTOM LINE: A touching, funny, beautifully shot and brilliantly acted tale of the underbelly of Hollywood in Eisenhower's America, *Ed Wood* more than deserved the critical acclaim it received from most circles on its release. The sheer quality of the script is made all the more impressive by the speed with which it was written. Every single line is a gem. It must rank alongside *A Star is Born* (both William Wellman's 1937 original and George Cukor's 1954 remake), *Sullivan's Travels* (Preston Sturges, 1941), *Singin' in the Rain* (Gene Kelley and Stanley Donnen, 1952) and *The Player* (Robert Altman, 1992) as one of the all-time great movies about moviemaking. The film's poor box office showing and lack of subsequent availability is utterly unrepresentative of both its accessibility and its sheer ability to entertain and engage. Hopefully its DVD release will finally allow the public to appreciate it as much as it deserves. *Ed Wood* is Burton at his very best.

MARS ATTACKS! (1997)

Warner Brothers presents
A film by Tim Burton
Written by Jonathan Gems
Director of Photography: Peter Suschitzky
Production Designer: Wynn Thomas
Art Director: John Dexter
Produced by Tim Burton and Larry Franco
Casting by Victoria Thomas, Jeanne McCarthy, Matthew Barry
Music by Danny Elfman
Costumes Designer: Colleen Atwood
Edited by Chris Lebenzoz
Visual Effects Supervisors: Jim Mitchell, Michael Fink, David Andrews
Based upon 'Mars Attacks!' by Topps
Directed by Tim Burton

CAST: Jack Nicholson (*President James Dale/Art Land*), Glenn Close (*First Lady Marsha Dale*), Annette Benning (*Barbara Land*), Pierce Brosnan (*Professor Donald Kessler*), Danny DeVito (*Rude Gambler*), Martin Short (*Press Secretary Jerry Ross*), Sarah Jessica Parker (*Nathalie Lake*), Michael J Fox (*Jason Stone*), Rod Steiger (*General Decker*), Tom Jones (*Himself*), Lukas Haas (*Richie*

Norris), Natalie Portman (*Taffy Dale*), Jim Brown (*Byron Williams*), Lisa Marie (*Martian Girl*), Sylvia Sidney (*Grandma Florence Norris*), Christina Applegate (*Sharona, Billy Glenn's Girl*), Joe Don Baker (*Richie's Dad*), Pam Grier (*Louise Williams*) Paul Winfeld (*General Casey*), Jack Black (*Billy Glenn Norris*), Brian Haley (*Mitch, Secret Service Man*), O-Lan Jones (*Sue Ann Norris*).

TAGLINE: 'Nice planet, we'll take it!'

TRAILER: Trailer one begins with the Warners logo against a pale blue sky, a flying saucer slides out from behind a cloud and across the screen, and we're into clips from the movie. A voice-over announces the presence of 'Alien life!' and goes on to say, 'Once you believe, Once you rise above fear; Then you'll be prepared to meet with a new people – More powerful than the might of America, more advanced than the brains of Britain, but be prepared for a few changes to what we know and love, as we must learn to dance to a new tune'. Slim Whitman's tune, presumably. The voice then tells us that we expect this picture 'From Director Tim Burton' and goes on to list the major stars of the picture, starting with Jack Nicholson and moving in order down the list above.

Trailer two simply has the standard Warners logo, minus the saucer embellishment, and much less voice-over. Many of the same clips are employed, as yellow letters inform us of Tim Burton's involvement, and the main cast are name checked. This time Nicholson is mentioned twice, once for each of his roles.

Danny Elfman specially scored these trailers in a separate session to the recording for the film's own score. Although trailers are usually backed by appropriate-sounding music from the archives (for example, the trailer for *Maverick* (Richard Donner, 1994) was backed with music from the most recent comedy western available, *Back To The Future Part III* (Robert Zemeckis, 1990)), this was simply not good enough in this instance, as Danny Elfman explains that Burton's films are 'very hard to "temp" for previews; the tone is so odd it's hard to nail his stuff. He gets very anxious to get original music. *Edward Scissorhands* is the only other time I've ever scored a trailer. They just couldn't find anything, and the trailers were coming out well before the scoring sessions, so we did a special session.'[1] That this was the case on *Mars Attacks!* is clearly a measure of both Warners' faith in the project and their financial commitment to it.

Both trailers are amusing and appropriate, with exactly the same tone as the picture. They remain, thus far, easily the most effective trailers for any Tim Burton movie.

TITLE SEQUENCE: The classic Warner Brothers logo appears with the cloudy blue sky behind. As distinctively Elfman mood music undulates quietly in the background, a lone, metallic 50s-style flying saucer appears through the clouds, rotating as it wafts from the top right to bottom left corners of the screen. Cut to a farmhouse '4 miles outside Lockjaw, Kentucky, Tuesday, May 9 – 6:57 P.M.,' where a hillbilly farmer (Tommy Bush) is asking his incongruously Filipino neighbour (Chi Hoang Cai) what's cooking on the barbecue. Just as he says he's not cooking anything, an orange glow appears, and a herd of cows, burning alive, run down the road, still mooing – the rarest steaks it's possible to get. As the locals look on in shock, a silvery flying saucer flies up from behind the farmhouse, and we follow it out of the Earth's atmosphere on another trademark Burton title-sequence journey as it heads towards the bright terracotta surface of Mars, where more saucers are rising from the canyons and craters of the planet's crust. The camera follows them as they spin and wobble their way through the gloom of space in triangular formations of eight, the camera rotating round and through them, showing layer upon layer from all different angles, all to Elfman's wavering, retro, theremin-based score, with its hints of wails and screams, until we see Earth surrounded by the Martian fleet, thousands strong. The credits appear over the saucers, first rotating around an invisible sphere, Saturn's rings of text, then drifting into space in 1950s B-movie-style perspective.

SUMMARY: Some Martians attack. A bunch of different people, including the President of the United States, the US Military, a Las Vegas sleaze ball, a hick family, a dumb TV presenter and Welsh entertainer Tom Jones, react to the threat in different ways. Humanity is saved by dumb luck. The chance of reconstruction in any meaningful sense is slim. The End.

SOURCE MATERIAL: Although Burton claimed 'there is not one overriding idea. It really is an amalgam of a bunch of information,'[2] the most obvious direct source, indeed one which was traded on (pun intended) in the pre-publicity, were the infamously graphic Mars Attacks! trading cards.

Produced in 1962, the 55 original *Mars Attacks!* cards were produced by Bubbles Inc (an alternative name for The Topps Company Inc, producers of the ever-popular baseball cards) and included in packets of five cent bubblegum. Based around a story by Woody Gelman and Len Brown where (surprise) Martians attack the Earth, they were inspired by 1950s B-movies, Hugo Gernsback's pulp magazine, *Amazing Stories*, and (for the self-consciously highbrow), 'the early science fiction films of Fritz Lang.'[3] Brown recalled that he and Gelman 'were both fans of science fiction movies, so we decided to do a space invasion series . . . In many ways we were trying to do every science fiction movie cliché: we had big-headed aliens, giant attacking bugs, ray guns and the like. It was *War of the Worlds* all over again.'[4] They were pencilled by Bob Powell (most famous for his work on *The Shadow* comics) and Wally Wood (artist for the first 11 issues of Stan Lee's *Daredevil*) and painted by pulp cover artist Norm Saunders.

The cards' graphic depiction of mutilation and death at the hands of the big-brained invaders and their enormous bug minions (the cards' Martians seemed to have a strange fascination with creating giant creepy-crawlies, from spiders the size of large houses, to skyscraper-sized caterpillars) led to a flurry of complaints by concerned parents and distributors alike. The already small run of cards was rapidly halted, 'perfectly ridiculous censorship'[5] in Burton's view, as, after all, 'I grew up watching things like *The Brain That Wouldn't Die* (Joseph Green, 1962) on Saturday afternoon television. There's a guy with his arm ripped off and his blood smeared all over the wall. I was eight years old while watching this on TV. I never saw it as negative.'[6] and their cult status was assured – complete sets have since been known to fetch as much as $2,000.

After a brief early 80s resurgence of interest in the cards on the back of a comics mini-series, a new series, *Dinosaurs Attack!*, a cash-in/thematic sequel to the original set, appeared in 1988. These again were published by Topps, and written by Brown and Gelman, and this time contained 55 cards plus 11 stickers.

When, in 1994, the original *Mars Attacks!* cards were re-issued along with 45 new cards, another comic book series, and a limited amount of tie-in merchandise, Burton convinced Warners to buy the rights to both series (see **PRODUCTION**). As he later explained, 'I just really liked the spirit of them. They were so beautiful, with stylish painting. They had a great naive quality to them that I liked very much – the luridness of the colors. It was really pure. It wasn't campy. It had a quality I like in most of the movies of the time as well . . . They're graphic, but they're fun.'[7]

REFERENCES: The saucers seem to have been taken not from the cards, but primarily from Fred F Sears' *Earth vs. the Flying Saucers* (1956), the special effects for which were done by Burton's idol, Ray Harryhausen. The Martians' jerky movement was likewise in deliberate imitation of Harryhausen's skeletons in *Jason and the Argonauts* (Don Chaffey, 1963) on Burton's orders, with the added touch of Norma Desmond's big eyes and wild movements in *Sunset Boulevard* (Billy Wilder, 1950), put in by initial designer, Barry Purvis. In addition, much of Pierce Brosnan's dialogue appears to have been lifted from *The Day The Earth Stood Still* (Robert Wise, 1951).

The idea for the Martians to be defeated by the dulcet tones of Slim Whitman may have originally come from a sketch entitled 'Slim Whitman VS The Midget Aliens From Mars,' performed on the WNBC *Howard Stern Show* back in 1982. It has been claimed that when Burton appeared on Stern's show in the early 90s, the sketch was played for the director, who greatly enjoyed it. An alternative possibility is that both Stern and Burton/Gems separately took the notion of attacking monsters being repelled by music from *The Attack of the Killer Tomatoes* (John de Bello, 1978), which is, after all, exactly the sort of low-budget, tongue-in-cheek movie Burton openly delights in. In this scenario the Slim Whitman connection is entirely coincidental.

The interiors of the Martian spaceships were consciously modelled on *Forbidden Planet* (Fred M Wilcox, 1956).

The initial attempts at translating the Martian dialogue come up with, amongst other things (see **DIALOGUE TO SKIP BACK FOR**), 'bodily fluids' – a reference to General Jack D Ripper's (Sterling Hayden) pet obsession in *Dr Strangelove or: How I Learned to Stop Worrying and Love the Bomb* (Stanley Kubrick, 1964). Rod Steiger's General Decker is also based loosely on General Ripper, and the White House's War Room is likewise based on Ken Adam's classic set from Kubrick's movie.

Paul Winfield's careful General Casey is clearly modelled on US General Colin Powell, one of the architects of the Gulf War, and later Secretary of State in the administration of 43rd US President, George W Bush.

PRODUCTION: According to Thomas Lassally, the then Executive Vice-President of production at Warner Brothers, as early as late 1994 Burton 'was talking about doing a series of smaller films – Friday night-date-type movies.'[8] These were the movies Burton loved whilst growing up: 'I lived in a rather sterile environment . . . These films ignited your imagination. Their imagery transported you elsewhere, opened new horizons to you.'[9]

Ed Wood had been something of a commercial disappointment, but it had garnered consistently favourable reviews, and won two Academy Awards. Furthermore, its depth and complexity had raised yet further critical and public opinion of Burton as a filmmaker, *and* it had somehow managed to instigate a minor revival of interest in, and appreciation of, the work of its subject. It sat centre-ground in many critics' 'Top Ten of the year' lists, and most of those moviegoers who saw it came away with the firm opinion that it was Burton's best picture yet.

Despite his in-built hatred of sequels, and his experience of the backlash to *Batman Returns*, it seemed as though Burton wanted his next project to be not a literal, but a thematic sequel to *Ed Wood* – showing what that director might have been aiming to create, given sufficient resources. However, despite knowing the *sort* of film he wanted to do next Burton, it seems, had no solid notion of the plot, screenplay or even subject matter he wanted to accompany his 'feeling'.

Enter Burton's friend, the British screenwriter Jonathan Gems, best known for helping adapt George Orwell's *Nineteen Eighty-Four* for the screen, and who had done some uncredited script work on *Batman*, as well as developing one version of the floundered *Beetlejuice* sequel. Gems had come across the *Mars Attacks!* cards in 'Whacko', a shop on Melrose Avenue in LA in Summer 1994. He bought them, and later showed them to Burton, who instantly fell in love with their 'classic, simple concepts and slightly naive painting style.'[10]

Burton claimed to remember the cards from his childhood anyway, but later admitted, 'Because the cards had come out and gone so quickly, I didn't know if it was a dream or something I made up. After rediscovering them, however, I couldn't get them out of my head.'[11] (Considering he would have been four at the time of the cards' release, and on the West coast, several thousand miles away from where they had their limited retail run, it is unlikely that he would have come across them, although they do seem like exactly the sort of thing the young Burton would have been into.)

Jonathan Gems saw the attraction of combining Burton's idea for a big budget B-movie with these graphic, infamous pieces of cardboard kitsch – 'Here was a chance to do something like *Plan 9 From Outer Space* – with a bit more money of course! We thought that was wonderful.'[12] Burton said later, 'We were able to do stuff that [Wood] wished he could have done ... These kinds of movies are the kind I like, and I remember reading stuff when I was doing *Ed Wood* about how much he was into them. For a lot of people, myself included, they are the inspiration in wanting to do movies.'[13]

This attitude resulted in *Mars Attacks!*, which arguably became the most expensive B-movie ever made, a star-filled alien-packed romp with more production values in its little finger than all the drive-in Friday-night monster movies of the 50s that inspired it put together. In other words, the film ended up exactly as Burton intended: 'I just wanted to capture the spirit of those old 50s alien movies. Part of what was so beautiful about them was the cheese factor. Everything from the aluminium foil spaceships to the little green guys looked so cheesy that they had a certain kind of charm.'[14]

Gems and Burton seemed ideally suited as the project's creative partners. As Gems explained, 'Tim and I had very similar tastes in a lot of things. I grew up with all the same Saturday morning matinees in England. We're both big fans of Herschell Gordon Lewis ... low-budget horror movies – C-features that were very lurid and appealed to very basic instincts.'[15] (Lewis' films typically had titles like *Blood Feast* (1963), *Goldilocks and the Three Bares* (1963), or *The Wizard of Gore* (1970) – letting the audience know exactly what they would be seeing on entering the cinema, not unlike the *Mars Attacks!* cards' title.)

Beginning work, Burton and Gems were initially unaware that the card series actually had a plot of its own. 'Nobody will believe this,' said Gems when interviewed, 'because nobody would think Tim and I were so stupid: there's a story on the back of the cards

– but we never looked on the back! We thought it was just some trading card bullshit. I only found out there was a story much later when someone asked. What inspired us were the images – in that lurid *Analog*-type cover style of pulp science-fiction.'[16]

In the story on the back of the cards the Martians had something they'd managed to lose by the time Burton's *Mars Attacks!* hit theatres – a motive for their invasion of Earth. According to the cards, Mars was about to explode, and so its denizens needed a new planet to inhabit. They are eventually defeated by a full-scale counter-invasion of Mars, and the destruction of the red planet.

Working without the strictures of being faithful to the cards' own plot, Gems and Burton cobbled their story together William S Burroughs style – 'by taking the cards and throwing them on the ground and picking out the ones that we liked,'[17] said Burton. He and Gems 'wanted to make sure we had certain images that we liked in there, not necessarily in the order they were originally presented, but they're in there somewhere.'[18] These seem to have included the following; listed in the approximate order they appear in the film:

- Card #22 (Burning Cattle) is one of the most obvious sources of the lot – the cattle charging past a farmhouse similar to that of the film; there is even a farmer standing in the background watching in horror.
- Card #2 (Martians Approaching) gives one of the best views of the Martians in their space suits, which were adapted very faithfully for the film, right down to the cute red nitrogen tanks.
- Card #19 (Burning Flesh) shows a soldier being disintegrated from the stomach outwards by a Martian ray gun, in exactly the same posture and with the same look of shock as General Casey when this happens to him.
- Card #21 (Prize Captive) is the most obvious source for Nathalie's abduction, as a leering Martian molests a screaming blonde.
- Card #5 (Washington in Flames) depicts the Martians attacking the Capitol building, from the same side as they do in the film, with troops ineffectually massed outside.
- Card #13 (Watching From Mars) is the most obvious inspiration for the Martians' twisted humour, as they rock back in laughter, pointing at the destruction of the Capitol dome while apparently getting drunk on decanters of wine.

- Card #4 (Saucers Blast Our Jets) is self-explanatory, and resulted in the very brief scene of a fighter plane being blasted out of the sky.
- Card #50 (Smashing the Enemy) depicts soldiers breaking open the skulls of Martians, although on the cards their blood is red, not green as it is in Burton's film.
- Card #32 (Robot Terror) is the source for the giant robot that chases Richie away from the trailer park – again, the film's rendering is incredibly faithful to the cards.
- Card #40 (High Voltage Electrocution) provided a way of dealing with the giant robot, although in the original card it was a giant insect that got tangled in power cables.
- Card #36 (Destroying a Dog) was one of the most infamous of the set, and led to the Presidential pooch's untimely death in the film.
- Card #11 (Destroy the City) shows Martians running amok through a burning town, with piles of charred bodies strewn about the streets, just as we see them at the height of the movie.
- Card #41 (Horror in Paris) depicts the destruction of the Eiffel Tower, just as in the film, except for the enormous caterpillar . . .
- Card #24 (The Shrinking Ray) provides the source for General Decker's demise.

The cover of the fifth *Mars Attacks!* comic and Card #76 of the 1994 set (drawn by John Pound, creator of *The Garbage Pail Kids*) showed a woman pulling off her head to reveal she is a Martian beneath – the inspiration for the 'Martian girl' scenes with Lisa Maric (although she claims that 'the girl I played was really designed by Tim'[19]).

In addition, Card #92, one of the additional cards added to the 1994 set, features a Martian holding JFK hostage with a gun to his head – just as President Dale is held hostage in the film. It was drawn by Norm Saunders' daughter, Zina.

Some ideas were also taken from the *Dinosaurs Attack!* cards – most obviously from card #43 (Business Lunch), featuring a dinosaur breaking through the plate glass windows at the back of a conference room – as a Martian saucer does in the Vegas hotel. Furthermore, card #24 (London in Flames), as its name suggests showed the British capital under attack, as in the film; card #45 (Anchorman's Peril) may have been the inspiration for the character of Jason Stone; and #30 (A Kid Strikes Back) seems a possible source for Richie to be the saviour of humanity – although on the card the 'kid' was a small girl in pigtails that only very vaguely resembles Lukas Haas . . .

Having worked out which images they wanted to use, Gems drew up a first draft screenplay with Burton in just three weeks. Initially budgeted at $200 million, several rewrites became necessary to get the budget down, because even with Tim Burton aboard the studio was 'worried about the money being spent on something that's not mainstream . . . If you do something like [*Mars Attacks!*], you've got to spend the money to do it properly.'[20] The need to cut the budget meant that soon Gems 'burned out. I was getting three hours of sleep at night. Tim said have a holiday.'[21] In his place, Burton brought in *Ed Wood* writers Scott Alexander and Larry Karaszewski. 'We had a lot of fun working on it,' confirms Karaszewski. They did two drafts of the screenplay, refining some elements and adding others: 'When we came on the project, the script had so many characters that there was literally a three-page index at the back of the script to help you keep track. We just did a lot of work on the reordering and clarifying who the characters are, and trying to really define everybody, so you know who they are and what they want.' It was Alexander and Karaszewski who introduced the character of Taffy Dale, the First Daughter, and expanded the role of Barbara Land. Karaszewski remembers, 'She was just like five lines, and we made her into a major character, gave her her own storyline. All the scenes with Nicholson and her with the New Agey stuff and meditating and all that nonsense.'

Despite the pair's undeniable knack for dialogue, the basic story was beginning to shift too far from Burton and Gems' original intentions, and Gems returned, refreshed and ready to restart the rewrites. By the time shooting began, the script was on its fifteenth draft. When the movie was finally released Alexander and Karaszewski's work went entirely unrecognised on the film's credits. Karaszewski again, 'At the end of the day, we thought that we deserved [some] credit on the movie, but the credit arbitration said that we did not. I think we probably feel most responsible for probably the first hour of the movie. Definitely the third act was certainly not ours.'

Meanwhile, work had begun on creating the Martians. Burton knew from the start that he wanted the Martians to resemble Ray Harryhausen's stop-motion skeletons in *Jason and the Argonauts*

(Don Chaffey, 1963). He first approached Henry Selick, *The Nightmare Before Christmas*' director, but he was still in the middle of making *James and the Giant Peach*. Instead, Burton turned to Barry Purvis, an animator from England, who headed a group of 70 animators, and began pre-production work on the project before it had even been green-lit. Purvis' initial designs for the Martians and their movements were the basis for the finished article.

However, as the stop-motion process was taking so long, the decision was made to switch to the less time-consuming and cheaper CGI. Here, Producer Larry Franco, who had just finished work on *Jumanji* (Joe Johnston, 1995), came in, and arranged a test CGI sequence with the Martians with Mark Miller at George Lucas' Industrial Light and Magic, replacing the marauding elephants trashing a car from a scene in *Jumanji* with marauding Martians. As Franco explained, 'Tim was really insisting at the time to go along with stop-motion animation and see how that looked. I had seen the early stages of computer effects for *Jumanji*, and whether you're moving a model physically with your hands, or if you're manipulating an image on a screen with a keyboard it's still frame-by-frame animation.'[22] 'With stop-motion animation, you get to a point where you're perceiving it to be alive, but it's just herky-jerky. If you stop at some point and don't smooth out computer animation, it pretty much looks like stop-motion.'[23] Franco believed that, although Tim *knew* this was the case, his love of stop-motion had blinded him to the potential of CGI. On top of this, switching to CGI would eradicate the problem of fingerprints appearing on the Martians' helmets, which had to be removed between each shot to manipulate the aliens' facial expressions.

The CGI test was good enough to convince Burton that: 'In some ways, the technique doesn't really matter. I wanted to go for a "feeling" of the stop-motion that I grew up on. Now, we're able to achieve that feeling in a few different ways ... [with CGI] I really didn't have to do much about cumbersome set-ups. I could pretty much do whatever I needed to do. It was really cool, real easy.'[24] Furthermore, as all the Martian characters looked almost identical, it would take far, far less time for a computer to animate them than to painstakingly shoot them in stop-motion. Purvis was naturally not pleased, as he and his crew received neither official credit nor a severance package – they had been working without contracts – as a further indignity they were even searched as they left the lot. He later complained, 'The same day big knobs at the studio had been applauding our rushes, they came in two hours later, while I had my hand up a Martian, and said, "sorry folks".'[25]

With the special effects sorted out, principle photography began at 7 a.m. on 26 February 1996 at Stage 6 at Warner Hollywood Studios, the other side of the hills from the main Warner Brothers lot in Burton's hometown of Burbank. Set construction had started in mid-December 1995 – using six of the seven sound-stages for the first six weeks of production. In April, location work began, first in Washington, DC.

Filming in the nation's capital involved negotiating with the department of parks and recreation, the local city police, and the federal police to use land for scenes outside the Capitol, but negotiations were smooth and production went well.

One innovative use of location was with the remains of Pam Grier's apartment block at the very end of the picture, a fire-damaged building on the corner of 4th and Massachusetts. With a small amount of dressing, the burned up apartment, with one exterior wall missing, was a perfect symbol of the state of DC following the Martian attack.

Production then moved to Burns, Kansas (aka Perkinsville) circa 40 miles northeast of Wichita, a minor town with a population under 300. They also filmed the opening cattle scene in Lawrence, Kansas, a neighbouring town, plus Wichita, for the retirement home scenes.

When the time came to shoot in Las Vegas Burton opted to record the casino sequences in the Luxor Casino. His first choice, Caesar's Palace – in many ways the epitome of Vegas' style – was available for only a few short hours each day, the result of its lengthy hours of business. As it was, Burton and his crew could only shoot at the Luxor between 11 p.m. and 8 a.m. each day they were there. Equally, it was only possible to shoot on the Las Vegas Boulevard itself between midnight and 6 a.m., meaning a number of 'short' but tiring shooting days for director and crew.

The initial Martian incursion in 'Pahrump, Nevada' was actually staged in a dry lakebed 20 miles outside Kingman, Arizona – a costly sequence involving over 1,200 cast, crew and extras.

The countrywide location shooting schedule clearly demon-strated how high Burton's stock had risen since budget restrictions on *Pee-wee* had forced them to choose locations with a 30 kilometre radius of their Los Angeles base.

CASTING: As so many of the movie's roles were small, and the characters were mostly unlikeable losers, there was, at least according to Gems, some initial reluctance from agents and stars to take part. 'At one point we actually thought we were going to have to cancel the film. The guy who saved our butt was Jack Nicholson.'[26] Burton had remained on good terms with Nicholson since *Batman,* and the two had worked on the abortive *The Hawkline Monster.* As Burton recalled, 'I asked him if he'd read the script, and he said he thought it was funny. I asked, "So, Jack, which part do you want to play?" and he replied, "How 'bout *all* of them?"'[27]

However, Producer Larry Franco has a somewhat different take on the casting process: 'Once the word got out and people started hearing what kind of project it was – a lot of cameos, a couple of weeks' work with Tim Burton on a big project – it was fairly easy to get everyone on the same wavelength. Logistically it was tricky working around people's schedules, but in terms of getting people's interest, that wasn't a problem at all. The first two people to jump on board were Pierce Brosnan and Sarah Jessica Parker, then Lukas Haas and Sylvia Sidney,' then Nicholson, after which 'it became a little bit easier.'[28]

In terms of the cast themselves, many had their own reasons for wanting to be involved. Danny DeVito, no stranger to this kind of madness thanks to his stint on the frequently surreal sitcom Taxi, as well as his appearance in Burton's *Batman Returns,* claims he did the picture just 'so I could stand around in Vegas and smoke cigars with Tom Jones,'[29] after all, 'when do you get a chance to do stuff like that? You run down there and do that, baby!'[30] Burton had used the legendary big-voiced Welshman's music already in *Edward Scissorhands,* and felt it was now time to give him some screen time. Jones was only too happy to oblige after Burton went in person to propose the idea to him in Vegas.

Pierce Brosnan, also no stranger to heavy FX movies thanks to his then recently acquired role as James Bond 007 was perhaps called upon to suffer greater indignities in the name of his character than anyone else. Asked about the experience of flirting with a woman with the body of a puppy dog whilst his disembodied head smokes a pipe, Brosnan simply laughed and said, 'I don't mind taking the piss out of myself. [*Mars Attacks!*] was just a hoot.'[31] Michael J Fox came to his decision after he thought, 'How many chances in your life are you going to get to work with somebody like Tim Burton? ... My son would have killed me if I didn't do it ... Another reason ... is the idea of being in a film ... where you just never know who's going to pop up and what's going to happen to them was really an exciting prospect.'[32] In the opinion of Rod Steiger, *Mars Attacks!* had 'one of the best casts since *On the Waterfront* (Elia Kazan, 1954). I was flattered.'[33]

For Paul Winfield, 'When they told me all the people involved, it really turned my head around. It's unusual to have an all-star cast in a science-fiction romp. Usually, the budget is spent on the effects, so there's very little left over for any sort of leading or respected actors in this sort of thing.'[34]

Screenwriters Larry Karaszewski and Scott Alexander took particular pleasure in Paul Winfield's character, later commenting, 'Just before Paul Winfield's going to meet the Martians, he's calling his wife, and he goes, "See honey, I told you, if I just keep my mouth shut and don't stand up for myself, things'll go well." What happened there was he was this guy, this character that we liked, and who had not done one bad thing, and we knew he was about to get blown up by the Martians. So basically, on the way to being blown up we just wanted to show him to be not that great. It was really great to see that scene with a full audience. Just great.'

Burton was delighted with the size, quality and eclecticism of his cast: 'You have to wonder what the hell you're doing with all these great performers ... I had all these great actors running through a field screaming. There's something funny about that ... watching these people who are Academy Award winners, some of them just acting to nothing. I had no real hard-core Method people. "I can't see the Martians! Where are the Martians? Where are they? What's my motivation?" Being chased by little green men, that's your motivation!'[35] Furthermore, it seemed to Burton that his cast were actually having as much fun as he was watching them: 'The actors [who] took part in this film did it purely for pleasure. This is particularly true of those which would normally never appear in a film of this kind.'[36]

BURTON REGULARS: Sylvia Sidney had played Juno, the Maitlands' afterlife guidance counsellor, in *Beetlejuice*. *Mars*

Attacks! was her last film, nearly 70 years after her first – she died of throat cancer on 1 July 1999, aged 89.

Art Director John Dexter would go on to have the same role on *Sleepy Hollow*, and acted as Supervising Art Director on *Planet of the Apes*. Rance Howard (father of film director and *Happy Days* star Ron Howard) had appeared in Burton's previous film, *Ed Wood*. He was also in *Independence Day* (see **AFTERLIFE**), as was Voice Artiste Frank Welker.

For trivia-hungry people, looking for a few more connections, Christina Applegate appeared in *21 Jump Street*, the TV series that starred Johnny Depp. Applegate appeared in the episode 'I'm OK – You Need Work' (series 2, no.15 – aired 21 February 1988). Paul Winfield, Jim Brown and Pam Grier had all previously worked together on *Original Gangstas* (Larry Cohen, 1996). Grier would go on to star alongside Burton regular Michael Keaton in Quentin Tarantino's *Jackie Brown* (1997). Lukas Haas and Natalie Portman had previously appeared together in Woody Allen's *Everyone Says I Love You* (1996). Portman would, of course, go on to star alongside *Sleepy Hollow* actors Ian McDiarmid, Christopher Lee and Ray Park in George Lucas' second trilogy of *Star Wars* films (1999–2005).

CRITICS: Generally speaking, the critics hated *Mars Attacks!*

The *New Yorker* drew the comparison that ' "Mars Attacks!" is like one of those messy, deliberately alienating albums that rock groups sometimes make after they've been embarrassed by commercial success.'[37] *Newsweek* argued it was 'so defiantly inconsequential it makes *Pee-wee's Big Adventure* look weighty,'[38] although at least admitted that it was amusing in places. Others moaned that 'Never has a movie so brimming with potential failed so utterly to deliver . . . the film looks great, but there's nothing inside'[39] and that the film 'blows most of its inspired moments because of its mean-spirited, deafening siege mentality, which turns rich promise into a tiresome array of half-baked skits. Hilarity never seemed so tedious.'[40] Others simply felt that it was 'disappointingly frivolous after the inventiveness of *Ed Wood*.'[41]

In a more positive vein, the *Los Angeles Times* was fairly sure that 'Burton fans won't be disappointed,'[42] and the *Village Voice* praised its 'near-Preston Sturges-like density of character,' arguing that it was 'inconsistent . . . [but] who cares?'[43] *Time* also claimed that it was 'curiously refreshing,'[44] but these three positive voices were largely drowned out by the torrent of negative opinion.

Burton, however, seemed unaffected by the criticism, he had made the film he wanted to make, after all. 'Negative criticism prevents me from getting big-headed. And it's not new for me. I remember taking flack for my first films. On a scale from 1 to 10, I was usually awarded less than 1. That armed me against critics and criticism.'[45]

MUSIC: After their split in the run-up to *Ed Wood*, *Mars Attacks!* saw a renewal of the Burton/Elfman creative partnership. As Elfman explained it, 'I would call what happened between the two of us a family feud. We had worked for ten years and on six films together, and we finally had a creative blow-up.' Elfman and Burton had often joked that their relationship was like that of musician Bernard Herrmann and director Alfred Hitchcock, who after working successfully together for many years had a major creative/personal disagreement over *Torn Curtain* (1966) and never worked again. Elfman felt 'that prophecy kind of self-fulfilled itself. Then we realized that we both missed each other and did good work together. And sometimes in a family you have a fight and you're mad at them, but as time goes by, you recognize that this can't last forever and make amends.'[46] Although Howard Shore's score for *Ed Wood* slotted perfectly into Burton's film, some fans had felt that a Burton film wasn't really a Burton film without Elfman's distinctive musical touch. Elfman partially reclaimed his place on *Ed Wood* here by using a variation of the Vampira TV show and title sequence music from *Ed Wood* within his *Mars Attacks!* score.

As a vehicle for reviving their collaborative relationship, *Mars Attacks!* was ideal. Just as Burton was paying homage to the B-movies he loved as a child, it allowed Elfman to pay homage to his favourite composer, whom he had discovered through just such a B-movie, as well as to play around with one of the weirdest instruments ever invented, which had already been put to good use by Howard Shore in *Ed Wood*: 'I wouldn't dream of going into the session without a theremin. The score that started me, that led me to becoming a film composer, was *The Day the Earth Stood Still*. That was the first time where I noticed the music and was aware as a kid that the music isn't just there by magic, that there was a name attached to it. I started to look for that name.

When I saw Bernard Herrmann's name on other science fiction movies as I was growing up I went, "Oh boy! This is gonna be good!" It was an awareness that there was a difference in the music; there was a personality, an individual, and it did make a difference. When his music was in the movies, they were better movies! It would be inconceivable for me not to be paying homage to that. What started the whole thing was a flying saucer movie.'[47]

CINEMATOGRAPHY: Cinematographer Peter Suschitzky has been David Cronenberg's first choice for his films ever since *Dead Ringers* (1988). This and his other work, which includes *The Empire Strikes Back* (Irvin Kershner, 1980) and *The Rocky Horror Picture Show* (Jim Sharman, 1975), suggests that he was an ideal choice to work with Burton, whose usual gloomy visual style is similar in many ways to Suschitzky's best work. In fact, he had initially been considered by Burton to shoot *Batman*.

The fact that Burton and Suschitsky could combine their back-catalogues full of dark, depressing images into such a jolly-looking, brightly-shot, colourful, and yet utterly bloodthirsty movie is something no one could have predicted. Burton had already realised Hollywood's dislike of darker images in its effects blockbusters, going on record as early as 1991, stating that 'they always resist darkness in Hollywood, even if it makes 'em money. I'm amazed. Their only successes could be dark films, and they'd *still* always resist it.'[48] The lack of award ceremony recognition for *Batman Returns* only further underlined this conviction, and everyone involved in *Ed Wood* knew that the decision to shoot in black and white would hurt the film's box-office chances. However, *Mars Attacks!* is one of Burton's brightest and most colourful films to date, rivalled only by the cartoonish vibrancy of *Pee-wee's Big Adventure*. Considering the people involved, this in itself must surely have been part of the film's joke.

PLOT PROBLEMS: The only real plot 'problem' in *Mars Attacks!* is impressively minor. We're never given any suggestion that Barbara and Byron know each other until Barbara runs to Byron for help in the final reel. It all hangs together as well as a deliberately episodic, utterly chaotic, plotless comedy can be expected to – perhaps slightly better.

DEATH: Soldiers, dogs, women, children, the inhabitants of the British Houses of Parliament and the US Congress, possibly the entire population of France, and certainly the Presidents of both France and the USA. Loads. Tons. In this film, however, death – although omnipresent – is given no gravity. It has no sting. It's a joke, the punchline to gleefully well-organised mayhem. This is pretty much the only film Burton has made in which death is meaningless. Even the likeable Taffy doesn't mourn the death of her parents.

CHILDREN AND FAMILIES: For Burton, the Martians were simply 'anarchistic kids you can't understand. You don't really know what they want, and there's really no clear motivation. They're just like bad, hyperactive teens'[49] albeit with spaceships and ray guns.

There are three families, all of which are dysfunctional to a greater or lesser degree. The presidential family is perhaps the most disjointed, with each member off in their own little world: President Dale constantly searching for good PR, Martha hunting for her own particular brand of tasteless style, and Taffy playing the typical self-important teenager, and reading Hermann Hesse's *Siddhartha*, the classic existentialist novella of individualism and enlightenment.

The Norris family, typical trailer trash though they are, are a close-knit group of three, although the family is actually five members strong. It is the two excluded members of this group who manage to save the world, but we are made constantly aware of their inadequacies too – Grandma is utterly senile, and it is made abundantly clear that Richie is only a little brighter than his parents and brother.

Both Taffy and Richie only seem to become content once their parents have been killed. In fact, the family that seems to work best is the Williams family, Byron, Louise, Cedric and Neville, even though the parents here are living separate lives, and the children are mostly off doing their own thing.

CLOWNS AND THE CIRCUS: Vegas – the biggest circus in the world, full of freaks, losers and misfits, and as such an ideal pool from which to draw out innumerable bizarre characters. The gaudy lights and colour schemes of Burton's Vegas vision owe more to the late 60s and early 70s – the Vegas of *Diamonds Are Forever* (Guy Hamilton, 1971) and Hunter S Thompson – with an added dash of 80s glam and tackiness. Burton saw Vegas as 'this constantly evolving fantasy land,'[50] and as such it seemed like a perfect locale for one of his films – it could be moulded into whatever image he saw fit, while retaining its inherent character. As costume designer Colleen Atwood put it, 'Vegas is a fantasy place . . . it was definitely the place to push the envelope as far as we could with colour and design,'[51] and this they certainly did. Even in the Egyptian-themed, expensive-looking casino there is a hint of something cheap – punters in polyester suits queuing up at one-armed bandits underneath flashing lights, like children waiting to throw a ball at a coconut in some tatty sideshow.

Outside the casino the circus theme continues, as Barbara, Byron, Tom Jones, the waitress and DeVito's gambler try to make their escape to the airfield, they pass through the Yesco Sign Yard, a dumping-ground for old casino and hotel signs, which distinctly resembles a rather ramshackle circus sideshow. Just like all the characters in the film, Vegas is a cliché in Burton's vision – an enormous fairground where people can get lost in the wonder, and even attacking aliens don't seem too out of place.

At first glance, it seems that Burton may have forgotten to put a clown in here, despite all the circus imagery of Vegas. This is where sharp eyes and a DVD come in. On the Martian spaceship where Nathalie and then Kessler are held captive, look at the glass orbs in the background. Some contain hundreds of eyes, others giant brains, one holds something that looks disturbingly like a mutilated cow crossed with a pig. However, in two shots (the first as Nathalie's head is brought through the ship, the second as Kessler and Nathalie flirt again), a clown, strangely reminiscent of the Fat Clown the Penguin kills in *Batman Returns*, can clearly be seen floating in one of the balls.

DOGS: This is one of Burton's ultimate dog movies, featuring as it does, his own pet pooch, Poppy the chihuahua. Just as Vincent Molloy dreamed of doing in *Vincent*, and as Victor Frankenstein succeeds in doing in *Frankenweenie*, here Burton himself performs CGI experiments on his beloved mutt, grafting Sarah Jessica Parker's head onto its body, and its head on to Parker's. The end result is rather more amusing and disturbing than either of the canine experiments of Burton's earlier films.

Also the presidential dog's disintegration, whilst taken from the original card series, clearly delights the director.

LOVE TRIANGLES: There's a fairly simple three-way split of affections between the Professor, Nathalie and Jason (up to the point where Jason is obliterated by a ray gun, at least).

AUTOBIOGRAPHY?: There have been suggestions of Haas and Portman being Burton alter-egos. Ken Hanke asserts that 'where Taffy represents his more detached, more amusedly cynical self, Richie is clearly Burton the innocent,'[52] but this seems to stretch his remit to near breaking point. This not only doesn't work in relation to Hanke's attempt to analyse Burton the man, it also misses the point that Richie is fairly worldly, if a trifle dense, and that Taffy is actually quite a warm figure, even making a nervous romantic move on Richie at the end. If, like Hanke, one takes the view that Burton's films are largely autobiographical, *Mars Attacks!*, along with *Planet of the Apes*, can only be seen as an exception. Searching either of these films for Burton avatars, or any really personal elements, is a task that can only realistically prove fruitless. In the final analysis, even Hanke has to admit that *Mars Attacks!* was, at the time of his writing at least, 'Burton's most calculatedly impersonal movie.'[53] The key word there is 'calculatedly' – this again, let's face it, is part of the joke.

JUST PLAIN WEIRD: Firstly, a tank full of women's shoes on the Martian ship. Secondly, pretty much everything else in the movie, but especially Richie Norris' left-field assertion that living in teepees is better than living in houses. Also, full executive authority seemingly passes to President Dale's daughter on his death – which is unconstitutional to say the least.

DIALOGUE TO SKIP BACK FOR:
Jerry Ross: 'For some picky reason, the secret services don't want the executive branch and the legislative branch in the same room at the same time.'
The initial translation of the Martian's dialogue says, 'All green of skin, 800 centuries ago, their bodily fluids include the birth of halfbreeds. For the fundamental truths of the determination of the cosmos. For dark is the suede that mows like the harvest.'
President Dale: 'I want the people to know that they still have two out of the three branches of Government working for them, and that ain't bad.' (This line of dialogue, arguably the best in the film, was the work of uncredited screenwriters Alexander and

Karaszewski. 'One of my favourite lines that we've ever written,' Karaszewski later commented.)

AFTERLIFE: According to Gems, initially Burton 'really liked *Dinosaurs Attack!* and we discussed a movie about dinosaurs attacking suburbia. But after *Jurassic Park*, he thought it would be too similar. So he chose to go with *Mars Attacks!*'[54] Ironically, *Mars Attacks!* suffered due to the prior release of the similarly-themed (but much more 'serious') *Independence Day* (Roland Emmerich, 1996).

Rare was the critic who missed the chance to point out the similarities, with *Newsweek* and the *Los Angeles Times* agreeing it was a sendup of Emmerich's movie, and *Entertainment Weekly* positing that 'the very form of *Mars Attacks!* is a swipe at *ID4*.'[55] The similarities between the two films are indeed painfully apparent. Not only do saucer-like alien craft invade Earth's atmosphere, but in both films locations include a New York TV station, a Midwestern farming district, the White House, and some kind of war room. Both also feature presidential advisors with conflicting views on how to approach the situation – one advising an all-out attack, one suggesting a more pacifistic approach, and both demonstrate that a pre-emptive strike would have been the best policy. Both have jets being blown out of the sky by alien vessels, and failed nuclear assaults. Both have similar breeds of pet dogs, although only *Mars Attacks!* is daring enough to kill off man's best friend. Both also have a President plead directly with one of the invaders for peace, arguing that humans and aliens can learn from each other. But where Bill Pullman's premier (obviously modelled on then Vice President Al Gore) suggests that 'we can learn to co-exist,' Jack Nicholson's Nixonian leader instead steals a line from Rodney King who, while attempting to quell the Los Angeles riots that exploded after the white police officers who brutally beat him on camera on 3 March 1991 were acquitted, pleaded, 'Why can't we all just get along?'

The *Village Voice* assumed the similarities between the two were 'likely a function of market-testing,'[56] but few, if any, critics seemed to acknowledge the obvious point that, as *Mars Attacks!* was actually sending up the low-budget monster/saucer movies of the 1950s, the fact that it could be seen as spoofing *Independence Day* was the ultimate proof of how successfully Emmerich's film had aped its source material. Yes, the special effects are pretty, and there are a few nods and winks to the more sophisticated audiences of the mid-90s but the only meaningful difference between the self-styled *ID4* and the B-movies of the 50s is the colour of heroic USAF pilot Will Smith's skin.

Although Emmerich's gung-ho piece of feel-good jingoism went into production some time after *Mars Attacks!*, the movie was released first, enjoying a very lucrative box office run during summer 1996, six months before Burton's film came out. Although Burton claimed that he was 'well into making it before I even heard about *Independence Day* so we just continued on,'[57] Producer Larry Franco thought that 'we were aware [of *Independence Day*] from the very first meeting I had. We made sure to separate ourselves from that. From that moment it became something to think about, but – hey – Tim Burton is Tim Burton. I don't give a shit how many films are about aliens attacking the earth. None of them are going to be even close to what Tim Burton's is.'[58] Even so, the two films shared at least two special effects crewmembers, model maker Michael Joyce, and pyrotechnician Joseph Viskocil, whose knowledge of Emmerich's film may have been a contributing factor in the decision to avoid showing the destruction of the Empire State Building, as had been originally planned.

Despite Burton's claim, 'I didn't worry about the *Independence Day* comparisons, I just like monsters,'[59] it would be incredible if no attempts were made to either capitalise on or gain distance from the earlier film's success in the months between its release and that of *Mars Attacks!* Yet Franco also maintained, 'I don't think anything we're doing would have been based on the success or failure of *ID4*. Most people don't know how long it takes to generate one of these films. This project has been on the boards for a long time – even long before there was an *ID4*. Besides, these are two very different movies.'[60] Equally, in one interview Gems argued, 'That movie was like a trailer for *Mars Attacks!* We should be very grateful,' while also separately and mysteriously claiming that 'Something happened that was unethical.'[61]

Whether *Independence Day*'s earlier release really did hurt *Mars Attacks!* at the box office is impossible to say. The massive commercial success of Emmerich's film could have ensured that people had already seen enough of aliens that year, so gave Burton's movie a miss. But the commercial failure of *Mars*

Attacks! could equally have been down to its Christmas release date – 'Fryday' 13 December in the US. A film set in a rather sunny May, despite the seasonal red and green of the skeletons left by the Martian ray-guns, was hardly the traditional Christmas fare.

Before the switch to CGI, the release had been planned for spring 1997, but the increased speed led Warners to push the date forward. *Screen International* pondered as early as October 1996 that 'the timing might be off. How many alien invasion movies can Americans handle in one year? Hot on *ID4*'s blockbusting heels, this spoof could well be burnt to cinders in its wake.'[62]

Many critics also compared the relative commercial successes of *Independence Day* and *Mars Attacks!* to the similar relationship between Stanley Kubrick's *Dr Strangelove* (1963) and Sidney Lumet's *Fail-Safe* (1964). In both cases, the two films covered very similar ground – *Mars Attacks!* and *Independence Day* both being loosely derived from HG Wells' *War of the Worlds*, and *Dr Strangelove* and *Fail-Safe* both being explicitly derived from Eugene Burdick and Harvey Wheeler's 1962 novel *Fail-Safe*.

In both cases, one film took a 'serious' stance, the other a satirical one. In both cases, the first film to be released did far better at the box office. When Jonathan Gems, in an interview published in January 1997, compared *Independence Day* to *Fail-Safe*, and *Mars Attacks!* to *Dr Strangelove*, his intention was to underline the tone. With the earlier films, Gems argued, 'both had similar story points, but their tones were completely different. The same is true here. In our film we take a very illogical approach to the reasoning for what's happening in the movie – which in that sense is similar to *ID4*, which was totally illogical. In our case, though, it was intentional, while in *ID4*, it wasn't.'[63]

Trying to work out the reasons for his film's lack of blockbuster status, Burton later explained that he thought the audience was confused because he was looking at the film from various simultaneous points of view. 'When I was making it, I kept thinking of it as an animated film in a sense, like it was about a bunch of different ideas that don't necessarily link up, thrown together ... Often what I think is funny, other people don't. It's like I have trouble identifying what's correct or incorrect.'[64]

AWARDS: Danny Elfman's score was honoured with a Saturn Award, whilst the picture was nominated for the 1997 Hugo for 'Best Dramatic Presentation.'

At the 1997 Golden Satellite Awards, *Mars Attacks!* was nominated for Best Motion Picture (Animate d or Mixed Media) and for outstanding Visual Effects (David Andrews, Michael L Fink, Jim Mitchell). Jack Nicholson was nominated for his performance and Danny Elfman's score too received a nod. The film didn't win any statuettes however.

Perhaps best of all Jim Brown's fist fight with a Martian was nominated for 'Best Fight' at the MTV Movie awards.

TRIVIA: As President Dale confronts the Martian ambassador in the War Room, his tie shifts positions between shots. This was not in fact a continuity error, but a deliberate spoof of courtroom drama *A Few Good Men* (Rob Reiner 1992), in which the same thing happens to Colonel Jessup's tie – Jack Nicholson played both characters.

The Landmark Hotel, which is visibly demolished during the Las Vegas sequences, was opened in 1969 by mogul Howard Hughes. A total of 361 feet high and with 31 stories, it was for many years the tallest building in Nevada. Before it closed in 1990, Burton had stayed there several times.

Taffy Dale was obviously modelled, to some extent, on Chelsea Clinton, at that point the only teenage daughter of a serving US President in modern history.

Some sources contend that Paul Newman was offered the role of President Dale, but turned it down, unhappy with the tone of the piece.

Several crew members reported that Jack Nicholson frequently entered the set to the sound of 'Hail to the Chief' – the piece of martial music traditionally played when the US President arrives in his official capacity. This was supposedly accompanied by a lap of honour around the set and being addressed as 'Mr President' – apparently it assisted the then twice Oscar winner to get into character.

EXPERT WITNESS: Producer Larry Franco: 'Tim does things in a way you can't quite anticipate. You talk about a scene in a living room with two people, and you conjure up in your mind what that is. What you're *really* going to shoot is a living room the size of a football field, painted black, with no ceiling. The walls are 18 feet high, and there's a red table in the corner with two people in white jumpsuits. That's Tim's version of two people in a living room talking.'[65]

Rod Steiger: 'He reminds me of a European director ... I knew Fellini and worked with some others out there. They don't come on the set with a script that's loaded with the directions. Burton comes on the set with nothing ... He's got it in his head ... By and large, very few directors in this town finish a film the way they want – which is a crime. But Burton does, because they don't know what he's going to do! And he's just smart enough to do just what he needs.'[66]

Jonathan Gems: 'He is the only director I know who thinks like an artist ... He's interested in the film itself ... Nobody has his visual sensibility, and that's one of the things that makes Tim's films very distinctive ... He also has this really quirky sense of humour and a love of the unexpected. The reason why his films are so popular is that Tim tries to undermine the genre and turn it into something fresh and new each time.'[67]

ANALYSIS: The essential difference between the world of *Independence Day* and that of *Mars Attacks!* is that, in *ID4* the characters rally around an inspirational leader in order to defeat the invaders – and in doing so confirm the triumphant nature of the human spirit – whereas in *Mars Attacks!* people react to the trauma of the Martian attack by lying, cheating, sneering or simply ignoring the whole ghastly business in order to go and watch Tom Jones in Vegas.

Essentially each character in *Mars Attacks!* sees the crisis through the very specific perspective of their own concerns and reacts to it within the very simple confines of their own personality, their own personal universe. This can make them act selfishly (Art Land) aggressively (General Decker) or with very real maturity and concern (Byron Williams – the closest thing the film has to a recognisable hero.) It can make them see it in scientific terms (Donald Kessler), metaphysical terms (Barbara Land) or as a PR opportunity (Jerry Ross.) In the end, no one has the perspective or skill to deal with the unknowable Martians and a combination of dumb luck and the bravery of the most disenfranchised of American society (an old woman abandoned by her family, a mistreated teenage boy, and a middle-aged washed up African American couple) saves the human race.

Perhaps Burton's most pessimistic (yet at face value his funniest) film, *Mars Attacks!* ultimately judges the whole of the human race to be a bit rubbish, a trifle embarrassing – and with very few exceptions (Byron, Louise, perhaps Taffy and Richie) undeserving of our compassion. There's no doubt at all that it is with the gleefully slaughtering Martian hordes that the director's sympathies truly lie. 'The Martians are such malicious characters ... they're like little children: they make fun; they're mocking; they do things just to be wicked! They're not like insects destroying the planet – they know they're being wicked and they take great glee in it ... it's just pure Tim.'[68]

AVAILABILITY: *Mars Attacks!* is available on DVD on both sides of the Atlantic. A nicely mastered but special features light edition was one of Warner Brothers' earliest ventures into the DVD market. It includes the movie's trailers but little else. Early (R1) US printings of the disc were 'flippers', with the wide-screen edition of the film on one side and a full-frame 4:3 pan and scanned version. Later printings have solely the wide screen edition of the film.

THE BOTTOM LINE: *Mars Attacks!* is slick, starry and very, very funny. Considering how wildly critical judgements on *Mars Attacks!* have varied (see **CRITICS**) perhaps in this instance, it is sensible to judge the picture by ascertaining how well it achieves that which its creators set out to do. And so, *Mars Attacks!*, a sometimes blissful splicing of screwball comedy, disaster movie and alien invasion antics, which somehow manages to retain a nihilistic core, surely cannot count as anything other than a brilliant, near total, success. It's also perhaps the only film in motion picture history to entirely take place, philosophically speaking, in inverted commas – there's not a single shred of sincerity in the entire film.

THE DEATH OF SUPERMAN (1998)
Or a potted history of a failed attempt to bring an icon back to films.

By November 1993, the cinematic rights to the DC Comics hero Superman were back in the hands of DC's parent company, Warners. They were previously owned by Alexander Salkind, who (along with his son, Ilya) was behind the four Superman films that starred Christopher Reeve as the eponymous man of steel. Warners had distributed the first three, between 1978 and 1983, although Cannon Films handled the fourth, Sidney J Furie's *Superman IV: The Quest for Peace* (1987).

Two years after the rights reverted to Warners, with ABC's Dean Cain/Teri Hatcher-starring TV series *Lois & Clark: The New Adventures of Superman* (also produced by Warners) a growing success, *Batman* producer Jon Peters took *Superman* in hand and approached Warner Brothers staff writer Jonathan Lemkin, who penned several episodes of the Johnny Depp-starring *21 Jump Street*, to produce a script.

The idea was for it to be based loosely on the phenomenally successful run of early 90s Superman comics that dealt with the hero's death and messianic resurrection. The storyline had unfolded over more than a year, and had dozens of major characters, so clearly some alterations would be necessary in order to trim the plot down to a two-hour feature. Lemkin's script kept many aspects of the death/resurrection arc, jettisoned many others, and featured old time Superman foe Brainiac (who hadn't featured in the comics version) as the main villain. However it did not work, partly being a bit too close to the then in production *Batman Forever*, and partly for being too dark in tone.

Enter (briefly) screenwriter Gregory Poirier, later to work with Peters on *Rosewood* (John Singleton, 1997), keeping the dark tone of Lemkin's draft, but focusing more on Superman's struggle with his dual nature as both Alien and American.

Come August 1996 little progress had been made, and Indie filmmaker Kevin Smith (of *Clerks* fame) was brought on board to lighten the project up a bit, injecting his trademark smart dialogue and wit. A self-professed comics geek whose movies are littered with in-jokes and references to comic books, Smith seemed a dramatically sensible choice. (Years after the Superman project floundered Smith would move into writing actual comics, turning Marvel Comics' financially and artistically bankrupt *Daredevil* into one of the world's ten biggest selling comic books, and resurrecting the ailing *Green Arrow* for DC.) Smith seems to have found the experience rather peculiar, telling of one occasion he met Jon Peters to discuss the project: 'I go out to his house in Bel Air, and Peters lies on his couch and I tell him a few of my ideas and he listens quietly. Then he looks at me in the eye and says, "There's just one thing I need from you – a fight with a giant spider in the third act." ' Back at the studio Smith was asked if Peters had liked my ideas and whether he had mentioned a giant spider. When Smith confirmed Peters had, 'they mumbled, "He's been going on about that spider for years".'[1] (Peters went on to produce the troubled *Wild Wild West* (Barry Sonnenfeld, 1999), a movie which featured – yes – a fight with a giant (metal) spider in the third act).

Smith's script, despite its introduction of numerous obscure characters from the DC Comics universe (such as L-Ron the robot) and perhaps overly wordy nature, managed to avoid Peters' giant spider. It also demonstrates a real love for, and understanding of, the characters and their world. Smith's draft caught the attention of (another self-confessed comics fanboy) Nicolas Cage, as well as Burton, who signed on as star and director, with pay or play contracts that allegedly guaranteed them $20 million and $5 million respectively, whether the project came to fruition or not.

However, Burton inexplicably decided to jettison Smith's script by May 1997, despite favourable responses to the screenplay (which remains easy to find on-line). He brought on Wesley Strick, who had written *The Saint* (Philip Noyce, 1997) and done touch-ups on Daniel Waters' *Batman Returns* screenplay, to redraft the film and make it darker once again. Strick was also quickly replaced, this time with Dan Gilroy, the screenwriter of *Chasers* (Dennis Hopper, 1994). Burton wanted to concentrate 'more on the fact that he's an alien, and maybe for the first time feel what it's like to be Superman . . . Here's this guy who's from another planet and he's really strong, and he's got to hide it. What if he gets angry? How does he have to hide that? You would have to be careful.'[2] (Interestingly, this was an idea briefly explored as a joke in Kevin Smith's 1995 cult classic, *Mallrats*).

Burton and Rick Heinrichs continued to develop the look of the film, picking Pittsburgh as a substitute Metropolis, and continuing to look around for other potential cast members. Rumours began to circulate that Kevin Spacey might become involved as Lex Luthor, with comedian Chris Rock mentioned – in a piece of unorthodox but potentially genius casting – for Clark Kent/Superman's photographer friend, Jimmy Olsen.

By late 1997 the project seemed to be faltering once again, trapped in endless development with an estimated budget of well over $100 million, and more than $30 million already having been spent on its development. Earlier in the year, Warners had experienced a huge-budget flop in Kevin Costner's *The Postman*, there were poor ratings for the third series of *Lois & Clark* and the fourth Batman feature, Joel Schumacher's *Batman & Robin*, was a critical and commercial disaster. Executives at the studio began to fear that Superman – and superheroes in general – was simply not popular enough to warrant the spending necessary to bring Burton's vision to the screen.

On 1 May 1998 Warners shut down the Superman offices, announcing that the company was concentrating on smaller films. Warner Brothers president of production Lorenzo di Bonaventura explained to *Entertainment Weekly* that 'It's not like building a house. You're creating a world where a guy flies around, something new where it takes a lot of time between when you create a wild scene and when ILM puts a price tag on it. We were never able to wrestle the budget down.'[3]

Frustrated, Burton complained that, 'I worked hard on Superman. I "made" the movie only I didn't film it. You'd have to ask Warner Brothers why. It was going to be expensive, and they were a little sensitive that they had screwed up the *Batman* franchise. Corporate decisions are all fear-based decisions. They were afraid.'[4]

Rumoured replacement directors, as the project was (and at the time of writing still is) *officially* in development, have included the big names of Oliver Stone and John Woo, as well as the lesser-known Ralph Zondag and Brad Sibering. Other rumoured stars have included Russell Crowe and John Cusack. There have been further scripts commissioned from *Terminator 2*'s William Wisher (mid-2000) and *Donnie Brasco*'s Paul Attanasio (April 2001), with additional rumours that Warners were returning to Kevin Smith's draft in August 2000. The project remains stuck in limbo, with Nicolas Cage also finally deciding to call it a day in March 2000.

Few people involved in the project seem to have enjoyed the experience, or understood how and why it became so problematic. Kevin Smith has publicly expressed that 'The whole process was like getting 400 people to sculpt a papier-mâché replica of their idea of the Man of Steel, using $100 bills as the paper strips and Dom Perignon as the water,'[5] and has tried to play down the reports of a public slanging match between him and Burton over the project. Burton, on the other hand, explained to one interviewer that, 'I basically wasted a year . . . A year is a long time to be working with somebody that you don't really want to be working with.' His rather melancholy conclusion was simply that 'If we could have just cut through some of the bullshit and done it, it would have been interesting.'[6]

Looking back over the project a few years later, Burton reflected on the reasons for its failure: 'I think it was a matter of lots of things, not logistics so much as probably cost and just studio politics at the time and . . . I think probably because I had a couple of failures . . . I think I've always had a somewhat uneasy alliance with the studios, I somehow . . . surprised them . . . they don't ever quite get it . . . when you have a failure, then it kind of confirms their suspicions about you, like "Yeah, he is a weirdo . . . out of control . . . loser," so I think there's a lot of dynamics that probably go into what their decisions are. There were some evil people involved. Life's too short.'[7]

In spring 2001, Jon Peters left Warners and the project, sparking hopeful rumours that Burton might return to *Superman* as the project to follow *Planet of the Apes*. This seems unlikely, but then at one point so did Burton directing a sequel to *Batman*.

SLEEPY HOLLOW (1999)

Mandaly Pictures presents
A Tim Burton Film
Screen Story by Kevin Yagher and Andrew Kevin Walker
Screenplay by Andrew Kevin Walker

Director of Photography: Emmanuel Lubezski ASC, AMC
Production Designer: Rick Heinrichs
Art Director: Les Tomkins
Produced by Scott Rudin and Adam Schroeder
Co-producer: Kevin Yagher
Associate Producer: Mark Roybal
Executive Producer: Francis Ford Coppola
Executive Producer: Larry Franco
Casting by Ilene Starger, Susie Figgis
Music by Danny Elfman
Costume Designer: Colleen Atwood
Edited by Chris Lebenzon
Based upon the story 'The Legend of Sleepy Hollow' by
Washington Irving
Directed by Tim Burton

CAST: Johnny Depp (*Ichabod Crane*), Christina Ricci (*Katrina Van Tassel*), Miranda Richardson (*Lady Van Tassel/Crone*), Michael Gambon (*Baltus Van Tassel*), Casper Van Dien (*Brom Van Brunt*), Jeffrey Jones (*Reverend Steenwyck*), Christopher Lee (*Burgonmaster*), Richard Griffiths (*Magistrate Philipse*), Ian McDiarmid (*Doctor Lancaster*), Michael Gough (*Notary Hardenbrook*), Marc Pickering (*Young Masbeth*), Lisa Marie (*Lady Crane*), Steven Waddington (*Killian*), Claire Skinner (*Beth Killian*), Alun Armstrong (*High Constable*), Mark Spalding (*Jonathan Masbeth*), Jessica Oyelowo (*Sarah*), Tony Maudsley (*Van Ripper*), Peter Guiness (*Lord Crane*), Nicholas Hewetson (*Glenn*), Orlando Seale (*Theodore*), Sam Stephens (*Thomas Killian*), Gabrielle Lloyd (*Doctor Lancaster's wife*), Robert Sella (*Dirk Van Garrett*), Michael Feast (*Spotty Man*), Jamie Foreman (*Thuggish Constable*), Philip Martin Brown (*Constable One*), Sam Fior (*Young Ichabod*), Tessa Allen-Ridge (*Young Lady Van Tassel*), Cassandra Farndale (*Young Crone*), Lily Phillips (*Girl 2*), Bianca Nicholas (*Little Girl*), Paul Brightwell (*Rifleman*), Christopher Walken (*Hessian Horseman*), Martin Landau (*Peter Van Garrett* – uncredited), Keely O'Hara (*Widow Winship* – uncredited).

TAGLINE: 'Heads will roll'. 'Close your eyes, say your prayers, sleep if you can . . .'

TRAILER: There are two trailers for *Sleepy Hollow*, and both are excellent. The first uses footage of the Hessian's massacre of the Killian family, and is deliberately misleading about the nature of the plot, suggesting that Ichabod is right about the non-supernatural nature of the Hessian. 'The assassin is a man of flesh and blood and I will catch him' is given great prominence. It uses small amounts of footage not in the finished film and suggests the style and tone without giving away plot details.

The second trailer features some more overtly supernatural footage, but ends with Ichabod waking from a nightmare, implying that some of the more outrageous moments seen in the trailer may, in the film, be part of some kind of dream sequence. Both trailers mention Burton by name, indicating how bankable a name he was considered to be, despite the relative commercial failures of both *Ed Wood* and *Mars Attacks!* and the fact that he had not made a film for over a year.

TITLE SEQUENCE: Smokey initial credits appear with the soft wailing that underlies much of Elfman's score, effectively highlighting the spooky nature of the film. We then enter a long pre-credit sequence, first showing the deaths of Peter Van Garrett and his son, before Ichabod is introduced in New York and dispatched to solve the murders. We follow Ichabod's carriage as it moves along the Hudson River towards Sleepy Hollow, watching the colour bleach from the land and the lighting grow darker as it does so. Over this the credits shimmer in and out, all backed by one of Danny Elfman's most effective opening themes.

SUMMARY: 1799. Unorthodox, scientifically minded New York police constable Ichabod Crane is sent to the upstate town of Sleepy Hollow to investigate the murders of several prominent local citizens. Upon arriving he finds the entire town convinced that the murders are being committed by a supernatural figure, the spirit of a Hessian Horseman sent to America during the revolutionary war, who is buried beneath a tree out in the woods. Determined to prove their backward superstitions wrong, he sets about hunting down the human killer he is convinced lies behind the deaths. After several more deaths, one of which Ichabod witnesses, he also becomes convinced that the Horseman is indeed the ghost of the Hessian, and his plan shifts to finding the mysterious human figure who is evidently controlling the Horseman as part of some devious conspiracy (see **PLOT PROBLEMS**). It seems someone has stolen the Hessian's skull, and that each night the horseman does as the thief commands because of the promise that the head will be one day returned and the horseman allowed to return to hell. Once the figure controlling the horseman has been revealed, Ichabod confronts them at the Tree of Dead, and returns to the horseman his head. The horseman departs for hell, carrying his controller with him.

SOURCE MATERIAL: As the credits say, the movie is based upon 'The Legend of Sleepy Hollow' by Washington Irving, which first appeared in his collection of stories, *The Sketch Book of Geoffrey Crayon, Gent.* in 1819–20.

The original story centred on the local schoolteacher, Ichabod Crane, who was a partial outsider to Sleepy Hollow, having originally hailed from Connecticut. His description bears little resemblance to that of Johnny Depp in the film, as he was 'tall, but exceedingly lank, with narrow shoulders, long arms and legs, hands that dangled a mile out of his sleeves, feet that might have served for shovels, and his whole frame most loosely hung together. His head was small, and flat at top, with huge ears, large green glassy eyes, and a long snipe nose, so that it looked like a weather-cock, perched upon his spindle neck ... one might have mistaken him for the genius of famine descending upon the earth, or some scarecrow eloped from a cornfield.' Furthermore, rather than being a scientifically-minded sceptic, Ichabod 'was a perfect master of Cotton Mather's *History of New England Witchcraft*, in which ... he most firmly and potently believed ... no tale was too gross or monstrous for his capacious swallow.' The tale that he appears to have most firmly believed was that of the Headless Horseman, buried in the local church-yard, and 'said by some to be the ghost of a Hessian trooper, whose head had been carried away by a cannon-ball ... the ghost rides forth to the scene of battle in nightly quest of his head.' Having decided to woo Baltus Van Tassel's heir, Katrina ('a blooming lass of fresh eighteen; plump as a partridge; ripe and melting and rosy-cheeked as one of her father's peaches'), Ichabod ends up in a feud with her other suitor, Brom Van Brunt, the popular, prankster leader of the local youths. One night, after a party at the Van Tassel's, Katrina apparently refuses Ichabod's advances. On his way home, the horseman appears and chases Ichabod, before throwing a pumpkin at him. The hapless schoolteacher leaves town without telling anyone, and is presumed taken by the horseman by the townsfolk until news reaches Sleepy Hollow that he has simply moved to another part of the country. Brom marries Katrina, and it is strongly suggested that it was he who was the horseman who chased Ichabod.

It becomes very clear that Andrew Kevin Walker's script really only takes the setting, a few character names, and some of the iconography from Irving's novella. Burton explained this: 'The film is very different to the original story. It was necessary to bring it closer to my universe and my obsessions,'[1] although practically all of the story changes had already been made by the time Burton came onto the project.

Walker's script adds a rather different explanation for the Horseman's actions (although his lost head is still a central part of his motivation), and alters the nature of the Horseman himself to being a supernatural creature. The Horseman's grave is also shifted to the foot of 'the Tree of the Dead', which appears to be based on 'Major André's tree' in Irving's novella, described as towering 'like a giant above all the other trees of the neighbourhood ... Its limbs were gnarled, and fantastic, large enough to form trunks for ordinary trees, twisting down almost to the earth, and rising again into the air,' and which is the centre of a lot of local superstitions.

The script also makes Ichabod a police constable from New York City and thus much more of an outsider in the shadowy world of Sleepy Hollow. Walker also makes Baltus' wife the central villain of the piece, whereas in Irving's story she is barely mentioned, and appears simply to be a typical housewife, as well as his first and only spouse. There is no mention whatsoever of a conspiracy to inherit land in Irving's tale, other than Ichabod's own plans to marry Katrina and gain her father's wealth. Also added are a whole host of other local citizens, none of whom are mentioned in Irving's story.

Another influence on the production was the Disney Company's animated version from the 1960s: 'I was more familiar with the Disney cartoon than the actual story,'[2] Burton admitted. 'I didn't read that until recently. It's funny, because most kids in America have never read it either, yet they know about the Headless

Horseman. I don't know where that comes from.'[3] 'One of my teachers at CalArts worked on the design stages of the [Disney] film,'[4] he commented on another occasion, enthusing that he loved the Disney cartoon's 'visceral power in creating a figure that's mythical, yet feels real. The cartoon's mixture of energy, colour, design and excitement . . . was one of my inspirations for getting into animation.'[5]

There were further, less familiar screen versions of the tale too, including three silent films before 1922, and more recently a made-for-TV movie, *The Legend of Sleepy Hollow*, with Jeff Goldblum and Meg Foster in 1980.

REFERENCES: Once again, 'The inspirations were manifold,' and that goes for the film's reference points too. Burton, on numerous occasions, stated that, 'One of the reasons I wanted to do this was to capture the beautiful, lurid atmosphere of the old Hammer films,'[6] as 'They were quite strong in a graphic way but still not so far over so that I couldn't watch them as a child.'[7] The cult films were, for Burton, 'very lurid and very gutsy. There's a simplicity to them, a certain emotional simplicity which is great, and I've tried to inject the joy I got from them into this, in a way.'[8]

Set up in 1932 by William Hinds and Enrique Carreras, twenty years later the mini-studio had become more ambitious, gaining American distribution deals, and trying to break out of the B-movie crime drama mould – it even created its own star, Diana Dors, with *The Last Page* (Terence Fisher, 1952). However, it was with the release of Val Guest's 1955 *The Quatermass Xperiment* (based on the controversial Nigel Kneale/Rudolph Cartier BBC television serial of 1953) that Hammer began to branch out into the horror films with which it will forever be associated. Many of the best of these starred either Peter Cushing and/or Christopher Lee, following their second appearance together in *The Curse of Frankenstein* (Terence Fisher, 1957). Yet despite the obvious influence of a few specific Hammer movies, such as the Peter Cushing/David Peel-starring *The Brides of Dracula* (Terence Fisher, 1960) and the Christopher Lee vehicle *Dracula Has Risen From the Grave* (Freddie Francis, 1968), the style of which resonates throughout Rick Heinrich's sets, it was more the atmosphere than any specifics that influenced *Sleepy Hollow*.

On top of this were many of Burton's usual influences, such as Whale's *Frankenstein* (again via his own *Frankenweenie*) and early German Expressionist movies. On top of the Hammer influences, Rick Heinrichs admitted that 'Some of the designs are reminiscent of the old German Expressionist films *The Cabinet of Dr Caligari* [Robert Wiene, 1920] and *Nosferatu* [FW Murnau, 1922] which have a very strong, graphic, two-dimensional look within a three-dimensional environment. That's something Tim and I have always liked to play with in the films we've done together.' Burton was adamant that, 'We really wanted to evoke the spirit of the old Hammer horror films, Vincent Price movies, Roger Corman's work,' as, like Ichabod Crane in Burton's *Sleepy Hollow*, 'The heroes in those films are always kind of separate, ambiguous, absorbed in their work. They're there, but you don't know much about them.'[9] Yet as Burton also admitted, Hammer films are 'often more intense in your memory than they are when you actually watch them again.' The influence was more aesthetic than specific, with the added impact that many Hammer films also tried to blend stage and location work into one slightly surreal world. Burton suggested that the Hammer pictures didn't so much provide a rigid look as suggest an atmosphere: 'it was more the *idea* of those films that inspired us ... I might like to draw a certain feeling or flavour out of an older movie, but I'm not trying to make a Xerox copy of it.'[10]

Director of Photography Emmanuel 'Chivo' Lubezki downplayed the Hammer influence: 'I was familiar with the most famous Hammer films, like their Frankenstein and Dracula movies, but I've never been as big a fan of them as Tim is. I find them to be funny and a bit campy, which I don't think Hammer intended them to be ... I don't think *Sleepy Hollow* resembles the Hammer films, except in the way it was made.' For Lubezki, 'Our biggest frame of reference was *Black Sunday*. That film is really interesting, because all the images are very clear and strong.'[11] *Black Sunday*, better known as *Revenge of the Vampire* in the UK or as *Mask of Satan* (the closest translation to its original Italian title, *La Maschera del demonio*), was a low-budget black and white horror classic from director Mario Bava, released in 1960. Many feel it to be the film which kick-started the Italian horror cinema of the latter half of the twentieth century, enabling directors such as Dario Argento (of 1977's *Suspiria* fame) and George (*Dawn of The Dead*) Romero to gain their cult status. It also launched the career of horror icon Barbara Steel, whose demise at the start of the movie, killed at the stake for witchcraft with a spiked iron 'Mask of Satan' nailed to her face, provided the inspiration for Lisa Marie's demise in Burton's film (with added touches of Roger Corman's 1961 movie, *The Pit and the Pendulum*). For Burton, Bava's classic picture was 'one of the first films that made me understand the power of cinema in the sense of images as part of the story,' and led him into an appreciation of some of Bava's later, even more stylised colour work, such as the 1964 Boris Karloff-starring *Black Sabbath* (aka *I Tre volti della paura*) and the same year's *Blood and Black Lace* (*Sei donne per l'assassino*) which, like *Sleepy Hollow*, featured a black-clad killer, and highly stylised colour cinematography. Burton explained of *Black Sunday* that, 'I've seen it many times, and the images stayed with me for years, like a dream. Some scenes went straight into my subconscious and I love [Bava's] way of making movies because it's so unique. I love it when I see a film and I can tell who made it just by the images. I think that's a very powerful thing.'[12]

CASTING: Johnny Depp was a shoo-in for the role of Ichabod, his third lead role in a Burton movie. Although Brad Pitt and Liam Neeson were both mooted in the press, Burton only ever wanted Depp, stating unequivocally that 'yes, he is first choice,'[13] and once again explaining, 'I love Johnny because he's willing to try anything. I appreciate actors who like to transform and are not afraid to get messy, dirty and dragged through the mud.'[14] Depp, for one, seemed unsurprised to be working on a further Burton picture: 'He knows how I work and I know how he works and I think we both kind of want the same thing,'[15] adding that 'The initial attraction was the opportunity to work with Tim again . . . The added plus was that I loved the story and have always loved this cult idea of the Headless Horseman. It's a great classic story, but with Tim's twist on it. I knew it would be special.'[16]

Burton's interest in Hammer pictures was transferred to his star, who revealed: 'Tim gave me a couple of Hammer tapes initially and we talked about the style. What I find fascinating about them is that there's a style of acting that's borderline bad, but it's so borderline that it's actually brilliant,' adding, 'I think Peter Cushing was a master craftsman, and Christopher Lee definitely is, and it's a style of acting that I find very interesting.'[17] Depp liked the challenge of trying to 'ride the fine line between honest acting and just a bit over the top, the style of Hammer horror films . . . I also liked the idea of playing a romantic lead who is not your typical romantic lead.'[18] In this version of the story, Ichabod was to be 'the first male action adventure hero who's portrayed like a thirteen-year-old girl,'[19] an interesting assignment for any actor.

Burton was ultimately unwilling to let Depp cover himself with prosthetics to make himself look more like Irving's description of Crane, as the actor had initially hoped, but was totally prepared to accept the actor's wildly unorthodox chosen role-model for his performance, Angela Lansbury in *Death on the Nile* (John Guillermin, 1978).

Former child star turned adult actress and pin-up, Christina Ricci, was cast as red herring/love interest Katrina Van Tassell. Joking about Ricci's unusual looks, Burton revealed the thinking behind her casting: 'You're talking about this place Sleepy Hollow and you think about people from upstate New York and the kind of weird inbreeding that goes on, and you just think about these weird-looking people and she just seemed to be appropriate.'[20] Depp approved of the casting. He'd first met Ricci nearly ten years before, when she was working on *Mermaids* (Richard Benjamin, 1990) with his then girlfriend Winona Ryder. One aspect of the casting struck him as rather odd, though: 'One of the first things that popped into my head was that, "My God, I've known her since she was nine years old and we're going to be kissing and stuff!" That was a little odd at first.'[21] Ricci simply 'really wanted to work with Tim,' whilst at the same time realising that 'it was a great opportunity to play a romantic lead, which I've not done before.' At the same time, the actress 'realized they wanted people to go "Christina Ricci's in the movie, she must be the bad one",'[22] thanks to her previous association with playing slightly sinister characters, such as the semi-evil Wednesday in the *Addams Family* films.

Cameo-ing in a pre-credits role as the Burgomeister was Hammer's own Dracula, Christopher Lee. Burton said of meeting another of his idols that, 'When I first met him, we were sitting there for two hours, and it's like, you're looking at Dracula. Even now, you're like looking at him, and he's talking to you, and you're hypnotised, you know.'[23] Lee's take on working with Burton was characteristically self-deprecating: 'Although it's a huge honour and an immense compliment, there's always the fear in your mind . . . that I wasn't going to live up to their expectations . . . I had trouble with some of the lines because the wretched cape was so heavy and I was trying to keep myself in position . . . I hope I did live up to their expectations.'[24]

Most of the other major roles went to British actors. This was both a sensible budgetary move considering the picture was to be shot entirely in England, and an artistic choice based on Burton's desire for the film to reflect aspects of Hammer's output. Exceptions were Burton regular Jeffrey Jones, given the pivotal role of Reverend Steenwyck, and Casper van Dien who was cast as Brom Van Brunt. Amongst the British cast members was Michael Gough, four times Batman's butler, who Burton called out of the blue, though he had effectively retired by this time.

For his grand villainess Lady Van Tassel Burton sought out Miranda Richardson – a hugely versatile actress and minor sex symbol probably best known to audiences for her performance as Queen Elizabeth I in television's *Black-Adder II*. Richardson's film work had included the TS Eliot biopic *Tom & Viv* (Brian Gilbert, 1994) and *Fatale* (USA:*Damage*, Louis Malle, 1992) in which she achieved the rare distinction of giving an extraordinary performance in a dreadful film. For her pains she was awarded a BAFTA statuette and both Oscar and Golden Globe nominations.

Sir Michael Gambon, a former member of the National Theatre and the star of perhaps British television's single greatest accomplishment, Dennis Potter's *The Singing Detective*, was cast as patriarch Baltus Van Tassel. Gambon's film career has been erratic, thanks to his concentration on theatre and television work, but his performance in *The Cook, The Thief, His Wife and Her Lover* (Peter Greenaway, 1989) deserves a place on anyone's DVD shelf.

Ian McDiarmid, cast as Doctor Lancaster, is a celebrated actor/director, greatly respected in Britain for his assured stewardship of the Almeida Theatre, based in London's Islington. His film work ranged from the small-scale, such as the magnificent *Sir Henry at Rawlinsford End* (Steve Roberts, 1980), to the hugely profitable *Return of the Jedi* (Richard Marquand, 1983) in which he played the embodiment of the dark side of the force, the evil Emperor. Shortly before *Sleepy Hollow* began production McDiarmid had finished returning to this character, albeit as a younger man, in *Star Wars: Episode I – The Phantom Menace* (George Lucas, 1999), a role he has already reprised once since, and is likely to do so again on at least one more occasion.

Richard Griffiths is, despite a long and illustrious career, destined for immortality for his role as Uncle Monty in *Withnail & I* (Bruce Robinson, 1986).

Burton was delighted with the highly stylised acting his cast brought to the picture, commenting, 'we tried to make a serious movie at the beginning, until the actors stepped into their costumes and we started to laugh and realised that was impossible.'[25]

PRODUCTION: In 1993 Kevin Yagher, an experienced makeup/FX artist, starting working on the idea of a film script based on Irving's novella. He contacted Andrew Kevin Walker, whose superlative script for *Se7en* (David Fincher, 1997) was winning him many plaudits in Hollywood even though the film had not yet been made. The two men pitched the idea to producer Scott Rudin (*The Addams Family*) who commissioned a script, and sold it to Paramount. There production stalled, partly due to Paramount's early 90s cash difficulties. Adam Schroeder, one of the credited producers on the eventual motion picture elaborates, 'I wouldn't say that they weren't enthusiastic about it, but they didn't see the commercial viability. They never really saw this as a commercial movie, even though we always had a passion for it, and Andrew Walker's script really redefined it. The studio thinks old literary classic and they think *The Crucible* [Nicholas Hytner, 1996]. There was a fear about that. So everybody saw this as a bit of a labour of love.'[26]

At this stage the movie was not thought of as the big budget, blockbusting star vehicle it later became. Yagher had plotted *Sleepy Hollow* as a low budget effects showcase, with a spectacular murder every five minutes or so. Schroeder again: 'When we started developing it, it was before horror movies came back . . . Certainly this is no *Scream* [Wes Craven, 1997] but the fact is, people think Ichabod Crane is Jeff Goldblum or John Malkovich. We never had that in mind. It was always going to be a young, sexy Ichabod, very different from what people think of from the Disney cartoon or some of the descriptions of him in the novella.'[27]

During development Yagher was contracted to act as director on the project as well as provide the film's makeup FX, but Rudin and Schroeder had wanted to work with Burton for several years, and when his *Superman* project finally fell through, they sent him a copy of Walker's screenplay.

After a year out of work due to *Superman*, Burton jumped at the chance to make a picture that seemed to have been purpose-built for his directorial style. Walker's script, he said, 'reminded [me] of . . . old Hammer horror films. It had a fresh take, but . . . respected the source . . . which has a . . . Germanic tone. I always liked . . . any story that has symbolic meaning [and] this script had a good, strong folktale vibe that I liked very much.'[28]

Those already working on the project were thrilled by Burton's declared interest. Schroeder felt, 'When the opportunity of Tim Burton came along, I came to Kevin [Yagher] and he said, "This is the person we always talked about directing this movie; this is who *should* be directing it." '[29] Yagher gracefully bowed out to take a writing, co-producing and effects credit, knowing his project would be in safe hands. With Burton on board, Paramount put *Sleepy Hollow* on the fast track.

It was Producer Scott Rudin's idea to shoot the film in England. While this may seem like a bizarre choice in an era of disadvantageous dollar/sterling exchange rates and when making one of America's few homegrown myths, the decision wasn't made lightly. After hunting throughout upstate New York, the Hudson Valley, and even as far as Massachusetts, Rudin found that suitable locations no longer existed, and that there was too little studio space in the New York area. However, they ended up with the same problem across the Atlantic: 'We came here [England] figuring we would find the perfect little town, and then, of course, we had to build it anyway,'[30] Rudin sighed. However, according to Burton there were other reasons for the continental shift: 'if you're doing a heavily designed movie, the only two places where you can really do it are Los Angeles and London. Even New York doesn't have the same level of resources that those two cities offer.'[31]

'I love upstate New York. It's such a haunted place,' said Burton when asked about the setting he would be recreating on the other side of the Atlantic. 'I wanted to make Sleepy Hollow a special place, like those strangely Japanese paintings of the Hudson Valley that show the rolling hills and towns nestled in misty valleys.'[32] Japanese Shinto paintings were an especially appropriate source for the look of *Sleepy Hollow*, considering that their fog/mist element is meant to indicate, symbolically, the presence of a god or some other supernatural element.

With Burton's intentions in mind, it had been decided that a totally controlled environment was required to create Burton's version of *Sleepy Hollow*. Although many exteriors would be shot outside, on location on the specially constructed outdoor village set, many others would be lensed on forced perspective sets within a studio. Production Designer, Rick Heinrichs, confirms why, 'You don't see them doing many exteriors on stage anymore, because it doesn't really fit the overall look of the films, the naturalism that movies tend to gravitate towards. We're not going for naturalism, we're going for a kind of natural expressionism.'[33]

'My intent was not to come up with any very precise historical recreation,'[34] explained Burton of the movie's atmosphere. 'I'd never have bet . . . that I'd ever be doing a movie where the people were dressed like George Washington!' he laughed. 'We didn't want . . . a bunch of people dipping candles and watching them dry. That's not the most exciting thing to see at the movies.' It was this logic that led the film's extreme stylisation, and the desire to blur the line between studio and location work in an unusual way. By pushing both towards a third aesthetic of the film's own, rather than trying to make the former more like the latter. 'We were trying to create our own reality for the film – a fantasy feel that would still seem *real* . . . I feel very good about what we achieved.'[35]

Construction of the required outdoor village began in September 1998 and lasted well into December. Shooting there would occupy about a month during January and February the next year. Before location filming began, however, there were interiors to shoot at Leavesden Studios. Leavesden was a relatively new facility, built in the shell of an old Rolls Royce factory, that had been used for the James Bond picture *GoldenEye* (Martin Campbell, 1995) and by George Lucas for both his *Young Indiana Jones* TV series and the first of his new trilogy of *Star Wars* prequels.

Shooting there began in November 1998, finally finishing in April the following year, Burton using many of the same crew he'd worked with on *Batman* a full decade before.

Ironically the first scene of the final picture was absolutely the last to be shot – and it was shot on a different continent to the rest of the movie long after the film was edited. Burton began to feel that the character of Peter Van Garrett, so vital to the movie's central conspiracy, should be seen rather than merely discussed and therefore constructed a pre-credits sequence around him. Martin Landau, who appeared in a wordless and uncredited performance as the patriarch, remembers, 'The picture was already finished. Tim called me, and he said, "Would you do this for me?" He had a couple of days in Yonkers, New York, in this old warehouse with a stage coach. I said, "Yes I would." Then he called me a few days later and he said, "Have you thought about it?" And I said, "Tim, yes! Take yes for an answer!" ' Burton for his part has claimed that he asked Landau to play Van Garrett as he knew his friend could be relied on to give sufficient impact to the wordless scene. That and 'Martin looks good in these kinds of clothes, and very few people do.'[36]

Filming was a quick process. After receiving the call from Burton on the Monday, Landau found himself flying into New York 'that Friday and on Saturday I watched the whole movie in the screening room because Tim wanted me to digest the texture of the movie. That night Johnny Depp was there doing a couple of pick-up shots, with Miranda Richardson and Tim, and afterwards we all went out for dinner down at Caroline's downtown, which was wonderful. Come Monday morning I was on the set, and shooting. Again, Tim sort of opened the door and lets me go. In two and a half days we did the entire prologue. On the last day Danny Elfman came on the set, because the score had already been finished, but he had to score this piece. Within a week he and Tim went to London with the orchestra there, scored the prologue, and then four weeks later the movie was in 2,500 theatres in America. Four weeks from the day we finished, which must be a record!'

CRITICS: Praise for *Sleepy Hollow*, although forthcoming, was rather qualified. It wasn't venerated as art in the way that *Batman Returns* had been, but given the kind of grudging respect afforded a well-produced and entertaining blockbuster. *Variety*'s reviewer was one publication equivocal in its praise for the movie, 'As beautifully crafted a film as anyone could ever hope to see . . . a supremely stylish *objet d'art* that has enough flair, drama and gory action to emerge as a strong . . . holiday [box office] attraction,' he opined, holding back on some of the praise because *Sleepy Hollow* seemed, to its reviewer, to be rarely about anything but plot and atmosphere. Despite this perceived shallowness they were willing to give the film the benefit of the doubt, if only due to the combination of the production design, cinematography, costume design and the perfect blend of studio and location work which, it argued, 'took the picture to a truly rarefied level in the visual department'.[37]

Kim Newman, writing in *Sight and Sound*, also found the film philosophically unsatisfying, feeling it to be 'not merely torn between rationality and superstition, but torn apart by the dichotomy, with each of the film's several significant creators drawing subtly different, mutually exclusive readings from the material.' He too was willing to excuse this because the film was 'never less than ravishing to look at – courtesy of . . . Emmanuel Lubezki and . . . Rick Heinrichs, though Burton's eye is evident in every composition.'[38]

Entertainment Weekly's critic thought he detected unnecessary restraint in Burton's film, calling it 'a harmlessly retro-quaint horror bash that keeps throwing things at you, right down to the inevitable stagecoach chase. Personally, I'd rather see Burton so intoxicated by a movie that he lost his head.' Depp's performance was singled out for some complaints too, apparently he 'just acts sillier and more innocuous as the movie goes on.' In the end the picture was both 'vintage Burton – ghoulish yet whimsical, funny in its disjunctive kookiness' and disappointing, 'it's store-bought mystery in place of the real thing.'[39]

The *Village Voice* was kinder, claiming *Sleepy Hollow* to be a 'splendid, shuddering contraption [with] a dazzling purity of vision' with a mood not 'grim but Grimm. Burton directs the grisly action as though it were a jolly puppet show, another *Nightmare Before Christmas*.'[40]

Although *Time* felt that 'The director wants to turn this fairy tale into a full-blooded ghost story,' disapproving of the director's take on the material, it (like many others) had to admit that the film was Burton's 'richest, prettiest, weirdest since *Batman Returns*. The simple story bends to his twists, freeing him for an exercise in high style. *Sleepy Hollow* may be late for Halloween, but this trick is a real treat.'[41]

MUSIC: Elfman's luscious score is one of his most pervasive yet, seeping into every nook and cranny, and filling the entire film with a sense of foreboding and dread. Unusually for Elfman, who often seems to relish the use of silence, here the music appears to be a near-constant presence, rumbling quietly in the background in almost any scene, heightening the suspense as the audience remains aware that it could rise at any moment, heralding another shock. Here the music is as important to the atmosphere as the ever-present mist, becoming almost unnoticeable in its casual acceptance, but ever wafting through the trees, ready to strike. A masterful piece of work.

CINEMATOGRAPHY: Irving's description of the Sleepy Hollow area, 'A drowsy, dreamy influence seems to hang over the land, and pervade the very atmosphere,' provided the basis for the film's surreal look, as designed by Rick Heinrichs. The unusual feel was further enhanced by Mexican Director of Photography Emmanuel Lubezki's hugely stylised visuals. He had the difficult task of melding the location and set work, providing a coherence between the two whilst maintaining the slightly odd, slightly unreal atmosphere that Irving describes, and that Burton had determined to maintain in a homage to his beloved Hammer films and Bava's *Black Sunday*.

Lubezki explained that at the start Burton would have shot the movie in black and white if the studio had allowed it. 'But then we talked about it and he said, "You know, maybe not – maybe it's better just to do it in colour and keep everything very monochromatic, but still keep all those shades of grey, dark blue, very dark brown and green." '[42]

After the difficulties of trying to get *Ed Wood* made in black and white, Burton felt that 'The saturated look I'm going for is not that big of a deal. It's more the quality of the film; it's not as extreme as black and white . . . but it helps when we go from stage to the set work. It's not sepia, it's not monochromatic, it's just a colour filter with a slightly muted quality.'[43] In deciding on this look, Burton could enjoy many of the advantages of black and white filmmaking, whilst being able to use sudden flashes of colour at key moments to emphasise elements of the shot that might otherwise have been missed by the audience (as well as adding to the shock of the numerous decapitations). The only real problem was that, due to the nature of the filters being used, the colour red ended up looking almost black, ensuring that all blood effects had to either be rendered in post-production, or be created with a garish orange liquid on set, that appeared red through the camera.

The set work created additional difficulties from the Director of Photography's perspective. On their first scouting trip in England, Lubezki thought the sets were a joke – the stage ceilings were low, less than 20' high. In order to disguise the low ceilings, a huge amount of smoke was necessary: 'I hate using smoke, but on this film we used it in almost every shot, because it really helped us to hide the stage ceilings and create some atmosphere,' Burton revealed. 'That was our biggest nightmare, because smoke can be very hard to control and it's very unpleasant to have to breathe it in all the time.'[44]

Lubezki explained another reason for the decision to go for such an unusual look: '*Sleepy Hollow* is not a realistic movie, and I didn't want it to be like a typical movie, where if you have a candle, the light is coming strictly from the candle ... For example, the candle might be on the left with the lighting coming from the right.' Burton and Lubezki 'wanted the audience to feel that the sets were slightly unreal. We wanted to create a hint of artificiality in the look, but not enough to take you out of the movie.'[45] Furthermore, this helped create the impression of 'a timeless place, with everything happening at a dreamy dusk. We wanted to create an atmosphere that was nostalgic and sad, a time of day where *anything* could happen.'[46] Burton would later praise Lubezki's intuition on set, emphasising the months of planning that went into creating the unique look of the film, and stressing, 'I feel very in synch, and it's the most fun I've had in a long time working with somebody. He's like another character on the movie.'[47]

The decision to go for such an unusual, muted colour tone for the film may have initially been based on the desire to hide the transition from location to stage-work, but it helped create one of the most beautifully shot and visually consistent movies of Burton's career. As Burton told French journal *Postif*, 'I actually conceived *Sleepy Hollow* as a silent movie. Of course, it's got an abundance of dialogue, but it's the visual aspects which are prime. The film represents my love for cinema. It's a silent and visceral experience.'[48]

PLOT PROBLEMS: The film's plot is hugely convoluted. In order to identify errors, it is first necessary to outline how and why the various murders in the film come about.

As a child, Lady Van Tassel lived in a cottage owned by Peter Van Garrett. When her father died, she, her mother and her twin sister were evicted by Van Garrett, and as her mother was a witch, no one in Sleepy Hollow would take them in. After their mother

– who had schooled them both in witchcraft – died, the twin girls were left to raise themselves in the Western Woods. Baltus Van Tassel, his wife and daughter (Katrina) had meanwhile moved in to their old home.

Witnessing the Hessian's death, the future Lady Van Tassel made a pact with the devil to control his ghost in order to get revenge on Van Garrett for evicting her family, and on Baltus Van Tassel for achieving the wealth and success from her father's old farm which she felt should be hers. By becoming Katrina's mother's nurse, she ensured that the first Lady Van Tassel died, and managed to take her place as the lady of the house, plotting to gain Baltus's wealth. Baltus would also, should Peter Van Garrett and his son both die, become the heir to the Van Garrett estate.

However, Peter Van Garrett had secretly got married to the Widow Winship, and got her pregnant, changing his will so that she, and not his son, would inherit his wealth and lands. Finding out about this, Lady Van Tassel managed to pressure the town elders into covering up the new will. They went along with her thanks to her affair with the Reverend Steenwyck (who performed the ceremony), blackmail of Doctor Lancaster (who had attended the pregnant widow and who was having an affair with the Van Tassels' maid, Sarah), and (presumably) their fear of the town's ownership reverting to outsiders if it passed to Widow Winship's heirs. As the widow's heirs are not visible at any point during the film, it appears they are from outside Sleepy Hollow itself, and thus for the town elders, their friend and local, Baltus, would be a preferable landlord.

To complete the coup, Lady Van Tassel then sent the Horseman to murder Peter Van Garrett, his son, and the pregnant Widow Winship, thus ensuring that Baltus would inherit the Van Garrett estate. To help cover up the new will further, Jonathan Masbeth, who had witnessed its signing, also had to be killed. Lady Van Tassel then found out that the Midwife Killian and her husband had been told of the secret marriage and pregnancy by the Widow Winship, so they too had to die to protect the conspiracy. Thanks to his helping Ichabod discover the Widow Winship's pregnancy, Magistrate Philipse also had to die before he revealed any more of the plot. Lady Van Tassel's sister was also killed, thanks to helping Ichabod discover the secret of how the Horseman was being controlled. Just as Doctor Lancaster is about to tell Baltus of the plot, Reverend Steenwyck kills him to protect Lady Van Tassel's secret, before being killed in turn by Baltus. The Horseman then kills Baltus. This just leaves Katrina, after whose death Lady Van Tassel would have inherited the whole of the Van Garrett and Van Tassel estates.

However, this still leaves a few deaths. Brom Van Brunt's demise is simple enough to explain – he just got in the way of the Horseman too much. His head is not taken, so it seems that Lady Van Tassel did not order his death. Notary Hardenbrook commits suicide in preference to being killed by the Horseman having, like Magistrate Philipse, inadvertently helped Ichabod discover the nature of the conspiracy.

There is no script reason for the Horseman to murder the midwife's little boy, Thomas Killian; in fact his killing *creates* a plot problem. After the Horseman has killed Brom Ichabod correctly deduces that it was reluctant to destroy him until he posed a threat to it because it only kills those whom it has been ordered to. Neither of the Horseman's two stated reasons for killing (either he has been ordered to by Lady Van Tassel or he is protecting himself) apply in this instance; the child is neither aware of the conspiracy nor a threat to the horseman (he is hiding and the Horseman very deliberately searches for, finds and then murders him). Notice also that the Horseman collects the child's head, something he only does with those he has been ordered to kill. This arguably means that Lady Van Tassell ordered the boy's death, except that the Horseman was preparing to leave the house when he heard the boy's movements. Does this mean that he was leaving with his task half done? No, it means the scene makes no sense.

On the DVD commentary Burton describes the cutaway of the Horseman putting the child's tiny skull into his bag as 'one of my favourite shots.' The quite brutal sequence of the Hessian hunting the boy was kept in, despite suggestions that it be cut because Burton remembered, 'As a child, I hated movies with children because they were always treated differently, given the break and we decided . . . treat 'em like everybody else.'[49] In other words, Thomas is killed because of the assumption that audience sentimentality allows children to always survive horror movies (a similar reasoning had underpinned the death of the presidential dog in *Mars Attacks!*).

There is a bigger, yet subtler problem, however. Lady Van Tassel also kills her maid, Sarah, explaining her disappearance with the plausible excuse that she has run off in fear of the Horseman, as have some of the other townsfolk. She then uses Sarah's decapitated corpse as a stand-in for her own body, after Baltus sees the Horseman approach her as if to kill her. Due to the lack of forensic knowledge at the time, it is a safe bet that everyone would assume that a headless female body of about her size, in one of her dresses, and with a cut in the same place as the one she made such a fuss over receiving on her hand, would indeed be Lady Van Tassel. (Only the scientifically-minded Ichabod realises that this is the wrong body due to the lack of bleeding from the wound – even though there is clearly some blood-flow as Sarah's hand is cut.) But why does Lady Van Tassel go to all the trouble of faking her own death, even providing a body that will be assumed to be hers, when the whole plan revolves around her being the last heir to the combined Van Garrett and Van Tassel estates? If she were thought to be dead, there would be a lot of difficult questions when she suddenly reappeared to claim the inheritance. It is possible that she could simply claim to have been injured in the woods, but then there would be awkward questions about whom the body belongs to. Furthermore, after the planned untimely demise of Katrina, Lady Van Tassel would be the most obvious prime suspect for the killings, as the sole remaining heir. Providing a substitute body would actually increase suspicions on Lady Van Tassel's eventual return.

DEATH: As one would expect in a murder mystery, and as can be seen in **PLOT PROBLEMS**, there are numerous (often quite wonderfully brutal) deaths. If we've got our maths right, the final tally sees twelve decapitations, with various other on-screen deaths, and numerous references to other people dying off-screen. It's quite a body-count.

CHILDREN AND FAMILIES: Families and bloodlines lie at the very heart of *Sleepy Hollow*'s complex conspiracy. It is further made clear that the entire town is loosely related either through blood or marriage, and Burton has expressed a delight in the odd-looking, inbred nature of its inhabitants.

Furthermore, all the children in the film have parents murdered, and end up orphans. In his dreams, Ichabod remembers his childhood, where his puritanical father brutally tortured his mother to death for her witchcraft. The experience both physically and psychologically scarred the young Crane, who had wiped his memory of the horror of discovering his mother's body, and lost his faith in both God *and* magic in the process. Katrina witnesses her father's demise in the Church, having already lost her mother thanks to the machinations of her stepmother. The Killians' son has the unpleasant experience of witnessing both his parents being murdered by the Horseman, with his mother's severed head staring down at him through cracks in the floorboards as he hides beneath the house. He is then unceremoniously decapitated himself (see **PLOT PROBLEMS**). Young Masbeth, motherless since early childhood, is also deprived of his father after the Horseman kills him for his part in the drafting of the new Van Garrett will.

By the end of the film, the surviving orphans, Ichabod, Katrina and Young Masbeth, seem to have formed a new family of their own. On the surface, Katrina and Ichabod would appear to be the parental figures, with Young Masbeth as their child. However, considering how much braver than Ichabod Young Masbeth and Katrina are it is apparent that, in this family, Ichabod is the child-figure. Both Katrina and Young Masbeth attempt to physically protect him from harm when danger approaches, and both need his help far less than he needs theirs. On top of this, there is a 'masculinity' to Katrina's role as the wealth-provider of the trio, and Masbeth with his wisdom, his compassion, and in his desire to look out for Ichabod and Katrina has many motherly qualities. They are an unconventional family unit, with traditional role attributes distributed in an unorthodox manner between the three of them.

LOVE TRIANGLES: There's the initial split between Ichabod, Brom and Katrina, as in Irving's story, until the Horseman dispatches Brom. Added to this are the loveless machinations of Lady Van Tassel, who disposed of her predecessor to win her way into Baltus' affections, before cuckolding him with the Reverend Steenwyck. Doctor Lancaster is also cheating on his wife with Sarah, the maid. Also, Ichabod finds himself trying to reconcile his firm belief in reason and deduction with the growing realisation that some things simply cannot be explained with science – another three-way division of feelings.

AUTOBIOGRAPHY?: Kim Newman, in *Sight and Sound*, argued that 'an experiment in expressionist autobiography is yet again in evidence'[50] in *Sleepy Hollow*. *Variety* was more specific, drawing parallels between Burton and his main character: 'Ichabod, obviously like Burton himself, is adamant about seeing things his own way,'[51] but this is hardly overly autobiographical.

Burton provided a clearer personal comparison, revealing, 'I always like characters who think they know things, but don't . . . You're in these meetings in Hollywood and halfway through the meeting you hear yourself talking and realise you don't know what the fuck you're talking about and yet you're pretending like you do. That's what the whole trip is about in a way.'[52] He later elaborated: 'If I'm a morally principled citizen, I retain an aversion for that type of person that represents bureaucracy, the establishment, whether it's in politics or in film,'[53] hence his delight in showing most of the town elders (with the exception of Baltus) in such an unfavourable light. Burton has also said that the script 'did get my mind going in a very visual direction. That type of strong visual response happens more often when a story really speaks to you personally.'[54]

Burton further added that, after the demise of the *Superman* project, 'When it was gone it was like having your head cut off . . . the symbolism of the headless horseman – which I had known since childhood – seemed very appropriate.' Aspects of the director's childhood surfaced in the depiction of Sleepy Hollow itself, as in Burbank people are supposed to be friendly and kind, but appearances are deceptive: 'Behind this facade of normality is not normal at all; they can treat you as an outcast if you challenge the system, the authority or the institutions and so there's this feeling of falseness around.'[55] This feeling was emphasised by Ichabod, whom Burton saw as indicative of the falseness of society as a whole, presenting himself 'in a way that doesn't correspond to his actual emotions. In a way, that's the idea on which the American way is founded! That's one of the aspects of modern people. Everything in America is in the image . . . and not in the substance.'[56]

DIALOGUE TO SKIP BACK FOR:

Ichabod: 'We have murders in New York without benefit of ghosts and goblins.'

Masbeth: 'Is he dead?'

Ichabod: 'That's the problem. He was dead to begin with.'

AWARDS: Rick Heinrichs and Peter Young received the Best Art Direction-Set Decoration Academy Award, with Heinrichs also picking up a BAFTA, a Sierra Award (from the Las Vegas Film Critics Society) and a Los Angeles Film Critics Association Award for Best Production Design, with an additional Award for Excellence in Production Design from the American Society of Motion Picture and Television Art Directors. Heinrichs, along with Ken Court, John Dexter, Andy Nicholson and Leslie Tomkins, also received a Golden Satellite Award.

Emmanuel Lubezki was nominated for the Best Cinematography Oscar, an American Society of Cinematographers Award for Outstanding Achievement in Cinematography in Theatrical Releases, a Chicago Film Critics Association Award and a Sierra Award, whilst winning a Santa Fe Film Critics Circle Award, an Online Film Critics Society Award, a Boston Society of Film Critics Award and a Golden Satellite.

Colleen Atwood also received an Oscar nomination for Best Costume Design, whilst winning at the BAFTAs and Golden Satellites, and gaining a Costume Designers Guild Award for Excellence for Costume Design for Film – Period/Fantasy. She received further nominations at the Saturn and Sierra Awards.

Danny Elfman won a Saturn Award for Best Music, and a Golden Satellite for Best Original Score, with a further nomination at the Sierra Awards.

Of the cast, Christina Ricci won a Saturn Award and a Blockbuster Entertainment Award, whilst being nominated for a Young Artist Award. Johnny Depp also won a Blockbuster Award and was nominated for a Saturn Award and a Golden Satellite. Miranda Richardson received a Blockbuster Award (with Marc Pickering receiving a nomination), with a nomination for a Saturn Award along with Christopher Walken, who was also nominated as Best Villain at the MTV Movie Awards.

Other nominations include those for Best MakeUp, Best Special Effects, and Best Writer (for Andrew Kevin Walker) at the Saturn Awards, and for Best Achievement in Special Visual Effects at the BAFTAs, with further nominations for Best Film Editing and Best Visual Effects at the Golden Satellites, where the film also won for Best Sound. A further nomination was from the American Motion Picture Sound Editors Awards. Another trophy came from the

Hollywood Makeup Artist and Hair Stylist Guild Awards for Best Character Makeup in a feature film.

The film was nominated as Best Horror Film at the Saturn Awards, where Burton also received a nomination as Best Director. It was also nominated as Best Film by the International Horror Guild, and Burton won the Silver Ribbon for Best Foreign Director from the Italian National Syndicate of Film Journalists – appropriate, given the influence of Mario Bava on the project.

TRIVIA: The first time one of the light boxes used for the location work was raised, people in the surrounding villages phoned the police to report a UFO.

The sequence in which the flesh grows around the Horseman's skull was dubbed a 'Large Marge' moment by the FX crew (see **Pee-wee's Big Adventure**).

An uncredited rewrite was performed on Walker's script by British playwright and screenwriter of the Oscar-laden *Shakespeare In Love* (John Madden, 1998), Tom Stoppard. He expanded the nature of Ichabod and Katrina's romance and emphasised the comic nature of Ichabod's character. He had provided similar rewrites on (amongst others) *Indiana Jones And The Last Crusade* (Steven Spielberg, 1989).

Filming the horse chase scenes on a soundstage proved difficult because of the necessity of getting the horses up to speed on such a relatively short running space. They were filmed in approximately three-second bursts from the back of a 4-wheel drive vehicle the crew nicknamed 'the Batmobile'.

Gaffer John Higgins came up with the idea of using full-on 250-ton construction cranes to light the location work. Having worked on rigs in the North Sea oil fields in the past, Higgins was able to work out the complex construction and lighting dynamics required by this approach.

EXPERT WITNESS: Johnny Depp: 'The characters that I've played in Tim's films are all . . . kind of deeply damaged. Which I think of as a good thing. The damaged individual dealing with the world. That is probably, at its very root, why Tim does what he does, and why I do what I do.'[57]

Michael Gough: 'He's great to work for. He's one of the sweetest people to get his own way – come hell or high water, he'll get his way without making waves, without any problems from anybody. He has a wonderful, strong personality and I trust him implicitly. You can put your life in his hands and he'll see you're all right.'[58]

ANALYSIS: It could be said that *Sleepy Hollow* is a fight between instinct and reason in which reason is defeated. Ichabod Crane's journey is away from his being, as Masbeth puts it, 'bewitched by reason' towards accepting that there are more things in heaven and Earth than are dreamt of in the philosophy he propagates.

Yet, whilst it is true that in discovering love and magic, and unlocking his capacity for both, Ichabod grows as a person, he never entirely abandons his belief in scientific *method* (indeed it is his very adherence to this method that forces him to accept the supernatural). Furthermore, it is his medical knowledge, rather than his gut instinct, that proves to him that Katrina is not his enemy. Had he followed his feelings in this instance events would have concluded very differently. Only by a compromise, a (literal) marriage between Ichabod and Katrina and their contrasting methods and outlooks, can the horror be stopped and the world made safe for everyone.

The film also rejects organised Christianity – all the religious characters are hypocrites and liars, with Reverend Steenwyck a letch to boot, conducting an illicit affair with a married woman. Furthermore, Ichabod's father was a religiously motivated murderer, 'a Bible black tyrant behind a mask of righteousness.' It also appears to be Katrina's white magic, not the simple fact of being in a church, which protects the townspeople from the Hessian's advances. Although he appears to be unable to cross the threshold of the consecrated ground, Katrina has already begun her spell of protection as he first attempts to enter.

On top of this, the film is a ringing criticism not just of the Sleepy Hollow community leaders, but perhaps community leaders in general. A conspiracy that kills nearly a dozen people starts at the very top of the social hierarchy and in the end destroys those who began it. Burton has claimed to have an aversion to bureaucrats and other establishment figures (see **AUTOBIOGRAPHY?**), and *Sleepy Hollow* demonstrates this more clearly than any of his other films. The outsiders are the heroes, as a witch, a much-derided police inspector and a child provide the solution to a problem created by society's leaders.

AVAILABILITY: A luscious DVD is freely available on both sides of the Atlantic. The UK one is very slightly trimmed of horror content, unfortunately.

THE BOTTOM LINE: Sharper, faster and wittier than any of the Hammer films it occasionally resembles, *Sleepy Hollow* is a triumph. The cast are divine, the atmosphere and design are unique, the action scenes are beautifully choreographed and the entire thing is stunningly shot. And doesn't that final scene just scream out for a sequel? 'It could well be the ultimate Tim Burton film,'[59] mused Johnny Deep during production. We might be prepared go along with that.

STAINBOY (2000)

Created in response to having to give up on the *Superman* film, and the feeling of inertia that had accompanied that project, Stain Boy is Burton's very own superhero. Unable to do anything other than 'leave a nasty stain' Burton knew that 'Next to Superman and Batman, I guess he must seem tame. But to me he is quite special, and Stain Boy is his name.'[1]

When the people at www.shockwave.com decided to try to further diversify the animations on their website in early 2000, one of the ideas was to try to get well known filmmakers to help. Along with *The Simpsons'* producer James L Brooks, *South Park* creators Matt Stone and Trey Parker, and director David Lynch, Burton was asked to contribute. As it turned out Burton was interested, and this offer provided him with an ideal introduction to the world of web animation. (At the time of writing, his official website, www.timburton.com remains inactive, populated solely by an animated drawing of his little superhero.)

Burton chose 'Stain Boy', a character from his book *The Melancholy Death of Oyster Boy and Other Stories*, as the idea he would like to develop, turning the character's name into one word for the animated version, and signing a deal to create 26 'webisodes' of original animation for Shockwave, all of which Burton, in an unusual departure from his usual working method, also wrote. Glenn Shadix explained that this was the sort of opportunity Burton had been looking for: 'with *Stainboy* Tim wanted to be able to work with a character and own it outright, outside of the studios, and to use the Internet to experiment with characters, to see how they played.' Burton felt strongly that 'Medium and idea share a chemistry. For some stories you have to wait for the right medium. I think [the Internet]'s the perfect forum to tell a sad little story like this one. Stainboy is a character that doesn't do much. He's just perfect for four-minute anima-tions.'[2]

In order to bring his vision to computer monitors across the globe, Burton approached Flinch Studios, an animation and web-media production studio based in Los Angeles. Burton brought them a series of colour storyboards and pencil sketches, made up of a mix of watercolours, greys, and dark-shaded colours with accents of bright pastels. It was unlike anything ever seen on the web, and initially the ideas seemed as if they would be impossible to animate while maintaining their distinctive look.

Burton was adamant that he wasn't interested in the garish, over-the-top look of Saturday morning cartoons, concentrating instead on minimal effects, and presenting the rather bizarre characters in realistic settings. Senior Producer Michael Viner elaborated that 'It is important that *Stainboy* not act like a normal cartoon. We didn't want it to look like an animator had done it. We wanted it to look alive – within the medium – to let time and space into the animation. There's a free-floating sense of anxiety that permeates *Stainboy*. We wanted the viewer to feel that, too.'[3] Art Director Will Amato 'wanted to create an effect that looked like a brush had painted them onto the screen,' and after a few months of experimentation, with some assistance from Shock-wave staff in the early stages, he 'found a way to paint the gradient, as if it were popped right into wet watercolour. I did it section by section of the drawing. It was a deliberate effort to mimic Tim's pure gesture. I was an art forger.'[4] The end result manages to look as if it is hand-painted frame-by-frame, despite having been created digitally.

One of the other innovations of *Stainboy* was in its use of sound. With a lush score provided by Danny Elfman, the atmosphere of the piece was heightened further. 'Our goal,' says Amato, 'was to create an animation that was not driven by incident or event.'[5]

Glenn Shadix voiced much of the dialogue, playing Sgt Glen Dale of the Burbank Police, one of the project's new characters: 'I went over to Tim's place, and we recorded the first episode on a little hand-held mic, I read the copy, we talked about it, and we just played with it. Then after that, the subsequent episodes, Mike Viner from Flinch would come to my house and we would try to knock off a couple of episodes at a time. But being that the Internet can't really support real high-tech sound quality it was not necessary to do it at a studio, so we just did it wherever.'

The first in the series went online in early October 2000, and within the first six days had generated over a million hits. *Variety* praised 'The simplicity of the ink and watercolour drawings, the odd details in each frame ... and the skilful way Burton uses colours against the black-and-white backgrounds,' also singling out Elfman's score as a significant contributory factor to 'the brilliant new animated series'.[6]

Sadly, after episode six, no new *Stainboy* appeared, as Burton found himself having to rush ahead with *Planet of the Apes*. Shadix feels, 'It's still evolving, I'm sure he has other ideas which he'd like to play with. With Tim it's all a matter of how much time he has for various endeavours, I mean he's thinking all the time, and I'm sure he has to prioritise his ideas, and when he works on them ... I think Tim would like to do more – it's all going to be his availability, because he writes them – I don't know. Right now there are none that are currently being produced ... I'm sure that at some points he'll have more to do with various Internet projects.' Whether these projects will include *Stainboy* remains unclear, but the prominent place given to the character on the front page of Burton's website suggests that we haven't heard the last from the silently grubby superhero.

The episodes can be found at http://atomfilms.shockwave.com/af/spotlights/stainboy/

EPISODE LOG

Episode 1: Staregirl

With no explanation of the situation or the characters, the first episode of *Stainboy* leaps right into the 'action'. Dale explains to Stainboy that no one 'will enter the house of the girl who just stares', and our hero trudges off to find his adversary. Derived from 'Staring Girl', in *Oyster Boy*, she poses no discernible threat to herself or to others, simply staring at herself in the mirror as Stainboy arrives, before fixing her attention on him. This episode consists primarily of Stainboy and Staregirl staring at each other, with occasional theremin wails, courtesy of Danny Elfman. Stainboy desperately tries to distract his opponent's gaze, and then to meet her stare without falling asleep. Eventually he can take it no longer, and uses his stain to dislodge a ceiling lamp, crushing her to death. Back at the Police Station, Sgt Dale thanks him 'for ridding our society of another no good freak of nature.'

The episode is simple, effective, and appears to capture precisely what Burton was aiming to achieve.

Episode 2: Toxicboy

Stainboy is sent to the house of Toxicboy (from 'Roy, the Toxic Boy' in *Oyster Boy*), due to complaints from nearby residents of foul smells, burning eyes and nausea. He finds his legless, green foe eating drain deblocker, slug pellets, and other unpleasant substances. After narrowly avoiding being dissolved by green vomit, he approaches Toxicboy with a Christmas-tree-shaped car air freshener. Stainboy manages to touch him on the head with the tree, causing him to scream in agony, thrashing around the room, before collapsing to the floor, dead, face down in a dog's water bowl. The dog in question, a chihuahua, appears through a cat-flap and takes a bite of Toxicboy's head, before turning blue and dropping dead.

Again, very simple, but with a bit more action, and here Stainboy's brand of reluctant justice begins to become less ambiguous – unlike Staregirl, Toxicboy did at least appear to be causing harm to others. Whether that deserves the death penalty or not is another matter . . .

Episode 3: Bowling Ball Head

According to Sgt Dale, 'the bowlers of Burbank are in an uproar' due to an evil menace. Stainboy is dispatched to a dark alley next to the 24 hour Burbank Bowl 10 Pin Lounge. As he nervously creeps down the passageway, hopping bowling pins hide and snigger behind him, before blocking the exit with a dumpster. Dark music wells up as a huge shadow appears . . . It's Bowling

Ball Head (a new character; he is also voiced by Glenn Shadix). He claims, 'Who I am is not important. But what I am is most certainly so ... Once bowling was the sport of kings ... these times are past, replaced with a plague of drunk loud people with hairstyles that resemble small dead animals.' His giant head detaches, and rolls after Stainboy as he flees on his stain down the alley. At the last minute, Stainboy avoids being crushed, Bowling Ball Head's bowling ball head smashes into the dumpster his pin minions trapped our hero with earlier, and the dead bodies of the bowlers he has killed are revealed. Bowling Ball Head is defeated, and Stainboy gets his first piece of real satisfaction in defeating a true villain, standing proudly atop his cracked head, cape flying in the wind. Sgt Dale congratulates him: 'You've made our streets safe again for overweight balding losers who consider themselves athletes for being able to roll a ball in a straight line.'

Sinister and scary, Bowling Ball Head is the first true villain that Stainboy is pitted against, and the little superhero can be proud of a job well done.

Episode 4: Robot Boy

Sgt Dale is incensed: 'There's a brownout in Burbank – there's more energy being wasted here than on my last three marriages.' It looks like he may even have to miss his favourite TV programme ('Cops Without Tops'), so 'get out there and pull the plug on that pervert!' Stainboy heads to Robot Boy's home, where there seem to be no signs of life. He picks up a magazine (*Mechanics Confidential*, with the intriguing headline 'Man Turns Son into Hedge Trimmer'), not noticing Robot Boy slowly assembling himself in the background, until Elfman's score reaches fever pitch as cogs and springs go flying to the sound of electric drills. The clawed villain approaches, zapping a passing mouse with his laser eyes, and evidently set on killing Stainboy. Our hero backs away, with Robot Boy slowly but threateningly pursuing, until the end of his power cord is reached, and the plug falls out of the socket, leaving him (literally) powerless. Dale, standing around the Department with his topless police buddies, is grateful: 'Thank you, Stainboy, for making it safe once again for citizens to waste huge amounts of power and energy, thus rapidly speeding up the destruction of our planet ... Now get the hell out of here!'

Most intriguing for the background details (such as an air freshener much like that used to defeat Toxicboy), this episode, based around the character of the same name in *Oyster Boy*, suggests that Burton and the team at Flinch had begun to know their material and their limitations much more. Robot Boy crops up again in the next episode, being used as a rubbish bin at the Burbank Police Department, much like in Burton's original poem, where 'Robot Boy grew up to be a young man. Though he was often mistaken for a garbage can.'[7]

Episode 5: Stainboy: Match Girl

At the Burbank Petrol Station, the Lisa Marie-voiced Match Girl (who describes herself as 'your match made in heaven') is, according to Sgt Dale, 'making guys pay at the pump – if you know what I mean!' She and Stainboy evidently have a history, as Dale refers to her with a bad pun as 'an old flame of yours'. Match Girl lights herself, destroying the gas station, before expiring. Dale's words of wisdom are typically blunt: 'This should teach you once and for all that you mustn't play with matches, and that it's much safer to play with yourself instead,' before he orders her body to be dumped.

Once again based on an *Oyster Boy* poem, 'Stick Boy and Match Girl in Love', this is one of the least effective episodes. Perhaps a prequel might be in order?

Episode 6: The Birth of Stainboy

As Stainboy enters, Sgt Dale is asleep. He wakes to reveal that 'Not a single criminal activity has been reported in Burbank today,' and sends Stainboy home. After trying to shake the boredom by checking his newspaper clippings and watching a TV advert for stain remover (featuring the blood left by Staregirl's death as an example), Stainboy falls asleep.

He dreams he is back in his mother's womb. Her voice (Lisa Marie again) is heard: 'I think my water just broke,' before her husband worriedly chips in, 'Honey, I don't think that's water . . .'

A crack of light appears, and widens. It becomes clear that we are seeing Stainboy's birth from his point of view, with his mother screaming in horror as the doctor juggles the child, the stains spreading uncontrollably. Cut to a week later, and Stainboy's father is complaining, 'We've had this thing less than a week, and the dry-cleaning bills have already put us in the poor house ... he's a freak!'

His parents decide to leave him at Burbank Charity Home for unusual cases ('or, as we like to call it, the Burbank House of Horrors!'), next to the noticeably smaller maternity hospital. Stainboy wanders around, meeting a few of the other unfortunate inhabitants, before Patrolman Glen Dale turns up as a special treat to give a talk. He begins, 'Hello children, and hello – Stainboy!'

Stainboy awakes, apparently in the Burbank Police Department first of all, before he realises he's at home, with Dale standing over him, shouting at him to wake up: 'Did we enjoy our little nap?' Inexplicably, Dale and Stainboy can also be seen on Stainboy's TV set in the background ...

By far the best, weirdest, most ambitious, and most disturbing of all the Stainboy episodes so far, this belated origin story throws in-joke after in-joke at Burton fans, from the Joker-like hand at the start of the 'Super Creepy Theatre' TV show, to the numerous references to other Stainboy instalments. There are even cameos from a number of *Oyster Boy* characters not seen before, including 'Brie Boy', 'The Girl With Many Eyes', 'Jimmy, the Hideous Penguin Boy' and 'The Boy with Nails in his Eyes'. Unlike the other episodes, which lose their appeal after a couple of viewings, this (currently final) foray into the world of Stainboy can happily be watched time and again, simply due to the level of detail and interest that has been packed in.

PLANET OF THE APES (2001)

Twentieth Century Fox presents
A Zanuck Company Production
A Tim Burton Film
Screenplay by William Broyles Jr and Lawrence Konner and Mark Rosenthal
Based on a novel by Pierre Boulle

1968 theatrical feature script adapted by Michael Wilson
and Rod Serling
Director of Photography: Phillipe Rousselot, AFC/ASC
Production Designer: Rick Heinrichs
Art Directors: Sean Haworth, Philip Toolin
Produced by Richard D Zanuck
Executive Producer: Ralph Winter
Casting by Denise Chamian
Music by Danny Elfman
Costume Designer: Colleen Attwood
Edited by Chris Lebenzon, ACE
Special Makeup Effects designed and created by Rick
Baker
Special Animation and Visual Effects by Industrial Light and
Magic
Directed by Tim Burton

CAST: Mark Wahlberg (*Captain Leo Davison*), Tim Roth (*General Thade*), Helena Bonham Carter (*Ari*), Michael Clarke Duncan (*Colonel Attar*), Paul Giamatti (*Limbo*), Estella Warren (*Daena*), Cary-Hiroyuki Tagawa (*Krull*), David Warner (*Senator Sandar*), Kris Kristofferson (*Karubi*), Erick Avari (*Tival*), Luke Eberl (*Birn*), Evan Dexter Parke (*Gunnar*), Glenn Shadix (*Senator Nado*), Freda Foh Shen (*Bon*), Chris Ellis (*General Vasich*), Anne Ramsay (*Lt Col Grace Alexander*), Andrea Grano (*Major Maria Cooper*), Michael Jace (*Major Frank Santos*), Michael Wiseman (*Specialist Hansen*), Lisa Marie (*Nova*), Eileen Weisinger (*Leeta*), Deep Roy (*Gorilla Kid/Thade's Niece*), Chad Bannon (*Red Ape Soldier/Man Hunt Ape*), Kevin Grevioux (*Limbo's 1st Handler/Ape Commander/2nd Ape Soldier*), Isaac C Singleton Jr (*Limbo's 2nd Handler/1st Ape Soldier*), Quincy Taylor (*Ape Soldier*), John Alexander (*Ape Dinner Guest/Old Man Servant/Old Ape #1*), Jay Caputo (*1st Ape Teenager/2nd Ape Soldier*), Philip Tan (*2nd Ape Teenager/Gossiping Male Ape*), Callie Croughwell (Little Human Girl), Allie Habberstad (*Girl Pet*), Brett Smrz (*Human Kid #1*), Howard Berger (*Gorilla*), Rick Baker (*Old Ape #2*), Emmy Collins (*Gorilla/Human Outcast*), Charlton Heston (*Zaius – Thade's Father*).

TAGLINE: 'Rule the planet'

TRAILER: The teaser trailer begins with the caption 'From the director of *Batman* and *Sleepy Hollow*' – once more indicating just how much box office clout the director of these two huge financial successes is expected to have. Climactic clips from the movie are interspersed with screens full of static, which emphasise Leo's isolation. 'This summer, rule the planet' suggests another caption. It all sets the pulse going – at least partly due to Danny Elfman's hugely evocative music.

The full trailer opens with shots of the desert, with Helena Bonham Carter's voice saying, 'Someday they'll tell a story, and some will say it is just a fairy tale, about a human who came from the stars and changed our world.' A caption then reads, 'from Tim Burton, the director of *Batman* and *Sleepy Hollow*' before a voice-over kicks in over vista shots and clips of random violence: 'in a world where freedom is history', it claims, 'brutality is law, the powerful rule by fear.' This trailer is lyrical and impressive, showcasing the picture's more philosophical dialogue, and it builds to a rousing climax.

TITLE SEQUENCE: The 20th Century Fox logo appears as normal before its colours slowly fade to muted grey-purple, and the sky behind the Fox monolith becomes filled with stars. Elfman's vaguely tribal, vaguely Jerry Goldsmith-influenced music begins, and the stars themselves begin to fade as the camera pulls back onto a slow tracking close-up of an object that's not recognisable until the last minute, when it quickly rotates off-screen – it was an ape's head, encased in some kind of armour. The camera then sinks into a rich redness, peppered with dome-like mounds, on which the film's title logo appears, before the screen fades to black. The titles continue over tracking shots across what at first appears to be a painting of an ape reaching out to some unknown deity, Sistine Chapel-style. We then cut to shiny black metal, with flame-like bronze details overlaid – some kind of spear-head or helmet – and then bronze runes on black. Despite the fact the camera movements are slow, the magnification is high enough to keep all these images separate and interesting. Next, the camera rolls over a rounded piece of armour and the ape which started the last sequence of shots. We see that it was not to a god, but to an ape that the primate was reaching. Behind these is superimposed a reddish, heart-shaped object, its edges covered in metal flames. This is eclipsed by a long conical

TIM BURTON

object, down which the camera tracks before stopping on a pair of dark closed eyes. They open, and we're back amongst the stars, from where the camera pans down, past a distant sun and over an identifiable planet's surface, into the cockpit of a futuristic spacecraft, where a hairy hand is pressing at the controls. All in all, a pretty impressive sequence.

SUMMARY: 2029, a crew of United States Air Force personnel and government scientists are aboard the space station Oberon, training simians to fly spaceships for deep space missions. A pod containing the ape Pericles is sent out to study a storm, despite the protestations of pilot/ape trainer Captain Leo Davidson. Pericles' pod disappears into the storm and, directly disobeying orders, Leo launches himself out in a pod to attempt a rescue. Leo too gets lost in the storm and crash-lands in a jungle, his pod sinking to the bottom of a lake as he barely escapes with his life.

Running into a party of primitive humans who are being hunted, Leo is also captured by their pursuers – talking Apes – who take the humans to a slave dealer, an orang-utan called Limbo, in the Apes' principal (only?) city. Amongst Limbo's customers are the brutal chimp General Thade and Ari – a sensitive female chimpanzee who objects to the way her society treats humans. Ari buys Leo and a young woman called Daena and installs them in the house of her father – an ageing and respected liberal politician.

Leo and Daena escape from the house. Accompanied by Ari and her faithful gorilla servant Krull, Leo and his mixed-species party make their way back to the wreckage of Leo's pod, where he collects various pieces of technology from the craft, including a tracer that will enable him to discover the position of the Oberon in relation to him. The party is confronted by Limbo and his bodyguards – after a short fight, he is taken along as a prisoner.

Meanwhile, Thade takes the opportunity to declare martial law and visits his dying father who tells him their society's greatest secret: 'In the time before time, we were the slaves and the humans the masters.' To prove this to him he shows Thade a handgun, hidden inside a holy relic – a symbol of the humans' lost technology and power. He tells him to capture the human as quickly as possible, as others will come to save him, and against their technology the Apes' civilisation will have no chance. Thade resolves to take an army to find and destroy Leo.

According to Leo's tracer, the rescue party he is expecting is in an area that the Apes call Calima. According to their mythologies, it was here that the creator breathed life into Semos, the first ever Ape – from whom General Thade is descended.

Leo's party reach Calima and discover that it is the wreckage of the Oberon, which has attracted his tracer and which has lain there for thousands of years. Leo's shipmates somehow arrived on the planet before he did whilst out searching for him, and all the Apes and humans on this planet are descendants of the primates and personnel onboard the crashed Oberon. While he doesn't understand what's going on, Leo doesn't have a chance to either mourn or attempt to fully work out the situation, as it becomes clear that Thade's army will soon attack.

Suddenly a large group of humans appear around the Oberon. They have heard of Leo, as a human-who-defies-the-apes, and have come to follow him in the belief that he can save them from lives of servitude. When Thade's army arrives, human and simian battle it out, with Leo trying every idea which occurs to him in a desperate attempt to win. Just as the humans are being bested a space pod arrives. It's Pericles, who left Earth's solar system before Leo but has arrived after him, just as the Oberon left after him but arrived before.

Thade attacks and wounds Pericles, apparently unaware or not caring that this primitive creature is a distant ancestor of his. Leo traps Thade inside a sealed area in the Oberon, and the maniacal Ape General appears to have some sort of nervous breakdown.

Leo leaves in Pericles' pod, believing that if he follows its reverse trajectory he might get home.

Arriving in Earth's solar system, Leo crashes his pod in what appears to be Washington DC. Climbing out of its wreckage, he faces what should be the Lincoln memorial – yet it is not Abe's features, but those of General Thade that stare back at him. Surrounded by Police-apes and fire trucks driven by Apes he stares in incomprehension at this perversion of history.

SOURCE MATERIAL: French novelist Pierre Boulle, the author of *The Bridge on the River Kwai* (1954), first published his satirical novella *La Planète des Singes* (*Monkey Planet*) in 1963. In the late 1960s it provided the basis for a much celebrated, and highly profitable, film adaptation which in itself spawned four sequels of varying quality, a spin-off television series (all of which are now available on DVD) and even cartoons. Heavily merchandised at the time, and in the exhaustive manner which some critics always insist began with *Star Wars* (George Lucas, 1977) it was, in America at least, one of the big crazes of the early 1970s. *Planet of the Apes* (Tim Burton, 2001) borrows equally and liberally from *Planet of the Apes* (Franklin J Schaffner, 1968) and its four sequels as well as the novella.

The basic thrust of the plot, the arrival of a human space-traveller on a far distant Ape planet is taken from Boulle, but filters it through the first film adaptation, which made the space-man American rather than French, and established him as a career military man rather than a journalist. Burton's film's difficult ending (see **JUST PLAIN WEIRD**), in which Leo returns to Earth, only to find it run by Apes, draws on the novella's penultimate chapter in which the main character, Ulysses, returns to a France where the Eiffel Tower is intact (just as the George Washington memorial is still visible as Leo approaches Washington DC). But upon leaving his 'capsule' Ulysses is shocked to see a world perhaps more primitive and old-fashioned than the one he left behind, and then horrified to see that the 'men' he has seen operating trucks and wearing uniforms are gorillas. The ending of Burton's picture then, echoes the book's conclusion not only in featuring an ape-controlled Earth, but also one which appears decidedly more primitive than the one he left.

This complex backwards/forward time travel dénouement (Ulysses confidently expects to return to an Earth 700 years after his own period due to the way he understands time to be disrupted by space travel) is never sufficiently explained in the book, either, but the scene immediately after it is more sophisticated than anything in any of the *Apes* films – the entire novella is revealed to be a story being read by two apes. The fantasy in Monkey Planet isn't that apes could rule a world, it's that such a thing as a talking human who has come from space can exist at all. This ending, which relegates the action of the book to 'fairy tale' status, is hinted at in one of the two trailers for the 2001 feature, and it's a shame that no adaptation of the novella has used it. Given Burton's declared interest in fairy tales and non-literal storytelling, his decision that his film shouldn't utilise this element of the novella's ending is rather surprising.

The 'explanation' for the Ape-run Earth offered, obliquely, in *Planet of the Apes* (2001), seems to be partially influenced by events in the third to fifth *Apes* movies. In *Escape from the Planet of the Apes* (Don Taylor, 1971) two ape characters from the first two films, Cornelius and Zira, travel back to the Earth of the 1970s via the space-warp through which Taylor originally arrived on their world (similar in a sense to how Leo returns home). Once there, they are killed by the CIA, but not before Zira has given birth to a child. She places this child with a human circus owner sympathetic to their plight. In *Conquest of the Planet of the Apes* (J Lee Thompson, 1972) this child grows up to lead a group of contemporary apes that he has educated, in open rebellion against their human masters. This is presumably (in some sense) what the time-travelling General Thade does in order to create the world Leo witnesses at the end of Burton's picture.

Furthermore, some minor character names in *Planet of the Apes* (2001) are taken from the novella and/or the first film, including Nova (a human woman in the book and the 1968 film, an ape courtesan in the 2001 version) and Zaius (an ape scientist in the 1968 adaptation, General Thade's father in 2001). Other aspects that appear to be drawn from the *Apes* sequels include the striking image of monkeys in space-suits (from *Escape from the Planet of the Apes*) and the strongly hinted at possibility of different species of apes engaging in civil war, taken from both *Beneath the Planet of the Apes* (Ted Post, 1970) and *Battle for the Planet of the Apes* (J Lee Thompson, 1973).

REFERENCES: There are a couple of paraphrases from the first *Planet of the Apes* film in the dialogue. The first 'Get your hands off me you damn dirty human', parodying a line of Charlton Heston's dialogue from the 1968 version, is very funny and rather effective. The second, with Heston himself in the Ape role of General Thade's father, delivering his own final lines 'Damn them, damn them all to hell' from the original movie, just doesn't work at all. The in-joke (it's Charlton Heston dressed as a monkey. See?) overwhelms the necessary plot-exposition (the secret of the society revealed, or at least hinted at) and capsizes, in the final seconds, one of the best scenes in the entire film.

Another returning actor from the original films was Linda Harrison, who played the human love interest in the first two films. Here she returns as one of the humans captured along with Leo.

From behind, the smashed remains of the USAF Oberon resemble the top of the Statue of Liberty in an effective homage to the shock ending of the original *Apes*, where Heston comes across the ruins of the monument, and realises he was on Earth all along. This is a subtle and devious piece of production design from Rick Heinrichs, hinting at something that does not come to pass in this version.

The revelation that the name of the holy land of Calima is in fact a corruption of the phrase 'Caution Live Animals' (etched into the wall of the Oberon i.e. a piece of damaged space hardware) is reminiscent of the way that in *Star Trek – The Motion Picture* (Robert Wise, 1979) the name of the robotic menace V'ger is revealed to be a corruption of the word Voyager the name of . . . a piece of damaged space hardware.

PRODUCTION: As with the production of 1989's *Batman*, the production of *Planet of the Apes* (2001) began long before Tim Burton became involved in the project. Fox first began looking at the possibility of reviving/remaking their monkey-related property in 1988, when a new script by Adam Rifkin (*Small Soldiers*, 1998) was commissioned. Little more was reported for another five years, until Fox announced pre-production in 1993. At this time Don Murphy, Jane Hamsher, and Oliver Stone were on board to act as producers after work finished on *Natural Born Killers*, with Terry Hayes, the screenwriter of impressively violent Australian post-apocalyptic flick, *The Road Warrior: Mad Max 2* (George Miller, 1981), working on a screenplay. A few months later press reports suggested Arnold Schwarzenegger was interested in playing the lead in the picture, and that Philip Noyce (*Patriot Games*, 1992) would direct. By early 1995 Noyce had moved on, helming *The Saint* with Val Kilmer, and *Home Alone* director Chris Columbus had become attached to the project. A new screenplay (possibly a rewrite of one of the previous drafts) was being prepared by *Batman* scribe Sam Hamm, working closely with Columbus – who himself had prior screenwriting experience with *Gremlins* (Joe Dante, 1984) and *The Goonies* (Richard Donner and Steven Spielberg, 1985). Presumably due to Schwarzenegger's prior working relationship with him on the very successful time travel *Terminator* movies, James Cameron then entered the frame as a producer. At some point during the next year Columbus departed from the project.

During 1996 both *Bad Taste*'s Peter Jackson and *Stargate*'s Roland Emmerich were suggested as possible directors, but by

1998 Robert Rodriguez, of *El Mariachi* fame, was felt by the trade press to be the most likely to finally lens the picture. Sam Hamm's script, then still apparently the favoured version, was widely thought to be a time-twisting plot reminiscent of Cameron's own *Terminator*, and is repeatedly reported as ending with human explorers returning to Earth from the Ape Planet only to discover that Apes have taken over their homeworld, and that the face of the Statue of Liberty (so integral to the climax of the original film) has been rechiselled into the face of an Ape.

During 1998 further rumours circulated of a new Cameron-penned script, which featured scenes with Charlton Heston playing his original-series character of Taylor (who had been killed in a nuclear explosion in *Beneath the Planet of the Apes*), enormous amounts of time-travel theory and endless continuity links to the original series. The storyline that circulated on-line during this period is virtually incomprehensible to anyone without a degree in *Apes*, and although widely believed looks more like the work of a fan with too much time on his hands than that of a respected Hollywood screenwriter. The end of 1998 saw Cameron no longer linked with the project (according to some unconfirmed reports on the Internet he was fired by Fox, though for no obvious reason). Further casting, script and director rumours, none credible, continued to circulate for the next year.

In summer 1999 yet another new writer was appointed: William Broyles Jr, screenwriter on *Apollo 13* (Ron Howard, 1995), was asked to begin afresh. Advised not to read any of the previous attempts, and not to feel limited by the constraints and conceits of the existing films, Broyles optimistically began work. As instructed he went entirely where his imagination took him, calling his version *The Visitor, Episode One in the Chronicles of Aschlar*, his name for the planet. 'It was originally conceived as the first of three movies in a whole new cycle. But that was when it was only me and nobody else, and I could do whatever I wanted.'[1]

In order to assist in the construction of his radically new version, Broyles indulged himself in huge amounts of research into periods of human history that moviegoers wouldn't normally directly associate with the planet of the apes as previously glimpsed. He investigated ancient and medieval warfare, siege instruments, and methods of fighting. Broyles' research opened his eyes to more than technical issues, and suggested a new approach to characterisation for the series. He would move away from the Apes equals bad/humans equals good (or vice versa depending on the individual film) simplicities of the original series, and the perhaps painfully earnest attempts at 'racial' allegory most of the films had indulged in. Looking at Roman history he saw a broad cross-section of human behaviour: nobility, betrayal, lust for power and cowardice. 'Then, if you could assign that kind of behaviour both to humans and apes, depending upon not just whether they were human or ape but what their character was like, that could be interesting.' A character who emerged out of the writing process at this time was a clear villain, an albino gorilla named General Thade. 'His name is an [anagram of] death, because that was the way that he was leading [his people].'[2]

In early 2000 new Fox Filmed Entertainment chairman/CEO Bill Mechanic and Fox Film Group president Tom Rothman decided to take personal control of the project. It seems that Fox, finding themselves with few summer movies for the year 2001, needed to put a 'popcorn' movie into quick turnaround so as to not miss out on a share of the lucrative period's market.

With Broyles' script judged nearly ready for production, and copies of it going directly from Fox execs to directors themselves (with none freely available for agents to read), word was that the studio was looking for a director ready to proceed quickly into casting and pre-production. Broyles recalls this time, 'I gave it to Tim and he said, "Yes, I'll do it." It happened fast.'[3] Burton himself remembers the process as being somewhat slower: 'I had to think about doing this movie. The original was a classic and I didn't want to do a remake. But I was intrigued by the mythology of a reverse world.'[4] Producer Richard D Zanuck, who as head of Fox had overseen the original *Planet of the Apes*, committed towards the end of March 2000 as, according to *Variety*, did Burton. Initial rumours of the director's potential involvement had only begun circulating a month earlier.

Before production could begin in earnest there were issues that needed resolving. Fox had budgetary concerns with Broyles' script, concerns that Burton shared. 'It would have cost us $200 million if we'd done half of what was in that script,'[5] he explained not long before release. These budgetary worries, combined with script alterations required for thematic, plot and character reasons (and additionally to 'make it less like [Ridley Scott's] *Gladiator*'[6] which had been produced and released while Broyles' *Apes* was in development) would necessitate the hiring of some fresh writers to take a pass at Broyles' script. Burton also had ideas of his own that he wanted to put in the picture, particularly in relation to the portrayal of the Ape-suit contingent: 'You're watching apes, but they're like humans, and you never quite know where you stand in relation to that. Just when you think you're going somewhere, something else happens. I love that. What this movie should do is put new images to unanswerable questions – the ones we all love to talk about and none of us have the answers to.'[7]

However, a delay of some months then ensued before Fox finally cleared the movie for production, during which time the Broyles script remained unaltered. It appears that during this period little work could be done on the project, although discussions were held with makeup maestro Rick Baker about providing the all-important monkey faces in early May, in place of former Burton collaborator Stan Winston, who had been attached to the project long before the director was finalised. Baker had been briefly involved with the project back in 1995, and had done some tests then, so knew the difficulties. His first discussions with Burton were just six months before filming, when the movie was suddenly on the fast track. 'If they had asked me how much time it was going to take, I would . . . have said "a year". From day one I said, "You're six months behind." '[8] 'The original film's make-up was great for the time,' Baker continues, 'but basically they had one sculpture – in gorilla, chimp and orang-utan versions – which they duplicated for everyone. They all had the same slicked-back hair and button noses. The teeth were in the mouth but you never saw them. I wanted to be sure our apes had lips that move so you can see the teeth. I think that seeing the teeth is very important to accept that they are speaking. In addition, I wanted each creature to be uniquely different. I like making them characters and bringing out the individual differences.'[9] 'I . . . had two weeks to do a bunch of designs. It was a really fun period, but not much of it applied when we finally got our actors and a script. It's kind of hard to do designs when you don't have the actors, because so much is dependent on the structure of the person's face.'[10] Unfortunately for Baker, the actors would not be finalised until as late as August (see **CASTING**). During pre-production, there were nearly 70 workers at Baker's Cinovation Studios headquarters in Glendale, CA, manufacturing appliances; 30 makeup artists worked on their application during production.

Production Designer Rick Heinrichs, returning from Burton's *Sleepy Hollow* to start work in May, relished the opportunity of reinventing a modern classic: 'Whenever you're taking on something someone else has done first – that's probably the biggest challenge.' His Ape City set was an astonishing 32,000 square feet, and took up Stage 30 at the Sony Culver City lot. Construction began in July 2000 and took four months to complete. No reshoots were possible on this set because the cast and crew of *Spiderman* (Sam Raimi, 2002) were booked to use the lot just a week after *Apes* was scheduled to finish. As he later revealed, 'I felt really good about the stuff we did on *Planet of the Apes*, I felt very fulfilled being on the set. The design of the Ape City set was really about getting the overall sense and then coming up with a lot of vignettes.' (see **EXPERT WITNESS**)

Once the go-ahead was given, the pressure was suddenly on all involved. Burton's friend, actor Glenn Shadix, recalls this period of production: 'It started without a script really completed, and it took six months to get a complete green light. When it did get going, the pressure [on Burton] was so intense.' Burton himself commented on the speed with which it was necessary to make the movie following this delay: 'It's a ridiculous kind of schedule. It took longer to green-light than to make, but that's the way things happen on movies like this. They're such big monsters that it takes an unnatural act to get them going and keep them moving.'[11]

After the film's *definite* go-ahead was announced, press speculation and rumour-mongering began in earnest. As no one outside the project had read Broyles' script (which was planned to be rewritten anyway) press reports were still confused over whether Burton's *Apes* would be a remake of the 1968 film, an addition to the existing Fox *Apes* series, or a separate adaptation of Boulle's novella. In the end it was explained that it would be all, and none, of the above. It would be a 'reimagining'.

Burton and Executive Producer Ralph Winter were now able to hire Mark Rosenthal and Lawrence Konner, who had experience of writing about apes with *Mighty Joe Young* (Ron Underwood, 1998), to rewrite Broyles' script; but the pressure of time affected them as well. Konner recalled: 'Mark and I were called early summer. So production was already sort of in motion – pre-production was already sort of finished.'[12] (According to *Variety*, Rosenthal and Konner were only officially hired at the start of October.) The production and release dates for the movie had already been set for 6 November 2000 and 4 July 2001 respectively, and were regarded as immovable – although by the end of October, the release had been pushed back by a mere three weeks to 27 July. Further delay would have meant the picture slipping into an autumn/winter season already packed with films expected to gross a sizeable amount of money, such as the first *Harry Potter* movie, and Peter Jackson's *The Fellowship of the Ring*. Any delay on top of that would have pushed *Apes* into 2002, where it would be expected to compete not only with the products of other studios, but also Fox's own *X-Men* sequel, and George Lucas' inevitably colossal *Star Wars: Episode II – Attack of the Clones*, which Fox would be distributing for Lucasfilm. Glenn Shadix recalls, 'It was put together and released on a schedule that was more concerned with the commercial aspects than anything else, because it was pushed for a summer release.'

Once shooting began (on schedule), new challenges presented themselves to Rosenthal and Konner, who continued to work on the rewrites during production. Konner revealed some of the difficulties they faced on top of the usual dilemmas of rewrites, including 'production problems and idiosyncratic notions of that ... in a sense every day [we were] being presented with a new problem that we had to go back and solve, and present the solution back to Tim and say what do you think of this way of getting the story ... and he would either like it or not like it.'[13] Burton confirms the hectic, improvisatory nature of the film's time on set: 'Every day was an experiment. These big fantasy films require constant daily exploration. We can sit around in a room like this talking about apes but it's a different story when you're on the set. You need to experiment to see what works.'[14]

The difficulties of shooting such a technically demanding picture in such a short space of time, and without a completed script, should be apparent to anyone. Any delay, no matter how small, could result in disaster. Despite the pressure it was often a happy set, with most actors, especially Tim Roth and Mark Wahlberg (see **CASTING**) reporting what a good time they had.

As well as studio shooting there was a period of location filming at Lake Powell, Utah, where some of the 1968 film had been shot. Although keen to avoid shooting there, the crew were eventually boxed in by the need to find locations within a small radius of their Los Angeles base. There are few areas of wasteland on Earth without any noticeable vegetation. There are even fewer within easy reach of Hollywood. Further location filming was done even closer to base, at Trona Pinnacles in California, a common movie location thanks to its unusual topography.

Typical of the problems encountered during location filming was the lake through which Leo's party escape. Initially under-full, it had to be pumped with water to bring it up to acceptable levels. But by the time the scene was filmed it was the middle of winter, and the American Humane Association adjudged the water too cold for horses to run through safely. A pump was installed to pour hot water into the mix in order to raise the temperature sufficiently to satisfy all concerned.

According to some reports, by the end of the shoot Burton had no less than three separate camera crews and a mobile editing unit operating on set. Whatever measures were taken seem to have worked – Planet of the Apes shooting finished on schedule and slightly under budget. Shortly afterwards the director reflected, 'Obviously, Planet of the Apes is a big investment . . . I feel a responsibility to that, to the studio, but it's all abstract; nobody knows what a successful movie is until it makes a billion dollars. On these kinds of things, there is a lot of pressure and you hope you can deliver whatever might be successful.'[15] 'I don't think about the comparisons 'cos that'll just be a nightmare,'[16] he told Mark Salisbury a few weeks later. Unfortunately comparisons were exactly what he was going to get.

CASTING: Despite press speculation that it was inevitable that the human space-traveller (a key figure in every single version of the story, including the novella) would be played by Johnny Depp, actor Mark Wahlberg eventually signed up to play USAF Captain Leo Davidson by the end of June 2000. Wahlberg, a former model and occasional recording artist, had begun to move into acting a few years previously. His work has included impressive roles in Boogie Nights (Paul Thomas Anderson, 1997) and Three Kings (David O Russell, 1999). Interestingly, he appears not to have been shown Broyles' screenplay (which Burton was still planning on altering) at this stage, taking the part based solely on the director's reputation: 'There was no script. I didn't need one,'[17] he commented. 'When you have a guy like Tim Burton, people come.'[18]

Helena Bonham Carter also became interested in the project because of Burton's involvement, although his approach to acquiring her services was unorthodox. 'He phoned me up and said, "Don't take this the wrong way, but you are the first person that I thought of to play this chimp." ' When she asked why Burton thought of her, the director said, ' "Well, you know, I just had this sort of hunch that you'd like to try something very different." It was so refreshing.'[19] In the role of the conventional love interest, model and former synchronised swimmer Estella Warren was cast in early July.

Another British actor not normally associated with this sort of role – indeed one who normally works away from studio films – was writer/director Tim Roth. At the end of July he turned down a part in the nascent *Harry Potter* franchise in order to play the part of the villainous General Thade, agreeing with Wahlberg that, 'We were all there because of Tim.'[20]

Michael Clarke Duncan, Oscar-nominated for his performance in *The Green Mile* (Frank Darabont, 1999), was selected by Burton because of his 'King Kong voice . . . there are not too many people I know where you just hear their voice and it makes you happy.'[21]

Paul Giamatti, whose previous roles included playing Bob Zmuda in *Ed Wood* screenwriters Scott Alexander and Larry Karaszewski's splendid Andy Kaufman biopic *Man on the Moon* (Milos Forman, 1999), also signed on board the film. He would play 'the Peter Lorre comic relief of this group'.[22] 'I had no qualms about the makeup at all,' he revealed. 'My agents asked me, "You want to play a human, right? So people can see your face?" And I said, "No way! What's the point of being in *Planet of the Apes* as a human?" '[23]

Despite at one time strenuously denying he would even consider a cameo in an Apes remake or sequel, Charlton Heston agreed to appear as General Thade's father. 'I have to say it helped a good deal when [producer Richard Zanuck] said there would be a large sum of money involved. But Burton is pretty good at his job and I think he's come up with an excellent movie,'[24] Heston joked, while also pointing out that 'There's no law against remakes,'[25] and that he had headlined remakes of *The Ten Commandments* and *Ben Hur*.

The actors playing Apes all had to attend what they referred to as 'Ape School' with stunt player Terry Notary (a former Cirque du Soleil performer), who taught them to loosen up so their movements approximated real ape body language.

Notary explains, 'A primate is a very liquid animal; he spirals into a chair. Generally speaking, they are very direct and grounded. They're easily distracted but when they're focused on one thing, the focus is total. In essence, we had to teach actors how to find their own sense of being primal.'[26]

Different ape actors reacted differently to the constraints and opportunities afforded by makeup. Tim Roth, though he hated spending all day in it, was delighted: 'I really, really enjoyed it, as far as what it gave me for acting ... it got me to vanish completely, which is perfect ... you're so liberated by not being yourself ... It gives you a chance to just go crazy and go wild and experiment.'[27] Helena Bonham Carter was not so keen, 'There were days when I thought the makeup was ridiculous and intolerable. I wanted to kill both my makeup artist and Tim Burton. It felt claustrophobic, like being buried alive, and your natural instincts are to tear it off.'[28] Other days, however, were less stressful – 'We were ... heavily disabled because we were wearing teeth which made it difficult to talk and we have fake ears so it makes it difficult to hear or listen. So it became very hilarious when you've got a bunch of us together because we can't hear a word we're saying and we're always going "What? What are you saying?" '[29]

CRITICS: Critical reaction to *Planet of the Apes* was varied, but a typical review was 'fascinating visuals ... spectacular costumes and makeup ... sloppy ending.'[30] Other comments included: 'Despite an undercooked script and the relative weakness of the main character, the movie delivers all the action and imagination you could ask from a summer blockbuster.'[31] Unfortunately, with Burton's name on the credits, and the insistence on the 'reimagining' rather than 're-make' tag, the majority of critics seemed to be expecting something rather more than just a popcorn film. It was thus inevitably a disappointment to learn that 'this picture has as much ambition about conquering the box office as General Thade does in taking over the monkey planet.'[32] Although a number of Burton's previous films had been huge money-makers, they had never before appeared to have been so cynically *designed* that way.

Some reviewers appeared to try and excuse the picture's deficiencies thanks to their affection for the director: 'The best that can be said is that it's still a Burton movie, with a singular combination of motley humour and visual majesty,' yet were usually forced to conclude in the negative: 'Burton continues to jam together jarring story points and clashing moods, and to tell his story from a point of view alternating between earnestness and camp.'[33] The film's inconsistent tone was not just bemoaned here, but the change in loyalty: you can be feeling for the humans (as Bonham-Carter's character led you to do) one minute; then suddenly you're 'trying not to enjoy the fact that a big ol' gorilla is giving some pathetic human such a whompin' that it takes three camera angles, four jump cuts, five pieces of the set being smashed up, and six crash-bang sound effects just to jam it all in your greedy, goin'-ape face.'[34]

Few films ever receive entirely bad notices, and *Apes* was no exception, with the *San Francisco Chronicle* opining that it was 'an amazing display of imagination,'[35] while the *Montreal Gazette* compared Burton with another reputed auteur director: 'some of the best space sequences since Stanley Kubrick ... *Planet of the Apes* is Hollywood at its very best – the perfect marriage of awesome big-screen technology and storytelling excitement.'[36]

Yet it cannot be denied that most reviews were more condemnatory than they were congratulatory, with *Variety* bitingly dismissing the movie as 'Largely listless and witless, [not] very exciting or imaginative; most surprisingly, given the material, it is also Burton's most conventional and literal-minded film, the one most lacking in his trademark poetic weirdness and bracing flights of fancy.' Furthermore, their critic felt that the scripting was obvious and the 'political' parallels were just cheap jokes. Moreover, the ending was 'really, really bad'.[37] Jay Carr of the *Boston Globe* had raved about Burton's previous films and had interviewed the director more than once, yet could find nothing worth praising in Burton's *Apes*, concluding that 'reimagined is precisely what the new film is not ... [it's] little more than a screenful of heavy-metal political correctness ... This will not be remembered as the finest hour for Burton's neo-Goth sensibilities ... The film has dissolved into self-parody ... Instead of reinvigorating a Hollywood classic, Burton only takes it to camp.'[38]

Many singled out the hastily rewritten script for scorn, although one (perhaps unfairly) suggested that disappointed punters should 'Blame the primary scriptwriter, William Broyles Jr ... [it] isn't a story about an alien in a strange new world. Rather, it's a travelogue about a tourist who visits a place where business is conducted in another currency.'[39] Others thought it was 'under-dramatised . . . its sporadic attempts at comic relief end up being neither comic nor a relief . . . it's just not very much fun to watch,'[40] or 'intermittently amusing and exciting, but also chaotic and befuddling . . . Some of the key plot strokes are feeble, relying on stupidities.'[41] Yet more pinned the film's failure on its lead: 'There's no emotional core . . . Wahlberg . . . is a dim, lunky presence without any of the charisma, emotional range or humour that might have made the film work.'[42] The short production time and unfinished script had ensured that 'While Franklin J Schaffner's *Planet of the Apes* had weight and depth, Burton's *Planet of the Apes* is nonsensical.'[43]

Being patronising was yet another criticism, in the *New York Times*: 'When Mr Burton's "Planet" fixes on being entertaining as single-mindedly as the gorillas bearing down on *Homo sapiens*, it succeeds. But the picture states its social points so bluntly that it becomes slow-witted and condescending; it treats the audience as pets.'[44]

But perhaps the most damning comment must be 'unoriginal' – 'its dialogue, action, and effects are as mired in formulas, clichés, and stereotypes as the simian world our hero finds himself imprisoned on . . . The only real surprise is how utterly unoriginal it has turned out to be.'[45] After a long and well-argued piece, which covered almost all of the problems mentioned above, *Sight and Sound* was forced to conclude that Burton's 'shallowness and cavalier attitude towards story are at least partly responsible for turning him into a hired hand,' and wondered, 'Is there a way back to Tim Burton's home planet from here, and does it still exist?'[46]

Planet of the Apes received the worst reviews of Burton's feature-filmmaking career.

MUSIC: Many of those working on *Planet of the Apes* felt the pressure of adding to an established series but composer Danny Elfman wasn't really one of them. He'd only seen the 1968 movie once as a kid and didn't know Jerry Goldsmith's score. Though he watched it on DVD – 'It was such an ethereal otherworldly score. Such an odd dissonant piece of work' – Elfman felt little compunction to imitate it, preferring instead to go his own way. 'Having just seen a rough cut of the film, I knew it was going to be very big, aggressive, muscular, kind of a tribal, driving score.'[47]

One unusual aspect of the soundtrack was that due to the demands of the film's merchandising, Elfman had to complete the commercial CD for release before the movie was ready. This means that some music on the CD was written especially for it, in the style of his score, rather than being from the score itself. In a further twist, on hearing the CD director Burton liked some of Elfman's consciously CD-only music sufficiently to ask for some of it to be worked into the finished film.

Shortly after the film's release the score was at the centre of a minor controversy, with suggestions in the press that some parties were unhappy with it and would have requested changes given more time. Elfman put the record straight in a letter to the *Los Angeles Times*: 'The facts are these: If anyone was unhappy in any way, they never told me. We not only didn't rescore anything, but I cancelled two sessions that I had been holding just in case we did need extra time and we were finished ahead of schedule.'[48]

CINEMATOGRAPHY: Burton had come to know French cinematographer Phillippe Rousselot during the preparations for *Mary Reilly*, which Rousselot shot, and which Burton pulled out of directing in favour of *Ed Wood*. Despite being in negotiations for another film, Rousselot quickly hopped on board with Burton: 'When you get a call from Tim Burton about a movie like this, there isn't a lot of hesitation.'[49]

Unlike his previous Oscar-winning work on Robert Redford's *A River Runs Through It* (1993), the Frenchman opted for a much more stylised look for *Apes*. The problem was that although 'this film is set in a totally different world [and] your imagination can run anywhere ... You have to find a balance between your dreams and what you *should* do.'[50] After several long discussions, Rousselot and Burton opted to go with several distinct filters, creating a slightly unreal look much like that achieved by Emmanuel Lubezki for *Sleepy Hollow*. Burton and his cinematographer 'tried to find a way of slightly distorting reality without going so far that the audience would think something is "wrong",'[51] and decided that having subtle shifts in the colour palette between the three main locations – the jungle, Ape City and the desert – was the best way to achieve this.

After various tests, Rousselot discovered that the best filters for the look they wanted to achieve were not designed for movie cameras, but for still photography – special Polarised lenses that can achieve two-tone colour gradations depending on the degree the filter is rotated. However, the effect of the particular filters he and Burton decided on is very random, creating problems in matching shots – when the camera's angle shifts, it also changes its relationship with the source of the light, which in turn changes the effect of the filters. Furthermore, 'when changing lenses, it's difficult to pull the filters apart and then find the exact rotation combination again.'[52] Added to this was the problem that, having managed to get custom-made filters for the film, none of the holders available would take them, making it necessary to simply tape them to the front of the cameras. Especially during location work in the desert, with strong winds, this created additional problems for the camera team.

Considering all the difficulties in achieving the look, it is impressive that much of the picture achieves Burton and Rousselot's intentions of an otherworldly feel. The purples and oranges of the desert scenes contrast strongly with the turquoise colour scheme of the jungle, and the softer, glowing night of Ape City. However, the difficulty of the technique is evident in certain shots, particularly during action sequences, as there seems to be a shift in colour tone as the camera moves about. The very short preparation time, and rapid pace of filming, again managed to detract from something interesting. When the filters work, the film looks fantastic, and the slightly unreal look further complements Rick Baker's makeup, Rick Heinrich's designs, and the general air of weirdness. It makes it all the more of a shame when a few shots seem out of place in the colour-scheme of the rest of the film.

PLOT PROBLEMS: Why does some of the Apes' religious iconography show Pericles, a single ape falling from the sky in a pod, an event which doesn't actually occur until the end of the movie?

The planet of the apes is not Earth. The only Earth-like elements, such as the humans, Apes and the vestiges of human civilisation seen in the Apes' culture, have come from Earth, more specifically from the crashed remains of the Oberon. So, where do the horses come from?

When slave trader Limbo catches up with Leo's party, he has two gorillas with him. Leo fires his gun, and in the ensuing panic Limbo is captured, but his gorilla companions simply disappear. Leo only agrees to bring Limbo along with them because he could go back and lead Thade to them, but this is nonsense as surely the escaped gorillas will inform on the party anyway?

Speaking of guns, Krull smashes Leo's gun in case he uses it on him or Ari, causing the spaceman to complain that it 'was going to keep us alive.' However, he still appears to have a flare gun, which would surely have been of some use against the primitive apes. By the end of the film, he acquires another explosive gun from Pericles' pod, which leads to another question – why do the USAF provide their monkey pilots with dangerous weapons they surely would have no need for, or ability to use, in deep space? When NASA sent primates into orbit in the 1950s, they didn't provide them with loaded Smith and Wessons, and it's hard to believe that Neil Armstrong and Buzz Aldrin were packing heat on the moon . . .

For the film's single biggest plot problem, see **JUST PLAIN WEIRD**.

DEATH: People die left right and centre, but there's no real feeling to the fatalities. None of the characters are given enough personality for us to mourn their passing. When Kris Kristofferson exits early on, neither his daughter nor his followers seem to care for more than a few seconds. Similarly, when Thade's father dies, all he seems to do is get *more* angry.

LOVE TRIANGLES: It is clear there's a romantic attachment between Ari and Leo, although this is left embryonic. One of the deleted scenes draws attention to it, but only in an oblique way. This is rendered vaguely triangular by the obvious, and more traditional, sexual tension between Leo and Daena. During production rumours abounded of this plotline, with suggestions that the tension between Ari and Leo would be more overt, or even that the relationship would be consummated at some point in the film. Responding to these suggestions, Burton laughed. 'Sex between animals and humans . . . I'd like to stay out of jail a little longer. I just felt the whole unrequited thing was more real and more bitter-sweet.'[53] To extend the love triangle into a quad-rangle, it's worth pointing out that General Thade has some sexual and/or romantic feelings for Ari, which she attempts to utilise as part of her attempt to get Thade to give up his pursuit of Leo. She doesn't succeed.

AUTOBIOGRAPHY?: Not so much autobiography, as art imitating life. 'As I got into it, I started thinking, well, here's a guy who doesn't really want to be here, he's trying to get out, he's got this huge responsibility that just keeps getting bigger and bigger and bigger, and finally he has to end up dealing with it, and I kind of related that to . . . making this movie.'[54]

JUST PLAIN WEIRD: The ending. It looks great and is actually rather unsettling to watch, but on first viewing it makes no sense at all. Reactions, even from the cast and crew, differed. 'When people see it again, they'll figure it out. There have been debates, but I thought it was fantastic. Doors are left open, and that is very intentional,'[55] announced Mark Wahlberg confidently, clearly believing that the conclusion both made story sense and was meant to.

On the other hand, Burton on one occasion stated that 'Movies should be open to interpretation,'[56] fuelling the idea that the picture's climax is a well-produced practical joke on the audience, with no internal logic of its own. Backing this up is Fox Head of Distribution Bruce Snyder. 'If the truth be known, it wasn't really supposed to make sense. It was just supposed to go "whoa", make you think . . . It's whatever you want it to be . . . but you've got to remember you just watched a movie about talking monkeys in outer space. Don't look for too much logic, you know?'[57] Snyder's attitude smacks of desperation, the argument being that because a film is fantastic or science fiction then it doesn't have to make sense, that it doesn't have to create its own rules which it then obeys. Whilst superficially similar to Burton's angle, Snyder's non-explanation actually comes from a very different place to Burton's anti-literalism.

Tim Roth, like Mark Wahlberg, sought to explain the final scene in plot terms: 'I thought that if my character is a direct descendant of Semos [and Semos was the son of Pericles] . . . then maybe he could have had it somewhere in him to press the right buttons to get into a pod and chase after the space man Marky Mark, right? And then go down a worm hole, into another time, and god knows what happens then.'[58]

Convoluted as Roth's theory sounds, he's nearly right. What actually happens (although it isn't sufficiently explained) is all to do with the electromagnetic storm through which Leo's pod passes. It's established elsewhere in the film that objects emerge from the event horizon in the reverse order to that in which they went in. So although Pericles, Leo and the Oberon cross the event horizon in that order, the Oberon arrives on the ape planet in the distant past, followed by Leo, followed by Pericles. Therefore, when Leo returns to Earth he will arrive in Earth's solar system *after* anyone who leaves after him. It follows then that at some point after Leo's abrupt departure from the battlefield, General Thade, who is not dead at the film's climax, finds a way to travel back through the event horizon to Earth (possibly utilising Leo's damaged pod, whose existence only he is aware of) and either on his own or with the assistance of other apes from the future, changes the history of the planet Earth, wiping out the entirety of human history in the process. Thus when Leo arrives after him he does not return to the world he came from, but a world changed by Thade's intervention. Got that?

That there is a cardboard erratum slip contained in the DVD of the movie to explain this plot point with the use of diagrams counts as one of the strangest things in the history of home cinema.

However, despite everything this explanation does not cover the following problems:

- When in Earth's past did the apes take control? If it was in the distant past why does the ape-ruled Washington look the same as the real one apart from the excess of monkeys? Even down to the architecture, the wording on the Lincoln memorial and the Washington DC Police Department logo? If it was in the recent past, why are they using the leftovers of human civilisation when they despise humans?
- Accepting that Thade returned to Earth in the past creates its own problems, even with race memories of Pericles' space skills, Leo's original pod was trashed beyond use, and the film states that apes can't emulate human technology.
- Furthermore, if we are to assume that the Lincoln Memorial was remodelled rather than built by the apes, this would place Thade's arrival at some point after 1914, when construction of the monument began. If we can trust the date readout in the space pods, then Leo returns to Earth (if it *is* Earth) in around 2155. So in less than a century and a half, Earth's apes have managed to evolve beyond the level of the apes descended from those on the Oberon, whose evolution apparently took several thousand years, mastering complex technology in the process.

- When Thade did arrive how *did* he evolve Earth's apes to the point that they could assist him in taking over Earth? Or did he bring an army *with* him? If so, how did they all fit in that (broken) one-man pod?

Perhaps the biggest question with the whole scene is why it exists at all. *Planet of the Apes* (2001) has a twist ending for one reason only: because *Planet of the Apes* (1968) does.

AFTERLIFE: During post-production it was rumoured that several endings had been shot, but the director was dismissive of the idea: 'We didn't have time! I often feel like I'm in some parallel universe that I'm not aware of – like I shot all these endings but I'm not aware of it.'[59]

Released as planned on 27 July, *Planet of the Apes* grossed $25 million on its opening day in the United States. The release of the VHS/DVD in the October of that year made $80 million in one week, and led to Burton being inducted into the Video Business Video Hall of Fame at a charity dinner held on 3 December at the Beverly Hilton Hotel, Hollywood. The award was presented to Burton, at his own request, by Martin Landau.

By that time the trauma of the production, combined with the movie's reception, had taken its toll on the director. 'If you drove a nail through my hand, I wouldn't feel it – I'm basically numb,' he told one British newspaper. 'They give you a script, and you do a budget based on that, and say, "This movie would cost $300m to make," and then they treat you like a crazy, overspending, crazy person! It's like, "Well, *you* gave me the script!" ' Much like after his difficult experience with *Batman*, Burton could not even consider going back to the same material again: 'The idea of doing a sequel – I'd rather jump out of the window, I swear to God.'[60]

AWARDS: At the time of writing, *Planet of the Apes* had been nominated for Best Costume Design (Colleen Atwood) at the 2002 Golden Satellite Awards, Best Score Soundtrack Album (Danny Elfman) at the Grammy Awards, and had won Rick Baker a Special Achievement Award from the Las Vegas Film Critics Society for his makeup work. Inexplicably Baker was not nominated for an Oscar.

TRIVIA: Strangely for a film that feels half finished, the (splendid) poster design was ready before principal photography began.

Burton has said, 'The first time they showed me the poster and on the bottom it said: "This film has not yet been rated," I said why not be accurate and say, "This film has not yet been shot"?'[61]

There was a much-reported public spat between Burton and former *Superman* scriptwriter Kevin Smith over the ending of *Planet of the Apes*. Smith had joked to one reporter that Burton had 'ripped off' the idea of the Lincoln Memorial with an ape's head from page nine of his third *Jay & Silent Bob* comic, drawn by Duncan Fegredo. The image certainly was in the comic, which had been out for at least two years before Burton's film. However, Smith's was not a serious allegation, simply a joke, possibly designed to emphasise the fact that his own imminent *Jay and Silent Bob Strike Back* had partially imitated the structure of *Pee-wee's Big Adventure* wholesale, *and* featured an elaborate spoof of *Planet of the Apes* itself.

ANALYSIS: Production difficulties and the timescale for the project forced casting and construction decisions to be based on a script that ended up too expensive to film, necessitating extensive rewrites while shooting was under way.

After his experience on *Batman*, Burton categorically stated that 'The responsibility of having this crew of over a hundred men waiting to shoot something unwritten was quite upsetting. Once you start shooting, you just can't be at that stage ... I'm never going to let that happen again.'[62] Another parallel with *Batman* can be seen in a comment made in June 1989 about the earlier film: 'My only real enemy was time ... This project had been floated around town for years, but we had just one year to make it from virtual scratch.'[63] With *Planet of the Apes* this was precisely the situation he found himself in once more, only the time-scale was even more extreme.

There are some great ideas in here. That Leo's arrogant refusal to control his impulsiveness leads to the destruction of all of human history is a brilliant concept, and there is yet another comprehensive rejection of organised religion in favour of a more personal spirituality, which is entirely in line with the director's work. The desire to present the apes as almost schizophrenic, genuinely alien and incomprehensible to the audience, even shows up how mundane the original pictures' portrayal of the creatures was. Even the time-warping electromagnetic storm, which demands that the audience think in a non-linear way, is potentially astounding. But none of these things are as developed on a story, emotional or character level, as they could be.

Burton, in arguing that his film was not for literal-minded people, was in a sense right. *Planet of the Apes*, if better developed, could have been defiantly anti-literal, deliberately, wondrously strange. But because it *doesn't* hold together on a literal, plot-driven level and yet fails to offer sufficient pleasures elsewhere (like, say, David Lynch's *Twin Peaks – Fire Walk With Me* (1994) or *Mulholland Drive* (2001) do), the picture suffers from charges of narrative incompetence rather than being praised for its subversion of the linear. Unlike *Batman Returns*, this picture's problems of narrative are not obscured and excused by the audience's connection with a greater emotional truth. The *Planet of the Apes* is hollow.

AVAILABILITY: A DVD was released in the US for Christmas 2001 and in the UK in February 2002. Loaded with thirteen hours of extras it has few equals in the format.

EXPERT WITNESS: Rick Heinrichs: '*Planet of the Apes* was a challenge for us all on many levels and a very gratifying experience for me. The opportunity to create another world with Tim out of character, texture and colour was exhilarating and one that Hollywood is uniquely set up to support. The challenge of the film was the attempt to get a sense of visual and historic scope through the efficient manipulation of sets and set pieces, a process that had served us well on *Sleepy Hollow*. We extended sets with huge walls of mirrors, experimented with front screen paint on walls, changed over and doubled one set for another and, where possible, shot the environment "in camera" rather than rely too heavily upon post production visual effects.'

Helena Bonham Carter: 'Tim ... has a strong vision and every single film of his has his stamp and signature on it. And yet to work with him is unbelievably collaborative, open, non-controlling and non-dictatorial ... He's great fun and thank God because frankly this wouldn't be tolerable if [he] wasn't.'[64]

Glenn Shadix: 'He has an instinctive respect and feel for actors. He doesn't make your choices for you. Some directors will tell you almost too specifically what they want ... He keeps the pressure that comes to bear on him away from the actors, so that we don't have to feel the pressure that *he's* under – and Tim was under, I think, more pressure on *Planet of the Apes* than he's ever been under on any film. By the time it was over, Tim looked like he had been hit by a truck, and I think he felt much the same way. But soon he'll be ready to do it all again – that I do know about him.'

THE BOTTOM LINE: *Planet of the Apes* is, to invoke cliché, far less than the sum of its parts. The production design is at times extraordinary, but the tension between the Roman-style slave blockbuster (*Spartacus* with chimps?) Broyles' script tries to be, and the non-literal fable that the director wants to make cripples both projects. On the plus side the movie retains the disturbing air that characterises the best moments from the first two *Apes* films, and features some great performances, particularly from Shadix and Giamatti. Tim Roth's hyperactive amoral chimpanzee is either a total delight or ranting caricature depending on your point of view. When the picture shudders occasionally to life (such as in the dinner party scene, or the wilfully perverse finale) it's possible to see the shadow of the film Burton wanted to make – but sadly not often. Tim Burton's take on the *Planet of the Apes* remains an enticing prospect. This film isn't it.

UNREALISED PROJECTS

It is frequently impossible to tell which rumours about a director are true, a problem compounded by the popularity of the Internet as a news source. Burton himself has said, 'I read on the Internet that I am attached to at least 20 different projects . . . but I know nothing of any of them.'[1] 'I feel like I'm living in my own parallel universe, or have my own evil twin out there doing things that I don't know about, but these projects combine with the Internet and you have to spend all day quelling rumors.'[2]

Below are some of the films Burton was allegedly involved with, or contemplating making, with information about them where a reliable source has confirmed it. But bear in mind that, as Burton puts it, 'These rumors could be coming from some pervert in his basement in Idaho, and now all of a sudden it's in *USA Today*.'[3] They are listed alphabetically, and are by no means a complete list.

Beetlejuice Goes Hawaiian

The ill-fated *Beetlejuice* sequel, which *Mars Attacks!* scribe Jonathan Gems helped Burton develop in the late 1980s/early 1990s. Gems explains: 'Tim thought it would be funny to match the surfing backdrop of a beach movie with some sort of German Expressionism, because they're totally wrong together . . . then all sorts of crazy stuff happens, including a surfing tournament Betelgeuse has to win by using magic.'[4] The story followed the Dietzes to Hawaii, where Charles had begun developing a hotel complex, in the process disturbing the ghosts of an ancient burial ground, necessitating a call to Betelgeuse, who agrees to help if he can finally have his way with Lydia. Michael Keaton and Winona Ryder were both keen to participate, but only if Burton returned as director. Warners eventually offered him the choice of either *Beetlejuice Goes Hawaiian* or *Batman Returns*, and he opted for the latter. In the late 1990s rumours of another *Beetlejuice* sequel, scripted by Billy Frolick with Burton producing, possibly titled *Beetlejuice in Love*, circulated briefly.

Catwoman

Initially planned as a spin-off from the *Batman* franchise, with Burton directing and Michelle Pfieffer picking up her whip once more. Now neither are involved, although the project is still in development at the time of writing, with Ashley Judd rumoured to take the title role.

Conversations With Vincent

Burton's documentary on his childhood hero and two-time collaborator, Vincent Price, was recorded between the making of *Edward Scissorhands* and Price's death in 1993. It is as yet incomplete, although it seems probable that Burton will finish it at some point.

The Fall of the House of Usher

A film version of Edgar Allan Poe's tale has long been rumoured. With Burton's fondness for Poe, it is unsurprising that he has been suggested as director. According to Jonathan Gems, he and Burton did get a script together in the mid-1990s: 'He wanted to make it a comedy set in Burbank. If you remember, Poe's story is an extremely depressing horror tale. Tim's idea was to give it a certain twist, make it funny and contemporary by setting it in the suburbs. It was such a brilliant approach. It's probably the best unproduced script I've written so far. Tim loves it and eventually he will make it.'[5]

Geek Love

The Internet has been rife with rumours that Burton acquired the rights to Katherine Dunne's 1983 novel a few years ago. It seems like ideal Burton material – a travelling circus which, to avoid bankruptcy, uses a variety of chemicals and toxins to create a truly freakish Freak Show. However, what connection (if any) Burton has to the book and its rights is unknown.

Go Baby Go

One of the more bizarre ideas that Burton asked Jonathan Gems to help develop. This was inspired by a dream Burton had, and is effectively a variation on *The Attack of the 50 Foot Woman* by way of cult master Russ Meyer. It was to revolve around three women dancing in the Nevada Desert in go-go outfits. They get hit by a nuclear weapon and grow to 300 feet. Gems elaborated further: 'The problem is they really love music, and so all they do is look for food, music and a place to dance. When they start getting bigger, the military is all embarrassed by this and wants to wipe them out and sweep it under the carpet.'[6] However, when HBO remade *The Attack of the 50 Foot Woman*, Burton scrapped the idea.

The Hawkline Monster

Another proposed project was an adaptation of Richard Brautigan's 1974 novel, which followed a couple of cowboys hoping to pull off one last job before retirement. The cowboys are eventually hired by twin sisters to kill a monster living in their basement. Clint Eastwood and Jack Nicholson signed on to star, with Jonathan Gems providing the script, but eventually Eastwood bowed out, and Nicholson soon followed because, in Gems' words, 'working with Clint is what appealed to him in the first place.'[7] After losing its stars, the project collapsed.

Lost in Oz

Burton signed up with Columbia TriStar TV Distribution to executive produce a TV series based around L Frank Baum's *The Wizard of Oz* in October 1998. It was planned to air in the autumn of 1999, with Burton directing the pilot, but he left the project after failing to get a commitment to an entire series before production began.

Mai, The Psychic Girl

Burton at one point signed with Mario Kassar and Andy Vajna at Carolco to direct *Mai, The Psychic Girl*, as his next project after *Batman Returns*. It was to be based on a Japanese comic book about world powers trying to kidnap a gifted medium in future Tokyo for international espionage. At the time, he explained, 'I'm directing it because I really liked Mario Kassar ... He's not into mega-budgets so much as unusual ways of how to approach film-making ... Film-making isn't about that with him and I admire his weird pioneer spirit.'[8]

Sweeney Todd

Burton owns the screen rights to the Broadway musical (by Stephen Sondheim and Hugh Wheeler). The film is currently in production.

X – The Man With the X-Ray Eyes

Rumoured in 1997, Burton was supposedly planning to direct a remake of the 1963 Roger Corman film for Dream Works SKG. Bryan Goluboff, who penned *The Basketball Diaries*, was supposedly working on a screenplay.

AFTERWORD

When I first met Tim, my general impression, and not just mine but that of everybody else who had gotten to know him at Cal Arts and at Disney, was that he clearly had an enormous talent and a fully formed vision. There was never a doubt when you looked at his design and film work what world the characters lived in. At Disney, there was always a question of when the powers-that-be would recognise what they had on their hands. This was due partly to a widespread cynicism among a highly talented group of young animators, disappointed with the sense of aimlessness in general at the highest levels of the studio. Thanks to production head, Tom Wilhite, and executive story editor, Julie Hickson, things began to turn around and Tim started to really spread his wings. We had no idea how he was going to grow in his career, but he did grow, and on his own terms.

As a filmmaker, he's really changed very little since then. The budgets have gotten bigger, there's more ambition, but still, in all of Tim's films, the animated and live action, his sensibility seeps into every corner – a Burtonesque feeling pervades. His aesthetic eschews the polish and patness that comes with cutting-edge technology because he's after an emotional connection that is much more immediate and involving.

His films often walk a live wire line between horror and humour, and manage to meld morbidity and sweetness in a way that is very compelling. Those closest to him recognise that his work represents a very important expression of who Tim is.

Ultimately I think that's what attracts people, why Tim's films have been so personal and so popular – the combination of those elements can be an enormously intoxicating mixture, and movie audiences relish the power of that intoxication.

Rick Heinrichs
January 2002

Rick Heinrichs has worked on more of Tim Burton's films than anyone apart from Tim Burton himself. His Production Design for *Sleepy Hollow* won an Academy Award.

NOTES

Introduction

1. Burton quoted in Alan Jones, 'Directing the Legend' in *Cinefantastique*, vol.20, n.1 (November 1989).
2. Burton quoted in Frank Rose, 'Tim Cuts Up' in *Premier*, vol.4, n.5 (January 1991).
3. Burton quoted in David Elliot, 'Tim Burton: The Man Behind "Batman"' in the *San Diego Union-Tribune*, 25 June 1989.
4. Burton quoted in Mark Salisbury, 'A Head of the Game' in *Fangoria*, n.189 (January 2000).
5. Burton quoted in Philip Thomas, 'The Misfit' in *Empire*, n.26 (August 1991).
6. Elfman in his commentary on the 10th Anniversary Edward Scissorhands DVD.
7. Burton quoted in John Clark, 'The Wood, The Bad, and The Ugly' in *Premiere*, vol.8, n.2 (October 1994).
8. Burton interviewed by Mark Kermode, the *Guardian* interview, NFT, 6 January 2000.
9. Jean Burton on the A&E *Tim Burton: Trick or Treat* documentary, 31 July 2001.
10. Ken Hanke, *Tim Burton: An Unauthorized Biography of the Filmmaker* (Renaissance Books; Los Angeles, 1999) p.xi.
11. Burton quoted in Jay Carr, 'Tim Burton's Big Adventure' in the *Boston Globe*, 17 October 1993.
12. Burton quoted in J. Rentilly, 'Tim Burton, Relying on Himself' from *www.audiencemagazine.com*

Early Life and Disney Times

1. Burton quoted in Andy Carvin, 'An Interview with Tim Burton' from EdWeb, http://sunsite.ust.hk/edweb/nightmare.burton.html
2. Burton quoted in Michel Ciment & Yannick Dahan, 'Entretien Tim Burton: Le conte de fées permet de décrire des vérités de façon plus subversive' in *Positif*, n.468 (January 2000).
3. *Ibid.*
4. Burton quoted in Elisabeth Perrin, 'Tim Burton Guides to the Screen Another Tale From the Dark Side' in the *Chicago Sun-Times*, 17 October 1993.
5. Ken Hanke, *Tim Burton: An Unauthorized Biography of the Filmmaker* (Renaissance Books; Los Angeles, 1999) p.xv.
6. Thompson quoted in Frank Rose, 'Tim Cuts Up' in *Premier*, vol.4, n.5 (January 1991).
7. Burton quoted in Mimi Avins, 'Ghoul World' in *Premier*, vol.7, n.3 (November 1993).
8. Burton quoted in Elisabeth Perrin, *op cit.*
9. Burton quoted in Lawrence French, 'The Nightmare Before Christmas' in *Cinefantastique*, vol. 24, n.5 (December 1993).
10. Burton quoted in Mimi Avins, *op cit.*
11. Burton quoted in Andy Carvin, *op cit.*
12. Burton quoted in Jay Carr, 'Tim Burton's Big Adventure' in the *Boston Globe*, 17 October 1993.
13. Burton quoted in Mimi Avins, *op cit.*
14. Burton quoted in Jay Carr, *op cit.*
15. Selick quoted in Mimi Avins, *op cit.*
16. Selick quoted in Lawrence French, *op cit.*
17. Burton quoted in Michael Dwyer, 'The Stuff that Dreams are Made of' in the *Irish Times*, 10 December 1994.
18. Burton quoted in Andy Carvin, *op cit.*

Luau

1. Selick quoted in Leslie Felperin, 'Animated Dreams' in *Sight and Sound*, vol.4, n.12 (December 1994).

Vincent

1. Burton quoted in Jay Carr, 'Can "Batman" Reach the Pot of Gold?' in the *Boston Globe*, 18 June 1989.

2. Burton interviewed by Mark Kermode, the *Guardian* interview, NFT, 6 January 2000.
3. David Coleman, 'Vincent' in *Cinefantastique* vol.13, n.4 (April–May 1983).
4. Heinrichs quoted in David Coleman, *ibid.*
5. Heinrichs quoted in David Coleman *ibid.*
6. Burton on the commentary track of the *Edward Scissorhands* 10th Anniversary DVD.
7. Burton interviewed by Mark Kermode, *op cit.*
8. Heinrichs quoted in David Coleman, *op cit.*
9. Vincent Price quoted in Steve Biodrowski, David Del Valle & Lawrence French, 'Vincent Price: Looking Back on Forty Years as Horror's Crown Prince' in *Cinefantastique*, vol.19, n.2 (January 1989).
10. David Coleman, *op cit.*
11. Taylor L White, 'Vincent' in *Cinefantastique*, vol.20, n.1/2 (November 1989).
12. Burton on the *Edward Scissorhands* DVD.
13. Burton quoted in Nina J Easton, 'For Tim Burton, This One's Personal' in the *Los Angeles Times*, 8 December 1990.
14. Burton on the *Edward Scissorhands* DVD.

Hansel and Gretel

1. Taylor L White, 'Hansel & Gretel' in *Cinefantastique*, vol.20, n.1/2 (November 1989).

Frankenweenie

1. Burton quoted in Michael Mayo, 'Frankenweenie' in *Cinefantastique*, vol.15, n.2 (May 1985).
2. *Ibid.*
3. *Ibid.*
4. Hickson quoted in Michael Mayo, *ibid.*
5. *Ibid.*
6. Burton quoted in Michael Mayo, *ibid.*
7. Hickson quoted in Michael Mayo, *ibid.*
8. Burton quoted in Michael Mayo, *ibid.*
9. Hickson quoted in Michael Mayo, *ibid.*
10. Michael Mayo, *ibid.*
11. Burton quoted in Michael Mayo, *ibid.*
12. Burton quoted in Michael Mayo, *ibid.*

Pee-wee's Big Adventure

1. Burton in 'commentary 1' on the *Pee-wee's Big Adventure* DVD (R1).
2. Reubens quoted in 'Return From Planet Pee-Wee' in *Vanity Fair* (September 1999).
3. *Ibid.*
4. *Ibid.*
5. Burton quoted in David Elliot, 'Paul Reubens proves there is life after Pee-wee' in the *San Diego Union-Tribune*, 4 August 1985.
6. Paul Reubens in 'commentary 1' on the *Pee-wee's Big Adventure* DVD.
7. *Ibid.*
8. *Ibid.*
9. *Ibid.*
10. Duval quoted by Reubens, *ibid.*
11. Burton in 'commentary 1' on the *Pee-wee* DVD.
12. Burton quoted in David Elliot, *op cit.*
13. Burton in 'commentary 1' on the *Pee-wee* DVD.
14. David L Schneider quoted in 'Sketches and Storyboards' on the *Pee-wee* DVD.
15. Burton in 'commentary 1' on the *Pee-wee* DVD.
16. Reubens, *ibid.*
17. David L Schneider quoted in 'Sketches and Storyboards' on the *Pee-wee* DVD.
18. *Ibid.*
19. *Ibid.*
20. *Ibid.*
21. Nigel Floyd, 'Pee-Wee's Big Adventure' in *Monthly Film Bulletin*, vol.54, n.643 (August 1987).
22. *Ibid.*
23. Ann Lloyd, 'Pee-Wee's Big Adventure' in *Films and Filming*, n.394 (July 1987).
24. *Ibid.*
25. Vincent Canby, 'Screen: "Pee-wee's Big Adventure," A comedy' in the *New York Times*, 9 August 1985.
26. Elfman quoted in Andy Carvin, 'An Interview with Danny Elfman' (October 1993) from EdWeb, http://sunsite.ust.hk/edweb/nightmare.elfman.html
27. Elfman quoted in Randall Larson, 'Danny Elfman, Director

Tim Burton's Rock Music Man' in *Cinefantastique*, vol. 20, n.1/2 (November 1989).

28. Elfman quoted in Diana Rico, 'A little fright music' in *Egg* (December/January 1990).
29. Elfman in 'commentary 2' on the *Pee-wee's Big Adventure* DVD (R1).
30. Elfman quoted in Andy Carvin, *op cit*.
31. Elfman quoted in Grammy Magazine from http://www.celluloidtunes.com/elfmangrammy.htm
32. Elfman quoted in Andy Carvin, 'An Interview with Danny Elfman' (October 1993) from EdWeb, quoted in Andy Carvin, *ibid*.
33. Reubens in 'commentary 1' on the *Pee-wee* DVD.
34. 'Pee-wee's Big Adventure' in *Variety*, 31 July 1985.
35. Elfman quoted in Diana Rico, *op cit*.
36. Elfman quoted in Randall Larson, *op cit*.
37. Reubens quoted in Lance Laud, 'Pee-wee Herman' in *Interview*, vol.xv, n.9 (September 1985).
38. Bryan Bruce, 'Pee Wee Herman: The Homosexual Subtext' in *CineAction!*, n.9 (July 1987).
39. Taylor White, 'Pee-Wee's Big Adventure' in *Cinefantastique*, vol.20, n.1/2 (November 1989).
40. *Ibid*.
41. Reubens in 'commentary 1' on the *Pee-wee* DVD.
42. Phil Trumbo quoted in Dan Persons, 'Building Pee-Wee's Playhouse' in *Cinefantastique*, vol.19, n.5 (July 1989).

Beetlejuice

1. Munro quoted in Jody Duncan Shannon 'Beetlejuice' *Cinefex* n.34 (May 1988).
2. Burton quoted in Frank Rose, 'Tim Cuts Up' in *Premier*, vol.4, n.5 (January 1991).
3. Munro quoted in Taylor L White, 'The making of Tim Burton's Beetlejuice & his other bizarre gems' in *Cinefantastique*, vol.20, n.1/2 (November 1989).
4. Munro quoted in Jody Duncan Shannon, 'Beetlejuice' in *Cinefex*, n.34 (May 1988).
5. Burton quoted in *ibid*.
6. Munro quoted in Taylor L White, *op cit*.

7. Kuran quoted in Dennis Fischer, 'Special Visual Effects' in *Cinefantastique*, vol.20, n.1/2 (November 1989).
8. Munro quoted in *ibid*.
9. Neil quoted in Taylor L White, *op cit*.
10. Burton quoted in Jody Duncan Shannon, 'Beetlejuice' in *Cinefex*, n.34 (May 1988).
11. Munro quoted in *ibid*.
12. Munro quoted in Taylor L White, *op cit*.
13. Heinrichs quoted in Taylor L White, *op cit*.
14. *Ibid*.
15. *Ibid*.
16. Short quoted in *ibid*.
17. Burton quoted in Jody Duncan Shannon, *op cit*.
18. Jones on the A&E *Tim Burton: Trick or Treat* documentary, 31 July 2001.
19. Burton quoted in Patrick Goldstein, 'Comic O'Hara Gets "Beetlejuice" Going' in the *Los Angeles Times*, 18 April 1988.
20. Kim Newman, 'Beetle Juice' in *Monthly Film Bulletin*, vol.55, n.655 (August 1988).
21. Patrick Goldstein, *op cit*.
22. Kevin Thomas, 'Gleeful Grand Guignol of "Beetlejuice" ' in the *Los Angeles Times*, 30 March 1988.
23. Rita Kempley, 'Great Goblins! It's "Beetlejuice"!' in the *Washington Post*, 30 March 1988.
24. Vincent Canby, ' "Beetlejuice" Is Pap For Eyes' in the *New York Times*, 8 May 1988.
25. Janet Maslin, 'Ghosts and Extra Eyeballs' in the *New York Times*, 30 March 1988.
26. Burton quoted in Frank Rose, *op cit*.
27. Burton quoted in the *Beetlejuice* production notes.
28. Ken Hanke, *Tim Burton: An Unauthorized Biography of the Filmmaker* (Renaissance Books; Los Angeles, 1999) p.72.
29. Welch quoted in the *Beetlejuice* production Notes
30. Munro quoted in Taylor L White, *op cit*.
31. Burton quoted in Jody Duncan Shannon, *op cit*.
32. Burton quoted in Frank Rose, *op cit*.
33. Munro quoted in Taylor L White, *op cit*.

Batman

1. Lance Parkin, *Pocket Essentials: Alan Moore* (not yet published).
2. Moore quoted in Ian Winterton, 'Murder, He Wrote' in *Hotdog*, n.20 (February 2002).
3. Les Daniels, *DC Comics: 60 Years of the World's Favourite Comics Heroes* (Bulfinch Press; 1995) p.119.
4. *Ibid*, p.119.
5. Jay Carr, 'Can "Batman" Reach the Pot of Gold?' in the *Boston Globe*, 18 June 1989.
6. Burton quoted in Alan Jones, 'Batman: Eccentric cinema stylist Tim Burton on bringing the comic book legend to the screen' in *Cinefantastique*, vol.20, n.1 (November 1989).
7. Jay Carr, *op cit*.
8. Gire in Dann Gire and Joseph Reboy, 'Batman: Two viewpoints on the trailer designed to quiet Bat fans up in arms' in *Cinefantastique*, vol.19, n.4 (May 1989).
9. Gire in *ibid*.
10. Reboy in *op cit*.
11. Burton quoted in Alan Jones, 'Batman', *op cit*.
12. Burton quoted in the *Batman* production notes.
13. Burton quoted in Alan Jones, 'Batman', *op cit*.
14. Hamm quoted in Stephen Rebello, 'Sam Hamm: A Profile of the hot new screenwriter who launched the Dark Knight's boxoffice torpedo' in *Cinefantastique*, vol.20, n.1 (November 1989).
15. Hamm quoted in Alan Jones, 'Batman', *op cit*.
16. Burton quoted in David Elliot, 'Tim Burton: The Man Behind "Batman" ' in the *San Diego Union-Tribune*, 25 June 1989.
17. Gough quoted in Paul Mount, 'What the Butler Saw' in *Starburst*, n.132 (August 1989).
18. *Ibid*.
19. Wuhl quoted in the *Batman* production notes.
20. Burton quoted in Alan Jones, 'Batman', *op cit*.
21. Hamm quoted in Stephen Rebello, *op cit*.
22. Burton quoted in Alan Jones, 'Batman', *op cit*.
23. Furst quoted in the *Batman* production notes.
24. Burton quoted in Alan Jones, 'Batman', *op cit*.
25. Furst quoted in the *Batman* production notes.
26. Burton quoted in Alan Jones, 'Directing the Legend' in *Cinefantastique*, vol.20, n.1 (November 1989).

27. Hamm quoted in Stephen Rebello, *op cit*.
28. Sheila Benson, 'Batangst in Basic Black' in the *Los Angeles Times*, 29 June 1989.
29. Henry Mietkiewicz, 'Batwimp no more' in the *Toronto Star*, 18 June 1989.
30. Jack Kroll, 'The Joker is wild, but Batman carries the night' in *Newsweek*, 26 June 1989 (US Edition).
31. Hal Lipper, 'A Classic Batman' in the *St Petersburg Times*, 23 June 1989.
32. Sheila Benson, *op cit*.
33. Hal Hinson, 'Batman with Dark Grandeur' in the *Washington Post*, 23 June 1989.
34. *Ibid*.
35. Jay Carr, 'Batophilia Strikes' in the *Boston Globe*, 23 June 1989.
36. West quoted in Joe Nazzaro, 'Bat Attitude' in *Starlog*, n.210 (January 1995).
37. Sheila Benson, *op cit*.
38. Elfman quoted in Daniel Schweiger, 'Danny Elfman Returns' in *Soundtrack! The Collector's Quarterly*, vol.11, n.43 (September 1992).
39. Elfman in a letter to the *Los Angeles Times*, 27 June 1989.
40. Burton quoted in the *Batman* production notes.
41. 'The Bat Mogul and the Abyss' in *The Economist*, 26 August 1989.
42. Burton quoted in Philip Thomas, 'The Misfit' in *Empire*, n.26 (August 1991).
43. Friedman quoted in Susan Spillman, 'Will Batman Fly?' in *USA Today*, 19 June 1989.
44. Burton quoted in Philip Thomas, *op cit*.
45. Burton quoted in Alan Jones, 'Batman', *op cit*.
46. Burton quoted in David Elliot, *op cit*.
47. Burton quoted in Alan Jones, 'Batman', *op cit*.
48. Burton quoted in Alan Jones, 'Cutting Remarks from Tim Burton' in *Starburst*, vol.13, n.11 (July 1991).
49. Burton quoted in Philip Thomas, *op cit*.
50. Sheila Benson, *op cit*.
51. Gough quoted in Paul Mount, *op cit*.
52. Burton quoted in Susan Spillman, *op cit*.

Edward Scissorhands

1. Burton on the *Edward Scissorhands* 10th Anniversary DVD commentary.
2. Burton quoted in Alan Jones, 'Cutting Remarks from Tim Burton' in *Starburst*, vol.13, n.11 (July 1991).
3. Burton quoted in Alan Jones, *ibid.*
4. Thompson quoted in Mark Salisbury, 'Caroline Thompson: Writer–Director/Horse Lover' in *Empire*, n.69 (March 1995).
5. Burton on the *Edward* DVD.
6. Burton quoted in Alan Jones, *op cit.*
7. Burton quoted in Graham Fuller, 'Tim Burton & Vincent Price' in *Interview*, vol.20, n.12 (December 1990).
8. *Ibid.*
9. Burton quoted in Alan Jones, *op cit.*
10. Burton quoted in Graham Fuller, *op cit.*
11. Burton quoted in Alan Jones, *op cit.*
12. Thompson quoted in Mark Salisbury, *op cit.*
13. Thompson quoted in Mike Lyons, 'Scripting Film Fantasies' in *Cinefantastique*, vol.28, n.3 (October 1996).
14. Thomspon quoted in Mark Burman, 'Caroline Thompson talks to Mark Burman about the script Lonely People' in *Sight & Sound*, vol.3, n.10 (October 1993).
15. Thompson quoted in Mike Lyons, *op cit.*
16. Burton quoted in Nina J Easton, 'For Tim Burton, This One's Personal' in the *Los Angeles Times*, 12 October 1990.
17. Burton on the *Edward* DVD.
18. Burton quoted in Alan Jones, *op cit.*
19. *Ibid.*
20. *Ibid.*
21. Roth quoted in Frank Rose, 'Tim Cuts Up' in *Premier*, vol.4, n.5 (January 1991).
22. Roth quoted in Nina J Easton, *op cit.*
23. Depp quoted in Laurie Halpern Smith, 'Look, Ma, No Hands, Or Tim Burton's Latest Feat' in the *New York Times*, 28 August 1990.
24. Depp quoted in Bob Thomas, '. . . And Beau Johnny Depp Is Earning More Respect' in the *Toronto Star*, 3 January 1991.
25. Welch quoted in Laurie Halpern Smith, *op cit.*

26. Thomspon quoted in Mark Burman, *op cit.*
27. Burton quoted in Graham Fuller, *op cit.*
28. Atwood quoted in Frank Rose, *op cit.*
29. Burton on the *Edward* DVD.
30. Burton quoted in Alan Jones, *op cit.*
31. Wiest quoted in Laurie Halpern Smith, *op cit.*
32. Wiest quoted in Tom Green, 'Wiest Finds It Hard To Let Go Of "Edward Scissorhands"' in *USA Today*, 17 December 1990.
33. Burton quoted in Frank Rose, *op cit.*
34. Burton quoted in Alan Jones, *op cit.*
35. Depp quoted in Nina J Easton, *op cit.*
36. Depp quoted in Laurie Halpern Smith, *op cit.*
37. Depp quoted in Bob Thomas, *op cit.*
38. Burton on the *Edward* DVD.
39. Depp quoted in Bob Thomas, *op cit.*
40. Burton quoted in Alan Jones, *op cit.*
41. Depp quoted in Bob Thomas, *op cit.*
42. Burton on the *Edward* DVD.
43. Burton quoted in Alan Jones, *op cit.*
44. Wiest quoted in Tom Green, *op cit.*
45. Burton quoted in Alan Jones, *op cit.*
46. Arkin quoted in Nina J Easton, *op cit.*
47. Roger Ebert, 'Edward Scissorhands' in the *Chicago Sun-Times*, 14 December 1990.
48. Derek Malcolm, 'Edward Scissorhands' in the *Guardian*, 25 July 1991.
49. Alan Jones, 'Edward Scissorhands' in *Starburst*, vol.13, n.11 (July 1991).
50. Peter Travers, 'A Cut Above the Rest' in *Rolling Stone*, 10 January 1991.
51. Joanna Berry, 'Edward Scissorhands' in *Empire*, n.26 (August 1991).
52. Stewart Klawans, 'Holiday Celluloid Wrap-Up' in the *Nation*, vol.252, n.1 (14 January 1991).
53. Mich LaSalle, ' "Scissorhands" Just Doesn't Cut It' in the *San Francisco Chronicle*, 14 December 1990.
54. Jay Carr, ' "Scissorhands" a Shear Delight' in the *Boston Globe*, 14 December 1990.
55. Richard Corliss, 'Shear Heaven: Edward Scissorhands' in *Time*, vol.136, n.35 (10 December 1990).

56. John Hartl, ' "Edward Scissorhands" Is A Fairy Tale Of Shear Purity' in the *Seattle Times*, 14 December 1990.
57. Peter Travers, *op cit.*
58. David Elliott, ' "Edward Scissorhands" Rises Several Cuts Above Usual Holiday Fare' in the *San Diego Union-Tribune*, 14 December 1990.
59. Mich LaSalle, *op cit.*
60. Susan Spillman, ' "Edward Scissorhands" Cuts To Tim Burton's Core' in *USA Today*, 10 December 1990.
61. Susan Spillman, 'The Shear Geniuses of "Scissorhands" Style in *USA Today*, 13 December 1990.
62. Roger Fritsoe, 'Edward Scissorhands; Johnny Depp Turns Cutup, Imaginatively' in the *Courier-Journal*, 14 December 1990.
63. Steven Frank, 'Cutting Up, Burton Style' in the *Daily Yomiuri*, 20 July 1991.
64. Frank Rose, *op cit.*
65. Janet Maslin, 'And So Handy Around The Garden' in the *New York Times*, 7 December 1990; Joe Pollack, 'Johnny Depp As Teen Who's Shy But Handy "Edward Scissorhands" ' in the *St Louis Post-Dispatch*, 14 December 1990.
66. Iain Johnstone, 'Fantasy With A Familiar Edge' in the *Sunday Times*, 28 July 1991.
67. Richard Scott, 'Pointed, Poignant' in *The Times*, 10 September 1994.
68. Catherine Dunphy, 'Burton's Off-Kilter Scissorhands A Fantastic Slice Of Suburban Life' in the *Toronto Star*, 14 December 1990.
69. Burton quoted in Alan Jones, *op cit.*
70. Elfman on the *Edward Scissorhands* 10th Anniversary DVD commentary.
71. Burton on the *Edward* DVD.
72. *Ibid.*
73. Burton quoted in Philip Thomas, *op cit.*
74. Jay Carr, *op cit.*
75. Burton quoted in Alan Jones, *op cit.*
76. Depp quoted in Nina J Easton, *op cit.*
77. Thompson quoted in *ibid.*
78. Burton quoted in Alan Jones, *op cit.*
79. Burton quoted in Frank Rose, *op cit.*
80. Burton quoted in Alan Jones, *op cit.*

81. Burton on the *Edward* DVD.
82. Burton quoted in Nina J Easton, *op cit*.
83. Thompson quoted in Susan Spillman, *op cit*, 12 December 1990.
84. Burton quoted in *ibid*.
85. Elfman on the *Edward* DVD.
86. Di Novi quoted in Nina J Easton, *op cit*.
87. Jay Carr, *op cit*.
88. Burton quoted in Graham Fuller, *op cit*.
89. Burton quoted in Laurie Halpern Smith, *op cit*.
90. Burton quoted in Susan Spillman, *op cit*, 12 December 1990.
91. Burton on the *Edward* DVD.
92. Burton quoted in Frank Rose, *op cit*.
93. Burton quoted in Philip Thomas, *op cit*.
94. John Hartl, *op cit*.
95. Elfman on the *Edward* DVD.
96. Burton quoted in Alan Jones, *op cit*.
97. Thompson quoted in Frank Rose, *op cit*.
98. Burton quoted in Nina J Easton, *op cit*.
99. Thompson quoted in Mike Lyons, *op cit*.
100. Burton quoted in Frank Rose, *op cit*.
101. Burton quoted in Alan Jones, *op cit*.

Batman Returns

1. Burton quoted in Jeffrey Ressner, 'Three Go Mad In Gotham . . .' in *Empire*, n.38 (August 1992).
2. Burton quoted in Brian D Johnson, 'Batman's Return' in *Maclean's*, vol.105, n. 25 (22 June 1992).
3. Burton quoted in Philip Thomas, 'The Misfit' in *Empire*, n.26 (August 1991).
4. Burton quoted in Fred Schruers, 'Bat Mitzvah' in *Premier*, vol.5, n.11 (July 1995).
5. Keaton quoted in the *Batman Returns* production notes.
6. Kane quoted in *ibid*.
7. Burton quoted in Fred Schruers, *op cit*.
8. *Ibid*.
9. Waters quoted in the *Batman Returns* production notes.
10. Burton quoted in Philip Thomas, *op cit*.
11. Burton quoted in Fred Schruers, *op cit*.

12. Welch quoted in Richard Corliss, 'Battier and Better' in *Time*, vol.139, n.25 (22 June 1992).
13. Ringwood quoted in the *Batman Returns* production notes.
14. *Ibid*.
15. Keaton quoted in Fred Schruers, *op cit*.
16. Burton quoted in Garth Pearce, 'Bat Talk' in *Movies*, vol.1, n.1 (July 1992).
17. DeVito quoted in the *Batman Returns* production notes.
18. Burton quoted in Fred Schruers, *op cit*.
19. DeVito quoted in Richard Corliss, *op cit*.
20. Keaton quoted in the *Batman Returns* production notes.
21. Burton quoted in Fred Schruers, *op cit*.
22. Keaton quoted in the *Batman Returns* production notes.
23. Keaton quoted in Fred Schruers, *op cit*.
24. DiNovi quoted in *ibid*.
25. Burton quoted in Alan Jones, 'Cutting Remarks from Tim Burton in *Starburst*, vol.13, n.11 (July 1991).
26. Burton quoted in Fred Schruers, *op cit*.
27. DiNovi quoted in *ibid*.
28. Pfeiffer quoted in the *Batman Returns* production notes.
29. Dave Kehr, 'Unhappy Outsides' in the *Toronto Star*, 19 June 1992.
30. David Ansen, 'A Gotham Gothic' in *Newsweek*, vol.119, n.25 (22 June 1992).
31. Richard Corliss, *op cit*.
32. Barbara Cramer, 'Batman Returns' in *Films In Review*, vol.43, n.9–10 (September/October 1992).
33. Frank Gabreny, 'Batman Returns Sequel more satirical, darker than original' in the *Columbus Dispatch*, 19 June 1992.
34. Brian D Johnson, *op cit*.
35. Dave Kehr, *op cit*.
36. John Simon, 'Batman and girls at Bat' in *National Review*, vol.44, n. 15 (3 August 1992).
37. *Ibid*.
38. Stanley Kauffman, 'The Odd Couple' in the *New Republic*, vol.207, n.5 (27 July 1992).
39. Derek Malcolm, 'Batman Fails To Take Flight' in the *Guardian*, 9 July 1992.
40. Peter Travers, 'Bat Girls on Line' in *Rolling Stone*, n.634–635 (9 July 1992).

41. Czapsky quoted in the *Batman Returns* production notes.
42. Derek Malcolm, *op cit.*
43. Frank Gabreny, *op cit.*
44. Dave Kehr, *op cit.*
45. Barbara Cramer, *op cit.*
46. Burton quoted in Fred Schruers, *op cit.*
47. Dave Kehr, *op cit.*
48. Burton quoted in Brian D Johnson, *op cit.*
49. Burton quoted in Fred Schruers, *op cit.*
50. Burton quoted in Jeffrey Ressner, *op cit.*
51. Burton quoted in Fred Schruers, *op cit.*
52. Di Novi quoted in the *Batman Returns* production notes.
53. Pfeiffer quoted in Brian D Johnson, *op cit.*
54. Keaton quoted in Garth Pearce, *op cit.*

Tim Burton's The Nightmare Before Christmas

1. Burton quoted in Elisabeth Perrin, 'Tim Burton Guides to the Screen Another Tale From the Dark Side' in the *Chicago Sun-Times*, 17 October 1993.
2. Burton quoted in Jay Carr, 'Tim Burton's Big Adventure' in the *Boston Globe*, 17 October 1993.
3. Burton quoted in Betsy Sharkey, 'Tim Burton's "Nightmare" Comes True' in the *New York Times*, 10 October 1993.
4. Burton quoted in Mimi Avins, 'Ghoul World' in *Premier*, vol.7, n.3 (November 1993).
5. Burton quoted in Andy Carvin, 'An Interview with Tim Burton' (October 1993) from *EdWeb*, http://sunsite.ust.hk/edweb/nightmare.burton.html
6. Hoberman quoted in Lawrence French, 'The Nightmare Before Christmas' in *Cinefantastique*, vol.24, n.5 (December 1993).
7. Burton quoted in Mimi Avins, *op cit.*
8. Katzenberg quoted in *ibid.*
9. Burton quoted in Steve Daly, 'Ghost in the Machine: Tim Burton's Animated "Nightmare" Haunts. Disney' in *Entertainment Weekly*, 29 October 1993.
10. Hoberman quoted in Mimi Avins, *op cit.*
11. Danny Elfman quoted in Andy Carvin, 'An Interview with Danny Elfman' October 1993 – from *EdWeb*, http://sunsite.ust.hk/edweb/nightmare.elfman.html

12. Di Novi quoted in Steve Daly, *op cit.*
13. Burton quoted in Andy Carvin, 'Tim Burton', *op cit.*
14. Selick quoted in John Hartl, ' "The Nightmare Before Christmas" Returns' in the *Seattle Times*, 22 October 2000.
15. Selick quoted in Mark Cotta Vaz, 'Animation in the Third Dimension' in *Cinefex*, n.56 (November 1993).
16. Selick quoted in Leslie Felperin, 'Animated Dreams' in *Sight and Sound*, vol.4, n.12 (December 1994).
17. Selick quoted in Steve Daly, *op cit.*
18. Leighton quoted in Mark Cotta Vaz, *op cit.*
19. Burton quoted in Andy Carvin, 'Tim Burton', *op cit.*
20. Elfman quoted in Mimi Avins, *op cit.*
21. Danny Elfman quoted in Andy Carvin, 'Danny Elfman', *op cit.*
22. David Ansen, 'Tim Burton Looks at Holiday Hell' in *Newsweek*, vol.122, n.18 (1 November 1993).
23. Harper Barnes, 'Gee Whiz: It's "Stop-Action" Again' in the *St Louis Post-Dispatch*, 22 October 1993.
24. Jay Carr, 'Tim Burton's "Nightmare" Is More Sweet than Scary' in the *Boston Globe*, 22 October 1993.
25. Roger Ebert, 'Burton's Dreamy Nightmare' in the *Chicago Sun-Times*, 27 October 2000.
26. Quentin Curtis, 'Amazing What you can do in a Fortnight' in the *Independent*, 27 November 1994.
27. Leslie Felperin, *op cit.*
28. Kim Newman, 'Tim Burton's The Nightmare Before Christmas' in *Sight and Sound*, vol.4, n.12 (December 1994).
29. Elfman quoted in Betsy Sharkey, *op cit.*
30. Kim Newman, *op cit.*
31. Jay Carr, *op cit* (22 October 1993).
32. Kim Newman, *op cit.*
33. Burton quoted in Michael Dwyer, 'The Stuff that Dreams are Made of' in the *Irish Times*, 10 December 1994.
34. Anna Everett, 'The Other Pleasures: The Narrative Function of Race in the Cinema' in *Film Criticism*, vol.xx, n.1–2 (Fall/Winter 1995–96).
35. Selick quoted in Leslie Felperin, *op cit.*
36. *Ibid.*
37. St Armand quoted in Mark Cotta Vaz, *op cit.*
38. Burton quoted in Michel Ciment 'Entrien avec Tim Burton – Un Optisme etrange et perverti' in *Postif*, n.412 (June 1995).

39. Betsy Sharkey, *op cit.*
40. Leslie Felperin, *op cit.*
41. Roger Ebert, *op cit.*
42. Kenneth Turan, 'Burton Dreams up a Delightful "Nightmare"' in the *Los Angeles Times*, 15 October 1993.
43. Selick quoted in Leslie Felperin, *op cit.*

Ed Wood

1. Boyington quoted in Paul M Sammon, 'Quick Cuts, Wood Works' in Cinefex n.61 (May 1995).
2. Burton quoted in Michel Ciment, 'Entrien avec Tim Burton – Un Optisme étrange et perverti' in *Postif 412* (June 1995).
3. *Ibid.*
4. Burton quoted in Lawrence French, 'An Ode to B-Movie Badness: Tim Burton's Ed Wood' in *Cinefantastique*, vol.25, n.6/vol.26, n.1 (December 1994).
5. Lehmann quoted in John Clark, 'The Wood, The Bad, and The Ugly' in *Premiere*, vol.8, n.2 (October 1994).
6. Karaszewski quoted in Susan S Davis, 'An Evening in Bipoia' on http://www.screenwritersutopia.com/pros/susan/002.html
7. Karaszewski quoted in Mark Carducci, 'Plan 9 From Outer Burton: Ed Wood' in *Cinefantastique*, vol.25, n.2 (April 1994).
8. Lehmann quoted in John Clark, *op cit.*
9. Burton quoted in Lawrence French, *op cit.*
10. Karaszewski quoted in *op cit.*
11. Burton quoted in John Clark, *op cit.*
12. Burton quoted in Lawrence French, *op cit.*
13. Burton quoted in Michael Dwyer, 'The Stuff that Dreams are Made of' in the *Irish Times*, 10 December 1994.
14. Parker quoted in John Clark, *op cit.*
15. Burton quoted in Lawrence French, *op cit.*
16. Burton quoted in Michael Dwyer, *op cit.*
17. Burton quoted in John Clark, *op cit.*
18. *Ibid.*
19. Burton quoted in Jay Carr, 'Tim Burton's Big Adventure' in the *Boston Globe*, 17 October 1993.
20. Burton quoted in Lawrence French, *op cit.*
21. Arquette quoted in John Clark, *op cit.*
22. Kathy Wood quoted in John Clark, *op cit.*

23. Kevin Lewis, 'Ed Wood' in *Films in Review*, vol.26, n.1–2 (January/February 1995).
24. Peter Travers, 'Auteur In Angora' in *Rolling Stone*, n.511 (July 1995).
25. Tom Gliatto, 'Ed Wood' in *People*, vol.42, n.15 (10 October 1994).
26. Kim Newman, 'Ed Wood' in *Sight and Sound*, vol.5, n.5 (May 1995).
27. Richard Alleva, 'In The Kingdom Of Cranks: Ed Wood & Road To Wellville' in *Commonweal*, vol.121, n.21 (12 February 1994).
28. Kim Newman, *op cit*.
29. Kevin Lewis, *op cit*.
30. David Ansen, 'Kitsch As Kitsch Can' in *Newsweek*, vol.124, n.15 (October 10 1994).
31. Peter Travers, *op cit*.
32. Burton quoted in Lawrence French, *op cit*.
33. Czapsky quoted in Lawrence French, 'Cinematography: DP Stefan Czapsky on the filming in black & white' in *Cinefantastique*, vol.25, n.6/vol.26, n.1 (December 1994).
34. Mark Carducci, *op cit*.
35. Burton quoted in Jay Carr, *op cit*.
36. Burton quoted in Lawrence French, *op cit*.
37. Burton quoted in John Clark, *op cit*.
38. Landau quoted in Jeff Dawson, 'The 67th annual academy awards' in *Empire* n. 71 (May 1995).
39. Kathy Wood quoted in John Clark, *op cit*.

Mars Attacks!

1. Elfman quoted in Steve Biodrowski, 'Mars Attacks!: Director Tim Burton brings the infamous cards to life' in *Cinefantastique*, vol.28, n.6 (December 1996).
2. Burton quoted in Steve Goldman, 'Spaced Invaders' in *Empire*, n.93 (March 1997).
3. Brown quoted in Stuart Taylor, 'Len Brown: Martian Madman' in *Alien Encounters*, n.6.
4. Brown quoted in Mark Cotta Vaz, 'Martial Art' in *Cinefex*, n.68 (December 1996).
5. Burton quoted in Michael Henry ' "Il ne faut pas se fier aux apparences," Entretien avec Tim Burton' in *Positif*, n.433 (March 1997).

6. Burton quoted in Frederick C Szebin and Steve Biodrowski, 'Mars Attacks: Tim Burton sends up the bubblegum alien invader genre' in *Cinefantastique*, vol.28, n.7 (January 1997).
7. Burton quoted in Steve Biodrowski, *op cit* (December 1996).
8. Lassally quoted in Karen R Jones – *Mars Attacks! The Art of the Movie* (Titan Books; London, 1996) p.x.
9. Burton quoted in Michael Henry, *op cit*.
10. Burton quoted in Susan Stark, 'Director Tim Burton Revels in the Weird in his New Space Comedy' in the *Detroit News*, 7 December 1996.
11. Burton quoted in the *Mars Attacks!* production notes.
12. Gems quoted in Szebin and Biodrowski, *op cit*.
13. Burton quoted in Steve Goldman, *op cit*.
14. Burton quoted in Cindy Pearlman, 'Today Vegas: Tomorrow, The World! Mean Little Green Guys Attack Earth' in the *Chicago Sun-Times*, 8 December 1996.
15. Gems quoted in Karen R Jones, *op cit*, p.24.
16. Gems quoted in Steve Biodrowski, *op cit* (December 1996).
17. Burton quoted in the *Mars Attacks!* production notes.
18. Burton quoted in Szebin and Biodrowski, *op cit*.
19. Lisa Marie quoted in John Epperson, 'Mars Attacks! Interview with actress Lisa Marie' in *Interview* (December 1996).
20. Gems quoted in Szebin and Biodrowski, *op cit*.
21. *Ibid*.
22. Franco quoted in *ibid*.
23. Franco quoted in Anthony C Ferrante, 'Duck for Cover when Mars Attacks' in *Fangoria*, n.159 (January 1997).
24. Burton quoted in Szebin and Biodrowski, *op cit*.
25. Barry Purvis quoted in Christine Spines, 'Men Are From Mars, Women Are From Venus' in *Premier*, January 1996.
26. Jonathan Gems quoted in *ibid*.
27. Burton quoted in the *Mars Attacks!* production notes.
28. Franco quoted in Szebin and Biodrowski, *op cit*.
29. DeVito quoted in Cindy Pearlman, *op cit*.
30. DeVito quoted in the *Mars Attacks!* production notes.
31. Brosnan quoted in Sylvia Patterson, 'Thomas Crown, back in town' in *Interview* (August, 1999).
32. Fox quoted in Frederick C Szebin, 'Martian Victim: Michael J Fox: Marty McFly on dabbling in another sci-fi universe' in *Cinefantastique*, vol.28, n.7 (January 1997).

33. Steiger quoted in Steve Biodrowski, 'Martian Victim: Rod Steiger: The Veteran Oscar-Winner on working with Burton' in *Cinefantastique*, vol.28, n.7 (January 1997).

34. Winfield quoted in Steve Biodrowski, 'Martian Victims: The Hawk & the Dove: Paul Winfield on challenging Steiger's warmongering' in *Cinefantastique*, vol.28, n.7 (January 1997).

35. Burton quoted in Szebin and Biodrowski, *op cit*.

36. Burton quoted in Christian Viviani, 'Mars Attacks! Small-town, USA' in *Postif*, n.433, March 1997.

37. Terrence Rafferty, 'The Current Cinema' in the *New Yorker*, 16 December 1996.

38. David Ansen, 'Aliens, Angels and Artiness' in *Newsweek*, vol.128, n.26 (23 December 1996).

39. Chris Kaltenbach, ' "Mars Attacks!" Crashes to Earth' in the *Baltimore Sun*, 13 December 1996.

40. Peter Slack, 'Scant Intelligent Life in "Mars": Starry Cast Can't Save Tim Burton's Interplanetary Gags' in the *San Francisco Chronicle*, 13 December 1996.

41. David Sterritt, 'High-Voltage Stars Can't Save "Mars Attacks!" ' in *The Christian Science Monitor*, 13 December 1996.

42. Mark Ehrman, 'Attack of the Martians Who Ate Hollywood!' in the *Los Angeles Times*, 16 December 1996.

43. J Hoberman, 'Creature Feature' in *Village Voice*, vol.41, n.51, 17 December 1996.

44. Richard Corliss & Richard Schickel, 'A Rich Film Fest' in *Time*, vol.148, n.29, 30 December 1996/6 January 1997.

45. Burton quoted in Christian Viviani, *op cit*.

46. Elfman quoted in Anthony C Ferrante, *op cit*.

47. Elfman quoted in Frederick C Szebin & Steve Biodrowski, 'Martian Music: Composer Danny Elfman: On Burtonizing the golden sci-fi scores of the past' in *Cinefantastique*, vol.28, n.7 (January 1997).

48. Burton quoted in Philip Thomas, 'The Misfit' in *Empire*, n.26 (August 1991).

49. Burton quoted in the *Mars Attacks!* production notes.

50. *Ibid*.

51. Atwood quoted in *ibid*.

52. Ken Hanke, *Tim Burton: An Unauthorized Biography of the Filmmaker* (Renaissance Books; Los Angeles, 1999) p.197.

53. *Ibid.* p.205.
54. Gems quoted in Steve Biodrowski, *op cit* (December 1996).
55. Owen Gleiberman, 'Our Favourite Martians' in *Entertainment Weekly*, 13 December 1996.
56. J Hoberman, *ibid.*
57. Burton quoted in Steve Goldman, *op cit.*
58. Franco quoted in Szebin and Biodrowski, *op cit.*
59. Burton quoted in Cindy Pearlman, *op cit.*
60. Gems quoted in Anthony C Ferrante, *op cit.*
61. Gems quoted in Szebin and Biodrowski, *op cit.*
62. *Mars Attacks!* Preview in *Screen International*, n.1081 (25–31 October 1996).
63. Gems quoted in Anthony C Ferrante, *op cit.*
64. Burton quoted in David Mills, 'One on One' in *Empire*, n.128 (February 2000).
65. Franco quoted in Karen R Jones, *op cit.* p.9.
66. Steiger quoted in Steve Biodrowski, 'Martian Victim: Rod Steiger' *ibid.*
67. Gems quoted in Anthony C Ferrante, *op cit.*
68. Elfman quoted in Steve Biodrowski, *op cit* (December 1996).

The Death of Superman

1. Smith quoted in 'Mr Smith Goes to Hollywood' in *Hotdog*, n.12 (May 2001).
2. Burton quoted in David Mills, 'One on One' in *Empire*, n.128 (February 2000).
3. Di Bonaventura quoted in Rebecca Ascher-Walsh, 'Cape Fear: Why the Super-Expensive Superman Lives Can't Seem to Get Off the Ground' in *Entertainment Weekly*, 29 May 1998.
4. Burton quoted in Stephen Schaefer, 'Tim Burton' From: http://mrshowbiz.go.com/news/Todays_Stories/991102/burton-sleepyhollow110 299.html
5. Kevin Smith, 'A Superman For All Seasons' in *TV Guide*, 3 December 2001
6. Burton quoted in David Mills, *op cit.*
7. Burton quoted in 'Interview Tidbits with Tim Burton' from http://www.aintitcoolnews.com/display.cgi?id=9860

Sleepy Hollow

1. Burton quoted in Michel Ciment and Yannick Dahan, 'Entretien Tim Burton: Le conte de fées permet de décrire des vérités de façon plus subversive' in *Postif*, n.468 (January 2000).
2. Burton quoted in Mark Salisbury, 'Heads Up for Sleepy Hollow' in *Fangoria*, n.188 (November 1999).
3. Burton quoted in Mark Salisbury, 'A Head of the Game' in *Fangoria*, n.189 (January 2000).
4. Burton quoted in Ciment and Dahan, *op cit*.
5. Burton quoted in Mark Cotta Vaz, 'A Region of Shadows' in *Cinefex*, n.80 (January 2000).
6. Burton quoted in *ibid*.
7. Burton quoted in Sandra Bordigoni – 'Heads and Tales' From: http://www.urbancinefile.com.au/scripts/cinefile/Interviews.idc?Article_ID=3184
8. Burton quoted in Mark Salisbury, 'A Head', *op cit*.
9. Burton quoted in Johnanna Schneller, 'Where's Johnny?' in *Premier*, vol.13, n.4 (December 1999).
10. Burton quoted in Stephen Pizzello, 'Head Trip' in *American Cinematographer*, vol.80, n.12 (December 1999).
11. Lubezki quoted in Stephen Pizzello, 'Galloping Ghost' in *American Cinematographer*, vol.80, n.12 (December 1999).
12. Burton quoted in Sandra Bordigoni, *op cit*.
13. Burton quoted in David Mills, 'One on One' in *Empire*, n.128 (February 2000).
14. Burton quoted in the *Sleepy Hollow* production notes.
15. Depp quoted in Mark Salisbury, 'Male of the Unexpected' in *Total Film*, n.37 (Feb 2000).
16. Depp quoted in the *Sleepy Hollow* production notes.
17. Depp quoted in Simon Braund, 'Village of the Damned!' in *Empire*, n.127 (January 2000).
18. Depp quoted in the *Sleepy Hollow* production notes.
19. Burton on the Director's Commentary on the *Sleepy Hollow* DVD.
20. Burton quoted in David Mills, *op cit*.
21. Depp quoted in Simon Braund, *op cit*.
22. Ricci quoted in Mark Salisbury, 'Wednesday's Child comes of age' in *Total Film*, n.37 (Feb 2000).
23. Burton quoted in Mark Salisbury, 'A Head', *op cit*.

24. Lee quoted in *ibid*.
25. Burton quoted in Sandra Bordigoni, *op cit*.
26. Schroeder quoted in Mark Salisbury, 'Heads Up', *op cit*.
27. *Ibid*.
28. Burton quoted in Stephen Pizzello, 'Head', *op cit*.
29. Schroeder quoted in Mark Salisbury, 'Heads Up', *op cit*.
30. Rudin quoted in *ibid*.
31. Burton quoted in Stephen Pizzello, 'Head', *op cit*.
32. Burton quoted in Mark Cotta Vaz, *op cit*.
33. Heinrichs quoted in Mark Salisbury, 'Heads Up', *op cit*.
34. Burton quoted in Ciment and Dahan, *op cit*.
35. Burton quoted in Stephen Pizzello, 'Head', *op cit*.
36. Burton on the *Sleepy Hollow* DVD.
37. Todd McCarthy, 'Sleepy Hollow' in *Variety*, 15 November 1999.
38. Kim Newman, 'The Cage of Reason' in *Sight and Sound*, vol.10, n.1 (January 2000).
39. Owen Gleiberman, 'Dead Heads' in *Entertainment Weekly*, 26 November 1999.
40. J Hoberman, 'Heads or Tails' in *Village Voice*, vol.44, n.47 (30 November 1999).
41. Richard Corliss, 'Tim Burton's Tricky Treat' in *Time*, 22 November 1999.
42. Lubezki quoted in Stephen Pizzello, 'Galloping', *op cit*.
43. Burton quoted in Mark Salisbury, 'Heads Up', *op cit*.
44. Burton quoted in Stephen Pizzello, 'Head', *op cit*.
45. Lubezki quoted in Stephen Pizzello, 'Galloping', *op cit*.
46. Lubezki quoted in Mark Cotta Vaz, *op cit*.
47. Burton quoted in Mark Salisbury, 'Heads Up', *op cit*.
48. Burton quoted in Ciment and Dahan, *op cit*.
49. Burton on the *Sleepy Hollow* DVD.
50. Kim Newman, *op cit*.
51. Todd McCarthy, *op cit*.
52. Burton quoted in David Mills, *op cit*.
53. Burton quoted in Ciment and Dahan, *op cit*.
54. Burton quoted in Stephen Pizzello, 'Head', *op cit*.
55. Burton quoted in Sandra Bordigoni, *op cit*.
56. Burton quoted in Ciment and Dahan, *op cit*.
57. Depp quoted in Johnanna Schneller, *op cit*.
58. Gough quoted in Mark Salisbury, 'Veterans in the "Hollow"' in *Fangoria*, n.188 (November 1999).

59. Depp quoted in Mark Salisbury, 'Male', *op cit*.

Stainboy

1. Tim Burton, *The Melancholy Death of Oyster Boy and Other Stories* (Faber & Faber; London, 1998) p.26.
2. Burton quoted in Dean Delandreville, 'Hollywood is Streaming' from http://www.zdnet.com/devhead/stories/articles/0,4413,2600198,00.html
3. Viner quoted in Sam McMillan, 'Tim Burton's Stainboy' from http://www.designinteract.com/features_d/stainboy/
4. Amato quoted in *ibid*.
5. *Ibid*.
6. Ramin Zahed, 'Stainboy' in *Variety*, 13 November 2000.
7. Tim Burton, *op cit*, p.9.

Planet of the Apes

1. William Broyles quoted in Daniel Argent, 'Time and Destiny' in *Creative Screenwriting* vol.8. n.4 (July 2001).
2. *Ibid*.
3. *Ibid*.
4. Burton quoted in Chris Betros, 'In Person: The Planet That Went Ape' from http://www.tokyoclassified.com/tokyointerview/384/tokyointerviewinc.htm
5. Burton quoted in Richard Natale, 'Remaking, Not Aping, An Original' in the *Los Angeles Times*, 6 May 2001.
6. William Broyles quoted in Daniel Argent, *op cit*.
7. Burton quoted in Michael Sragow, 'The Ape Man' in the *Guardian*, 3 August 2001.
8. Baker quoted in John Calhoun and Scott Essman, 'Show me the Monkey' (1 August 2001) from www.entertainmentdesign.com
9. Baker quoted in the *Planet of the Apes* production notes.
10. Baker quoted in Calhoun and Essman, *op cit*.
11. Burton quoted in Richard Natale, *op cit*.
12. Konner quoted in 'Interview: Planet of the Apes Scribes Mark Rosenthal and Lawrence Konner' from www.fandom.com
13. *Ibid*.
14. Burton quoted in John Hiscock, 'What a Piece of Work is an Ape!' in the *Daily Telegraph*, 27 July 2001.
15. Burton quoted in J Rentilly, 'Tim Burton, Relying on Himself' from www.audiencemagazine.com

16. Burton quoted in Mark Salisbury, 'Gorillas just Wanna have Fun' in *Premiere* vol.14, n.11 (July 2001).
17. Wahlberg quoted in Barbara Vancheri, 'Man vs. Ape' in the *Pittsburgh Post-Gazette*, 27 July 2001.
18. Wahlberg quoted in Richard Natale, *op cit.*
19. Helena Bonham Carter quoted in the *Planet of the Apes* production notes.
20. Roth quoted in *ibid.*
21. Burton quoted in Cindy Pearlman, 'A Strange New Planet' in the *Ottawa Citizen*, 20 July 2001.
22. Richard D Zanuck quoted in the *Planet of the Apes* production notes.
23. Giamatti quoted in Benjamin Svetkey and M Raftery, 'Ape Crusaders' in *Entertainment Weekly*, n.593 (27 April 2001).
24. Heston quoted in 'Heston Does It For The Money' from: http://www.empireonline.co.uk/news/news.asp?3178
25. Heston quoted in the *Planet of the Apes* production notes.
26. Notary quoted in *ibid.*
27. Roth quoted in Barbara Vancheri, *op cit.*
28. Bonham Carter quoted in Janine Dallas Steffan, 'Celebrities: See, Heard, Said' in the *Seattle Times*, 30 July 2001.
29. Bonham Carter quoted in Anthony C Ferrante, 'Helena Bonham Carter on Getting AADD – Attention Ape Deficit Disorder – Filming the "Planet of the Apes" Remake' in *If Magazine*, n.27.3 (25 May 2001).
30. Francesca Chapman, ' "Apes" Opts For Style Over Substance' in the *Philadelphia Daily News*, 27 July 2001.
31. Joe Williams, 'New "Planet" Needn't Play Second Banana To Original' in the *St Louis Post-Dispatch*, 27 July 2001.
32. Elvis Mitchell, 'Get Your Hands Off, Ya Big Gorilla!' in the *New York Times*, 27 July 2001.
33. Michael Sragow, *op cit.*
34. John Mark Eberhart, 'For Better Or For Worse, This Isn't Apes By The Book' in the *Kansas City Star*, 26 July 2001.
35. Bob Graham, 'Great "Apes" ' in the *San Francisco Chronicle*, 27 July 2001.
36. Matt Radz, 'Jungle Land: Director Tim Burton reimagines a classic in Planet of the Apes' in the *Montreal Gazette*, 27 July 2001.
37. Todd McCarthy, 'Planet of the Apes' in *Variety*, 30 July 2001.

38. Jay Carr, 'When Hairy Met Silly' in the *Boston Globe*, 27 July 2001.
39. John Petkovic, 'This Time, The Humans Are Smarter And The Movie Is Dumber' in the *Plain Dealer*, 27 July 2001.
40. Kenneth Turan, 'Some Serious Monkey Business' in the *Los Angeles Times*, 27 July 2001.
41. Michael Sragow, 'Clunky Monkeys' in the *Baltimore Sun*, 27 July 2001.
42. Steven Mazey, 'Little More Than Monkey Business' in the *Ottawa Citizen*, 27 July 2001.
43. Gary Johnson, 'Movie review' in *Images Journal*, n.10.
44. Elvis Mitchell, *op cit*.
45. David Sterrit, ' "Planet" Remake Merely Apes The Original' in the *Christian Science Monitor*, 28 July 2001.
46. Andrew O'Hehir, 'Gorilla Warfare' in *Sight and Sound*, vol.11, n.9 (September 2001).
47. Elfman quoted in Ford A Thaxton, 'Danny Elfman revisits the Planet of the Apes' in *Soundtrack*, vol.20, n.79 (Fall 2001).
48. Elfman letter in the *Los Angeles Times*, 28 July 2001.
49. Rousselot quoted in David E Williams, 'Antisocial Darwinism' in *American Cinematographer*, vol.33, n.4 (August 2000).
50. *Ibid*.
51. *Ibid*.
52. *Ibid*.
53. Burton quoted in Jenny Cooney Carillo, 'Monkey Magic' in *Dreamwatch*, n.86 (November 2001).
54. Burton on the commentary track of the *Planet of the Apes* DVD (R1).
55. Wahlberg quoted in Matt Webb Mitovich – 'Wahlberg Tackles Apes Rumours' from *TV Guide Online*, 31 July 2001 – http://www.tvguide.com/newsgossip/insider/010731a.asp
56. Burton quoted in John Hiscock, *op cit*.
57. Snyder quoted in Brandon Grey, 'Planet of the Apes Ending Explained by Fox Exec' (29 July 2001) from www.zap2it.com
58. Roth quoted in Brandon Gray, 'Tim Roth Theorizes About "Planet of the Apes" Ending' (27 September 2001) from www.zap2it.com
59. Burton quoted in Jane Crowther, 'Tim Burton Interview: Planet of the Apes' from: http://www.bbc.co.uk/films/2001/08/14/tim_burton_planet_apes_interview.shtml

60. Burton quoted in Charlotte O'Sullivan, 'Numb and Number' in the *Independent*, 16 August 2001.
61. Burton quoted in Michael Sragow, *op cit.*
62. Burton quoted in Alan Jones, 'Directing the Legend' in *Cinefantastique*, vol.20, n.1 (November 1989).
63. Burton quoted in David Elliot, 'Tim Burton: The Man Behind "Batman" ' in the *San Diego Union-Tribune*, 25 June 1989.
64. Bonham Carter quoted in Anthony C Ferrante, *op cit.*

Unrealised Projects

1. Burton quoted in Sandra Bordigoni, 'Heads and Tales' from: http://www.urbancinefile.com.au/scripts/cinefile/Interviews.idc?Article_ID=3184
2. Burton quoted in J Rentilly, 'Tim Burton, Relying on Himself' from www.audiencemagazine.com
3. *Ibid.*
4. Gems quoted in Anthony C Ferrante, 'Hidden Gems' in *Fangoria*, n.160 (March 1997).
5. *Ibid.*
6. *Ibid.*
7. *Ibid.*
8. Burton quoted in Alan Jones, 'Cutting Remarks from Tim Burton' in *Starburst*, vol.13, n.11 (July 1991).

BIBLIOGRAPHY

Interviews

Tim Burton interviewed by Mark Kermode – the *Guardian* interview at the National Film Theatre (UK), 6 January 2000

Unless otherwise stated in the notes to each chapter, all quotes from the following were from interviews conducted by the authors on the dates shown, or from subsequent correspondence:

Glenn Shadix (14 November 2001)
Scott Alexander (18 December 2001)
Larry Karaszewski (18 December 2001)
Tom Duffield (5 January 2002)
Martin Landau (8 January 2002)
Rick Heinrichs (24 January 2002)

Books

Burton, Tim, *The Melancholy Death of Oyster Boy and Other Stories* (Faber & Faber; London, 1998)

Daniels, Les, *DC Comics: 60 Years of the World's Favourite Comics Heroes* (Bulfinch Press; 1995)

Fox, Ken, Grant, Ed and Imeson, Jo (eds), *The Seventh Virgin Film Guide* (Virgin Books; London, 1998)

Hanke, Ken, *Tim Burton: An Unauthorized Biography of the Filmmaker* (Renaissance Books; Los Angeles, 1999)

Irving, Washington, *The Sketch-Book of Geoffrey Crayon, Gent.*

Jones, Karen R, *Mars Attacks! The Art of the Movie* (Titan Books; London, 1996)

Konigsberg, Ira, *The Complete Film Dictionary* (Bloomsbury; London, second edition – 1997)

Merschmann, Helmut (trns. Kane, Michael), *Tim Burton: The Life and Films of a Visionary Director* (Titan Books; London, 2000)

Miller, Frank with Janson, Klaus and Varley, Lynn, *Batman: The Dark Knight Returns – Tenth Anniversary Edition* (DC Comics; New York, 1996)

Parkin, Lance, *Pocket Essentials Alan Moore* (Pocket Essentials; Harpenden, 2002)

Salisbury, Mark (ed.), *Burton on Burton* (Faber & Faber; London, 1995)

Salisbury, Mark (ed.), *Burton on Burton: Revised and Updated Edition* (Faber & Faber; London, 1998)

Schwartz, Carol (ed.), *Videohound's Complete Guide to Cult Flicks and Trash Pics* (Visible Ink Press; Detroit, 1996)

Walker, John (ed.), *Halliwell's Film & Video Guide 2001* (HarperCollins; London, 2000)

Walker, John (ed.), *Halliwell's Who's Who in the Movies* (HarperCollins; London, 1999)

Wasko, Janet, *Understanding Disney: The Manufacture of Fantasy* (Polity Press; Cambridge, 2001)

Articles

Abbott, Denise, 'Nightmare by Design' in *Hollywood Reporter*, vol.361, n.49 (29 February 2000)

Adamson, Rondi, 'Planet Of The Heartless, Arrogant Humans' in the *Ottawa Citizen*, 27 July 2001

Addiego, Walter, 'Mars Attacks!' in the *San Francisco Examiner*, 13 December 1996

Alleva, Richard, 'In the Kingdom of Cranks: Ed Wood & Road to Wellville' in *Commonweal*, vol.121, n.21 (2 December 1994)

Anderson, Jeffrey M, 'Snoopy Dances: An Interview With Johnny Depp' (12 November 1999) from http://www.combustiblecelluloid.com/intdepp.shtml

Anderson, John, 'Something Simian, Something Sinister' in *Newsday*, 27 July 2001

Anonymous, 'Pee-wee's Big Adventure' in *Variety*, 31 July 1985

Anonymous, 'Guest Star Catherine O'Hara on the set of Beetlejuice' in the *Toronto Star*, 2 October 1988

Anonymous, 'The Bat Mogul and the Abyss' in *The Economist*, 26 August 1989

Anonymous, *Mars Attacks!* Preview in *Screen International*, n.1081 (25–31 October 1996)

Anonymous, 'Return From Planet Pee-Wee' in *Vanity Fair* (September 1999)

Anonymous, ' "Sleepy Hollow" Gallops Into New Millennium; Most Ambitious Online Launch of Motion Picture to Date' in *Business Wire*, 29 October 1999

Anonymous, 'Interview: Planet of the Apes Scribes Mark Rosenthal and Lawrence Konner' from www.fandom.com

Anonymous, 'Heston Does It For The Money' from http://www.empireonline.co.uk/news/news.asp?3178

Anonymous, 'Mr Smith Goes to Hollywood' in *Hotdog*, n.12 (May 2001)

Anonymous, 'Interview Tidbits with Tim Burton' from http://www.aintitcoolnews.com/display.cgi?id=9860

Ansen, David, 'A Gotham Gothic' in *Newsweek*, vol.119, n.25 (22 June 1992)

Ansen, David, 'Tim Burton Looks at Holiday Hell' in *Newsweek*, vol.122, n.18 (1 November 1993)

Ansen, David, 'Kitsch as Kitsch Can' in *Newsweek*, vol.124, n.15 (10 October 1994)

Ansen, David, 'Aliens, Angels and Artiness' in *Newsweek*, vol.128, n.26 (23 December 1996)

Argent, Daniel, 'Time and Destiny' in *Creative Screenwriting*, vol.8, n.4 (July 2001)

Ascher-Walsh, Rebecca, 'Cape Fear: Why the Super-Expensive Superman Lives Can't Seem to Get Off the Ground' in *Entertainment Weekly*, 29 May 1998

Avins, Mimi, 'Ghoul World' in *Premier*, vol.7, n.3 (November 1993)

Barbieri, Susan M, 'Florida Hairdresser the Real "Scissorhands" ' in the *Toronto Star*, 10 January 1991

Barker, Olivia, 'Mark Wahlberg doesn't dare to bare for "Apes" ' in *USA Today*, 23 February 2001

Barnes, Harper, 'Gee Whiz: It's "Stop-Action" Again' in the *St Louis Post-Dispatch*, 22 October 1993

Barrett, Amy, 'Going Ape' in the *New York Times*, 24 December 2000

Barth, Jack, 'Pee Wee TV' in *Film Comment*, vol.22, n.6 (November–December 1986)

Bealing, Stephen, 'Beetlejuice' in *Films and Filming*, n.407 (August 1988)

Beck, Marilyn, 'Cruise Juggling Schedule for "Scissorhand"' in the *Courier-Journal*, 15 November 1989

Benshoff, Harry M, 'Mars Attacks! ID4-Independence Day' from http://www.nottingham.ac.uk/film/journal/filmrev/id4-and-mars-attacks.htm

Benson, Sheila, 'Batangst in Basic Black' in the *Los Angeles Times*, 29 June 1989

Berry, Joanna, 'Edward Scissorhands' in *Empire*, n.26 (August 1991)

Betros, Chris, 'In Person: The Planet That Went Ape' from http://www.tokyoclassified.com/tokyointerview/384/tokyointerviewinc.htm

Biodrowski, Steve, Del Valle, David & French, Lawrence, 'Vincent Price: Looking Back on Forty Years as Horror's Crown Prince' in *Cinefantastique*, vol.19, n.2 (January 1989)

Biodrowski, Steve, 'Mars Attacks!: Director Tim Burton brings the infamous cards to life' in *Cinefantastique*, vol.28, n.6 (December 1996)

Biodrowski, Steve, 'Martian Victims: The Hawk & the Dove: Paul Winfield on challenging Steiger's warmongering' in *Cinefantastique*, vol.28, n.7 (January 1997)

Biodrowski, Steve, 'Martian Victim: Rod Steiger: The Veteran Oscar-Winner on working with Burton' in *Cinefantastique*, vol.28, n.7 (January 1997)

Biodrowski, Steve, 'Martian Design: Art Direction: Designer Wynn Thomas on devising the sci-fi look' in *Cinefantastique*, vol.28, n.7 (January 1997)

Biodrowski, Steve, 'Martian Effects: Special Effects: ILM shows off CGI to stop-motion fan Burton' in *Cinefantastique*, vol.28, n.7 (January 1997)

Bonin, Liane, 'Apes of Wrath' in *Entertainment Weekly*, n.549 (14 July 2000)

Bordigoni, Sandra, 'Heads and Tales' from: http://www.urbancinefile.com.au/scripts/cinefile/Interviews.idc?Article_ID=3184

Braund, Simon, 'Village of the Damned!' in *Empire*, n.127 (January 2000)

Broeske, Pat H, 'Dusting Off Burton' in the *Los Angeles Times*, 20 January 1991

Bruce, Bryan, 'Pee Wee Herman: The Homosexual Subtext' in *CineAction!*, n.9 (July 1987)

Brumley, Al, 'Fablelike "Scissorhands" Stands Out 10 Years Later' in the *Arizona Republic*, 22 September 2000

Burman, Mark, 'Caroline Thompson talks to Mark Burman about the script Lonely People' in *Sight & Sound*, vol.3, n.10 (October 1993)

Busch, Anita M, 'Burton Lands on "Planet of the Apes" in Fox's Remake' in *Hollywood Reporter*, vol.361, n.45 (22 February 2000)

Cagle, Jess, 'Making Faces' in *Time*, vol.156, n.5 (31 July 2000)

Calhoun, John, 'Headless in Sleepy Hollow' in *Entertainment Design*, vol.33, n.10 (November 1999)

Calhoun, John and Essman, Scott, 'Show me the Monkey' (1 August 2001) from www.entertainmentdesign.com

Canby, Vincent, 'Screen: "Pee-wee's Big Adventure," A comedy' in the *New York Times*, 9 August 1985

Canby, Vincent, ' "Beetlejuice" is Pap for the Eyes' in the *New York Times*, 8 May 1988

Carducci, Mark, 'Plan 9 From Outer Burton: Ed Wood' in *Cinefantastique*, vol.25, n.2 (April 1994)

Carducci, Mark, 'Deadringer for Tor: Wrestler George Steele on playing the horror icon' in *Cinefantastique*, vol.25, n.5 (October 1994)

Carducci, Mark, 'Ve Neil on working with designs by Rick Baker' in *Cinefantastique*, vol.25, n.5 (October 1994)

Carr, Jay, 'Can "Batman" Reach the Pot of Gold?' in the *Boston Globe*, 18 June 1989

Carr, Jay, 'Batophilia Strikes' in the *Boston Globe*, 23 June 1989

Carr, Jay, ' "Scissorhands" a Shear Delight' in the *Boston Globe*, 14 December 1990

Carr, Jay, 'Batman to Battle DeVito's Penguin' in the *Boston Globe*, 3 March 1991

Carr, Jay, 'Tim Burton's Big Adventure' in the *Boston Globe*, 17 October 1993

Carr, Jay, 'Tim Burton's "Nightmare" Is More Sweet than Scary' in the *Boston Globe*, 22 October 1993

Carr, Jay, 'Carving Out an Affectionate Look at Ed Wood' in the *Boston Globe*, 2 October 1994

Carr, Jay, 'When Hairy Met Silly' in the *Boston Globe*, 27 July 2001

Carvin, Andy, 'An Interview with Tim Burton' (October 1993) from EdWeb – http://sunsite.ust.hk/edweb/nightmare.burton.html

Carvin, Andy, 'An Interview with Danny Elfman' (October 1993) from EdWeb – http://sunsite.ust.hk/edweb/nightmare.elfman.html

Chapman, Francesca, ' "Apes" Opts For Style Over Substance' in the *Philadelphia Daily News*, 27 July 2001

Ciment, Gilles, 'Vincent, Frankenweenie: Apprentim Burton' in *Postif*, n.412 (June 1995)

Ciment, Michel, 'Entrien avec Tim Burton, Un Optisme étrange et perverti' in *Postif*, n.412 (June 1995)

Ciment, Michel and Dahan, Yannick, 'Entretien Tim Burton: Le conte de fées permet de décrire des vérités de façon plus subversive' in *Postif*, n.468 (January 2000)

Clark, John, 'The Wood, The Bad, and The Ugly' in *Premiere*, vol.8, n.2 (October 1994)

Coleman, David, 'Vincent' in *Cinefantasique*, vol.13, n.4 (April–May 1983)

Colton, David, 'Lee Still Scaring Up Work' in *USA Today*, 6 August 1999

Cooney Carillo, Jenny, 'Monkey Magic' in *Dreamwatch*, n.86 (November 2001)

Corliss, Richard, 'Shear Heaven: Edward Scissorhands' in *Time*, vol.136, n.35 (10 December 1990)

Corliss, Richard, 'Battier and Better' in *Time*, vol.139, n.25 (22 June 1992)

Corliss, Richard, 'A Monster to be Despised!' in *Time*, vol.144, n.15 (10 October 1994)

Corliss, Richard & Schickel, Richard, 'A Rich Film Fest' in *Time*, vol.148, n.29, 30 December 1996/January 1997

Corliss, Richard, 'Tim Burton's Tricky Treat' in *Time*, 22 November 1999

Cotta Vaz, Mark, 'Animation in the Third Dimension' in *Cinefex*, n.56 (November 1993)

Cotta Vaz, Mark, 'Martial Art' in *Cinefex*, n.68 (December 1996)

Cotta Vaz, Mark, 'A Region of Shadows' in *Cinefex*, n.80 (January 2000)

Cramer, Barbara, 'Batman Returns' in *Films In Review*, vol.43, n.9–10 (September/October 1992)

Crowther, Jane, 'Tim Burton Interview: Planet of the Apes' from http://www.bbc.co.uk/films/2001/08/14/tim_burton_planet_apes_interview.shtml

Curtis, Quentin, 'Amazing What you can do in a Fortnight' in the *Independent*, 27 November 1994

Dallas Steffan, Janine, 'Celebrities: See, Heard, Said' in the *Seattle Times*, 30 July 2001

Daly, Steve, 'Ghost in the Machine: Tim Burton's Animated "Nightmare" Haunts Disney' in *Entertainment Weekly*, 29 October 1993

Davis, Susan S, 'An Evening in Biopia: MAN ON THE MOON's Scott Alexander and Larry Karszewski' from http://www.screenwritersutopia.com/pros/susan/002.html

Dawson, Jeff, 'The 67th annual Academy Awards' in *Empire* n. 71 (May 1995)

Delandreville, Dean, 'Hollywood is Streaming' from http://www.zdnet.com/devhead/stories/articles/0,4413,2600198,00.html

Doherty, Thomas, 'Pee-Wee Herman: Thoughts on the peculiar appeal of Paul Reubens as a perennial man-child' in *Cinefantastique*, vol.19, n.5 (July 1989)

Dudek, Duane, 'With technology, "Planet of the Apes" evolves into purer version of original' in the *Milwaukee Journal Sentinel*, 27 July 2001

Dunphy, Catherine, 'Burton's Off-Kilter Scissorhands A Fantastic Slice Of Suburban Life' in the *Toronto Star*, 14 December 1990

Dwyer, Michael, 'The Stuff that Dreams are Made of' in the *Irish Times*, 10 December 1994

Easton, Nina J, 'For Tim Burton, This One's Personal' in the *Los Angeles Times*, 8 December 1990

Eberhart, John Mark, 'For Better Or For Worse, This Isn't Apes By The Book' in the *Kansas City Star*, 26 July 2001

Ebert, Roger, 'Batman' in the *Chicago Sun-Times*, 23 June 1989

Ebert, Roger, 'Edward Scissorhands' in the *Chicago Sun-Times*, 14 December 1990

Ebert, Roger, 'Batman Returns' in the *Chicago Sun-Times*, 19 June 1992

Ebert, Roger, 'Tim Burton's The Nightmare Before Christmas' in the *Chicago Sun-Times*, 22 October 1993

Ebert, Roger, 'Mars Attacks!' in the *Chicago Sun-Times*, 13 December 1996

Ebert, Roger, 'Burton's Dreamy Nightmare' in the *Chicago Sun-Times*, 27 October 2000

Ehrman, Mark, 'Attack of the Martians Who Ate Hollywood!' in the *Los Angeles Times*, 16 December 1996

Elliot, David, 'Is America Ready for a Nut Who's a Genius?' in the *San Diego Union-Tribune*, 18 July 1985

Elliot, David, 'Paul Reubens proves there is life after Pee-wee' in the *San Diego Union-Tribune*, 4 August 1985

Elliot, David, 'Tim Burton: The Man Behind "Batman" ' in the *San Diego Union-Tribune*, 25 June 1989

Elliott, David, ' "Edward Scissorhands" Rises Several Cuts Above Usual Holiday Fare' in the *San Diego Union-Tribune*, 14 December 1990

Epperson, John, 'Mars Attacks! Interview with actress Lisa Marie' in *Interview* (December 1996)

Everett, Anna, 'The Other Pleasures: The Narrative Function of Race in the Cinema' in *Film Criticism*, vol.xx, n.1–2 (Fall/Winter 1995–96)

Felperin, Leslie, 'Animated Dreams' in *Sight and Sound*, vol.4, n.12 (December 1994)

Ferrante, Anthony C, 'Duck for Cover when Mars Attacks' in *Fangoria*, n.159 (January 1997)

Ferrante, Anthony C, 'Hidden Gems' in *Fangoria*, n.160 (March 1997)

Ferrante, Anthony C, 'Helena Bonham Carter on Getting AADD – Attention Ape Deficit Disorder – Filming the "Planet of the Apes" Remake' in *If Magazine*, n.27.3 (25 May 2001)

Ferrante, Anthony C, 'A Visit to the Set of Planet of the Apes . . .' in *If Magazine*, n.29.3 (27 July 2001)

Fleming, Shaun, 'Interview' from http://www.glennshadix.com/beetlejuice/main.html

Fink, Mitchell and Rubin, Lauren, ' "Apes" Actors Held Their Fire When Heston Made His Cameo' in the *New York Daily News*, 26 June 2001

Finnigan, David, 'Is 20th Century Fox Hedging Its Bets With A Reserved Apes Campaign?' in *Brandweek*, vol.42, n.28 (16 July 2001)

Fischer, Dennis, 'Special Visual Effects' in *Cinefantastique*, vol.20, n.1/2 (November 1989)

Floyd, Nigel, 'Pee-Wee's Big Adventure' in *Monthly Film Bulletin*, vol.54, n.643 (August 1987)

Frank, Joe, 'Lights, Camera, Big Bucks' in the *St Petersburg Times*, 17 April 1990

Frank, Steven, 'Cutting Up, Burton Style' in the *Daily Yomiuri*, 20 July 1991

French, Lawrence, 'The Nightmare Before Christmas' in *Cinefantastique*, vol. 24, n.5 (December 1993)

French, Lawrence, 'Playing Bela Lugosi: Martin Landau stars as the revered horror actor' in *Cinefantastique*, vol.25, n.5 (October 1994)

French, Lawrence, 'Tim Burton's Ed Wood: Burton on his black & white ode to a different kind of auteur' in *Cinefantastique*, vol.25, n.5 (October 1994)

French, Lawrence, 'An Ode to B-Movie Badness: Tim Burton's Ed Wood' in *Cinefantastique*, vol.25, n.6/vol.26, n.1 (December 1994)

French, Lawrence, 'Cinematography: DP Stefan Czapsky on the filming in black & white' in *Cinefantastique*, vol.25, n.6/vol.26, n.1 (December 1994)

French, Lawrence, 'Writing the Script: How a would-be documentary turned quirky biopic' in *Cinefantastique*, vol.25, n.6/vol.26, n.1 (December 1994)

French, Lawrence, 'Lugosi's Makeup: Designer Rick Baker on transforming Martin Landau into Bela Lugosi' in *Cinefantastique*, vol.25, n.6/vol.26, n.1 (December 1994)

French, Lawrence, 'Production Design: Tom Duffield on matching Wood's B-movie look' in *Cinefantastique*, vol.25, n.6/vol.26, n.1 (December 1994)

Fritsoe, Roger, 'Edward Scissorhands; Johnny Depp Turns Cutup, Imaginatively' in the *Courier-Journal*, 14 December 1990

Fuller, Graham, 'Tim Burton & Vincent Price' in *Interview*, vol.20, n.12 (December 1990)

Gabrenya, Frank, 'Batman Returns Sequel more satirical, darker than original' in the *Columbus Dispatch*, 19 June 1992

Garsault, Alain, 'Méliès retrouvé (*Beetlejuice*)' in *Postif*, n.336 (February 1989)

Gire, Dann & Reboy, Joseph, 'Batman: Two viewpoints on the trailer designed to quiet Bat fans up in arms' in *Cinefantastique*, vol.19, n.4 (May 1989)

Gleiberman, Owen, 'Our Favourite Martians' in *Entertainment Weekly*, 13 December 1996

Gleiberman, Owen, 'Dead Heads' in *Entertainment Weekly*, 26 November 1999

Gliatto, Tom, 'Ed Wood' in *People*, vol.42, n.15 (10 October 1994)

Glionna, John M, 'A Different Beat' in the *Los Angeles Times*, from http://elfman.filmmusic.com/elfman_la_times.html

Goldman, Steve, 'Spaced Invaders' in *Empire*, n.93 (March 1997)

Goldstein, Patrick, 'Comic O'Hara gets "Beetlejuice" Going' in the *Los Angeles Times*, 18 April 1988

Gorchov, Jolie, 'Fantasy Fashions' in *Los Angeles Business Journal*, 28 February 2000

Gordinier, Jeff, 'Danny Elfman Interview' in *Entertainment Weekly*, n.422 (13 March 1998)

Graham, Bob, 'Great "Apes" ' in the *San Francisco Chronicle*, 27 July 2001

Green, Tom, 'Wiest Finds It Hard To Let Go Of "Edward Scissorhands" ' in *USA Today*, 17 December 1990

Grey, Brandon, 'Planet of the Apes Ending Explained by Fox Exec' (29 July 2001) from www.zap2it.com

Gray, Brandon, 'Tim Roth Theorizes About "Planet of the Apes" Ending' (27 September 2001) from www.zap2it.com

Hagen, Bill, ' "Pee-wee's Big Adventure" Nothing but a Giant Bore' in the *San Diego Union-Tribune*, 17 September 1985

Hagen, Bill, 'Innovative "Beetlejuice" Tweaks Ghost Tales Deliciously' in the *San Diego Union-Tribune*, 13 April 1988

Halpern Smith, Laurie, 'Look, Ma, No Hands, Or Tim Burton's Latest Feat' in the *New York Times*, 28 August 1990

Hartl, John, ' "Edward Scissorhands" Is A Fairy Tale Of Shear Purity' in the *Seattle Times*, 14 December 1990

Hartl, John, ' "The Nightmare Before Christmas" Returns' in the *Seattle Times*, 22 October 2000

Hartney, Michael, 'Kaboom! A Kitschy Invasion From Mars' in the *Buffalo News*, 7 January 1997

Hassler-Forset, Dan, 'Tim Burton: *Auteur* or Marketing Concept?' from http://www.euronet.nl/users/mcbeijer/dan/burton/title.html

Henry, Michael, ' "Il ne faut pas se fier aux apparences" Entretien avec Tim Burton' in *Postif*, n.433 (March 1997)

Hinson, Hal, 'Batman with Dark Grandeur' in the *Washington Post*, 23 June 1989

Hiscock, John, 'What a Piece of Work is an Ape!' in the *Daily Telegraph*, 27 July 2001

Hoberman, J, 'Creature Feature' in *Village Voice*, vol.41, n.51 (17 December 1996)

Hoberman, J, 'Heads or Tails' in *Village Voice*, vol.44, n.47 (30 November 1999)

Hobson, Louis B, 'Such a Softie' in the *Toronto Sun*, 1 March 2001

Howe, Desson, 'A Nifty "Christmas" Bizarre' in the *Washington Post*, 22 October 1993

Howe, Desson, ' "Mars Attacks!": We Lose' in the *Washington Post*, 13 December 1996

Howell, Peter, 'Recurring Nightmare' in the *Toronto Star*, 22 October 2000

Hughes, Kathleen A, 'Beetlejuice Batman has Fans in Flap' in the *Toronto Star*, 26 December 1988

Hunter, Allan, 'Pumpkin Power' in *Scotland on Sunday*, 4 December 1994

Huskey, Melinda, 'Pee-wee Herman and the Postmodern Picaresque' in *Postmodern Culture*, vol.2, n.2 (January 1992)

Issue, Marc, 'Geeks and Fruitgums' in *City Limits*, 13–20 August 1987

Jackson, Mike, 'Glenn Shadix Interview' (16 December 2000) from www.timburtoncollective.com

Jaratz, Lea, 'Mars Attacks! Played For Laughs' in the *Plain Dealer*, 16 December 1996

Johnson, Brian D, 'Batman's Return' in *Maclean's*, vol.105, n. 25 (22 June 1992)

Johnson, Brian D, 'Two Exercises in Style: From B-Movie Camp to Stereotypical Romance' in *Maclean's*, vol.107, n.41 (10 October 1994)

Johnson, Gary, '*Mars Attacks!* Provides Campy, Sci-Fi Fun' from www.imagesjournal.com

Johnson, Gary, 'Movie review' from www.imagesjournal.com

Johnstone, Iain, 'Fantasy With A Familiar Edge' in the *Sunday Times*, 28 July 1991

Jones, Alan, 'Batman: Eccentric cinema stylist Tim Burton on bringing the comic book legend to the screen' in *Cinefantastique*, vol.20, n.1 (November 1989)

Jones, Alan, 'Directing the Legend' in *Cinefantastique*, vol.20, n.1 (November 1989)

Jones, Alan, 'Cutting Remarks from Tim Burton' in *Starburst*, vol.13, n.11 (July 1991)

Jones, Alan, 'Edward Scissorhands' in *Starburst*, vol.13, n.11 (July 1991)

Jones, Bill, 'He Kept His Nightmare Alive' in the *Phoenix Gazette*, 22 October 1993

Kaltenbach, Chris, ' "Mars Attacks!" Crashes to Earth' in the *Baltimore Sun*, 13 December 1996

Kauffman, Stanley, 'The Odd Couple' in the *New Republic*, vol.207, n.5 (27 July 1992)

Kehr, Dave, 'Unhappy Outsiders' in the *Toronto Star*, 19 June 1992

Kempley, Rita, 'Great Goblins! It's "Beetlejuice"!' in the *Washington Post*, 30 March 1988

Kempley, Rita, ' "Edward Scissorhands": Winter's Fable' in the *Washington Post*, 14 December 1990

Kempley, Rita, 'Plan 9 1/2 From Hollywood' in the *Washington Post*, 13 December 1996

Kirkland, Bruce, 'Ooo, Scary Stuff' in the *Toronto Sun*, 30 October 2000

Klady, Leonard, 'Bats at the Box Office' in *Movies*, vol.1, n.1 (July 1992)

Klawans, Stewart, 'Holiday Celluloid Wrap-Up' in the *Nation*, vol.252, n.1 (14 January 1991)

Kral, Petr, 'L'ére du bric-à-brac sur Pee-Wee Big Adventure' in *Postif*, n.317–318 (July–August 1987)

Kroll, Jack, 'The Joker is wild, but Batman carries the night' in *Newsweek*, 26 June 1989 (US Edition)

Larson, Randall, 'Danny Elfman, Director Tim Burton's Rock Music Man' in *Cinefantastique*, vol. 20, n.1/2 (November 1989)

Laud, Lance, 'Pee-wee Herman' in *Interview*, vol.xv, n.9 (September 1985)

LaSalle, Mich, ' "Scissorhands" Just Doesn't Cut It' in the *San Francisco Chronicle*, 14 December 1990

Laski, Beth, 'Zanuck Revisits "Planet of the Apes" for Fox, Burton' in *Hollywood Reporter*, vol.362, n.14 (21 March 2000)

Lazarus, David, 'How Not to Wield a Movie Camera' in the *Ottawa Citizen*, 7 October 2000

Lewis, Kevin, 'Ed Wood' in *Films in Review*, vol.46, n.1/2 (Jan/Feb 1995)

Lida Rubin, Rosina, 'Cameos: Production Designer Bo Welch' in *Premier*, vol.5, n.11 (July 1995)

Lipper, Hal, 'A Classic Batman' in the *St Petersburg Times*, 23 June 1989

Lipper, Hal, 'Something's Strange in Suburbia' in the *St Petersburg Times*, 22 May 1990

Littleton, Cynthia, 'Burton Goes to "Oz" for CTTD' in *Variety*, 12 October 1998

Lloyd, Ann, 'Pee-Wee's Big Adventure' in *Films and Filming*, n.394 (July 1987)

Lyons, Mike, 'Scripting Film Fantasies' in *Cinefantastique*, vol.28, n.3 (October 1996)

McCarthy, Todd, 'Mars Attacks!' in *Variety*, 2 December 1996

McCarthy, Todd, 'Sleepy Hollow' in *Variety*, 15 November 1999

McCarthy, Todd, 'Planet of the Apes' in *Variety*, 30 July 2001

MacIntyre, Ben, 'Is Batman a Racist Bigot?' in *The Times*, 4 August 1992

McMillan, Sam, 'Tim Burton's Stainboy' from http://www.designinteract.com/features_d/stainboy/

Macor, Alison, 'Mars Attacks!' in the *Austin Chronicle*, 13 December 1996

Ron Magid, 'Strange Invaders' in *American Cinematographer*, vol.77, n.12 (December 1996)

Malcolm, Derek, 'Edward Scissorhands' in the *Guardian*, 25 July 1991

Malcolm, Derek, 'Batman Fails To Take Flight' in the *Guardian*, 9 July 1992

Malcolm, Derek, 'They Came, They Saw, They Got Too Clever' in the *Guardian*, 28 February 1997

Malmquist, Allen, 'Beetlejuice' in *Cinefantastique*, vol.18, n.5 (July 1988)

Maslin, Janet, 'Ghosts and Extra Eyeballs' in the *New York Times*, 30 March 1988

Maslin, Janet, 'And So Handy Around The Garden' in the *New York Times*, 7 December 1990

Maslin, Janet, 'Infiltrating the Land of Sugar Plums' in the *New York Times*, 9 October 1993

Maslin, Janet, 'Mars Attacks!' in the *New York Times*, 13 December 1996

Mathews, Jack, ' "Apes" Remake Sorta Tame' in the *New York Daily News*, 27 July 2001

Mathews, Jack, 'Simian Skin Color Variations are Raising Eyebrows' in the *New York Daily News*, 27 July 2001

Mayo, Michael, 'Frankenweenie' in *Cinefantastique*, vol.15, n.2 (May 1985)

Mazey, Steven, 'Little More Than Monkey Business' in the *Ottawa Citizen*, 27 July 2001

Mietkiewicz, Henry, 'Batwimp no more' in the *Toronto Star*, 18 June 1989

Mills, David, 'One on One' in *Empire*, n.128 (February 2000)

Mitchell, Elvis, 'Get Your Hands Off, Ya Big Gorilla!' in the *New York Times*, 27 July 2001

Morris, Gary, 'It's an Ed Wood World After All' in *Bright Lights Film Journal*, n.16 (May 1996)

Mount, Paul, 'What the Butler Saw' in Starburst, n.132 (August 1989)

Nashawaty, Chris, 'A Head of its Time' in *Entertainment Weekly*, 19 November 1999

Natale, Richard, 'Remaking, Not Aping, An Original' in the *Los Angeles Times*, 6 May 2001

Natale, Richard, ' "Apes" Rules Planet' in the *Los Angeles Times*, 30 July 2001

Nazzaro, Joe, 'Bat Attitude' in *Starlog*, n.210 (January 1995)

Newman, Kim, 'Beetle Juice' in *Monthly Film Bulletin*, vol.55, n.655 (August 1988)

Newman, Kim, 'Tim Burton's The Nightmare Before Christmas' in *Sight and Sound*, vol.4, n.12 (December 1994)

Newman, Kim, 'Ed Wood' in *Sight and Sound*, vol.5, n.5 (May 1995)

Newman, Kim, 'The Cage of Reason' in *Sight and Sound*, vol.10, n.1 (January 2000)

O'Hehir, Andrew, 'Gorilla Warfare' in *Sight and Sound*, vol.11, n.9 (September 2001)

O'Sullivan, Charlotte, 'Numb and Number' in the *Independent*, 16 August 2001

Patterson, Sylvia, 'Thomas Crown, Back in Town' in *Interview* (August 1999)

Patterson, Troy, 'Head of the Class' in *Entertainment Weekly*, 26 May 2000

Pearce, Garth, 'Bat Talk' in *Movies*, vol.1, n.1 (July 1992)

Pearlman, Cindy, 'Today Vegas: Tomorrow, The World! Mean Little Green Guys Attack Earth' in the *Chicago Sun-Times*, 8 December 1996

Pearlman, Cindy, 'A Strange New Planet' in the *Ottawa Citizen*, 20 July 2001

Perrin, Elisabeth, 'Tim Burton Guides to the Screen Another Tale

From the Dark Side' in the *Chicago Sun-Times*, 17 October 1993

Persons, Dan, 'Building Pee-Wee's Playhouse' in *Cinefantastique*, vol.19, n.5 (July 1989)

Petkovic, John, 'This Time, The Humans Are Smarter And The Movie Is Dumber' in the *Plain Dealer*, 27 July 2001

Pizzello, Stephen, 'Head Trip' in *American Cinematographer*, vol.80, n.12 (December 1999)

Pizzello, Stephen, 'Galloping Ghost' in *American Cinematographer*, vol.80, n.12 (December 1999)

Pollack, Joe, 'Johnny Depp As Teen Who's Shy But Handy "Edward Scissorhands"' in the *St Louis Post-Dispatch*, 14 December 1990

Radz, Matt, 'Jungle Land: Director Tim Burton reimagines a classic in Planet of the Apes' in the *Montreal Gazette*, 27 July 2001

Rafferty, Terrence, 'The Current Cinema' in *New Yorker*, 16 December 1996

Rea, Steven, 'The Verdict's in: Batpurists Love Keaton' in the *Toronto Star*, 7 July 1989

Rebello, Stephen, 'Sam Hamm: A Profile of the hot new screen-writer who launched the Dark Knight's boxoffice torpedo' in *Cinefantastique*, vol.20, n.1 (November 1989)

Rentilly, J, 'Tim Burton, Relying on Himself' from www.audiencemagazine.com

Ressner, Jeffrey, 'Three Go Mad In Gotham . . .' in *Empire*, n.38 (August 1992)

Rico, Diana, 'A little fright music' in *Egg* (December/January 1990)

Robins, Jane, 'Hollywood Plays it Safe by Remaking Old Classics' in the *Independent*, 26 October 2000

Rose, Frank, 'Tim Cuts Up' in *Premier*, vol.4, n.5 (January 1991)

Saada, Nicolas, 'Du mécanique plaqué sur du vivant' in *Cahiers du Cinema*, n.511 (March 1997)

Salem, Rob, 'Beetlejuice a Comedy of Terrors' in the *Toronto Star*, 30 March 1988

Salisbury, Mark, 'Caroline Thompson: Writer-Director/Horse Lover' in *Empire*, n.69 (March 1995)

Salisbury, Mark, 'Blood Jones' in *Empire*, n.90 (December 1996)

Salisbury, Mark, 'Heads Up for Sleepy Hollow' in *Fangoria*, n.188 (November 1999)

Salisbury, Mark, 'Veterans in the "Hollow"' in *Fangoria*, n.188 (November 1999)

Salisbury, Mark, 'A Head of the Game' in *Fangoria*, n.189 (January 2000)

Salisbury, Mark, 'Male of the Unexpected' in *Total Film*, n.37 (February 2000)

Salisbury, Mark, 'Wednesday's Child comes of age' in *Total Film*, n.37 (February 2000)

Salisbury, Mark, 'Gorillas just Wanna have Fun' in *Premiere* vol.14, n. 11 (July 2001)

Sammon, Paul M, 'Quick Cuts, Wood Works' in Cinefex n.61 (May 1995)

Schneller, Johnanna, 'Where's Johnny?' in *Premier*, vol.13, n.4 (December 1999)

Schruers, Fred, 'Bat Mitzvah' in *Premier*, vol.5, n.11 (July 1995)

Schweiger, Daniel, 'Danny Elfman Returns' in *Soundtrack! The Collector's Quarterly*, vol.11, n.43 (September 1992)

Scott, Richard, 'Pointed, Poignant' in *The Times*, 10 September 1994

Schaefer, Stephen, 'Tim Burton' from: http://mrshowbiz.go.com/news/Todays_Stories/991102/burtonsleepyhollow110299.html

Sharkey, Betsy, 'Tim Burton's "Nightmare" Comes True' in the *New York Times*, 10 October 1993

Sheehan, Henry, 'Yak-Yak Is Way Martians Communicate' in the *Seattle Times*, 27 December 1996

Sherman, Paul, 'Disney Has Dreams of Profits From "Nightmare"' in the *Boston Herald*, 22 October 2000

Simon, John, 'Batman and girls at Bat' in *National Review*, vol.44, n.15 (3 August 1992)

Slater, Lydia, 'Paws For Effect' in the *Sunday Times*, 26 November 2000

Sloane, Judy & Caro, Jason, 'Hollow Pursuits' in *Starburst*, vol.24, n.7 (February 2000)

Slotek, Jim, 'The Humans' Planet is Buzzing: Apes All Set to Swing into Theatres' in the *Toronto Sun*, 24 July 2001

Smith, Adam, 'Where Are They Now? Jeffrey Jones: Demon Headmaster ...' in *Empire*, n.90 (December 1996)

Smith, Kevin, 'A Superman For All Seasons' in *TV Guide*, 3 December 2001

Spillman, Susan, 'Will Batman Fly?' in *USA Today*, 19 June 1989

Spillman, Susan, ' "Edward Scissorhands" Cuts To Tim Burton's Core' in *USA Today*, 10 December 1990

Spillman, Susan, 'The Shear Geniuses of "Scissorhands"' Style' in *USA Today*, 13 December 1990

Spines, Christine, 'Men Are From Mars, Women Are From Venus' in *Premier*, January 1996

Sragow, Michael, 'Clunky Monkeys' in the *Baltimore Sun*, 27 July 2001

Sragow, Michael, 'The Ape Man' in the *Guardian*, 3 August 2001

Stack, Peter, 'Scant Intelligent Life in "Mars": Starry Cast Can't Save Tim Burton's Interplanetary Gags' in the *San Francisco Chronicle*, 13 December 1996

Stark, Susan, 'Director Tim Burton Revels in the Weird in his New Space Comedy' in the *Detroit News*, 7 December 1996

Stark, Susan, 'Tim Burton goes "Apes" in this high-style remake' in the *Detroit News*, 29 July 2001

Sterritt, David, 'A Wacko Comedy that Harks Back to Jerry Lewis' in the *Christian Science Monitor*, 3 September 1985

Sterritt, David, 'A Fable of Social Understanding' in the *Christian Science Monitor*, 16 January 1991

Sterritt, David, 'High-Voltage Stars Can't Save "Mars Attacks!"' in the *Christian Science Monitor*, 13 December 1996

Sterrit, David, ' "Planet" Remake Merely Apes The Original' in the *Christian Science Monitor*, 28 July 2001

Strickler, Jeff, 'Merry Scary Christmas' in the *Star Tribune*, 22 October 1993

Svetkey, Benjamin and Raftery, M, 'Ape Crusaders' in *Entertainment Weekly*, n.593 (27 April 2001)

Szebin, Frederick C and Biodrowski, Steve, 'Mars Attacks: Tim Burton sends up the bubblegum alien invader genre' in *Cinefantastique*, vol.28, n.7 (January 1997)

Szebin, Frederick C, 'Martian Victim: Michael J. Fox: Marty McFly on dabbling in another sci-fi universe' in *Cinefantastique*, vol.28, n.7 (January 1997)

Szebin, Frederick C & Biodrowski, Steve, 'Martian Music: Composer Danny Elfman: On Burtonizing the golden sci-fi scores of the past' in *Cinefantastique*, vol.28, n.7 (January 1997)

Frederick C Szebin, 'Martian Victim: Pierce Brosnan: Suave James Bond on playing a clueless scientist' in *Cinefantastique*, vol.28, n.7 (January 1997)

Taylor, Stuart, 'Len Brown: Martian Madman' in *Alien Encounters*, n.6

Thaxton, Ford A, 'Danny Elfman revisits the Planet of the Apes' in *Soundtrack*, vol.20, n.79 (Fall 2001)

Thomas, Bob, '... And Beau Johnny Depp Is Earning More Respect' in the *Toronto Star*, 3 January 1991

Thomas, Kevin, 'Gleeful Grand Guignol of "Beetlejuice" ' in the *Los Angeles Times*, 30 March 1988

Thomas, Philip, 'The Misfit' in *Empire*, n.26 (August 1991)

Thomas, Philip, 'Batman Returns' in *Empire*, n.38 (August 1992)

Thompson, Patricia, 'Emmanuel Lubezki, ASC, AMC: *Sleepy Hollow*' in *American Cinematographer*, vol.81, n.6 (June 2000)

Thorpe, Vanessa, 'Heston Returns to Planet of the Apes' in the *Observer*, 3 December 2000

Travers, Peter, 'A Cut Above the Rest' in *Rolling Stone*, 10 January 1991

Travers, Peter, 'Bat Girls on Line' in *Rolling Stone*, n.634–635 (9 July 1992)

Travers, Peter, 'Auteur in Angora' in *Rolling Stone*, n.511 (July 1995)

Turan, Kenneth, 'Burton Dreams up a Delightful "Nightmare" ' in the *Los Angeles Times*, 15 October 1993

Turan, Kenneth, ' "Mars Attacks!"; Tim Burton's "Plan 9" ' in the *Los Angeles Times*, 13 December 1996

Turan, Kenneth, 'Some Serious Monkey Business' in the *Los Angeles Times*, 27 July 2001

Vachaud, Laurent, 'L'Étrange Noel de monsieur Jack: La mort lui va si bien' in *Postif*, n.406 (December 1994)

Vancheri, Barbara, 'Man vs. Ape' in the *Pittsburgh Post-Gazette*, 27 July 2001

Veck, Pierre, 'Vincent: La Magie Du Noir et Blanc Retrouvée' in *Banc-Titre*, n.33 (September 1983)

Viviani, Christian, 'Mars Attacks! Smalltown, USA' in *Postif*, n.433 (March 1997)

Viviani, Christian, 'Sleepy Hollow: Le reniement de la mère sorcière' in *Postif*, n.468 (January 2000)

Wagner, Chuck, 'Martian Inspiration: The Bubblegum Cards: Public outrage halted sales, but the series lived on' in *Cinefantastique*, vol.28, n.7 (January 1997)

Webb Mitovich, Matt, 'Wahlberg Tackles Apes Rumours' from *TV Guide Online*, 31 July 2001

Webb Mitovich, Matt, 'Apes Director's Secret Fear' from *TV Guide Online*, 3 August 2001

Welsh, James M, 'Edward Scissorhands' in *Films in Review*, vol.42, n.3–4 (March/April 1991)

Westbrook, Caroline, 'Lisa Marie' in *Empire*, n.128 (February 2000)

Wilmington, Michael, 'Soft-Hearted Fairy Tale of an Outsider' in the *Los Angeles Times*, 14 December 1990

White, Taylor L, 'Vincent' in *Cinefantastique*, vol.20, n.1/2 (November 1989)

White, Taylor L, 'Aladdin's Lamp' in *Cinefantastique*, vol.20, n.1/2 (November 1989)

White, Taylor L, 'Other Weirdness' in *Cinefantastique*, vol.20, n.1/2 (November 1989)

White, Taylor L, 'Hansel and Gretel' in *Cinefantastique*, vol.20, n.1/2 (November 1989)

White, Taylor L, 'Frankenweenie' in *Cinefantastique*, vol.20, n.1/2 (November 1989)

White, Taylor L, 'Pee-Wee's Big Adventure' in *Cinefantastique*, vol.20, n.1/2 (November 1989)

White, Taylor L, 'The making of Tim Burton's Beetlejuice & his other bizarre gems' in *Cinefantastique*, vol.20, n.1/2 (November 1989)

White, Taylor L, 'Makeup Effects' in *Cinefantastique*, vol.20, n.1/2 (November 1989)

White, Taylor L, 'The Betelsnake' in *Cinefantastique*, vol.20, n.1/2 (November 1989)

White, Taylor L, 'Transformations' in *Cinefantastique*, vol.20, n.1/2 (November 1989)

Williams, David E, 'Galactic Antics' in *American Cinematographer*, vol.77, n.12 (December 1996)

Williams, David E, 'Antisocial Darwinism' in *American Cinematographer*, vol.33, n.4 (August 2000)

Williams, Joe, 'New "Planet" Needn't Play Second Banana To Original' in the *St Louis Post-Dispatch*, 27 July 2001

Wilner, Norman, 'Quality Attacks!' in the *Toronto Star*, 14 June 1997

Winterton, Ian, 'Murder, He Wrote' in *Hotdog*, n.20 (February 2002)

Woodward, Sarah, 'Tim Burton Fashions Narrow Escape with Timex' in *Shoot*, 9 June 2000

Woof, William, 'In Praise of Tim Burton: Finding the Masterpiece in *Mars Attacks!*' in *Kinema* (Spring 1998)

Wright, Kenneth, 'Shear Misery' in the *Glasgow Herald*, 8 February 1992

Zahed, Ramin, 'Stainboy' in *Variety*, 13 November 2000

INDEX